accounting 1

accounting 1

by

G. E. SYME

B. Com., C.A.

PRENTICE-HALL  OF CANADA, LTD.

Scarborough · Ontario

PRENTICE-HALL, INC., ENGLEWOOD CLIFFS, NEW JERSEY
PRENTICE-HALL OF AUSTRALIA, PTY., LTD., SYDNEY
PRENTICE-HALL OF INDIA PVT., LTD., NEW DELHI
PRENTICE-HALL INTERNATIONAL, INC., LONDON
PRENTICE-HALL OF JAPAN, INC., TOKYO

Library of Congress Catolog Card No. 73-109491
13-001438-9
3   4   5   74   73   72   71
PRINTED IN CANADA

The teaching of introductory accounting is taking a different direction than in the past. It is concerned with the development of a more positive understanding of accounting principles and concepts, as well as with a broader appreciation of the office environment. It aims to prepare the student of accounting for the technologically dynamic society in which he will one day be employed.

Objectives

For the first six chapters **Accounting I** follows fairly traditional lines in developing a firm understanding of basic concepts. Then, it breaks away —proceeding along new and original lines in an attempt to satisfy the following objectives:
1. To provide for the student the means of acquiring a thorough understanding of basic accounting principles, concepts, and procedures.
2. To provide a solid foundation for possible further study.
3. To develop in the student the qualities of versatility, flexibility, and initiative that will be of certain benefit to him in a world of persistent change.
4. To achieve the above three objectives through the application of genuinely functional practice material which of itself will benefit the student.

Organization

The broad coverage of the text, together with the availability of independent optional chapters, provides the teacher with a flexible tool that can be adapted to suit the needs of all students in regular courses.

The text consists of fifteen chapters. The first nine chapters are considered to be the minimum coverage for a satisfactory one-year course. However, it is expected that most students will proceed beyond this point.

The first ten chapters are developed on a continuous basis. After completing Chapter 10, the student may proceed to any of four additional independent units of study. These are:
Ch. 11—Cash Registers, Banking, Bank Reconciliations.
Ch. 12—Basic Accounting Systems and Procedures.
Ch. 13—Payroll.
Ch. 14 and Ch. 15—Adjustments, Closing Entries, Classified Financial Statements, Reversing Entries.

Where it is desirable to offer a two-year course, **Accounting I** may be combined with one semester of an additional subject such as Applied Accounting or Data Processing.

Individualized Instruction

Accounting I explains the subject matter thoroughly, an approach that benefits both the student and the teacher.

It enables the student to work more independently. This is a habit that he should develop, in many instances wants to develop, and often is forced to practice. For the superior student, complete independent study is possible.

Because the student can rely on the text, the teacher is provided with a less demanding classroom situation, a very important consideration in view of the popularity of individual student progress.

Problems and Exercises

A wealth of exercise material of varying degrees of difficulty is included. It is not expected that all students will work all of the exercises, but rather that by careful selection the needs of all students will be satisfied.

Scope of Business Transactions

This text attempts to include every routine business transaction that falls within the domain of the accounting clerk. Sales Tax, Petty Cash, Cash Registers, Returns and Allowances, Credit Notes, Cash Refunds, Cash Discounts, Payroll, N.S.F. Cheques, Bank Debit and Credit Notes, and Bank Reconciliations are among the many topics discussed.

Office Systems and Procedures

The last ten to fifteen years have witnessed tremendous changes in accounting techniques. During that time, the traditional role of the bookkeeper has disappeared and the role of the accounting clerk has emerged in a new accounting environment of systems, procedures, and automation.

Accounting I reflects the new state of accounting and relates accounting theory to current practices.

Total Business Concept

The text is organized so that it is not necessary to devote a separate chapter to each of the Purchases Journal, the Sales Journal, the Cash Receipts Journal, and the Cash Payments Journal. The organization of **Accounting I** makes it possible to introduce these four special journals all in one chapter. This method has the advantage of showing all transactions in their proper perspective; that is, in relationship to total business activity.

Subsidiary Ledgers and Control Accounts

Subsidiary Ledger accounting is an important phase of every business and is the type of accounting work most likely to fall to a new or junior employee. Therefore, the study of

Subsidiary Ledgers and Control Accounts is given an early and prominent place in **Accounting I.**

Flowcharts

This text teaches basic flowcharting techniques and utilizes them to describe graphically the basic accounting systems and procedures. With the advent of greater use of mechanical and electronic accounting techniques, flowcharts have become the accepted method of effectively describing business systems.

Business Source Documents

The entire accounting process is dependent on a variety of business documents. Accounting systems and procedures are geared to the flow of business papers. These business papers represent a means of communication from business to business and from person to person. They represent the supporting evidence of most business transactions and the source of most

accounting entries. As such, they deserve a place of importance in a text on introductory accounting and receive it in **Accounting I.**

Adjusting and Closing Entries

The text includes two different treatments of adjusting entries. Either or both methods may be studied according to the individual's preference. The first is the traditional method, using adjusting entries. The second is the professional's method, by means of which the adjustments are effected through the closing entries.

Mechanical and Electronic Accounting

This text is designed to provide a thorough introduction to fundamental accounting principles and practices. Where appropriate, mechanical and electronic devices are acknowledged and discussed. However, it is not a purpose of this text to overlap into the field of Data Processing.

ACKNOWLEDGMENTS

The author wishes to express his appreciation to those who assisted him in the preparation of this manuscript. The contribution of two people in particular is gratefully acknowledged:

DOUGLAS DIXON, *Commercial director, Hammarskjold High School, Thunder Bay, Ontario, who taught from this text while it was still in*

manuscript form and was thus able to offer many helpful suggestions and to confirm many of the ideas incorporated therein. He was also responsible for the preparation of The Teachers' Guide and The Answer Key.

JOHN LITT, *Assistant Commercial director, Hammarskjold High School, Thunder Bay, Ontario, who*

experimented with a new course in applied bookkeeping and accounting which required the writing of a great deal of exercise material. He also wrote the chapter on payroll for this text.

A word of thanks is also due to the Lakehead Board of Education for its co-operation.

G. E. S.

CONTENTS

Introduction

ACCOUNTING AND YOUR FUTURE

Accounting and related functions play an important role in the structure of our economy. You will find that in numerous ways a knowledge of Accounting can be of considerable value to you in your career.

Those of you who decide to go into the working world of business, commerce, trade and industry, will find employment in one of the countless numbers of business establishments that make up our economic system. Within these business establishments, however, so many of the individual jobs are either directly or indirectly involved in the accounting and recording processes that there is every chance of your job being one of them. It is not difficult to see that an understanding of Accounting may help to perform your duties and increase your value as an employee.

As an employee improves his position in the business world he finds that his responsibilities grow accordingly. The higher positions in business require a more able and knowledgeable employee. If you hope to improve your position in business, either by moving up the ranks or by changing employers, an understanding of Accounting will be helpful. It will round out your appreciation of the aims and objectives of the whole business organization, the interdependence of the various departments and the relationship of your own job to the whole enterprise. Also, it will direct your attention to matters that concern management, such as profit, systems and procedures, and efficiency.

It is the ambition of many a person one day to become the owner of a business. Anyone who achieves this goal will soon find himself concerned with matters related to Accounting. There is the banking, the customers' accounts, the paying of bills, the sales tax, the income tax, the payroll, and so on. For the owner of a business, a knowledge of Accounting is of obvious benefit.

Some of you may choose a career as a professional accountant. By completing the requirements of one of the professional bodies of accountants, you can become a Chartered Accountant (C.A.), a Certified General Accountant (C.G.A.), or a Registered Industrial Accountant (R.I.A.). The work performed by a qualified accountant depends to some extent on which particular group he is associated with. In general, qualified and experienced accountants are eligible for senior management positions and have the right to practise as public accountants; that is, to offer their services to the general public for a fee in the same manner as a doctor or lawyer. Professional accountants earn good incomes and enjoy a respected place in the community.

An appreciation of Accounting will also influence your personal and social life. By understanding the financial aspects of the family, and various community organizations, you will be better able to take your place in the community.

Chapter 1

THE BALANCE SHEET

Purpose of Accounting

Although the science of accounting is useful to business people in a variety of ways, it is fundamentally a system designed to accomplish two things. These are–

1. To maintain an accurate and up-to-date record of the **financial position** of a business or individual.
2. To keep a detailed record of the changes which occur in the **financial position.**

Financial Position

' The concept of financial position is simple and logical. Ask yourself this question–How can I determine someone's (e.g., an ordinary home-owner's or my parents') financial position? Then, using pure common sense, find the answer.

You will likely decide that the following three steps are necessary:

1. List and total the things he owns that have some monetary value; these are called his **Assets.**
2. List and total his debts; these are called his **Liabilities.**
3. Calculate the difference between his total **Assets** and his total **Liabilities;** this difference is called his **Capital** or **Equity.**

Example

To determine the financial position of A. R. Proctor on June 30, 19—.

Step 1

List and total the things of value that he owns. These **Assets** might be as follows:

Cash on Hand	$ 35.60
Bank Balance	647.40
Government Bonds	1,200.00
Amount Loaned to Jack Burns	300.00
Automobile	2,700.00
House and Lot	16,500.00
Furniture and Equipment	1,956.00
Total Assets	**$23,339.00**

Step 2

List and total his debts. These **Liabilities** might be as follows:

Acme Finance Co. (Automobile)	$ 962.00
Western Furniture Company	264.00
Mortgage on Home	11,363.50
Total Liabilities	**$12,589.50**

Step 3

Calculate the difference between total assets and total liabilities. The calculation is as follows:

Total Assets	$23,339.00
Less Total Liabilities	12,589.50
Difference	$10,749.50

The difference of $10,749.50 is the amount that A. R. Proctor is worth. It is generally referred to as his **Capital** or **Equity.**

Note:

Other less common terms for Capital are **Proprietorship** and **Net Worth.**

The Balance Sheet

A. R. Proctor's financial position may be presented formally by means of a financial statement or financial report called a **Balance Sheet.** A simple form of Balance Sheet is illustrated at right.

A. R. Proctor Balance Sheet June 30, 19—				
Assets		**Liabilities**		
Cash on Hand	35 60	Acme Finance Co.		962 00
Bank Balance	647 40	Western Furniture Company		264 00
Government Bonds	1 200 00	Mortgage Payable		11 363 50
Jack Burns	300 00			12 589 50
Automobile	2 700 00	**Capital**		
House and Lot	16 500 00	A. R. Proctor, Capital		10 749 50
Furniture and Equipment	1 956 00			
	23 339 00			23 339 00

The above Balance Sheet is that for a person. It is just as easy to prepare a Balance Sheet for a business, club, church or any orangization. Some additional sample Balance Sheets are shown on the right.

Wesley Saxton Lawyer Balance Sheet December 31, 19—				
Assets		**Liabilities**		
Cash	1 407 10	Bank Loan		2 000 00
R Mason	350 00	Mercury Finance Co.		1 475 00
H. Moran	1 056 75			3 475 00
Office Supplies	264 00	**Owner's Equity**		
Furniture and Equipment	2 600 00	Wesley Saxton, Capital		5 467 85
Automobile	3 265 00			
	8 942 85			8 942 85

Balance Sheet for a small business

Center High School Student Council Balance Sheet March 31, 19—				
Assets		**Liabilities**		
Cash	156 50	Glendale Company		52 03
D. Fraser	37 24			
Art Supplies	17 00	**Net Worth**		
Decorating Materials	56 00	Student Council Net Worth		214 71
	266 74			266 74

Balance Sheet for a small organization

Important Features of the Balance Sheet

1. A three-line heading is used. The heading tells three things–
   (a) the name of the business, organization, or individual;
   (b) the name of the financial statement–Balance Sheet;
   (c) the date on which the financial position was determined.

2. The Assets are listed on the left side of the Balance Sheet and the Liabilities and the Capital are listed on the right side.

3. The details of any item are fully disclosed on a Balance Sheet. For example, on the Balance Sheet of A. R. Proctor, shown above, his automobile is shown in the Assets section at its value of $2,700 and the amount that he owes on the automobile, $962 to Acme Finance Co., is shown in the Liabilities section. This is a more informative presentation than to show the car at a value of $1,738, the amount that Mr. Proctor has paid on it.

4. Abbreviations are not used on financial statements except when listing a company name which includes an abbreviation; for example, International Trading Co.

5. The two final totals, one for each side of the Balance Sheet, are recorded on the same line.

Use of Columnar Paper

It is important for a student of accounting to learn to use columnar paper. When columnar paper is used, notice how the figures are placed carefully in the columns; this is to help total the columns correctly. Observe also the omission of dollar signs, periods, and commas when recording amounts of money in the columns.

It is permissible when using columnar paper to indicate even dollar amounts by inserting a dash in the cents column as shown below.

	506	21
1 000	—	
	51	20
	12	—

Debtor and Creditor

When a sum of money is owed to our business or organization it is listed on our Balance Sheet as an asset. Conversely, when a sum of money is owed by our business or organization it is listed on our Balance Sheet as a liability.

Considering this from a different viewpoint, whenever the name of a business or an individual appears on our Balance Sheet in the Assets section, that business or individual owes us a sum of money. Such a business or individual is one of our **Debtors.**

Similarly, whenever the name of a business or an individual appears on our Balance Sheet in the Liabilities section, we owe a sum of money to that business or individual. Such a business or individual is one of our **Creditors.**

Note:

It is customary when discussing the business for which we work to use terms such as 'we', 'us', 'our', and so on. On the other hand when talking about another business it is customary to use terms such as 'they', 'their' and so on.

Use of Ruled Lines

If a column of figures is to be totaled (added or subtracted) a single line is drawn beneath the column and the total is placed beneath this single line as shown below.

131	10
14	11
31	05
176	26

If a total happens to be a final total, such as the last amounts on the Balance Sheet, a double ruled line is drawn immediately beneath the total as shown below.

14	62
194	75
30	—
12	65
252	02

Sometimes it is desirable to leave one or more unused lines between the figures in the column and the total. When this is done, place the single ruled line immediately above the total and not immediately beneath the figures in the column. Examine the following examples:

Incorrect	*Correct*

46	10		46	10
92	05		92	05
19	64		19	64
137	88		137	88
295	67		295	67

This technique is required on many Balance Sheets when placing the two final totals on the same line.

Neatness

It is most important that an accountant's work be neat and perfectly legible. He must see to it that no one misinterprets his writing or figuring. Although his work should never be unsightly, at the same time it is not necessary that it be beautiful—only neat and legible.

From the very beginning you should make it a habit to strive for neatness and clarity in all of your exercises. Be sure to use your ruler to underline headings.

The Fundamental Accounting Equation

It is a fundamental truth in Accounting that a Balance Sheet always balances. It is not possible to prepare a correct Balance Sheet that is not balanced.

The relationship between the Assets, Liabilities, and Capital as shown on the simple Balance Sheet indicates the 'fundamental accounting equation' (also known as the 'fundamental bookkeeping equation'). This equation is shown by the illustration on the right.

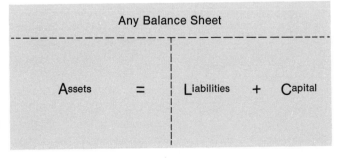

Any Balance Sheet

Assets = Liabilities + Capital

The fundamental accounting equation is:

$$A = L + C$$

By simple mathematical rearrangement:

$$A - L = C$$

This relationship is an extremely important concept in the study of Accounting. As you will soon see, the whole science of Accounting is based on it.

Bookkeeping and Accounting Terms

Balance Sheet: A statement showing the financial position (the Assets, Liabilities, and Capital) of an individual, company, or other organization on a certain date.

Asset: Something owned that has a monetary value.

Liability: A debt, owed to another individual, company, or organization.

Capital:
Equity:
Proprietorship:
Net Worth:
Each of these four terms means the same thing–the difference between the total assets and the total liabilities.

Creditor: An individual, business, or other organization to whom our business owes a sum of money.

Debtor: An individual, business, or other organization that owes a sum of money to our business.

Review Questions

1. Name the two basic purposes of Accounting.
2. Describe how a person's financial position is arrived at.
3. Define 'Asset'. Name five different assets.
4. Define 'Liability'. Name three different liabilities.
5. Define Capital (or Equity).
6. Name two other less commonly used terms that mean the same as Capital.
7. What is a Balance Sheet?
8. What three things must the heading of a Balance Sheet show?
9. When may the name of the owner of a business be used in the heading?
10. On which side of the Balance Sheet are the Assets listed? On which side are the Liabilities listed?
11. Describe the way in which an automobile that is only partially paid for is shown in a Balance Sheet.
12. When listing figures on columnar paper, what items may be omitted?
13. Define 'Creditor'.
14. Define 'Debtor'.
15. Describe where debtors and creditors are listed on a Balance Sheet.
16. What is meant by a single ruled line drawn beneath a column of figures?
17. What is meant by drawing a double ruled line beneath a total?
18. What is the exception to the rule "never use short forms or abbreviations on financial statements"?
19. Give two forms of the fundamental accounting equation.

Exercises

Study the Balance Sheets illustrated on page 4. Then complete the following exercises using the illustrated Balance Sheets as a guide.

Note:

You will never be a successful accountant if, as you work through the exercises in this text, you merely memorize the solutions. Therefore, as you proceed through the text, always do your best to understand each topic completely.

1. (a) List eight assets that a small business might own.
   (b) List three liabilities that a small business might owe.
   (c) If the total assets of a business are $37,486.49, and the total liabilities are $11,749.71, calculate the owner's equity.

2. Classify each of the following as an Asset, Liability, or Capital item: office furniture; an amount owed to H. Smith; land; buildings; cash on hand; the owner's investment in the business; an amount owed by R. Jones; an unpaid heating bill; trucks; supplies; bank loan.

3. From the following information prepare a Balance Sheet for M. H. Clark, a public accountant, on December 31, 19—.

Cash	$ 356.75
R. Swift (a debtor)	100.00
G. K. Falls (a debtor)	500.00
Y. S. Banton (a debtor)	275.00
Office Supplies	135.50
Office Equipment	462.00
Automobile	2,850.00
Colewell Office Supply (a creditor)	225.00

4. The Western News Company, owned by C. D. Proctor, had the following assets and liabilities on March 31, 19—. Prepare a Balance Sheet for the company on that date.

Cash	$ 896.52
S. Miller (a debtor)	750.60
P. Hayes (a debtor)	400.00
Supplies	351.00
Automobile	1,850.00
Furniture and Fixtures	965.00
Bank Loan	2,500.00
Ace Finance Company (a creditor)	920.00
General Trading Co. (a creditor)	642.98

5. From the following list of assets and liabilities prepare the personal Balance Sheet of T. G. Russell as of June 30, 19—.

Cash on Hand	$ 402.16
Bank Balance	1,002.34
Stocks and Bonds	3,560.00
House and Lot	18,005.00
Household Furniture	4,095.00
Automobile	2,400.00
Mortgage Payable	12,569.00
Sabot Finance Co. (creditor)	853.50
Click Finance Co. (creditor)	1,235.40

6. From the following information as of June 30, 19— prepare a Balance Sheet for Morgan & Associates, which is owned by A. Morgan.

Bank Balance	$ 1,449.55
J. Arthur (a debtor)	75.00
N. Jackson (a debtor)	100.00
Land	4,000.00
Buildings	12,000.00
Equipment	1,975.00
Trucks	4,925.00
Hardware Supply Company (creditor)	461.20
General Merchants Co. (creditor)	1,105.63
Marvel Finance Co. (creditor)	163.00
Mortgage Payable	3,251.00

7. B. M. Kramer is the owner and operator of The Kramer Company. On September 30, 19— The Kramer Company had the following assets and liabilities. Prepare the September 30 Balance Sheet for The Kramer Company.

Assets

Cash on Hand	$ 106.70
Bank Balance	530.00
J. Crothers	100.00
R. Smart	370.00
Supplies	200.00
Furniture and Equipment	1,700.50
Delivery Equipment	2,100.00

Liabilities

Anglo Supply Co.	740.46
C. P. Gregg	1,000.00
Bank Loan	2,000.00

8. C. B. Travis, the proprietor of Travis and Company, gave the following list of assets and liabilities to a public accountant and asked him to prepare a Balance Sheet as of March 31, 19—. Prepare the Balance Sheet as if you were the public accountant.

Amounts Owed to Travis and Company

–G. Fordham	$ 42.16
–W. Gaines	743.86
–D. Samuelson	346.95

Amounts Owed by Travis and Company

–Raymond and Company	125.00
–Bank of Montreal	2,500.00
–Gem Finance Co.	1,236.45
–Dacana Insurance Co.	50.00
–Radelect Company	1,567.25
–Realmont Mortgage Co.	5,540.00

Office Supplies	326.40
Building	15,000.00
Bank Balance	946.03
Land	6,000.00
Office Equipment	1,960.00
Shop Equipment	535.00
Delivery Equipment	4,240.00

Chapter 2

CHANGING THE FINANCIAL POSITION

You now know how the financial position of a business (or individual) is found and how it is presented by means of a Balance Sheet. But the financial position does not remain constant. In an active business it is forever undergoing change. Whenever a payment is made, an article is bought, money is received, goods are sold, in fact, whenever any **transaction** takes place, the financial position of the business changes.

It is your next step in the study of Accounting to learn how the various business transactions affect and change the financial position. To begin, consider the Balance Sheet of Metropolitan Cartage on a certain date.

Metropolitan Cartage — Balance Sheet — - - DATE - - -

Assets			Liabilities		
Cash	1 500	00	Bank Loan	2 000	00
K. Lincoln	500	00	Garrott Supply Co.	1 574	00
Supplies	321	46	Central Hardware	656	74
Trucks	7 261	30	Mercury Finance Co.	600	00
Equipment	1 426	75		4 830	74
			Capital		
			H. Harrison, Capital	6 178	77
	11 009	51		11 009	51

TRANSACTION NO. 1

A regular monthly payment of $100 cash is made to the Mercury Finance Company.

After this payment is completed the financial position as shown by the above Balance Sheet will no longer be correct. Can you make the changes that are necessary to bring the Balance Sheet up to date? Try to do this before looking at the adjusted Balance Sheet shown at right.

Transaction No. 1 has had the following effect on the financial position of Metropolitan Cartage and is reflected in the new Balance Sheet:

(i) Cash has decreased by $100.

(ii) The amount owed to Mercury Finance Company has decreased by $100.

Metropolitan Cartage — Balance Sheet — - - DATE - - -

Assets			Liabilities		
Cash	1 400	00	Bank Loan	2 000	00
K. Lincoln	500	00	Garrott Supply Co.	1 574	00
Supplies	321	46	Central Hardware	656	74
Trucks	7 261	30	Mercury Finance Co.	500	00
Equipment	1 426	75		4 730	74
			Capital		
			H. Harrison, Capital	6 178	77
	10 909	51		10 909	51

K. Lincoln, who owes us $500, pays us $300 cash in part payment of his debt.

Can you make the changes necessary to bring the Balance Sheet up to date?

The corrected Balance Sheet is as shown at right.

In analysing transaction No. 2 note the following:
 (i)   Cash has increased by $300.
 (ii) The amount owed to us by K. Lincoln has decreased by $300.

You will see these changes by comparing this Balance Sheet with the preceding one.

Metropolitan Cartage — Balance Sheet
--- DATE ---

Assets			Liabilities		
Cash	1 700	00	Bank Loan	2 000	00
K. Lincoln	200	00	Garrott Supply Co.	1 574	00
Supplies	321	46	Central Hardware	656	74
Trucks	7 261	30	Mercury Finance Co.	500	00
Equipment	1 426	75		4 730	74
			Capital		
			H. Harrison, Capital	6 178	77
	10 909	51		10 909	51

A cash purchase of $50 of additional supplies is made.

Make the changes necessary to bring the Balance Sheet up to date.

The corrected Balance Sheet is as shown at right.

In analysing transaction No. 3 note that:
 (i)   Cash has decreased by $50.
 (ii) Supplies has increased by $50.

Metropolitan Cartage — Balance Sheet
--- DATE ---

Assets			Liabilities		
Cash	1 650	00	Bank Loan	2 000	00
K. Lincoln	200	00	Garrott Supply Co.	1 574	00
Supplies	371	46	Central Hardware	656	74
Trucks	7 261	30	Mercury Finance Co.	500	00
Equipment	1 426	75		4 730	74
			Capital		
			H. Harrison, Capital	6 178	77
	10 909	51		10 909	51

Mr. Harrison purchases for his store a piece of equipment costing $500 from Garrott Supply Co. Not wishing to pay the full price at the time of purchase, Mr. Harrison makes a cash down-payment of $125 and owes the balance of $375.

Make the changes necessary to bring the Balance Sheet up to date. The corrected Balance Sheet is as shown at right.

In analysing transaction No. 4 note the following:
 (i)   The Cash decreased by $125.
 (ii) The Equipment increased by $500.
 (iii) The Liability to Garrott Supply Co. increased by $375.

Metropolitan Cartage — Balance Sheet
--- DATE ---

Assets			Liabilities		
Cash	1 525	00	Bank Loan	2 000	00
K. Lincoln	200	00	Garrott Supply Co.	1 949	00
Supplies	371	46	Central Hardware	656	74
Trucks	7 261	30	Mercury Finance Co.	500	00
Equipment	1 926	75		5 105	74
			Capital		
			H. Harrison, Capital	6 178	77
	11 284	51		11 284	51

Metropolitan Cartage completes a storage service for G. Taylor at a price of $50. Mr. Taylor pays cash at the time the service is completed. (Remember that Metropolitan Cartage is in the business of providing a service to make a profit.)

Make the changes necessary to bring the Balance Sheet up to date.

The corrected Balance Sheet is as shown at right.

Metropolitan Cartage
Balance Sheet
--- DATE ---

Assets			Liabilities		
Cash	1 575 00		Bank Loan	2 000 00	
K. Lincoln	200 00		Garrott Supply Co.	1 949 00	
Supplies	371 46		Central Hardware	656 74	
Trucks	7 261 30		Mercury Finance Co.	500 00	
Equipment	1 926 75			5 105 74	
			Capital		
			H. Harrison, Capital	6 228 77	
	11 334 51			11 334 51	

It is a little more difficult to understand transaction No. 5 than it was to understand the previous four. But to understand the transaction is of the utmost importance. You must endeavour wholeheartedly to master completely the reasoning in one transaction before proceeding to the next.

Transaction No. 5 is explained as follows:

(i) Cash has increased by $50, the amount received from the customer, Mr. Taylor.

(ii) No other assets or liabilities have changed.

(iii) H. Harrison's Capital has increased by $50.

Remember that the fundamental accounting equation tells us to calculate Capital by subtracting total liabilities from total assets. In each of the first five Balance Sheets shown in this chapter you will find that the total assets minus the total liabilities is the same—$6,178.77. The total assets figure does not remain the same, nor does the total liabilities

figure, but the difference between them–capital–does remain the same.

The situation as a result of transaction No. 5 is different. After making the changes to any assets or liabilities affected by the transaction you will find that the difference between the total assets and the total liabilities is now $6,228.77–which is $50 more than it was before. The new figure of $6,228.77 is the up-to-date capital figure and the one that must be shown on the new Balance Sheet.

A piece of equipment which cost $120 and which is included in the equipment figure on the Balance Sheet at that amount is found to be no longer necessary and is sold to Morrison Brothers for $95 cash.

Make the changes necessary to bring the Balance Sheet up to date.

The corrected Balance Sheet is as shown at right.

Metropolitan Cartage
Balance Sheet
--- DATE ---

Assets			Liabilities		
Cash	1 670 00		Bank Loan	2 000 00	
K. Lincoln	200 00		Garrott Supply Co.	1 949 00	
Supplies	371 46		Central Hardware	656 74	
Trucks	7 261 30		Mercury Finance Co	500 00	
Equipment	1 806 75			5 105 74	
			Capital		
			H. Harrison, Capital	6 203 77	
	11 309 51			11 309 51	

The explanation for transaction No. 6 follows:

(i) Cash has increased by the amount of cash received, $95.

(ii) Equipment has decreased by $120. The item that was sold

was included in the Equipment figure at $120. Since it is no longer on hand, the Equipment figure must be $120 less than it was before in order to be correct.

(iii) Capital has decreased by $25. After changing the necessary assets and liabilities, the difference between total assets and total liabilities is $6,203.77, a decrease of $25.

You have studied the effect of six transactions on a financial position. You should now be ready to consider the concept of financial change in general.

The first step in the accounting process is the analysing of a transaction; that is, the breaking down of a transaction to determine the financial changes that result from it. It is imperative that you recognize the importance of performing this step correctly. As you will see later, the final product in accounting must be accurate. It is for this reason that you must be very careful in executing the first, or any step in the accounting process.

You must realize, too, that the possible number of different transactions is very large. To illustrate them all so that you might commit them to memory is not practicable. In the first place, it is unlikely that you could remember them all. But secondly, and more important, if you were to rely on the technique of committing transactions to memory, you could never become a truly accomplished accountant. A good accountant relies not on memory but on common sense, ingenuity, and clear thinking. He is able to handle any transaction, not just certain ones. In your work, you must endeavour to follow his good example.

The following suggestions will assist you in analysing transactions:

1. In general, endeavour to make your decision logically and to understand the results.
2. For each of the given transactions analyse the information carefully to decide what changes occur in any of the assets, liabilities, or both.
3. Recalculate the total assets and the total liabilities. Then calculate A–L to see if C has changed.
4. See that at least two of the individual items on the Balance Sheet (any of the assets, liabilities, or capital) have changed. It is possible that several items may have changed but never only one.

Exercises

1. Explain how a transaction is analysed.

2. In each of the following transactions name the accounts affected and indicate which accounts increase and which decrease.

Transactions

1. A cash payment is made to Ace Supplies, a creditor.
2. A new desk for the office is purchased for cash from Equipment Supply.
3. D. Murray, who owes us a sum of money, makes a cash payment on his debt.
4. We perform a service for a customer, J. Cooke, who pays us cash.
5. We purchase a new truck from Pine Motors but pay only one third of the cost in cash.
6. We buy stationery and supplies from Doug's Stationers but do not pay for them at the time of purchase.
7. The owner, J. Pitt, takes a sum of money out of the business for his personal use.

3. **P. Givens** is the proprietor of a business. The Balance Sheet at the close of business on January 31, 19— is as follows:

Givens' Cartage
Balance Sheet,
January 31, 19—

Assets		Liabilities	
Cash	$ 126.31	Francis Manley	$ 57.40
E. Foster	24.75	Burton Bros.	267.50
I. Noonan	10.50	Chartered Finance Co.	2,095.65
Trucks	4,946.00		$2,420.55
Supplies	115.00		
Equipment	1,150.00	*Capital*	
		P. Givens, Capital	3,952.01
	$6,372.56		$6,372.56

INSTRUCTION 1.

The business transactions of February 1 are listed below. Analyse each transaction and record the changes that are necessary. Show the Balance Sheet items that change, the amounts of the changes and whether they are increases or decreases.

Transactions

1. $24.75 cash is received from E. Foster in payment of his debt.
2. $150 cash is paid to Burton Bros. in part payment of the debt to that company.
3. A service is performed for a customer, G. Fields, at a price of $100. Mr. Fields pays cash at the time the service is performed.
4. $30 of supplies are purchased and received from Francis Manley but the supplies are not paid for.
5. A cash payment is received from I. Noonan in full payment of his debt.

INSTRUCTION 2.

After analysing all of the above transactions and recording the necessary changes, prepare the Balance Sheet at the close of business on February 1, 19—.

4. The Balance Sheet of Triangle Real Estate, at the close of business on September 30, 19— is as follows:

Triangle Real Estate
Balance Sheet,
September 30, 19—

Assets		*Liabilities*	
Cash	$ 216.00	Acme Supply	$ 562.00
P. Adams	375.00		
N. Serle	200.00	*Capital*	
J. Walker	150.00	J. Morse, Capital	1,521.40
Office Supplies	175.40		
Equipment	967.00		
	$2,083.40		$2,083.40

INSTRUCTION 1.

Analyse the transactions of October 1 listed below and record the necessary changes.

Transactions

1. Received $100 cash from N. Serle in part payment of the amount owed by him.
2. Paid $200 cash to Acme Supply in part payment of the debt owed to them.
3. Purchased supplies costing $29.50 from the Standish Company and paid cash for them.

4. Triangle Real Estate sells a home for Mr. A. J. Baxter. For this service Triangle Real Estate is paid a commission of $900 cash.
5. A new office desk is purchased from Ideal Office Outfitters for $195 cash.

INSTRUCTION 2.

Prepare the Balance Sheet at the close of business on October 1, 19—.

---

5. Merrymen Window Washers is a business owned and operated by C. Clyde. On November 30, 19— at the end of the day the financial position of Merrymen Window Washers is as shown by the following Balance Sheet.

Merrymen Window Washers
Balance Sheet
November 30, 19—

Assets		Liabilities	
Cash	$ 750.00	Simplex Finance	$1,560.00
D. Washer	75.00	Cleanall Supply	124.00
T. Bird	120.00	Piper's Garage	175.00
Supplies	80.00		$1,859.00
Truck	3,050.00		
Equipment	947.00	*Capital*	
		C. Clyde, Capital	3,163.00
	$5,022.00		$5,022.00

INSTRUCTION 1.

Analyse the transactions of December 1 listed below and record the necessary changes.

Transactions

1. Paid the regular monthly instalment payment to Simplex Finance; $125 cash.
2. Purchased $56 worth of supplies from Arthur Soaps but did not pay for them.
3. $100 cash is received from T. Bird in part payment of his debt to the business.
4. A new cash register is purchased from International Register Company. A cash down-payment of $100 is made; the balance of the $325 purchase price is to be paid at a later date.
5. The old cash register, included in the Equipment figure at $150, is sold to B. Lasby for $40 cash.

INSTRUCTION 2.

Prepare the Balance Sheet of Merrymen Window Washers at the close of business on December 1, 19—.

---

6. P. Severs is a lawyer in business for himself. On the morning of May 6, 19— the business has the following assets and liabilities.

Assets		Liabilities	
Cash	$ 761.25	Jack Wilson's Co.	$ 56.86
V. Brabson	100.00	Starter Finance Co.	1,320.00
T. Carlisle	50.00		
Office Supplies	42.00		
Office Equipment	330.00		
Automobile	2,500.00		

On May 6 Mr. Severs transacts the following business. Analyse the transactions and record the necessary changes.

Transactions

1. $750 cash is paid for an air-conditioner for the office.
2. Because the cash position of the business is very low, Mr. Severs transfers $500 cash from his personal bank account into the business.
3. A cash payment of $115 is paid to Starter Finance Co.
4. A. Bates, a client, is given legal advice by Mr. Severs. For the service performed for his client, Mr. Severs charged $75. Mr. Bates paid in cash.
5. Mr. Severs had his automobile washed and paid $2 cash.

INSTRUCTION 2.

Prepare the Balance Sheet of P. Severs at the close of business on May 6, 19—.

---

7. Alliance Appliance Service, owned by W. Wills, has the following assets and liabilities at the close of business on October 20, 19—.

Assets		*Liabilities*	
Cash	$ 516.20	Bank Loan	$1,000.00
N. Brock	100.00	Mortgage Payable	2,700.00
P. Jones	27.50		
Supplies	92.00		
Equipment	316.00		
Delivery Truck	2,750.00		
Building	10,000.00		

INSTRUCTION 1.

On October 21 the following transactions occur. Analyse them and record the necessary changes.

Transactions

1. The owner, in need of money for his personal use, draws $200 cash out of the business.
2. P. Jones comes to the store and pays his debt of $27.50.
3. A service is rendered for a customer. The customer pays the full amount of the bill in cash, $45.
4. A new electrical tester is purchased and paid for in cash, $110.
5. The regular monthly mortgage payment is made, $150 cash.

INSTRUCTION 2.

Prepare the Balance Sheet of the business as at the close of business on October 21, 19—.

Chapter 3

THE SIMPLE LEDGER

The exercises in Chapter 2 have given you practice in keeping certain 'financial positions' up to date. But the method employed–as you may already suspect–is not the one used by practising accountants. The method of Chapter 2 is much too cumbersome and untidy to be used in business. But if you fully understand the effect that transactions have on 'financial position', Chapter 2 has served a very worthwhile purpose.

In current accounting practice a most efficient and orderly system is used. But because of its design it cannot be explained in a few words, or even in a few chapters. Several chapters are necessary to unfold the full accounting story.

Financial Position Presented by Means of Ledger Accounts

The accounting function with which you are immediately concerned is the maintaining of an up-to-date 'financial position'. The universal method of performing this function is the **Double-Entry System of Accounting**. As you are about to see, it is a marvellously effective system.

Let us begin the study of this new method by looking at the Balance Sheet of City Moving and Storage. It presents 'financial position' in the form with which you are familiar.

City Moving and Storage Balance Sheet --- DATE ---					
Assets			**Liabilities**		
Cash	765	35	Bank Loan	3 000	00
R. Caswell	400	00	Packham Supply Co.	946	24
B. Atwell	220	00	Jenkins and Sons	1 000	00
W. Randall	150	00	Proctors Limited	516	28
Supplies	465	20		5 462	52
Trucks	5 075	00	**Capital**		
Equipment	4 674	00	B. J. Wilson, Capital	6 287	03
	11 749	55		11 749	55

You have already learned that the Balance Sheet itself is not a suitable means of dealing with a 'financial position' that is undergoing change. Accountants long ago recognized this problem and overcame it by developing a unique system of 'ledger' accounts. This system gives to each Balance Sheet item a separate and specially designed page on which the changes are recorded in a special way. Before explaining the system in detail let us examine the financial position of City Moving and Storage as presented by means of 'ledger' accounts.

There are a number of important features of this new presentation that must be carefully examined.

1. Each individual Balance Sheet item is given its own specially divided page with the name of the item at the top. Each of these pages is called an **Account.** In the illustration there are twelve accounts altogether. You must learn to refer to them as the Cash account, the R. Caswell account, the Merchandise Inventory account, the Bank Loan account, and so on.

2. The dollar value of each item, as taken from the previous Balance Sheet, is recorded in the account on the first line. It is especially important to record the dollar value on the correct side of the account. For any item, the correct side is the side on which the item would appear on a simple Balance Sheet. Observe that for each of the assets the dollar amount is placed on the left side of the account page and that for each of the liabilities and for the capital the dollar amount is placed on the right side of the account page.

Cash	
765.35	

R. Caswell	
400.00	

B. Atwell	
220.00	

W. Randall	
150.00	

Supplies	
465.20	

Trucks	
5,075.00	

Equipment	
4,674.00	

Bank Loan	
	3,000.00

Packham Supply Co.	
	946.24

Jenkins & Sons	
	1,000.00

Proctors Limited	
	516.28

B.J. Wilson, Capital	
	6,287.03

The Simple Ledger Accounts of City Moving and Storage.

3. All of the accounts together are called a **Ledger.** A ledger may be prepared in different forms. For instance, the accounts may be printed on cards, thus forming a card ledger; the accounts may be printed on loose-leaf pages, thus forming a loose-leaf ledger; or the accounts may be recorded on magnetic tape that can be read by a computer.

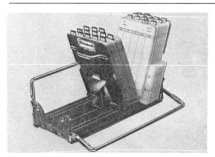

Card Ledger (Courtesy of Luckett Loose Leaf, Ltd.)

Loose-leaf Ledger (Courtesy of Luckett Loose Leaf, Ltd.)

Magnetic Tape (Courtesy of IBM Canada Ltd.)

4. The ledger and the Balance Sheet both show financial position, although in different ways. It follows, therefore, that given a ledger a Balance Sheet can be prepared from it, and conversely, given a Balance Sheet a ledger can be prepared from it.

Debit and Credit

In your work so far you have come to know that the matter of the left-hand side or the right-hand side is of considerable importance in accounting. When dealing with accounts, this is especially true. The theory of accounting by means of ledger accounts is based entirely on the understanding that there are two definite sides to every account page.

In referring to the two sides of an account, modern accountants use terms that have their origin in the Latin language. The left-hand side of an account is given the name **Debit** and the right-hand side is given the name **Credit.**

Any Account	
Left side is **DEBIT**	Right side is **CREDIT**
(short form **Dr.**)	(short form **Cr.**)

These two words have become what are probably the two most important words in the accountant's vocabulary. As the accounting system is developed you will see that they are used constantly.

Let us begin to use these two new terms right away. In looking back at the simple ledger on page 18 you will notice that the values of the assets were set up individually on the left-hand or debit side of their accounts, and that the values of the liabilities and of the capital were set up individually on the right-hand or credit side of their accounts. You may correctly conclude from this that the assets are considered to be debit accounts and that the liabilities and capital are considered to be credit accounts.

Now that you have been introduced to the simple ledger and to the terms 'debit' and 'credit', you must learn how they are used in performing the task at hand, namely, the recording of changes caused by transactions.

In order to record correctly the changes caused by transactions, follow the rules set out below:

Increases in Accounts

1. To increase an asset the amount of the increase is recorded on the debit side of the appropriate account.
2. To increase a liability or capital the amount of the increase is recorded on the credit side of the appropriate account.

Decreases in Accounts

1. To decrease an asset the amount of the decrease is recorded on the credit side of the appropriate account.
2. To decrease a liability or capital the amount of the decrease is recorded on the debit side of the appropriate account.

These rules are summarized in the chart below. It will be wise for you to impress them indelibly on your mind.

The importance of understanding the theory that is being introduced cannot be over-emphasized, for if you do not master the technique of analysing and recording transactions correctly, all of your subsequent work is apt to be so inaccurate as to render it useless.

To provide you with the opportunity of developing a facility with the new rules as quickly as possible, let us discuss a series of transactions pertaining to City Moving and Storage. In applying these new rules to the transactions, it is preferable that you perform the analysis mentally before reading the explanations that follow. You will remember, of course, that the beginning financial position of City Moving and Storage is represented by the ledger on page 18. It will be necessary for you to refer to this ledger in performing your analyses.

DEBIT AND CREDIT SUMMARY	TO INCREASE	TO DECREASE
ASSET	DEBIT THE ACCOUNT	CREDIT THE ACCOUNT
LIABILITY	CREDIT THE ACCOUNT	DEBIT THE ACCOUNT
CAPITAL (EQUITY)	CREDIT THE ACCOUNT	DEBIT THE ACCOUNT

TRANSACTION 1.

$200 cash is received from R. Caswell in part payment of his debt.

EXPLANATION

This transaction requires–
(i) That the Cash account be increased by $200. You will recall, of course, that Cash is an asset. As such, in accordance with the new rules, a debit entry (an amount recorded on the debit side of the account) is required to increase it. Or, as the bookkeepers say, "Debit Cash, $200."

(ii) That the R. Caswell account be decreased by $200. A look at the ledger tells you that the R. Caswell account is also an asset account and as such, in compliance with the rules, requires a credit entry to decrease it. In the language of the bookkeeper, "Credit R. Caswell, $200."

After recording the changes, the two accounts involved in the transaction appear as follows.

Cash		R. Caswell	
765.35		400.00	200.00
200.00			

TRANSACTION 2.

A storage service has been provided for a customer at a price of $100. As the storage contract has just been completed the customer pays cash for the service.

EXPLANATION

This transaction requires–
(i) That the Cash account be increased by $100. Since Cash is an asset, the rules require that it be debited for an increase; the amount, $100.
(ii) That the B. J. Wilson, Capital account be increased by $100. To increase Capital the rules state 'credit'. Therefore, credit B. J. Wilson, Capital, $100.

After recording the changes, the accounts involved in the transaction appear as follows.

Cash		B.J. Wilson, Capital	
765.35			6,287.03
200.00			100.00
100.00			

TRANSACTION 3.

A used moving truck costing $1,000 is purchased from Packham Supply Co. A cash down-payment of $250 is made at the time of the purchase and the balance is to be paid at a later date.

EXPLANATION

This transaction requires–
(i) That the Cash account be decreased by $250. According to the rules, since Cash is an asset, $250 must be entered on the credit side of the Cash account. Or, expressed in the new terminology, Cash must be credited $250.

(ii) That the Trucks account be increased by $1,000. According to the rules, since Trucks is an asset account, $1,000 must be entered on the debit side. Or, expressed in the new terminology, Trucks must be debited $1,000.
(iii) That the Packham Supply Co.

account be increased by $750. According to the rules, since the Packham Supply Co. account is a liability account, $750 must be entered on the credit side of the account. Or, expressed in the new terminology, Packham Supply Co. is to be credited $750.

After these changes are recorded, the accounts involved appear as follows.

Cash		Trucks		Packham Supply Co.	
765.35	250.00	5,075.00			946.24
200.00		1,000.00			750.00
100.00					

TRANSACTION 4.

$540 is paid to Jenkins & Sons.

EXPLANATION

This transaction requires–

(i) That the Cash account be decreased by $540. According to the rules, since Cash is an asset, $540 must be entered on the credit side. Expressed in the new terminology, Cash must be credited $540.

(ii) That the Jenkins & Sons account be decreased by $540. According to the rules, since Jenkins & Sons represents a liability, $540 must be entered on the debit side. Expressed in the new terminology, Jenkins & Sons must be debited $540.

After these changes are recorded, the accounts involved appear as follows.

Cash		Jenkins & Sons	
765.35	250.00	540.00	1,000.00
200.00	540.00		
100.00			

Finding the Balance of a T Account

The accounts used in this chapter are very simple accounts called T accounts. The T account obtained its name from the fact that its main rulings resemble the letter T. T accounts are used only for the purpose of explaining accounting theory. The formal account–the one used in actual practice–is introduced in Chapter 4.

In a ledger there are several accounts. Each account stores information about one specific item. The question to be answered now is this: What information does an account hold?

In addition to its name, which is written at the top, an account tells two things. These are–
1. The dollar value of the account.
2. The type of value it is–debit or credit.

These two things together are called the **Account Balance** or **The Balance of the Account**. To determine the balance of a T account two steps must be performed.
1. Add separately each of the two sides of the account. Write down the totals beneath the last figure on each side in tiny pencil as illustrated below. These tiny figures are called **Pencil Footings** or **Pin Totals**.
2. Subtract the smaller total from the larger total and write the difference beside the larger of the two totals. Circle the amount just written (as illustrated).

It now remains to interpret the information produced in these two accounts of City Moving and Storage. Looking at the two accounts below it should be easy enough for you to see that the Cash account has a debit balance of $275.35 and that the Jenkins & Sons account has a credit balance of $460.00. But it is not enough just to determine the balances; they must have some meaning for you. At this stage (as far as your knowledge has progressed), the fact that an account has a

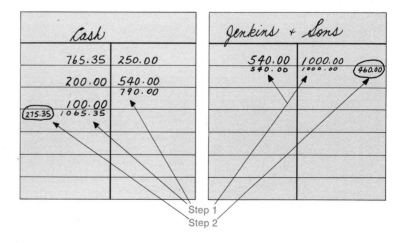

debit balance should mean to you that it is an asset account. Similarly, the fact that an account has a credit balance, and is not the Capital account, should mean to you that it is a liability account. The Jenkins & Sons account, for example, having a credit balance, is a liability account which means that City moving and Storage owes a sum of money to Jenkins & Sons. But, if by chance a debit balance had been produced in this account it would have been an asset account and would have meant that Jenkins & Sons owes a sum of money to City Moving and Storage.

On page 24 you will see the ledger of City Moving and Storage with all of the accounts showing the balances after transaction No. 9.

Accounting Entry

In addition to its use in its dictionary sense, "a writing or something in a book", the word entry is used in a special way. Whenever a transaction occurs and the resultant changes in accounts are decided upon, all of the account changes together are referred to as the accounting entry for the transaction.

In this chapter, so far, there have been four transactions and consequently four accounting entries. These four accounting entries are shown below.

If you have been observant, you will have noticed something about these four transactions that is very special, something that is basic to the whole accounting process. Each of these four transactions balances

within itself; that is, the total of the debit amounts is equal to the total of the credit amounts. This is a condition that will hold true for every possible transaction. If, in your work, you ever arrive at an accounting entry that does not balance within itself, you can be absolutely certain that the entry is not correct. On the other hand, just because you have worked out a balanced entry is no guarantee that the entry is correct. It merely means that it might be correct. If it doesn't balance, there is no such possibility.

Balancing the Ledger

A ledger is an alternate method of presenting the information on a Balance Sheet. Since a Balance Sheet must balance, so too then must a ledger.

When setting up a ledger, such as was done on page 18, it is the usual practice to obtain the information for the accounts from a Balance Sheet. This ensures that the ledger begins in a balanced position; that is, the money total of the accounts with debit balances is equal to the money total of the accounts with credit balances. Thereafter, the ledger is used to record the changes caused by business transactions. These changes are in the form of accounting entries. And, as was explained in the preceding section, each individual accounting entry itself balances. As a result, after each full accounting entry is recorded, provided of course that it is done correctly, the ledger will still be balanced.

The Trial Balance

The procedure to ascertain whether or not a ledger is in balance is quite simple. It is merely necessary to see if the total of all the accounts with debit balances is equal to the total of all the accounts with credit balances. If the two totals are the same the ledger is said to be **In Balance.** If they are not the same the ledger is said to be **Out of Balance** or **Not in Balance.** The whole process is called **Taking off a Trial Balance.**

In carrying out the balancing procedure your work may be done with pen and paper as illustrated on page 24, or it may be done by means of an adding machine. Other illustrations and a further discussion of trial balances will be found in Chapter 5.

Importance of the Trial Balance

It is important to an accountant to have his ledger in balance. He knows that if his ledger is not in balance his work cannot be accurate. To him a ledger out of balance is a sign that one or more errors have been made in the accounts and that he cannot rest until he finds and corrects them. He knows, too, that he must test the ledger fairly frequently. It is standard practice to take off a trial balance at least every month.

A ledger that is in balance proves only that it is mechanically or mathematically correct. It may be in balance and still have inaccuracies in it. These could be caused by the fact that the accountant made incorrect entries even though they were balanced ones.

When a ledger is not in balance it has mechanical errors in it. The errors may be in addition, or in entering an item on the wrong side, and so on. Sometimes, the error or errors can be found easily; at other times, they are quite obscure and difficult to detect. The technique for finding errors when a trial balance is out of balance is fully discussed in Chapter 5.

Trans-action No.	Account	Debit	Account	Credit
1	Cash	$200	R. Caswell	$200
2	Cash	$100	B. J. Wilson, Capital	$100
3	Trucks	$1,000	Cash Packham Supply Co.	$250 $750
4	Jenkins & Sons	$540	Cash	$540

Some additional transactions of City Moving and Storage are now given. Review the work of this chapter and then see if you can work out the entries for yourself before you look at the explanations that follow.

No. 5 The owner, B. J. Wilson, brings into the business $1,000 from his personal funds.

No. 6 $1,000 is paid to Packham Supply Company in part payment of the debt owed to that company.

No. 7 $85 of Supplies is purchased and paid for in cash.

No. 8 A $123 item of Equipment is purchased from Majestic Machinery Co., a new business supplier for City Moving and Storage. The item is not to be paid for until two months have passed, giving the store an opportunity to try out the new item.

No. 9 One of the lifting machines (part of Equipment) breaks down. $112 cash is spent on repairing the machine. (A common mistake made by beginners in respect to this type of transaction is to increase Equipment. To assist you over this hurdle, here is a clue: The owner is worse off financially because he had to repair the machine.)

EXPLANATIONS OF TRANSACTIONS 5 TO 9

No. 5 This transaction requires that—
 (i) Cash be increased by $1,000. (Increase an Asset.)
 (ii) Capital be increased by $1,000. (Increase Capital.)
The required accounting entry is:
Debit Cash, $1,000; Credit B. J. Wilson, Capital, $1,000.

No. 6 This transaction requires that—
 (i) Cash be decreased by $1,000. (Decrease an asset.)
 (ii) Packham Supply Co. be decreased by $1,000. (Decrease a liability.)
The required accounting entry is:
Debit Packham Supply Co., $1,000; credit Cash, $1,000.

No. 7 This transaction requires that—
 (i) Supplies be increased by $85. (Increase an asset.)
 (ii) Cash be decreased by $85. (Decrease an asset.)
The required accounting entry is:
Debit Supplies, $85; Credit Cash, $85.

No. 8 This transaction requires that—
 (i) Store Equipment be increased by $123. (Increase an asset.)
 (ii) Majestic Machinery Co. be set up as a liability of $123. (Increase a liability.) Since there is no account in the ledger at present for this company it will be necessary to prepare one.
The required accounting entry is:
Debit Store Equipment, $123; Credit Majestic Machinery Co., $123.

No. 9 This transaction requires that—
 (i) Capital be decreased by $112. (Decrease Capital.)
 (ii) Cash be decreased by $112. (Decrease an asset.)
The required accounting entry is:
Debit B. J. Wilson, Capital, $112; Credit Cash, $112.

The ledger of City Moving and Storage, after the nine transactions have been recorded and the up-to-date balances have been calculated, is shown on page 24. Notice in particular, in the Cash account, how an old balance is crossed out once a later one is determined.

Cash

765.35	250.00
200.00	540.00
	790.00
100.00	1,000.00
(278.35) 1065.35	
1,000.00	85.00
(78.35) 2065.35	
	112.00
	1987.00

R. Caswell

400.00	200.00
(200.00) 400.00	200.00

B. Atwell

220.00	
(220.00) 220.00	

W. Randall

150.00	
(150.00) 150.00	

Supplies

465.20	
	85.00
(550.20)	550.20

Trucks

5,075.00	
	1,000.00
(6075.00)	6,075.00

Equipment

4,674.00	
	123.00
(4797.00)	4797.00

Bank Loan

	3,000.00
	3,000.00 (3,000.00)

Packham Supply Co.

1,000.00	946.24
1,000.00	
	750.00
	1696.24 (696.24)

Jenkins + Sons

540.00	1,000.00
540.00	1,000.00 (460.00)

Proctors Limited

	516.28
	516.28 (516.28)

Majestic Machinery

	123.00
	123.00 (123.00)

B.J. Wilson, Capital

112.00	6,287.03
112.00	
	100.00
	1,000.00
	7387.03 (7275.03)

Trial Balance
--- DATE ---

Dr's	Cr's
78.35	3,000.00
200.00	696.24
220.00	460.00
150.00	516.28
550.20	123.00
6,075.00	7,275.03
4,797.00	
12,070.55	12,070.55

Balancing the Ledger.

Bookkeeping and Accounting Terms

Account: A specially ruled page used to record financial changes. There is one account for each different item affecting the financial position.

Ledger: A group or file of accounts that can be stored in the form of pages in a book, cards in a tray, or tape on a reel.

Debit: To record an amount on the left side of an account.

Credit: To record an amount on the right side of an account.

Account Balance: The present value of an account showing the dollar amount and an indication as to whether it is a debit or a credit value.

Accounting Entry: All of the account changes caused by one transaction expressed in terms of debits and credits. For each accounting entry the total of the debit amounts will equal the total of the credit amounts.

Trial Balance: A special listing of all the account balances in a ledger, the purpose of which is to see if the total of the accounts with debit balances is equal to the total of the accounts with credit balances. The process of obtaining this special listing is called 'balancing the ledger' or 'taking off a trial balance'.

Pencil Footings: / **Pin Totals:** Column or other totals written with tiny pencil figures.

Review Questions

1. What is an account?
2. What is a ledger?
3. Each side of an account is given a special name. What are they?
4. Describe the rule for recording an increase in an asset account; in a liability account; in the capital account.
5. Describe the rule for recording a decrease in an asset account; in a liability account; in the capital account.
6. Using a chart, summarize the rules of debit and credit.
7. Explain the procedure for finding the balance of a T account.
8. Three important pieces of information are stored in an account. What are they?
9. What are 'pin totals'? What is another name for pin totals?
10. If the R. Jones account has a debit balance, what does it mean?
11. The Hunt Brothers account has a credit balance. Explain.
12. What kind of balance does an asset account have? a liability account? the capital account?
13. Define 'accounting entry'.
14. Describe a special characteristic of all accounting entries.
15. Describe a special characteristic of the ledger.
16. What is a trial balance?
17. Explain the importance of a trial balance.
18. How does one know that the trial balance does not balance?
19. What is meant by a trial balance that does not balance?
20. Describe the procedure for taking off a trial balance.

Exercises

1.

Cash		Powell and Son		R. Smart, Capital	
250.00	190.00	200.00	250.00	150.00	3,140.00
1,210.00	48.00		90.00		
360.00	512.00				
29.00					

INSTRUCTION 1.

Calculate the balance of each of the above T accounts.

INSTRUCTION 2.

What does the debit balance in the Cash account indicate?

INSTRUCTION 3.

What does the credit balance in the Powell and Son account indicate?

INSTRUCTION 4.

What do you think the debit entry in the Capital account indicates?

2. In each of the following transactions indicate which account is debited and which account is credited.

Transactions

1. F. Baker invests cash to begin a business.
2. A supply of envelopes is purchased from Ace Stationers and paid for in cash.
3. A debt to Little Brothers is paid for in cash.
4. Cash is received from S. Mann, a debtor, in payment of his debt.
5. The owner withdraws cash from the business for his personal use.
6. A typewriter is purchased and received from Olympic Supply but is not paid for.
7. A service is performed for P. Glass. He agreed to pay for the service at the end of the month.

3. From the following information prepare a Trial Balance for the R. K. Smith Company. Date the Trial Balance September 30, 19—.

Account balances:

Cash, $7,000 Dr; W. Philips, $300 Dr; Equipment, $1,400 Dr; Land, $5,000 Dr; Buildings,

$10,000 Dr; Willwest Company,
$1,700 Cr; Mortgage on Build-
ing, $5,400 Cr; R. K. Smith,
Capital, $16,600 Cr.

---

4. Reliable Janitorial Service,
owned and operated by M. Fin-
ley, begins business with the following assets. There are no
liabilities.

Assets

Cash	$ 750.00
Supplies	56.00
Equipment	175.00
Truck	2,500.00

INSTRUCTION 1.

Set up the beginning financial
position in T accounts.

INSTRUCTION 2.

In the T accounts record the
accounting entries for each of
the transactions listed below.

Transactions

1. Purchased $150 of cleaning supplies from Special Chemicals Limited but did not pay for them.
2. Purchased a large vacuum cleaner from Proust Bros. and paid $300 cash.
3. Performed a cleaning service for S. Pearson at a price of $115. Mr. Pearson paid cash.
4. Performed a service for M. King at a price of $70. Mr. King agreed to pay in thirty days.
5. Paid $50 cash to Special Chemicals Limited.

INSTRUCTION 3.

After all of the transactions
have been completed, calculate
and record the balances in the
accounts.

INSTRUCTION 4.

Take off a trial balance to see
if the ledger is in balance.

---

5. T. Barkley, an accountant, is in
business with the following assets
and liabilities.

Assets		*Liabilities*	
Cash	$ 500.75	Proctors' Limited	$ 112.15
R. Burke	25.00	A. Rose and Son	64.25
P. Chapple	150.00	Familiar Finance	1,621.42
O. Patterson	78.00		
Supplies	85.00		
Equipment	1,956.25		
Automobile	3,050.00		

INSTRUCTION 1.

Set up the financial position of
T. Barkley in T accounts.

INSTRUCTION 2.

In the T accounts record the
accounting entries for the
transactions listed below.

Transactions

1. Received $78 cash from O. Patterson in
   payment of his debt to the business.
2. Paid $64.25 cash to A. Rose and Son.
3. The owner withdrew $250 cash from the
   business for his personal use.
4. An accounting service was performed for
   R. Burke at a price of $170. Mr. Burke
   agreed to pay for the service at a later date.
5. The office air-conditioner (included in the
   Equipment figure) broke down and had to
   be repaired at a cost of $47. Cash was paid
   for the repair.
6. An accounting service was performed for
   E. Green for $75 cash.

INSTRUCTION 3.

Calculate and record the balances in the accounts.

INSTRUCTION 4.

Take off a trial balance to see
if the ledger is in balance.

---

6. For each of the following transactions of East End Electric
   Repairs, owned by V. Marsh,
   record the accounting entry.
   Show the accounts that are
   debited and those that are credited as well as the corresponding
   amounts.

Transactions

1. Purchased $50 of supplies and paid cash
   for them.
2. Received $25 cash from C. Fells, a debtor.
3. Repaired a motor for a customer and received $35 cash.
4. Paid $100 cash to R. Tweed, a creditor.
5. The owner withdrew $110 cash from the
   business for his personal use.
6. $150 cash was paid for repairs to the de-
   livery truck which was damaged in a collision.
7. Performed a repair service for J. Wiley at a
   price of $82 but Mr. Wiley did not pay for
   it immediately.
8. A new typewriter was purchased for the
   office from Standard Typewriter Company
   at a cost of $350. $100 cash was paid at the
   time of the purchase and the balance was to
   be paid at a later date.
9. $200 cash was given to the bank for the
   purpose of reducing the bank loan.

---

7. A. Frost is a sign painter and
   truck letterer. His business has
   the following assets and liabilities.

Assets		Liabilities	
Cash	$ 216.00	Bank Loan	$ 500.00
G. Anderson	57.00	Consumers' Supply	375.20
N. Paul	102.00	Nu-Style Furniture	951.65
Office Supplies	80.00	Economy Finance	1,980.00
Painting Supplies	120.00	Mortgage Payable	5,092.25
Office Furniture	590.00		
Building	10,000.00		
Automobile	3,000.00		

INSTRUCTION 1.

Set up A. Frost's financial position in T accounts.

INSTRUCTION 2.

For the transactions listed below record the accounting entries in the T accounts.

Transactions

1. Received $25 cash from a customer for painting a sign.
2. Paid $100 to Consumers' Supply
3. Received $102 cash from N. Paul.
4. An extra office desk (which is included in the Office Furniture figure at $150) is sold to G. Brand at a price of $60. Mr. Brand paid $10 cash and owed the balance.

5. An additional $500 was borrowed from the bank.
6. Paid the regular monthly mortgage payment of $175 cash.
7. Paid the regular monthly finance payment to Economy Finance, $125.
8. Paid the balance owing to Consumers' Supply in cash.

INSTRUCTION 3.

Calculate the account balances and balance the ledger.

---

8. Rainbow Real Estate is a business owned by C. Rogers. The assets and liabilities of the business are as follows:

Assets		Liabilities	
Cash	$1,056.25	Bank Loan	9,000.00
A. Carlisle	516.00	Capitol Corporation	520.00
D. Murray	351.00		
Office Supplies	115.00		
Furniture and Equipment	916.00		
Properties Owned	8,042.00		
Automobile	2,965.00		

INSTRUCTION 1.

In T accounts set up the financial position of Rainbow Real Estate.

For the transactions which
follow record the accounting
entries in the T accounts.

Transactions

1. Received $516 cash from A. Carlisle.
2. Sold a home for V. Morris. For this service Mr. Morris owed $750 to Rainbow Real Estate.
3. Paid $35 cash for office supplies.
4. One of the properties owned by Rainbow Real Estate (included in the Properties Owned figure at $2,000) is sold for $3,000 cash.
5. $4,000 cash is paid to the bank to reduce the amount of the bank loan.
6. $100 cash is paid to Capitol Corporation.
7. $16 cash is paid for a new headlight for the automobile.
8. $351 cash is received from D. Murray.
9. The owner withdrew $200 cash for his personal use.
10. Received $250 cash from V. Morris.
11. Paid the balance of the debt to Capitol Corporation in cash.
12. Purchased a new office desk at a cost of $195 from Pioneer Furniture but did not pay cash for it.
13. Sold a home for A. McIntosh. Mr. McIntosh paid Rainbow Real Estate $900 cash for the service.

INSTRUCTION 3.

Calculate and record the
balances in the accounts and
take off a trial balance.

Chapter 4

FORMAL JOURNALIZING AND POSTING

Although the simple system described in Chapter 3 is theoretically sound and accurate, it is still not in the form used by today's businessmen. Businessmen and professional accountants have found that by modifying and expanding the simple system a far greater effectiveness is possible.

The Journal

The theory described so far suggests that only one device–the ledger–is used in the accounting process and that as accounting entries arise the only thing that happens to them is that they are recorded promptly in the accounts.

Unfortunately, this simple system contains a serious weakness. Since each accounting entry affects at least two, and sometimes several accounts, its various parts become scattered throughout the ledger. After a period of time, these scattered parts become buried in the accounts in a great mass of accounting entries, the result of continually occurring transactions. Eventually, for all practical purposes, it becomes impossible to reverse the accounting process; that is, to reconstruct any particular accounting entry from the bits and pieces that are spread throughout the ledger. But this reverse procedure is an essential function in the accounting process. For it seems always to be necessary to investigate some transaction which, for any of a variety of reasons, suddenly becomes troublesome.

To overcome this difficulty, another book is introduced into the system. This new book, called a **Journal**, is used expressly for the purpose of listing the accounting entries individually in the order in which they occur (chronologically). Each entry is first, or originally, recorded in the journal before being recorded in the ledger. The accounting entries as they appear in the journal are referred to as **Journal Entries** and the process of recording them in the journal is called **Journalizing**. And, because the journal entries are the first or original recording, the journal is known as a **Book of Original Entry**.

The Two-Column General Journal

There are several types of journals in actual use today, each one designed for a special purpose. The simplest journal and the one to be studied first in this text is the **Two-Column General Journal**. It is illustrated on page 32.

Familiarize yourself thoroughly with the two-column general journal. Examine the illustration on page 32, carefully noting the general appearance and the column headings. Then, more specifically, observe the following:

1. Each accounting entry is listed in a special way, balances within itself, and is separated from other accounting entries by a blank line. The debit accounts are listed first and are placed at the extreme left-hand side of the Particulars column. The debit amounts are placed in the Debit column. The credit accounts are listed in the Particulars column beneath the debit accounts but are indented approximately one inch. The credit amounts are placed in the Credit column.

2. Immediately beneath the accounting entry, and in the Particulars column only, a simple explanation is written. Each line of the explanation begins at the extreme left-hand side of the column. The explanations are simple, brief, and meaningful. They are to be thought out spontaneously–not memorized.

3. In respect to the date it is necessary to consider the year, the month, and the day separately.

   (a) On each page, the year is entered in small figures in the top half of the first line of the Date column. The year is not repeated for each journal entry; the figure at the top of the page is meant to serve all of the entries on the page. Occasionally, however, it may happen that the year changes before the page is completed. Then the new year is entered in small figures at the point on the page where the year changes (see illustration).

   (b) On each page, the month is entered in the month section of the Date column on the first line. It is not repeated for each journal entry, the intention being that the notation on the first line will serve all of the entries on the page. However, if the month changes before the page is completed, the new month is entered at the point of change.

   (c) For each journal entry, the day is entered once in the day section of the Date column on the line which corresponds with the beginning line of the journal entry. It is important to note that the day is recorded on the first line of each journal entry no matter how many journal entries may occur on any given day.

4. The Posting Reference (P.R.) column, often called the Folio (Fo.) column, is used to cross-reference the journal and the ledger. Cross-referencing is explained fully in a later section on 'Posting'.

5. It is permissible to use abbreviations in the journal (or in the ledger). The only place where abbreviations are not permitted is on financial statements, and the only financial statement with which you are acquainted up to this point is the simple Balance Sheet.

The Three-Column Account

In Chapter 3 the theory of entry making (the determining of accounting entries from the transactions) was demonstrated through the use of a simple two-sided account called the T account. It was explained at that time that the simple two-sided account, although ideal for theoretical explanations and discussion, is of little value in actual practice. Today's accounting requires an account that provides more detailed information in a more formal way.

The style of account that is most widely used today is the three-column account. Two illustrations of this type of account appear below and at the top of page 33.

At first glance, your normal reaction is probably that the formal account is radically different from the one used in Chapter 3. But you will find, upon closer examination, that the differences are logical and easily understood.

You will see in the formal account a Debit column and a Credit column. These two columns form the core of

Date		Particulars	P.R.	Debit	Credit
Dec.	17	Cash	1	17 42	
		T. Hill	2		17 42
		Paid the balance of his account			
	23	Supplies	6	50 00	
		Cash	1		50 00
		Letterhead and envelopes from Dover Stationery			
Jan.	7	Store Equipment	7	165 00	
		Cash	1		50 00
		Raynor Bros	22		115 00
		New Display cases			
	18	King Finance Co	21	126 74	
		Cash	1		126 74
		Monthly payment on auto			
	18	Cash	1	25 00	
		W. Foster	4	75 00	
		R. Jennings, Capital	31		100 00
		Sale to W. Foster			
	28	R. Jennings, Capital	31	200 00	
		Cash	1		200 00
		Owner's withdrawal			
Feb.	2	Raynor Bros	22	115 00	
		Cash	1		115 00
		Payment of balance of account			

General Journal — Page 16

A Page from a Two-Column General Journal

Account Cash							No. 1	
Date		Particulars	P.R.	Debit	Credit	DR. CR.	Balance	
June	3		J1	1 750 00		DR.	1 750 00	
	10		J2		106 00	DR.	1 644 00	
	12		J2	174 70		DR.	1 818 70	
	18		J3	64 26		DR.	1 882 96	
	30		J4		250 00	DR.	1 632 96	
July	2		J5	25 00		DR.	1 657 96	
	4		J5		135 46	DR.	1 522 50	

Account	Acme Finance Company					No. 23	
Date	Particulars	P.R.	Debit	Credit	DR. CR.	Balance	
19-1 Nov 15		J9		1 500 00	CR	1 500 00	
19-2 Feb 15		J11	150 00		CR	1 350 00	
May 15		J14	150 00		CR	1 200 00	
Aug 15		J16	150 00		CR	1 050 00	
Nov 15		J19	150 00		CR	900 00	

1. Obtain an unused page of account paper;
2. Write the name of the new item at the top of the page in the space designated. This is called the **Account Title**.
3. Write the number given to the new account in the space designated.
4. Place the new account in its proper place in the ledger.

The Basic Accounting Procedure

You know that there are two important books in the field of accounting. These two books–the journal and the ledger–are commonly referred to as the **Books of Account** or as the **Books**.

You have also learned that each accounting entry is recorded in the journal before it is entered in the ledger. This is a cardinal rule in Accounting except in advanced systems using complex equipment. As far as you are concerned, do not record entries in the ledger without their first being journalized.

For every transaction the basic procedure is:

1. Determine the accounting entry and record it in the journal. The method of doing this–journalizing–has already been discussed in this chapter.
2. Transfer the information shown in the journal to the appropriate accounts in the ledger. The routine for doing this, called **Posting**, is explained in the next section.

Posting

The process of transferring the information from the journal to the ledger is called **Posting**. Before beginning the actual posting, you should have both the journal and the ledger available on the desk or table in front of you with the journal open at the entry to be posted. Also, you should have a supply of ledger paper close at hand so that, if the entry to

the account and they correspond to the simple account that you have already used. In addition, the formal account has the following columns:

Date: This column is used to record the date on which the entry is recorded in the journal.* With the introduction of a Date column, it becomes necessary that each amount recorded in the account be entered on a separate line. The rules in respect to the year, month, and day are precisely the same as for the journal.

Particulars: This column is not used for every posting. You will not be required to use it until Chapter 7, at which point it will be used to record Invoice numbers. This column is often called **Items**.

Posting Reference: This column is used to cross-reference the journal and the ledger and is fully explained in a later section on 'Posting'. This column often goes under the name **Folio**.

Dr/Cr: This column is used to indicate the type of balance that the account has. It must be used in conjunction with the Balance column.

Balance: The Balance column is the most important addition to the account. With this column the balance in the account is now always readily available since, after each

*The word 'entry' has different meanings in Accounting. It may mean the full accounting entry with which you are already familiar. Or, as is intended in this instance, it may mean just one part of the full accounting entry.

new amount is entered, the new balance is usually calculated and recorded. Note carefully that the most recently determined balance is entered on the same line as the most recently entered amount and represents the balance up to and including that amount; it must not be entered on any other line. It is most essential that you become proficient in the handling of this important column.

Numbering the Accounts

Although it is not absolutely necessary, most bookkeepers number the accounts in the ledger in order to improve the efficiency of the system. The technique of numbering the accounts varies according to the size and complexity of the business and on the views of the bookkeeper. In this text the numbering system begins with the very simple arrangement shown below.

Assets ... No. 1 to No. 20 inclusive
Liabilities No. 21 to No. 30 inclusive
Capital ... No. 31

In larger businesses having automated bookkeeping systems, coding of the accounts by means of numbers is essential.

Opening an Account

As transactions occur in business, it often happens that an accounting entry affects an item for which there is no account in the ledger. When this happens, it is necessary to prepare an account for the new item and place it in the proper place in the ledger. This is called **Opening an Account**. To open an account it is necessary to:

be posted includes any item for which there is no account in the ledger, an account may be opened for that item. You are then ready to commence the posting routine.

In posting, **each debit and credit amount of each journal entry is dealt with individually.**

Step 1. Find the account in the ledger for the item to be posted (i.e., recorded in the ledger from the journal).

Step 2. In the account, on the first unused line and in the appropriate columns, record the amount and the date shown in the journal for this item. Naturally, the debit amounts of any journal entries will be recorded in the Debit columns of the accounts and the credit amounts of any journal entries will be recorded in the Credit columns of the accounts.

Step 3. In the account, on the same line as step 2 and in the Posting Reference column, record the journal page number from which the entry is taken, prefixed by a code letter or letters–e.g., J14. It is necessary to use a journal code because, in actual practice, several journals are used simultaneously and it is necessary to indicate which journal is being referred to. The code for the general journal may be any one of the following three: J, G, or G.J. But once having selected one of these, it must be used consistently throughout the ledger.

Step 4. Calculate and enter the new balance of the account in the Balance column and indicate whether it is a debit or a credit balance in the small column to the left of the Balance column.

Step 5. In the journal, in the Posting Reference column and on the same lines as the amount being posted, record the number of the account to which the posting was just made. Steps 3 and 5 constitute 'cross-referencing' to which reference has been made previously. The recording of the account

number in the journal is the final step in the posting of any one individual item. The presence of the account number in the journal is evidence that the posting of that item is completed. And the absence of the account number in the journal is evidence that the posting of that item is not completed. If for any reason, perhaps for a telephone call, your posting of the journal is interrupted, you will be able to tell by a glance at

the Posting Reference column where to recommence posting upon your return.

There are some accountants who do not number the accounts in the ledger. Where this occurs, a check-mark (√) or some other symbol (e.g. ✓) must be placed in the Posting Reference column of the journal instead of the account numbers to indicate that the posting of that amount has been completed.

A partially posted journal page. The P.R. column indicates that the first two entries have been posted but that the third one has not been posted:

Date	Particulars	P.R.	Debit	Credit
19— June 17	Supplies	7	37 50	
	Anderson Bros	25		37 50
	Ledger and typing paper			
18	Cash	1	100 00	
	C. Winston	4		100 00
	Partial payment of account bal.			
18	Office Furniture		125 00	
	Cash			50 00
	Office Supplies Company			75 00
	New desk from Office Supplies			

General Journal — *Page 3*

The ledger accounts needed to post the last entry in the journal above as they might appear before postings are made:

Account Cash — No. 1

Date	Particulars	P.R.	Debit	Credit	DR. CR.	Balance
19— May 31		J1	2 000 00		Dr.	2 000 00
June 6		J2		1 475 00	Dr.	525 00
12		J2	746 47		Dr.	1 271 47
18		J3	100 00		Dr.	1 371 47

Account Office Furniture — No. 11

Date	Particulars	P.R.	Debit	Credit	DR. CR.	Balance
19— May 31		J1	1 250 00		Dr.	1 250 00
June 15		J2	310 00		Dr.	1 560 00

Account Office Supplies Company — No. 24

Date	Particulars	P.R.	Debit	Credit	DR. CR.	Balance
19— June 2		J1		500 00	Cr.	500 00
7		J2	500 00			0

On the previous page there are two illustrations to be used to demonstrate the 'posting' process. These illustrations are—

1. A page of a general journal on which the latest recorded journal entry is not yet posted (as indicated by the absence of any account numbers beside that entry in the Posting Reference column).

2. The ledger accounts that are affected by this entry, as they appear before the posting of the entry under discussion. (You will see in the Office Suppliers Company account a good method of indicating that an account has no balance; i.e., that the balance is nil.)

To begin the posting of a journal entry, each amount in the entry is usually considered in turn. In this example, the first item to be considered is the debit of $125 to the Office Furniture account. Step 1 in the posting process, assuming that the journal is opened at the correct page, is to open the ledger at the Office Furniture account. Steps 2, 3, 4, and 5 (as stated on page 34) are then performed mechanically in turn as illustrated at top right.

The second item to be considered (in posting the sample entry) is the credit of $50 to the Cash account. Step 1 in the posting process is to turn to the Cash account in the ledger. Then, steps 2, 3, 4, and 5 follow mechanically (lower right).

Notice in the journal how the Posting Reference column serves to indicate the point at which the posting has been completed. If you were called away from your work at this point, you would be able to tell by a glance at this column upon your return that you should recommence your posting with the $75 credit to the Office Suppliers Company account.

The final item to be considered (in posting the sample entry) is

Account *Office Furniture* — Step 1: Open the ledger at this account — No. 11

Date	Particulars	P.R.	Debit	Credit	DR./CR.	Balance
May 31		J1	1 250 00		Dr	1 250 00
June 15	Step 3: Record the journal page number	J2	310 00		Dr	1 560 00
18		J3	125 00		Dr	1 685 00

Step 2: Record the date and the debit amount as shown in the journal entry

Step 4: Enter the new balance

General Journal — Page 3

Date	Particulars	P.R.	Debit	Credit
June 17	Supplies	7	37 50	
	Anderson, Bros.	25		37 50
	Ledger and typing paper			
18	Cash	1	100 —	
	C. Winston	4		100 —
	Partial payment of account bal.			
18	Office Furniture	11	125 —	
	Cash			50 —
	Office Suppliers Company			75 —
	New desk from Office Suppliers			

Step 5: Enter the account number

Account *Cash* — Step 1: Open the ledger at this account — ACCOUNTS — No. 1

Date	Particulars	P.R.	Debit	Credit	DR./CR.	Balance
May 31		J1	2 000 00		Dr.	2 000 00
June 6		J2		1 475 00	Dr.	525 00
12	Step 2: Record the date and the credit amount as shown in the journal entry	J2	746 47		Dr.	1 271 47
18		J3	100 00		Dr.	1 371 47
18	Step 3: Record the journal page number	J3		50 00	Dr.	1 321 47

Step 4: Enter the new balance

18	Office Furniture	11	125 —	
	Cash	1		50 —
	Office Suppliers Company			75 —
	New desk from Office Suppliers			

JOURNAL

Step 5: Enter the account number

the credit of $75 to the Office Suppliers Company account. It will be necessary for you to repeat the posting process for this item in a manner identical to that already executed for the first two items.

After completing the posting of this third item, the journal and the three accounts involved appear as illustrated in the first four figures shown at right.

		General Journal			Page 3		
Date		Particulars	P.R.	Debit		Credit	
June 17		Supplies	7	37	50		
		Anderson Bros.	25			37	50
		Ledger and typing paper					
	18	Cash	1	100	00		
		C. Winston	4			100	00
		Partial payment of account bal.					
	18	Office Furniture	11	125	00		
		Cash	1			50	00
		Office Suppliers Company	24			75	00
		New desk from Office Suppliers					

Account	Cash							No. 1		
Date		Particulars	P.R.	Debit		Credit		DR.CR.	Balance	
May 31			J1	2 000	00			Dr	2 000	00
June 6			J2			1 475	00	Dr	525	00
12			J2	746	47			Dr	1 271	47
18			J3	100	00			Dr	1 371	47
18			J3			50	00	Dr	1 321	47

Account	Office Furniture							No. 11		
Date		Particulars	P.R.	Debit		Credit		DR.CR.	Balance	
May 31			J1	1 250	00			Dr	1 250	00
June 15			J2	310	00			Dr	1 560	00
18			J3	125	00			Dr	1 685	00

Account	Office Suppliers Company							No. 24		
Date		Particulars	P.R.	Debit		Credit		DR.CR.	Balance	
June 2			J1			500	00	Cr	500	00
7			J2	500	00				—	
18			J3			75	00	Cr	75	00

The Opening Entry

You have already learned that, before any accounting entry is recorded in the ledger, it must first be listed in the journal. You must be sure to do this at all times, even for the very first entry–the one that begins the set of books.

To begin or 'open' a set of books, the beginning financial position must be set up in the accounts. But, in compliance with the rule above, before the amounts are placed in the accounts, they must be recorded in the journal as a journal entry. This **Opening Entry**, the one which starts the books off, is then posted to the ledger accounts in the usual way.

For example, Tom Wilson begins business on April 30, 19— with the financial position shown by the Balance Sheet shown to the right.

Tom Wilson
Balance Sheet
April 30, 19—

Assets			Liabilities		
Cash	1 564	67	Courier Mfg. Co.	3 649	16
C. Ferris	126	50	London Wholesale	1 472	90
J. Bancroft	300	00		5 122	06
Merchandise Inventory	7 641	32			
Office Supplies	125	00	Capital		
Equipment	4 765	00	Tom Wilson, Capital	9 400	43
	14 522	49		14 522	49

36

To open the books of Tom Wilson, it is necessary to record the beginning financial position in the form of a journal entry as shown at right. This journal entry, the opening entry, will then be posted to the ledger accounts in the usual manner.

The Opening Entry for Tom Wilson

Date		Particulars	P.R.	Debit	Credit
Apr.	30	Cash		1,564 67	
		C. Ferries		126 50	
		F. Bancroft		300 00	
		Merchandise Inventory		7,641 32	
		Office Supplies		125 00	
		Equipment		4,765 00	
		Courier Mfg. Co.			3,649 16
		London Wholesale			1,472 90
		Tom Wilson, Capital			9,400 43
		To open the books of Tom Wilson			
		- financial position of Apr. 30			

General Journal — Page 1

The Trial Balance

Periodically, it is necessary to test the mechanical accuracy of the ledger by means of a trial balance. This is usually done at the end of each month. The reasons for a trial balance being necessary have been discussed previously on page 22.

Three different types of trial balances are available to the bookkeeper. The method which he chooses will depend on his particular point of view.

One method of preparing a trial balance is to list separately on a piece of paper the debit balances and the credit balances from the ledger. When these two lists are totaled, the two totals should agree. The piece of paper on which the trial balance is prepared should be headed with the name of the business or individual, the words 'Trial Balance', and the date of the balances.

A second method of preparing a trial balance is to list the balances from the ledger on a paper tape using an adding machine. With this method the debit balances are entered into the machine as plus amounts and the credit balances are entered into the machine as minus amounts. The total of all the balances should be nil since the plus amounts entered into the machine should equal the minus amounts entered into the machine. As in the first method, the tape should be headed with the name of the business or individual, the words 'Trial Balance', and the date of the balances.

Although prepared in an informal manner, the first two methods are perfectly acceptable. Some accountants, however, use a third method, insisting that the trial balance be prepared in a formal way. With this method each account is listed in order and the account balance is placed in a Debit column or a Credit column depending on the type of balance. After all the accounts have been listed the two columns are totaled and agreed. The formal trial balance is headed in the same way as the two informal methods. It is illustrated at the top of page 38.

Regardless of the method used, a trial balance should be kept on file for a short time, at least until a subsequent one is prepared at the end of the following month, but more commonly until after the visit of the official auditors.

Correcting Errors in the Books

Over the years, it has become an established rule in the accounting profession that the making of erasures is never permitted. Since erasures may arouse the suspicions of the auditors (the official examiners of the books and records), it has become standard practice not to make erasures under any circumstances. Consequently, it is necessary to make the corrections in some other way.

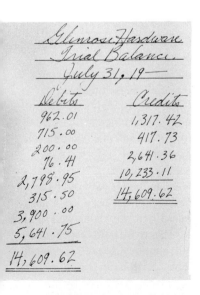

Glenrose Hardware
Trial Balance
July 31, 19—

Debits	Credits
962.01	1,317.42
715.00	417.73
200.00	2,641.36
76.41	10,233.11
2,798.95	14,609.62
315.50	
3,900.00	
5,641.75	
14,609.62	

Trial Balance (Method 1)

Glenrose Hardware
Trial Balance
July 31, 19—

```
            0 0 T
      9 6 2.0 1
      7 1 5.0 0
      2 0 0.0 0
        7 6.4 1
    2,7 9 8.9 5
      3 1 5.5 0
    3,9 0 0.0 0
    5,6 4 1.7 5
    1,3 1 7.4 2  −
      4 1 7.7 3  −
    2,6 4 1.3 6  −
  1 0,2 3 3.1 1  −
            0 0 T
```

Trial Balance (Method 2)

Trial Balance (Method 3—The Formal Method)

An error which is detected very soon after it is made usually presents no problem in making the correction. It is simply a matter of stroking neatly through the incorrect words or amount and inserting the correct words or amount immediately above. Examples of this type of correction are shown below.

It should be evident from the examples that a person who has a large style of handwriting will encounter difficulty in making corrections. In his regular work, an accounting clerk should make his letters and figures small enough to facilitate the subsequent correction of possible errors.

Any single error may necessitate the making of several corrections to completely rectify the books of account. For instance, a journal entry with a wrong amount could be posted to the accounts and the new account balances determined before the error is detected. To rectify this error it would be necessary to change the amount in the journal, to change the posting in the account, and to recalculate and enter the correct account balance.

On many occasions the accountant may not notice an error until after quite some time has elapsed. By the time it comes to his attention many subsequent entries, postings, balances, and even trial balances, all incorporating the effect of the error, may have been made. Making the correction in the manner just described usually requires a number of changes.

Some errors can be corrected by means of a correcting journal entry. Using this method the incorrect entry is left untouched and a new (correcting) entry is worked out and journalized. The correcting entry must cause the accounts to reflect correctly the original transaction.

For example, suppose that a clerk incorrectly recorded a cash purchase of supplies as a credit purchase of supplies. The incorrect journal entry made by the clerk might be as follows:

Supplies	105.00	
Weaver Brothers		105.00

On discovering the error, it will be necessary for the accountant to make the following correcting entry:

Weaver Brothers	105.00	
Cash		105.00

The two entries considered together reflect the correct position.

On Account

The term 'on account' is used extensively in modern business. For that reason, it is an absolutely essential part of business vocabulary.

The term is used in four specific ways.

1. When something is purchased but not paid for at the time the purchase is made, i.e., a credit purchase, it is commonly referred to as a purchase on account.
2. When something is sold but no money is received for it at the time of the sale, i.e. a credit sale, it is commonly referred to as a sale on account.
3. When money is paid out to a creditor for the purpose of decreasing the balance owed to him, it is said to be paid on account.
4. When money is received from a debtor for the purpose of reducing the balance owed by him, it is said to be received on account.

Correcting a name in the journal.

Correcting amounts in the account.

38

After a time, if an account page becomes filled, it is necesary to continue the account on a new page. It is customary to start the new page in a special way from the information on the last line of the finished page. This process is called **Forwarding**, and the steps involved are:

1. Prepare a new account page by entering the account title and the account number which will be the same as on the finished account page.

2. On the last line of the finished account page, and in the Particulars column, write the words 'Carried Forward' or more simply, just 'Forwarded'.

3. On the first line of the new account page write the following information (obtained from the last line of the completed page):
   (a) The date of the last entry.
   (b) In the Particulars column, the words 'Brought Forward', or more simply, just 'Forwarded'.
   (c) In the P.R. Column, a dash.
   (d) In the Balance column, the last balance including the balance indicator.

Notice that nothing is written at this time in the Debit or credit columns of the new page.

After completing the process, the completed account page and the new account page might appear as follows:

Account J. J. Barker						No. 4	
Date	Particulars	P.R.	Debit	Credit	DR. CR.	Balance	
Feb 7		J 1	150 62		DR	150 62	
9		J 3	374 50		DR	525 12	
11		J 5		150 62	DR	374 50	
12		J 5	216 51		DR	591 01	
16		J 8	75 62		DR	666 63	
18		J 9		374 50	DR	292 13	
19		J 9	583 62		DR	875 75	
21	Forwarded	J 10		292 13	DR	583 62	

The Finished Account Page After Being Forwarded.

Account J. J. Barker						No. 4	
Date	Particulars	P.R.	Debit	Credit	DR. CR.	Balance	
Feb 21	Forwarded	—			DR.	583 62	

The New Account Page With the Balance Brought Forward.

Bookkeeping and Accounting Terms

Journal: A specially ruled book in which accounting entries are recorded in the order in which they occur.

Journalizing: The process of recording accounting entries in a journal.

Book of Original Entry: Any journal, that is, the books in which the entries are originally recorded.

Two-Column General Journal:	The simplest type of journal, in which there are two money columns, one for the debit amounts and one for the credit amounts.
Three-Column Account:	The most commonly used type of account, in which there are three money columns, one for the debit amounts, one for the credit amounts, and one for the amount of the balance.
Opening an Account:	The process of setting up a new account in the ledger.
Account Title:	The name written at the top of an account.
Books of Account:	The journal and the ledger.
Posting:	The process of transferring the accounting entries from the journal to the ledger.
Opening Entry:	The first entry in the general journal, the one that records the beginning financial position and starts the books of account.
On Account:	(Refer to page 38 for the explanation of the four uses of this expression.)
Forwarding:	The process of transferring certain information from the bottom of a completed page to the top of a new page.
Opening the Books:	The whole process of beginning a set of books of account for a business, individual, or organization.

Review Questions

1. Define 'journal'.
2. In what order are accounting entries recorded in the journal?
3. What are journal entries?
4. Define 'journalizing'.
5. Define 'book of original entry'.
6. Briefly name and describe the simplest type of journal.
7. When journalizing, which accounts are listed first?
8. When journalizing, which accounts are indented?
9. On a journal page where does the accounting clerk enter the year? the month? the day?
10. What is another name for Posting Reference?
11. Is it permissible to use abbreviations in a journal? a ledger?
12. Briefly describe the three-column account.
13. Why do most accountants number the ledger accounts?
14. Explain the meaning of 'opening an account'.
15. What are the 'books of account'?
16. Briefly define 'posting'.
17. Give the five steps involved in posting.
18. How many of these steps are performed in the account? in the journal?
19. How is an accountant able to tell if a journal entry has been posted?
20. Briefly describe 'opening entry'.
21. Briefly describe three ways of preparing a trial balance.
22. Why are erasures not permitted in the books?
23. Describe two ways of correcting errors in the books.
24. Give four ways in which the term 'on account' is used.
25. Briefly describe the forwarding procedure.

Exercises

1. R. Bell begins business with the following assets and liabilities: Cash, $1,200; Office Equipment, $900; Land, $3,500; Building $5,900; amount owed to Diamond Equipment, $350; Mortgage on Building, $2,000.

    Record the opening entry for R. Bell in a two-column General Journal.

2. For each of the transactions listed below indicate which accounts are debited and which accounts are credited. Select the accounts from the following list:

    Cash
    Adams & Company
    Office Equipment
    Beck Brothers
    Clair Garage
    P. H. Morgan, Capital

    Transactions

    1. Received cash from Adams & Company on account.
    2. Paid cash to Clair Garage on account.
    3. Purchased a new adding machine from Beck Company on account.
    4. Performed a service for a customer for which he paid cash.
    5. Performed a service for Adams & Company, a customer, on account.

3. Identify each of the accounts listed below as an Asset account, a Liability account, or a Capital account.
    Automobile, Office Machines, Ace Equipment (creditor), Queen Repairs (debtor), Cash, Bank Loan.

4. The Balance Sheet of J. A. Munro, a lawyer, on March 31, 19— was as follows:

J. A. Munro
Balance Sheet
March 31, 19—

Assets		Liabilities	
Cash	$1,941.82	Elite Equipment	$ 174.00
P. O. Ewing	76.00	Legal Publishers	81.60
R. M. Keyes	178.50		$ 255.60
Law Library	565.50		
Office Equipment	724.90	*Capital*	
		J. A. Munro, Capital	3,231.12
	$3,486.72		$3,486.72

INSTRUCTION 1.

Journalize and post the opening entry on April 1, 19—.

INSTRUCTION 2.

Journalize and post the following transactions:

Transactions

April

2 Received $38 cash from P. O. Ewing on account.

3 Performed a service for a customer and received $50 cash.

4 Paid $100 cash to Elite Equipment on account.

5 Purchased $150 of additional books for the law library from Legal Publishers on account.

5 The proprietor withdrew $200 cash for his personal use.

8 Performed a legal service for R. M. Keyes who did not pay for it at the time. A bill for $70 was sent to him.

10 Received $178.50 cash from R. M. Keyes on account.

11 A typewriter which had originally cost $150 was sold for $100 cash.

12 P. O. Ewing paid the balance of his account.

15 Legal Publishers account was paid in full.

15 Performed a legal service for a customer and received $25 cash.

INSTRUCTION 3.

Balance the ledger.

---

5. Topflight Tool Rentals is a business owned and operated by Wm. R. Doyle. On October 1, 19—, the assets and liabilities of the business were as follows:

Assets		Liabilities	
Cash	$ 1,950.62	Apoca Equipment	$4,750.00
J. Hardie	110.00	Eastern Equipment	2,500.00
S. Seward	25.00	John's Garage	65.00
M. Singer	175.00		$7,315.00
Rental Tools	12,050.00		
Shop Equipment	2,470.00	Owner's Capital	
Delivery Truck	2,950.00		?
	$19,730.62		

INSTRUCTION 1.

Journalize and post the opening entry.

INSTRUCTION 2.

Journalize and post the following transactions:

Transactions

October

2 Received $50 cash from J. Hardie on account.

3 Purchased $120 of rental tools from Apoca Equipment on account.

3 Rented a tool to a customer who paid $15 cash for the use of it.

4 Rented a tool to a customer who paid $25 cash for the use of it.

5 $500 was paid to Eastern Equipment on account.

8 M. Singer paid his account balance in full.

10 S. Seward who had rented a large piece of equipment for three weeks was issued a bill for $400.

11 $750 was paid to Apoca Equipment on account.

12 S. Seward paid $300 on account.

15 John's Garage account was paid in full.

15 A tool valued in the accounts at $75 was broken beyond repair and was thrown out.

15 S. Seward paid the balance of his account in full.

INSTRUCTION 3.

Balance the ledger.

---

6. Journalize the following transactions of John Miller on page 14 of his General Journal. In preparing these journal entries use the account names that seem most appropriate to you.

Transactions

May

3 Received $180 from J. Jenson on account.

5 Paid $100 to Acme Supply Company on account.

6 A payment on account of $75 was made to City Finance Company.

7 Performed a service for P. Workman and received $40 cash.

10 Purchased $102 of supplies for cash from Anchor Supplies.

13 Performed a $100 service on account for O. R. Thomas.

13 A new delivery truck was purchased from Elite Motors. The cost price of the truck was $2,800. A cash down-payment of $1,000 was made at the time of the purchase, the balance to be paid later.

14 $150 of store machinery was purchased from The Standard Company on account.

15 The owner withdrew $27 for his personal use.

15 Borrowed $1,500 from the bank.

15 Paid $25 for repairs to the delivery truck.

---

7. The Crown Repair Shop, owned by W. T. Hall, is a business that has been in operation for several years. The trial balance of the business on March 31, 19— is as follows:

The Crown Repair Shop
Trial Balance
March 31, 19—

	Debit	Credit
Cash	$ 2,273.60	
J. Watson	47.20	
Amber Bros.	16.80	
Supplies	2,000.00	
Machinery	3,500.00	
Truck	2,068.00	
Office Furniture and Equipment	900.00	
Parker's Service Station		$ 27.60
Harold's Hardware		563.65
Regal Supply		729.56
W. T. Hall Capital		9,484.79
	$10,805.60	$10,805.60

INSTRUCTION 1.

Set up the ledger of The Crown Repair Shop as of March 31, 19—.

Note:

In this particular exercise, it is not correct for you to record and post an opening entry. An opening entry is proper only when a business is being started. In this exercise, the business has been in operation for some time.

To begin this exercise, set up each of the ledger accounts by merely entering the account balance and the date as shown on the trial balance.

INSTRUCTION 2.

Journalize and post the following transactions beginning on page 32 of the journal. (Remember that the business has been in operation for several years and as a result some portion of the journal will already have been used.)

Transactions

April

1 Received $500 cash from the owner to increase the cash position of the business.

2 Received cash from J. Watson in full payment of his account.

3 Paid cash to Parker's Service Station in full payment of the account.

4 Received $25 from Amber Bros. on account.

4 Paid Amber Bros. an amount sufficient to adjust their account which they had overpaid.

5 Purchased $800 of supplies from Regal

Supply on account.

8 Purchased new machinery, $246, from Peerless Machinery on account.

9 Paid $400 on account to Harold's Hardware.

9 Sold a piece of office equipment, which was no longer required, for $35 cash. The item had originally cost $50 and was included in the Office Furniture and Equip-ment account at $50.

10 Paid Regal Supply account in full.

10 Purchased a filing cabinet for $70 cash.

11 Paid $100 on account to Harold's Hardware.

15 The owner withdrew $200 cash for his personal use.

15 Paid the balance of Harold's Hardware account.

INSTRUCTION 3.

Balance the ledger.

---

8. The Northtown Gardening Service, owned by T. C. Harlow, begins business on February 1, 19—, with the following financial position.

Northtown Gardening Service
Balance Sheet
February 1, 19—

Assets		*Liabilities*	
Cash	$2,650.20	Holland Bulb Growers	$1,150.00
F. Greig	165.00	Baxter Chemical Co.	164.91
C. Charles	174.00		$1,314.91
M. Rogers	316.00	*Owner's Equity*	
Supplies	116.50		
Equipment	967.20	T. C. Harlow, Capital	3,073.99
	$4,388.90		$4,388.90

INSTRUCTION 1.

Journalize and post the opening entry. Number the accounts in the usual way.

INSTRUCTION 2.

Journalize and post the transactions which appear below.

INSTRUCTION 3.

Take off a trial balance as of February 15.

Transactions

February

1 Received $200 from M. Rogers on account.

2 Paid $700 on account to Holland Bulb Growers.

4 The proprietor withdrew $75 for his personal use.

5 Performed a gardening service for G. Easter and charged him $32, which he paid right away.

7 Performed a gardening service for F. Greig on account; $56.

9 Purchased $300 of fertilizer on account from Baxter Chemical Co.

12 The Baxter Chemical Co. account was paid in full.

15 M. Rogers paid the balance of his account.

Chapter 5

INCOME, EXPENSE AND DRAWINGS

The theory of double-entry accounting is being developed in a gradual way. In the first four chapters you have been introduced to a great deal of basic accounting theory. The work in Chapter 5 is the next logical step in the accounting process.

This is an extremely important chapter as it finalizes the rules for the making of accounting entries.

That is, the rules of debit and credit, except for more advanced transactions, will be completed.

Expanding the System

The rules of debit and credit, as developed so far, have been summarized in the chart at right.

These rules, with which you are familiar, will not be changed. But the chart itself is to be expanded–to make the whole accounting system more useful.

In particular, it is the Capital or Equity section of the chart that is to be expanded. The rules for Assets and Liabilities remain unchanged.

To date you have been accustomed to having a single account for Capital. Any change in the Equity of a business has been recorded in this single account. Now you must become familiar with a system in which the ledger, instead of having a single account for Capital, has a number of accounts in the Equity section.

DEBIT AND CREDIT SUMMARY	TO INCREASE	TO DECREASE
ASSET	DEBIT THE ACCOUNT	CREDIT THE ACCOUNT
LIABILITY	CREDIT THE ACCOUNT	DEBIT THE ACCOUNT
CAPITAL (EQUITY)	CREDIT THE ACCOUNT	DEBIT THE ACCOUNT

Purpose of Expanding the System

It is the principal purpose of the new accounts in the Equity section of the ledger to gather the information that is necessary for the preparation of another financial statement. This statement, The Profit and Loss Statement, is illustrated on the right.

HARRIS REAL ESTATE

Profit and Loss Statement

Month Ended January 31, 19-4

Income		
Commissions		$1,472.60
Expenses		
Advertising	$42.65	
Car Expenses	97.60	
Entertainment	104.73	
Miscellaneous	34.19	
Rent	200.00	
Wages	215.75	694.92
Net Profit		$777.68

A Simple Profit and Loss Statement

(Income Statement)

You can readily see from the illustration that the Profit and Loss Statement tells a great deal about the progress of the business for which it is written. You may rightfully ask why this statement is necessary in a business. The answer is twofold. First, it is vitally important that the owners and managers know if the business is being run profitably. Remember that their livelihood depends on its successful operation. To them, the Profit and Loss Statement is an extremely useful tool. From an analysis of it, these people are able to derive a great deal of useful information that guides them in their decision-making and assists them in formulating company policies. Second, the Profit and Loss Statement is needed to satisfy legal requirements. It must be prepared to comply with various government and income tax regulations.

It is absolutely essential in any business that the Profit and Loss Statement be prepared, and it is the principal purpose of the new Equity section of the ledger to gather the information necessary for its preparation. This new statement will be discussed more fully in the next chapter along with a new form of the Balance Sheet.

Equity Section of the Ledger

In the expanded accounting system the ledger has an Equity section that includes several accounts rather than a single Capital account. In this new section there are the following accounts:

1. A **Capital** account that is reserved for the beginning Capital balance.
2. An **Income** or **Revenue** account. (In some cases there will be more than one of these.)
3. Several **Expense** accounts.
4. A **Drawings** account.

These new accounts, Income, Expense, and Drawings accounts, are now discussed in detail.

Income (Revenue)

The first of the new accounts to be introduced is the **Income** or **Revenue** account. Income may be defined as:

An increase in Equity as a direct consequence of usual business activity.

Whenever a transaction occurs that involves an increase in Equity as a result of usual business activity, you must now be prepared to treat it differently.

An example of a business transaction that produces income is the following:

D. Peters, a lawyer, draws up a legal agreement for a client and for his services is paid a fee of $75 cash.

This transaction has the effect of increasing both Cash and Equity by the amount of $75. (If you need a review of the reasoning underlying changes in Equity refer back to page 11.) Previously, you would have debited Cash and credited D. Peters, Capital with the $75. But now, under the new and expanded system, you will debit Cash, as before, and credit an Income account which may be called Fees Income. In General Journal form the entry is:

| Cash | $75.00 | |
| Fees Income | | $75.00 |

Remember that Fees Income represents an increase in Equity. Since it has been established earlier that an increase in Equity requires a credit entry, it should come as no surprise to you that the Fees Income account normally receives credit entries. All Fees Income will be accumulated in this account and it will have a credit balance.

Usually, a business has only one Income account and it is given an appropriate name. A 'loan' company, for example, which earns its income by charging 'interest' on money loaned, will probably have an Income account called Interest Income or Interest Earned. Similarly, a 'real estate' company, which earns its income in the form of 'commissions' will very likely have an income account called Commissions Earned, Commissions Income, or just plain Commissions. Other suitable names for the Income account of other businesses might be: Rental Income, Fees Earned, Sales, Royalties, and so on.

Expense

The second new type of account to be introduced is the **Expense** account. Expense may be defined as:

A decrease in Equity as a direct consequence of usual business activity.

Whenever a transaction occurs that involves a decrease in Equity as a result of usual business operations, you must be prepared to deal with it in a special way.

An example of a transaction that involves expense is:

D. Peters pays to his secretary her regular weekly wage of $65 cash.

This transaction requires that both Cash and Equity be decreased by $65. The decrease to Cash is handled in the usual way, as a credit to that account. But the decrease to Equity is now to be debited to a new account called Wages Expense. In General Journal form the entry is:

| Wages Expense | $65.00 | |
| Cash | | $65.00 |

Keep in mind that Wages Expense represents a decrease in Equity and as such requires a debit entry. It follows logically, therefore, that the Wages Expense account, or any Expense account for that matter, will normally receive debit entries. All Wages Expense will be accumulated in the one account and it will have a debit balance.

A second example of a transaction

hat involves an expense is the fol-
owing:

D. Peters receives the monthly furnace oil bill for $25.65 from Municipal Oil but does not pay the bill immediately.

As a result of this transaction it s necessary to decrease Equity and o set up a liability to Municipal Oil. According to the rule just stablished, the accounting entry is:

Heat Expense $25.65
Municipal Oil $25.65

In any business, there are usually everal expense accounts, each one epresenting a reduction in Equity rom a specific cause. The name iven to each one of these accounts ·ill tell the nature of the reduction. n addition to those already men- oned, other typical expense ac- ounts are: Rent Expense, Delivery xpense, Insurance Expense, Bank harges, Postage, Property Taxes. otice that the word 'expense' is ot always included as part of the ccount title but is sometimes im- ied. With experience you will come o know the names customarily given the expense accounts.

rawings

he third of the new types of ac- ounts introduced in this chapter is e **Drawings** account. Drawings ay be defined as:

decrease in Equity that is not an xpense.

The Drawings account may be ought of as the owner's personal ithdrawal account. In it are ac- mulated any decreases in Equity at are not *bona fide* expenses of the siness and as such are considered be the personal responsibility of e owner. Such decreases are arged* or debited to the owner

Professional accountants often use the rd 'charge' instead of 'debit'.

through his Drawings account.

An example of the most common type of transaction that involves Drawings is the following:

D. Peters, the owner of the busi- ness, withdraws $125 cash for his personal use.

This transaction requires that both Cash and Equity be decreased by $125. The decrease to Cash is handled in the usual way, as a credit to that account. But the decrease to Equity, not falling within the classi- fication of an Expense, must be charged to the owner's Drawings ac- count. The correct accounting entry to record the transaction is:

D. Peters, Drawings $125.00
Cash $125.00

This and all entries affecting Drawings conform to the rules of debit and credit with which you are familiar. Since Drawings represents a decrease in Equity and since de- creases in Equity require debit entries, it follows that the Drawings account normally receives debit entries. All drawings will be accumu- lated in this one account and it will have a debit balance.

Another common type of trans- action that affects the Drawings ac- count occurs when the owner buys something for his personal use but has the business pay for it. He may do this in order to take advantage of a special price that is offered to businesses but is denied to individu- als. Or, he may do it just for the sake of convenience. In any event, the recording of the transaction re- quires that the debit be to Drawings and that the credit be either to Cash or to a creditor's account depending on whether the item is paid for or not.

A third type of transaction that affects Drawings occurs when the owner takes assets other than cash

permanently out of the business for his personal use. As an example, he may take home a spare office type- writer so that his family may have the use of it. If the typewriter is to be permanently left in the home, propriety requires that the value of it, as recorded in the books, be charged to him. The correct ac- counting entry will be one that debits Drawings and credits Office Equip- ment.

In your textbook exercises you will meet additional transactions that affect the Drawings account.

Relationship of Income, Expenses and Drawings

A definite relationship exists among Income, Expenses, and Drawings. This relationship, reduced to a very simple form, is discussed below.

The Income account together with the Expense accounts (but not the Drawings account) reflect what is known as the Profit or the Loss of a business. Profit occurs when the bal- ance of the Income account is greater than the total of all the Expense ac- counts. Loss occurs when the total of all the Expense accounts is greater than the balance of the Income ac- count.

Usually, a man who is in business for himself depends on the business for his source of livelihood. It is his hope and intention that the business will earn a substantial profit and that he will be able to withdraw this profit for his own purposes. Normally, he will withdraw as much of the profit as he can without squeezing the busi- ness; that is, leaving the business so short of funds that it cannot operate comfortably. If the business happens to suffer a loss, the owner may find himself hard pressed financially. Certainly no one will continue to carry on a business that loses money persistently.

To summarize, the Income and Expense accounts all together show the amount of the Profit or the Loss. The Drawings account shows the ex- tent of the owner's withdrawals.

There appears below an illustration of a ledger with the expanded Equity section. The accounts included in this ledger are much the same as those that you might find in a ledger in the business world today.

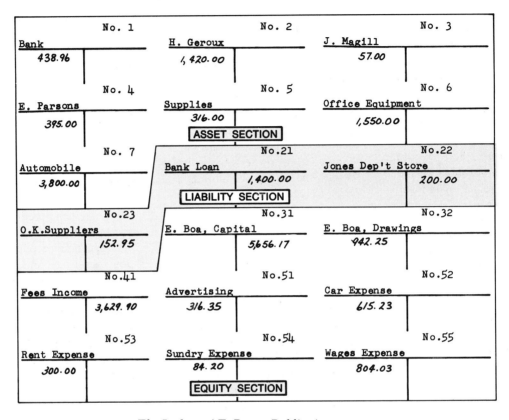

The Ledger of E. Boa, a Public Accountant

Examine the new ledger carefully and note the following:

1. The ledger has three sections: Assets, Liabilities, and Equity. These three sections still conform to the Fundamental Accounting Equation. If you were to evaluate the three sections you would find that the total value of the Asset accounts is equal to the combined total value of the Liability and Equity accounts.

2. In the Equity section are several accounts. The Capital account is intended to show the Capital balance at the beginning of the accounting period and the other accounts are intended to show the various changes in Capital since that time. The Expense and Drawings accounts have debit balances because they represent decreases in Equity. The Income account has a credit balance because it represents an increase in Equity.

Note:

There is one exception to the statement that the Capital account shows only the beginning Capital balance. At times in business, usually to tide the business over a difficult period, it is necessary for the owner to bring new capital into the business in the form of cash. In such circumstances, the Capital account is credited with the amount of the new investment.

3. The numbering system has been expanded to include the new accounts in the system. The complete numbering system used in this text is summarized below.

Assets	Nos. 1 to 20 inclusive
Liabilities	Nos. 21 to 30 inclusive
Capital	No. 31
Drawings	No. 32
Income	No. 41
Expenses	No. 51 and on.

4. The Expense accounts are often arranged alphabetically. This is not obligatory but is a practice employed by many accountants.

Debit and Credit Summary — Final Form

	TO INCREASE	TO DECREASE
Assets	Debit	Credit
Liabilities	Credit	Debit
Equity Capital	Credit	Debit
Income	Credit	Debit
Expense	Debit	Credit
Drawings	Debit	Credit

managers to keep more closely in touch with the progress of the business.

Chart of Accounts

A Chart of Accounts is simply a list of the ledger accounts and their numbers all arranged in ledger order. Most businesses, except very small ones, have copies of their Chart of Accounts available for the use of their own office staff, particularly new employees, and for their auditors. The Chart of Accounts of E. Boa, from the ledger on page 50, is shown at the foot of the page.

The Fiscal Period

At the time of the introduction of Income and Expense accounts, it is proper to introduce another new concept in the subject of Accounting. This new concept has to do with the measurement of earnings in relation to a certain period of time.

In order to have any meaning, the earnings figure of a business must be calculated in respect to a certain length of time. If not, the information is meaningless. If you were told that the profit of a business was $1,000, you would not be very well informed unless you also knew the length of time taken to earn it. For instance, if it took a period of one year, you would not be very favourably impressed, especially if you were the owner of the business and it was your only source of income. But if it took only one week to earn the $1,000 you would probably be very impressed indeed.

It is hoped that the foregoing paragraph has shown you that in respect to earnings it is necessary to know 'for how long?' as well as 'how much?' Bookkeepers and accountants accept this fact without hesitation and they refer to the period of time over which earnings are measured as the **Fiscal Period**, or as the **Accounting Period**, and sometimes as the **Bookkeeping Period**.

In business today, the usual length of time chosen for the fiscal period is one year. The choice of a year is a natural one. There are powerful forces at work in the world which have selected this period as the cycle of nature. It influences us in innumerable ways, from birthdays to income taxes. Its use as the most common accounting period should not surprise you, nor should the fact that it is the maximum length of fiscal period permitted by government regulations.

A period shorter than one year may be chosen as a fiscal period. Half-yearly, quarterly, or monthly fiscal periods are not uncommon. Short fiscal periods allow owners and

Debit and Credit Balances

It is very important that you be able to interpret readily the account balances in a ledger. At this stage it is not very difficult to tell whether an account is an Asset or an Expense, a Liability or Income. But there will come a time when it is not so simple. Be prepared for that day. As new accounting concepts are introduced, strive to understand them thoroughly.

At this point in the text, the accounts that have debit balances are either Assets, Expenses, or Drawings, and the accounts that have credit balances are either Liabilities, Capital, or Income.

E. Boa
Chart of Accounts

accounts receivable

accounts payable

Assets			Equity	
Bank	No. 1		E. Boa, Capital	No. 31
H. Geroux	2		E. Boa, Drawings	32
J. Magill	3		Fees Income	41
E. Parsons	4		Advertising	51
Supplies	5		Car Expense	52
Office Equipment	6		Rent Expense	53
Automobile	7		Sundry Expense	54
			Wages Expense	55
Liabilities				
Bank Loan	21			
Jones Dep't Store	22			
O.K. Suppliers	23			

Other Forms of Ownership

Except for this particular section, this textbook deals exclusively with a form of business organization known as a single-proprietorship. This is a business that is owned by one person whose investment is reflected by his Capital account.

As you are probably aware, there are other forms of business ownership. A partnership, for example, is a form of ownership by means of which two or more persons may carry on business together. A partnership is a type of business organization that is suitable for small- to medium-sized businesses having more than one owner. The accounts of a partnership are almost identical to those for a single-proprietorship. The only difference is in the Equity section where each partner must have his own Capital and Drawings accounts. It is in this way that the investment of each partner is accounted for separately.

Another major form of business organization is the corporation or limited company. Corporations are usually large enterprises requiring such large amounts of capital that it must be obtained from a number of people. Individuals invest their money in a corporation by purchasing share certificates which entitle them to a share in the ownership of the business. These investors are known as shareholders.

The accounts of a corporation are similar to those of the single-proprietorship and the partnership, except for the way in which the Capital is recorded. In the Equity section of the corporation's ledger, there is an account called Capital Stock or Shareholders' Equity, which shows the total capital contributions of all the shareholders. The individual contributions of the shareholders are kept track of in a separate record. The shareholders do not have Drawings accounts.

Buying and Selling on Credit

It is an accepted feature of our modern economy that businesses with good reputations are able to buy the things that they need on short-term credit, usually from 10 days to one month. By being able to delay payment for a short period of time, the buyer gains for himself the opportunity of thoroughly inspecting or testing the goods. If they are found to be unsatisfactory, the buyer is in a commanding position; he can simply refuse to pay for the goods until they are made right.

A great deal of buying and selling on credit goes on in the business world of today. Each time a sale is made on account, it is necessary for the seller to prepare a business document called a Sales Invoice. The Sales Invoice form, such as the one illustrated below, shows all the pertinent information in respect to the sale. One or more copies of the Sales Invoice are sent to the buyer for his records and also as a request for payment. (See also Chapter 12.)

Bank Account

Businessmen rely heavily on the banking system as the safest, cheapest, and most convenient way to make payments. It should be clear to you that the handling of large quantities of cash is unsafe. This is one important reason why a businessman chooses to keep his money in a bank account. Another and perhaps even more important reason is the convenience of being able to make payments by cheque. It is much easier to send a cheque to someone than it is to deliver cash to him in person. This is especially evident if the buyer and the seller are dealing with each other over a long distance. Except in the case of retail stores and their dealings with the general public, it is usual for all except very small payments to be made by cheque.

In the books of account, therefore, you can expect to see an account called Bank rather than one called Cash. You can also expect to see the paying of bills being effected through the issuing of cheques by the ones who owe the money and the receiving of cheques by the ones to whom the money is owed.

Income Tax Regulations

The various governments of the country impose strict requirements on businesses for taxation and regulatory purposes. One requirement that is very important to a business is that it must keep the documents or business papers (called 'vouchers') as evidence of the authenticity

STAR ✳ SUPPLY

419 Mill's Gate, Oak City

| SOLD TO | W. Hay, 16 Mark's Road, Oak City. | | INVOICE NUMBER 971 |
| DATE | March 15, 19-- | | TERMS 3/10,N/30 |

Quantity	Description	Unit Price	Amount
6 Pkg.	Typewriting paper 8 1/2 X 11	$7.50	$45.00
	5% Federal Sales Tax		2.25
			$47.25

of the business records. A government auditor may come at any time to verify the records by examining the supporting vouchers for the transactions.

Trial Balance Procedure Unchanged

With the introduction of the new types of accounts you might expect that the trial balancing procedure would need to be amended. But fortunately there is no change in principle. It is still only necessary to total the accounts with debit balances, total the accounts with credit balances, and see that the two totals agree.

Trial Balance Out of Balance

Now that you are able to journalize transactions, post them to the ledger, and take off a trial balance, you will be confronted with the problem of what to do when the trial balance does not balance. A trial balance out of balance indicates that one or more errors have been made in the journal, ledger, or trial balance. It is your responsibility as accountant to find and correct these errors.

Do not underestimate the importance of acquiring a real competence in this respect. For two reasons a real skill in the locating of errors can be extremely advantageous to the aspiring accountant. In the first place, it is not infrequent that a ledger is out of balance. In fact, in the more complex businesses it is a rare event when the trial balance is found to be in balance after the first attempt. Even in your relatively simple classroom exercises, you will find that on numerous occasions the trial balance does not balance.

Secondly, some errors are very elusive and can be detected only by a persistent and expertly conducted search. A person who does not possess the skill to conduct this search successfully is not a competent accountant. It is likely that this person will be constantly thwarted in his efforts to achieve success in business.

When a trial balance does not balance, it is a certainty that one or more errors have been made in the accounting process. To discuss all the ramifications of locating these errors is not practicable in a text of this nature. Instead, there is set out in brief form the general procedure to be followed when you are confronted with a trial balance out of balance. It will be wise for you to decide now to carry out this procedure to many successful conclusions. Only through persistent application will the necessary confidence and expertise be acquired.

Briefly, the steps to be taken and the order in which they should normally be followed are—

1. Re-add the trial balance columns.
2. Check the accuracy of transferring the account balances from the ledger to the trial balance.
3. Re-add the account balances beginning at the point at which the ledger was previously balanced. Ensure that the Dr. or Cr. prefix to the balance is correct.
4. Check the accuracy of the postings from the journal to the ledger, beginning at the point at which the ledger was previously balanced. In particular, watch for incorrect amounts, amounts not posted, amounts posted twice, and amounts posted to the wrong column. In performing step 4, it is generally necessary to make a distinguishing mark beside each of the amounts as they are checked.
5. Check to see that each individual journal entry is in balance.

Since on many occasions the error or errors will be detected at some intermediate stage, it is often not necessary to complete all of the five steps. On the other hand, if it so happens that after completing the five steps there still remain some undetected errors, it is not possible that the five steps were carried out properly. In this unhappy situation, it will be necessary that you go through the sequence again, remembering to work with greater care. It is a positive fact that if the steps are carried out correctly the errors will be detected.

Short-Cuts in Detecting a Single Error

It can be a tedious and time-consuming task to carry out the full routine just described, and experienced accountants try to avoid it where they can. There is a strong possibility, provided that only one error has occurred, that the error can be located quickly by the application of a few short tests. These tests are set out below.

First, it is necessary to determine the difference between the two totals of the trial balance. Then any of the following tests may be applied.

1. If the trial balance difference is 1¢, 10¢, $1, etc., it is very likely that an error in addition has been made, in which case steps 1 and 3 of the previously discussed sequence should be performed first.
2. If the trial balance difference is an even amount, divide it by 2. Then scrutinize (i) the trial balance, and (ii) the ledger accounts for this amount. If found, check to see if it is a debit amount placed in a credit column by mistake, or vice versa. An error of this type always produces a difference in the balance equal to twice the amount of the error.
3. Scrutinize the account balances to see if one of them is equal to the amount of the trial balance difference. It may be that one account has been overlooked in the preparation of the trial balance.
4. Divide the trial balance difference by 9. If it divides evenly, it is likely that a transposition error has occurred. A transposition occurs when, for example, $35.60 is posted as $36.50, or when $1,200 is transferred as $120. Such errors always pro-

duce a trial balance difference
that is exactly divisible by 9.
When this happens, steps 2 and 4
of the previous section should be
performed first.

Bookkeeping and Accounting Terms

Income: An increase in Equity as a direct consequence of business activity.

Expense: A decrease in Equity as a direct consequence of business activity.

Drawings: A decrease in Equity that does not fit the definition of Expense.

Charge: A word often used instead of debit.

Profit: The difference between total Income and total Expenses if the Income is greater than the Expenses.

Loss: The difference between total Income and total Expenses if the Expenses are greater than the Income.

Fiscal Period:
Bookkeeping Period:
Accounting Period: The period of time over which earnings are measured.

Chart of Accounts: A list of the ledger accounts and their numbers all arranged in ledger order.

Cash Sales Slip: A business form prepared by the seller of goods or services at the time of a cash sale showing a description of the goods, the price, and other information.

Sales Invoice: A business form prepared by the seller of goods or services, usually in respect to a credit sale, showing a description of the goods, the price, and other pertinent information.

Voucher: A business document establishing the validity of accounting records.

Transposition: An interchanging of the digits of a number when transferring the number from one place to another.

Review Questions

1. What is the purpose of expanding the ledger?
2. Give two important reasons for preparing the Profit and Loss Statement.
3. Name the four types of accounts that are to be found in the Equity section of a ledger.
4. Define Income.
5. Give an example of an increase in Equity that does not result from normal business activity.
6. Define Expense.
7. Define Drawings.
8. Give three examples of transactions that affect Drawings.
9. What is meant by 'charge'?
10. How is the Profit or Loss of a business determined?
11. What is the Fiscal Period?
12. Give two other names for Fiscal Period.
13. In today's business world what is the most common length of the Fiscal Period?
14. What type of balance is usually found in an Income account? an Expense account? the Drawing account?
15. Draw a chart summarizing debit and credit theory in its final form.
16. What is a Chart of Accounts?

Who uses a Chart of Accounts?

17. Why will a business that is buying something endeavour to arrange short-term credit with the seller?

18. Why do businesses rely heavily on the banking system?

19. What are vouchers? Explain the need for them.

20. Why is a real skill in locating errors an advantage to a junior bookkeeper?

21. List the five steps to be taken in locating errors in the books.

22. Is it always necessary to carry out the five steps? Explain.

23. Describe the four short-cuts in locating errors.

24. What is a transposition?

Exercises

Special Note on the Handling of Supplies

It is a fairly common practice in accounting to allow certain accounts to be incorrect during the accounting period and to make them correct at the end of the accounting period. This is a technique used by accountants for convenience. The Supplies account is one account to which this short-cut technique is applied.

During the accounting period, make your accounting entries for Supplies as follows:

1. Whenever supplies are purchased:
    Dr. Supplies
    Cr. Bank or the Creditor $\left.\right\}$ with the cost price of the supplies.

2. Whenever supplies are used in the business:
    Make no accounting entry

The effect of step 2 above is to permit the Supplies account to become incorrect. The technique for updating this account at the end of the accounting period is explained in Chapter 14.

---

1. From the following information for the month ended November 30, 19— prepare a Profit and Loss Statement for Atlas Associates.

    Fees earned, $8,000; Salaries Expense, $600; Rent Expense, $750; General Expense, $185; Advertising Expense, $120; Car Expense, $158; Light and Heat Expense, $40.

---

2. For each of the accounts listed on the following page indicate whether it would normally have a debit or credit balance.

Supplies; Advertising Expense; A. Bryce, Drawings; G. Wright, a creditor; Rent Expense; Fees Earned; Bank Loan; W. Magill, a debtor; A. Bryce, Capital; Mortgage Payable.

---

3. If a credit item for $265 in the General Journal is posted in error as a debit, by how much will this cause the trial balance to be out of balance? How might you detect such an error?

---

4. If the trial balance difference is $63, what type of error would you suspect? What steps would you take to locate the error?

---

5. T. J. Boyle, the owner of an engineering consultant business, has the following chart of accounts:

Assets		*Proprietorship*	
Bank	No. 1	T. J. Boyle, Capital	No. 31
M. Black	2	T. J. Boyle, Drawings	32
F. Rose	3	Fees Earned	41
Office Supplies	4	Bank Charges	51
Office Equipment	5	Car Expenses	52
Automobile	6	Miscellaneous Expense	53
		Rent Expense	54
Liabilities		Telephone Expense	55
Bank Loan	21	Wages Expense	56
Mason Brothers	22		
Regal Oil Co.	23		

INSTRUCTION.

In the two-column general journal of T. J. Boyle, on page 162, journalize the following transactions; use the accounts shown above.

Transactions

March

1 Issued cheque No. 615 for $165 to Royalty Trust Co. in payment of the monthly rent.

2 Issued cheque No. 616 for $200 to the owner, T. J. Boyle, for his personal use.

2 Received an invoice in the amount of $42.73 from Mason Brothers for office supplies that had been purchased.

3 Issued checque No. 617 in the amount of $355 to West End Garage, as directed by the owner. The payment was for repairs to Mrs. Boyle's personal car.

5 Issued invoice No. 214 to F. Rose for services rendered; $125.

5 Issued cheque No. 618 for $150 in payment of the wages of the office secretary for a two-week period.

9 Received an invoice from Regal Oil Company for gasoline and oil used in the business automobile; $56.46.

12 Received a cheque for $100 from M. Black on account. (It is a routine daily procedure in business to make a bank deposit of all cash and cheques received.)

15 Received a memorandum from the bank stating that $26.50 had been deducted by the bank from the business' bank account to pay for interest on the bank loan and other bank charges.

16 Issued cheque No. 619 for $15 to the post office to pay for the purchase of postage stamps.

19 Issued cheque No. 620 for $35 to the City Telephone Company in payment of the monthly telephone bill.

19 Issued cheque No. 621 for $150 to the office secretary in payment of her wages for two weeks.

22 Issued invoice No. 215 to M. Black for services rendered; amount, $500.

23 Received $25 from C. Sloan as a cash payment for services rendered. Cash sales slip No. 65.

25 Purchased several trade magazines for the office and paid for them by cheque No. 622 in the amount of $18.

---

6. The accounts required for this exercise are as follows:

No. 1 Bank
    2 Jenkins and Co.
    3 Office Supplies
    4 Office Equipment
    5 Automobile
  21 Office Supply Company
  31 N. A. James, Capital
  32 N. A. James, Drawings
  41 Fees Income
  51 Advertising Expense
  52 Car Expenses
  53 Donations Expense
  54 Miscellaneous Expense
  55 Rent Expense

N. A. James, a public accountant, decided to begin a business of his own on October 1, 19—. At that time he invested in the business a bank balance of $2,497 and an automobile worth $2,000. There were no business liabilities.

INSTRUCTION 1.

Journalize and post the opening entry.

INSTRUCTION 2.

Journalize and post the following subsequent transactions:

Transactions

October

2 Sundry office supplies were purchased from Martin Bros. at a cost of $165.55. Cheque No. 1 was issued in payment.

2 Issued cheque No. 2 to Premier Realty Co. for one month's advance rent; amount, $75.

5 An advertisement costing $15 was placed in a local newspaper; cheque No. 3 was issued in payment.

5 A desk, chair, and a filing cabinet were purchased on account from Office Supply Company; cost, $305.

8 Mr. James was engaged by a client, Jenkins & Co. At the conclusion of three days' work an invoice amounting to $170 was sent to Jenkins & Co.

9 A bookkeeping service was performed for B. Masters and $35 cash was collected from him. A tax return was prepared for W. Shields and $20 cash was collected from him. The total of $55 was deposited in the bank.

12 A $25 donation was given to the United Appeal. Cheque No. 4 was issued.

12 Received a cheque for $100 from Jenkins & Co. on account. The cheque was deposited.

13 Paid the Office Supply Company account in full. Cheque No. 5 was issued.

14 Issued cheque No. 6 to Louis' Service Station for gasoline and oil used in the business car; amount $16.50.

16 Performed a service for R. Andrews and received $100 cash in payment. The proprietor, N. A. James, did not deposit this money in the bank but kept it himself for his own use.

19 Purchased a quantity of office supplies from Daniel's and issued cheque No. 7 for $36.75 in payment.

22 Placed an advertisement in the local newspaper at a cost of $18. Cheque No. 8 was issued in payment.

23 Issued an invoice to Jenkins & Co. for several days' work; amount, $300.

26 Issued cheque No. 9 to the post office in payment for $20 worth of postage stamps.

27 Issued cheque No. 10 to N. A. James for his personal use; amount, $150.

INSTRUCTION 3.

Balance the ledger by means of a trial balance.

INSTRUCTION 4.

Determine the amount of the profit or loss.

---

7. S. P. Proctor began a business called the General Repair Shop for the purpose of providing cleaning, repairing, and general handyman services to the public. His beginning Balance Sheet was as follows:

General Repair Shop
Balance Sheet
August 31, 19—

Assets		Liabilities	
Cash	$1,000.00	Bank Loan	$1,500.00
Supplies	150.00		
Office Equipment	732.50		
Truck	3,957.00	*Capital*	
		S. P. Proctor, Capital	4,339.50
	$5,839.50		$5,839.50

INSTRUCTION 1.

Record the opening entry in the journal and post it to the accounts. The complete chart of accounts for this exercise is as follows:

Bank	No. 1	S. P. Proctor, Capital	No. 31
W. J. Thomson	2	S. P. Proctor, Drawings	32
G. D. Fraser	3	Sales	41
Supplies	4	Loss on Sale of Equipment	51
Office Equipment	5	Miscellaneous Expense	52
Truck	6	Rent Expense	53
Bank Loan	21	Truck Expense	54
Jones Hardware	22	Wages Expense	55
Imperial Garage	23		

A very important routine in business is to deposit in the bank daily all cash and cheques received. In this and all future exercises you are to assume that this function is performed as a matter of course—unless you are specifically told otherwise.

INSTRUCTION 2.

Journalize and post the following transactions.

Transactions

September

1 Issued cheque No. 1 to P. Jarvis for the rent for the month of September; amount, $120.

3 Received an invoice from Jones Hardware regarding a purchase of supplies on account; amount, $135.

5 Issued invoices to W. J. Thomson, $180, and G. D. Fraser, $150, in respect to services performed during the week.

9 Sold an office desk for $50 cash. The desk had originally cost $175 and was included in the Office Equipment account at that figure. (Although a sale has been made, this transaction does not affect the Sales account which is reserved for the normal sales of the business.)

10 Received $90 cash from a customer for services performed.

11 Issued Cheque No. 2 to the owner for his personal use; amount, $150.

12 Issued cheque No. 3 to Jones Hardware on account; amount, $75.

15 Received an invoice from Imperial Garage for gasoline and oil used in the truck; amount, $42.

16 Issued cheque No. 4 to Cochrane Bros. for a cash purchase of supplies; amount, $65.45.

18 Received a cheque from W. J. Thomson in full payment of his account balance.

19 Received a memorandum from the bank to the effect that $16.50 had been deducted from the bank account to pay for bank charges.

19 Issued cheques for wages as follows:
No. 5 to R. Barnes–$90
No. 6 to G. Bolton–$85

19 Received $300 cash from a customer for services performed over a period of one week.

22 The owner, S. P. Proctor, requested the bank to reduce the bank loan by $500.

24 Issued cheque No. 7 to the telephone company; $12.

25 Received a cheque on account from G. D. Fraser; $75.

26 Received $200 cash from a customer for services rendered.

26 The owner withdrew $150 cash for his personal use; cheque No. 8.

29 Issued Cheque No. 9 to Jones Hardware in payment of the balance of the account.

29 While on a job, S. P. Proctor needed some additional supplies immediately and purchased them at a local store paying cash from his personal funds; $19.

30 Received $75 cash from a customer for services rendered.

INSTRUCTION 3.

Take off a trial balance.

INSTRUCTION 4.

Determine the amount of the profit or the loss.

---

8. P. Simpson began business as an engineering consultant on October 1, 19—. He began business with the following assets and liabilities:

Assets		Liabilities	
Cash in Bank	$1,651.20	Ace Finance Company	$850.00
Office Equipment	465.00	Grand's Stationers	200.00
Automobile	2,460.00		

INSTRUCTION 1.

Journalize and post the opening entry. The accounts used in this exercise are shown in the following chart of accounts.

Bank	No. 1	P. Simpson, Capital	No. 31
P. Arthur	2	P. Simpson, Drawings	32
J. Morrison	3	Income from Fees	41
N. Martin	4	Car Expenses	51
Supplies	5	Office Expenses	52
Office Equipment	6	Rent	53
Automobile	7	Wages	54
Ace Finance Company	21		
Grand's Stationers	22		
Industrial Suppliers	23		
Star Oil Co.	24		

INSTRUCTION 2.

Journalize and post the transactions listed below.

October

1 Performed a service for S. Stewart and received $20 cash in payment.

2 Received an invoice from Grand's Stationers for supplies purchased on account; amount, $103.78.

4 Issued invoice No. 1 to P. Arthur for services rendered; amount, $200.

5 Issued cheques for the weekly wages as follows:
No. 1–O. Mack–$75.
No. 2–W. Moss–$87.50.

8 Received an invoice from Star Oil Co. for gasoline and oil used in business car; amount, $31.24.

9 Paid the regular monthly payment to Ace Finance Company; cheque No. 3 for $120.

10 Issued invoice No. 2 to J. Morrison for services rendered; amount, $420.

11 P. Simpson withdrew $200 for his personal use; cheque No. 4.

12 Issued cheques for the weekly wages as follows:
No. 5–O. Mack–$75.
No. 6–W. Moss–$93.50.

15 Issued cheque No. 7 to J. Mahoney for the rent for the month of October; amount, $175.

16 Received a cheque on account from P. Arthur; $200.

17 Issued invoice No. 3 to J. Morrison for services rendered; $300.

19 Issued cheques for the weekly wages as follows:

No. 8–O. Mack–$75.
No. 9–W. Moss–$77.75.

19 Issued cheque No. 10 to Grand's Stationers on account; amount, $200.

23 Received an invoice from Star Oil Co. for gasoline and oil used in the business automobile; amount, $55.80.

25 Received an invoice from Industrial Suppliers for the purchase of supplies on account; $76.40.

25 Received a cheque from J. Morrison on account; $300.

26 Issued cheque No. 11 to the owner to repay him for out-of-pocket expenses as follows:

Postage	$15.
Car Repair	$40.
Parking	$ 5.

26 Paid the weekly wages with the following cheques:
No. 12–O. Mack–$75.
No. 13–W. Moss–$90.

26 Issued invoice No. 4 to N. Martin for services rendered; $425.

29 Issued cheque No. 14 to Endovers' Garage for repairs and servicing to the business automobile, $68.92.

30 Issued cheque No. 15 to Star Oil Co. in full payment of the account balance.

31 Issued cheques as follows:
No. 16–Telephone Company–$22.50.
No. 17–Hydro-Electric Co.–$6.45.

INSTRUCTION 3.

Take off a trial balance at October 31.

INSTRUCTION 4.

Calculate the amount of the profit or loss for the period.

Chapter 6

THE SIMPLE WORK SHEET AND FINANCIAL STATEMENTS

You have been told throughout this text that a vital purpose of accounting is to make possible the preparation of financial reports. Now that you have mastered the simple basic principles of accounting, it seems appropriate to follow these principles through to their ultimate and logical conclusion–the preparation of the financial statements. Therefore, you will now be shown how to apply the information shown in the books and records of a business, to produce a Profit and Loss Statement and a Balance Sheet.

The purpose of introducing this topic at this time is to give to you a broader view of the ultimate purpose of the system of accounting as a whole.

At the conclusion of every accounting period, and at any other time required by management, financial reports are prepared from the information accumulated in the ledger. The preparation of financial statements may appear to be a simple matter to you in view of the knowledge you have gained so far, but in reality it is work of an advanced and important nature as you will see later. This work is usually done, not by a clerk but by an accountant, a person possessing expert knowledge in such matters.

The Simple Work Sheet

To assist him in organizing and planning for the financial statements, an accountant uses a working paper called a Work Sheet. This, as its name suggests, is a more informal type of business paper. It is ordinarily prepared in pencil so that any necessary changes can be made easily. The work is done on columnar bookkeeping paper; the number of money columns used depends on the complexity of the business and the technique of the accountant. For our simple exercises, six money columns are used.

The steps in the preparation of a Work Sheet are detailed below. The information used in the examples is obtained from problem No. 8 of the previous chapter.

Step 1. The first step in the preparation of a Work Sheet is to **write the heading on the columnar paper.** Examine the headings in the upper illustration very carefully. Observe, in particular, the precise way in which the accounting period is described.

Step 2. The second step in the preparation of a Work Sheet is to **record the trial balance in the manner shown above.** It is absolutely imperative that the trial balance columns be balanced and correct before any additional work is done on the work sheet.

Step 1. The Headings of a Work Sheet

Step 2. Recording the Trial Balance on a Work Sheet

63

Step. 3. The third step in the process is to **record each of the amounts from the trial balance columns into one of the four columns to the right**. The process is simple and logical. The Profit and Loss Statement columns of the Work Sheet receive the Income and the Expenses–the items that make up the profit or the loss. The Balance Sheet columns receive everything else–the Assets, the Liabilities, the Capital, and the Drawings. Remember that the Drawings is definitely not an element of profit or loss and therefore cannot be included in that section. Be careful to transfer the amounts accurately and to record debit amounts into Debit columns and credit amounts into Credit columns. Be sure, too, that no single amount is transferred to two places and that no item is missed.

Step 4. The fourth step in the process is that of '**balancing the Work Sheet**'. The objective in balancing the Work Sheet is–

1. To total the four right-hand money columns.
2. To see that the difference between the two Profit and Loss columns is equal to the difference between the two Balance Sheet columns. This difference is known as the 'balancing figure'.
3. To record the above information in a neat and orderly manner on the Work Sheet as shown to the right.

It is very important that the Work Sheet balances and so the 'balancing work' must be done very carefully. If the two differences mentioned in 2 above do not agree, then the Work Sheet does not balance. This means that one or more errors have been made in preparing it and that you may not proceed to the preparation of the financial statements until the errors have been found and corrected. It is mathematic-

ally impossible for the Work Sheet to be out of balance and be correct.

The 'balancing figure' on the Work Sheet will always tell you the amount of the Profit or the Loss for the accounting period. An intelligent look at the column totals of the Profit and Loss section of the Work Sheet will tell you which it is. When the credits (Income) are greater than the debits (Expense), a Profit has been earned; when the debits are

greater than the credits, a Loss has been suffered.

The lower illustration shows the 'balancing' work in a different colour for purposes of emphasis. 'Balancing' does not involve a great deal of work but it needs to be done carefully. Follow the lower example for a profit situation and the example on page 65 for a loss situation. Observe carefully the slight but important variations in the finalizing of the Work Sheet for a Loss situation.

Work Sheet	P. Simpson	Month ended Oct. 31, 19—					
Accounts	Trial Balance Dr	Cr	P.+L. Statement Dr	Cr	Balance Sheet Dr	Cr
Bank	582 54				582 54	
J Morrison	420 —				420 —	
N Martin	425 —				425 —	
Supplies	87 68				87 68	
Office Equipment	465 —				465 —	
Automobile	2 460 —				2 460 —	
Acc. Finance Company		730 —				730 —
Grand's Stationers		103 78				103 78
Industrial Suppliers		76 40				76 40
P Simpson, Capital		3 526 20				3 526 20
P Simpson, Drawings	292 50				292 50	
Income from Fees		1 365 —		1 365 —		
Car Expenses	200 96		200 96			
Office Expense	43 95		43 95			
Rent	175 —		175 —			
Wages	648 75		648 75			
	5 801 38	5 801 38				

Step 3. Transferring the Amounts on a Work Sheet

Work Sheet	P Simpson	Month ended Oct. 31, 19—					
Accounts	Trial Balance Dr	Cr	P.+L. Statement Dr	Cr	Balance Sheet Dr	Cr
Bank	582 54				582 54	
J Morrison	420 —				420 —	
N Martin	425 —				425 —	
Supplies	87 68				87 68	
Office Equipment	465 —				465 —	
Automobile	2 460 —				2 460 —	
Acc. Finance Company		730 —				730 —
Grand's Stationers		103 78				103 78
Industrial Suppliers		76 40				76 40
P Simpson, Capital		3 526 20				3 526 20
P Simpson, Drawings	292 50				292 50	
Income from Fees		1 365 —		1 365 —		
Car Expenses	200 96		200 96			
Office Expense	43 95		43 95			
Rent	175 —		175 —			
Wages	648 75		648 75			
	5 801 38	5 801 38	1 068 66	1 365 —	4 732 72	4 436 38
Net Profit			296 34			296 34
			1 365 —	1 365 —	4 732 72	4 732 72

Step 4. Balancing the Work Sheet (Profit Situation)

Work Sheet	R Graham Month Ended June 30, 19—					
Accounts	Trial Balance		P.&L. Statement		Balance Sheet	
	Dr	Cr	Dr	Cr	Dr	Cr
Bank	601 17				601 17	
C. Foster	125 —				125 —	
Wages Expense	316 —		316 —			
	4 701 17	4 701 17	2 172 47	1 816 40	5 167 21	5 523 28
Net Loss				356 07	356 07	
			2 172 47	2 172 47	5 523 28	5 523 28

Step 4. Balancing the Work Sheet (Loss Situation)

Financial Reporting

The completed Work Sheet possesses, in an organized and readily accessible form, all of the information that is needed for the preparation of the financial statements. Develop the habit of looking only to the Work Sheet for this information. Later, with more advanced work, it will not be available in any other place.

The financial statements represent the accountant's report to the owners or managers on the financial affairs of the business. Owners and managers rarely need to look at the actual accounting records since they rely on the skill of the accountant to maintain them accurately. All that the owners want to see are the finished financial reports of the accountant. It would be a foolish accountant indeed who did not take the trouble to prepare his statements flawlessly.

In today's business world financial reports are most often prepared in typewritten form by skilled secretarial personnel who copy from the accountants' handwritten work. But for you, as a student, it will probably be necessary to prepare your statements in handwritten form.

The Profit and Loss Statement

It is important that you recognize right from the start where to obtain the information necessary for the preparation of the Profit and Loss Statement. Establish firmly in your mind that it is found in the Profit and Loss columns of the Work Sheet. At an advanced level of study these columns will be the one and only source of the correct information.

The Profit and Loss Statement of P. Simpson appears below. It has been prepared from the Work Sheet on page 64. The style shown is not the only one possible.

Examine the lower illustration carefully. Observe in particular the following points:

1. The heading shows three things:
   (a) The name of the business or individual.
   (b) The description of the financial statement.
   (c) The exact fiscal period.
2. The Income and the Expenses are set out in separate sections.
3. The Net Profit (or Net Loss–see top of page 66) is shown as the final item on the statement.
4. When a money column is totaled and the total is to be used in further calculations on the statement (e.g., the Expenses column at the top of page 66) one standard way of showing the total is—
   (a) Rule a single line beneath the column.
   (b) Place the total in the next column to the right and beside the last figure in the column that was totaled.

P. Simpson Profit and Loss Statement Month Ended October 31, 19-6			
Income			
Income from Fees			1,365 —
Expenses			
Car Expenses		200 96	
Office Expense		43 95	
Rent		175 —	
Wages		648 75	1 068 66
Net Profit			296 34

Example of Profit and Loss Statement (Profit Situation)

Morris Real Estate
Profit and Loss Statement
Three Months Ended June 30, 19—

Income		
Commissions		$3,874.60
Expenses		
Advertising	$1,256.70	
Business Tax	57.50	
Car Expenses	746.51	
Miscellaneous Expense	92.46	
Rent	600.00	
Telephone Expense	96.24	
Wages	1,174.25	4,023.66
Net Loss		$ 149.06

Example of Profit and Loss Statement (Loss Situation)

The Balance Sheet

All of the figures that are needed for the preparation of a Balance Sheet are found in the Balance Sheet columns of the Work Sheet. Select them as you need them for the preparation of the statement.

The Balance Sheets illustrated in this chapter differ from those you have used heretofore in two major respects: **Appearance**, and **Content**. These two aspects are considered in turn.

Appearance. The Balance Sheets you are familiar with have had a horizontal or side-by-side arrangement as shown in the illustration, lower left. This arrangement is known as the 'Account Form' of the Balance Sheet.

The new style of Balance Sheet, introduced in this chapter, has a vertical or one-above-the-other arrangement as shown in the illustration, lower right. This new style is known as the 'Report Form' of the Balance Sheet. The 'Report Form', owing to the fact that it is more suitable for use with standard equipment and stationery, is a commonly used style.

Three sample Balance Sheets, in the new 'Report' form, are shown on pages 67-69.

Content. The Balance Sheet of Chapter 1 was very simple. The 'Report Form' Balance Sheets shown in this chapter are of a moderately more advanced nature. As well as including 'additional' information, this new form of Balance Sheet presents the usual information in more detail. You will find that much of the information is broken down into smaller classes or categories in order to make the statement more informative. It is at this stage that the Balance Sheet is considered to be a 'classified' financial statement.

Examine carefully the Balance Sheet samples that follow observing in particular the points listed below.

1. **Current Assets.** There is a separate section in the Balance Sheet for Current Assets. These consist of Cash and assets that will be converted into cash within one year in the ordinary course of business. Current assets are listed in the order of their 'liquidity'; that is, their ability to be converted into cash.

2. **Fixed Assets.** There is a separate section in the Balance Sheet for Fixed Assets. These are assets that normally last for more than one year; e.g., Buildings, Automotive Equipment, and Office Equipment.

3. **Current Liabilities.** There is a separate section in the Balance Sheet for Current Liabilities. These are debts of the business that are due to be paid within one year.

4. **Capital.** The new form of Balance Sheet has a section rather than a single figure for Capital. This section shows in broad terms the changes to Capital that have occurred during the accounting period. Specifically, the major elements of Capital–(a) the balance at the beginning of the period, (b) the Profit or the Loss for the period, and (c) the Drawings for the period–are arranged on the statement in a way that permits the calculation of the new Capital balance at the end of the accounting period.

It is important to note that variations in presentation occur in the

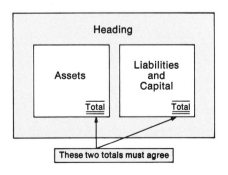

Account Form of Balance Sheet

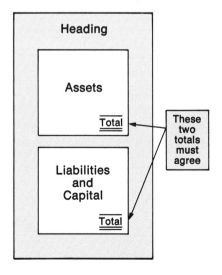

Report Form of Balance Sheet

Capital section depending on (a) whether the business has earned a profit or suffered a loss, and (b) whether the profit is greater or less than the drawings. It will be necessary for you to follow the samples in the textbook carefully when you are working your exercises.

Western Company					
Balance Sheet					
September 30, 19—					
Assets					
Current Assets					
Cash			1 246 02		
J. C. Duncan			75 —		
R. M. Prior			81 50		
P. G. Oliver			621 40		
Supplies			272 75	2 296 67	
Fixed Assets					
Furniture and Fixtures			863 20		
Delivery Equipment			3 500 —	4 363 20	
				6 659 87	
Liabilities and Capital					
Current Liabilities					
York Canning Company			951 —		
Maple Leaf Manufacturers			652 75	1 603 75	
A. M. Kendall, Capital					
Balance September 1			4 381 60		
Add: Net Profit	1 051 41				
Less Drawings	376 89		674 52		
Balance September 30				5 056 12	
				6 659 87	

Report Form Balance Sheet (Profit Greater than Drawings)
(Fiscal Period of One Month Indicated by Capital Section)

Eastern Company
Balance Sheet
March 31, 19—

ASSETS

Current Assets

Cash	$1,040.80	
B. Carson	225.40	
E. F. Fournier	443.27	
R. Nolan	72.00	
Supplies	132.60	$1,914.07

Fixed Assets

Furniture and Fixtures	$931.00	
Delivery Equipment	3,950.00	4,881.00
		$6,795.07

LIABILITIES AND CAPITAL

Current Liabilities

Bank Loan	$1,000.00	
Standard Company	1,247.61	$2,247.61

R. C. Jensen, Capital

Balance January 1		$4,696.86	
Deduct: Drawings	$1,400.00		
Less Net Profit	1,250.60	149.40	
Balance March 31			4,547.46
			$6,795.07

Report Form Balance Sheet (Drawings Greater than Profit)
(Fiscal Period of Three Months Indicated by Capital Section)

Notes:

1. When financial statements are typewritten, as they are in most cases, dollar signs are used in a limited way. For typewritten statements the rule for the use of dollar signs is: Use a dollar sign with the first figure in every money column and with the first figure beneath every ruled line in every money column.

2. On typewritten statements the 'cents' part of an even dollar amount is always shown by two ciphers and never by a dash.

3. In the Capital section the final Capital figure is dropped one line to permit a description to be written in the same line as the figure it describes. This is a common technique.

Northern Company
Balance Sheet
August 31, 19-6

Assets

Current Assets			
Cash		951 06	
Stewart and Martin		43 —	
Sevigny Bros		777 46	
D. F. Talbot		731 32	
Office Supplies		185 21	2 688 05
Fixed Assets			
Land		5 000 —	
Office Equipment		230 —	
Furniture and Fixtures		375 50	
Delivery Equipment		2 925 —	8 530 50
			11 218 55

Liabilities and Capital

Current Liabilities			
Central Supply Co		1 316 05	
Silvanite Company		871 63	2 187 68
H. H. Phillips, Capital			
Balance September 1, 19-5		9 893 47	
Deduct: Net Loss	512 60		
Drawings	350 —	862 60	
Balance August 31, 19-6			9 030 87
			11 218 55

Report Form Balance Sheet (Loss Situation)
(Fiscal Period of One Year Indicated by Capital Section)

The Accounting or Bookkeeping Cycle

During a fiscal period a certain number of procedures are required to be carried out in a precise and orderly manner. The first three of these procedures, journalizing, posting, and balancing of the ledger, are the responsibility of junior employees. The remaining procedures have to do with the preparation of financial statements and advanced accounting matters. They are the responsibility of the accountant and are discussed fully in Chapters 14 and 15. All of the steps together constitute the **Accounting or Bookkeeping Cycle,** the regular pattern of accounting functions that have to be carried out during each accounting period.

The Ledger and Automation

In relatively recent times, automation and the computer have had a tremendous impact in the field of accounting. And it appears that the computer's influence is not diminishing.

Although it has not changed the theory of accounting, the computer has had an effect on the form and appearance of accounting records, in particular the ledger.

A simulation of a computer-produced ledger is shown on page 70. It differs from the traditional ledger in two main respects.

1. The traditional ledger consists of a file of account cards or a book of account pages. There is a separate page or card for each account in the ledger.

   The computer-produced ledger consists of a particular kind of listing of the accounts. There is not a separate page for each account; one or more accounts may be listed on each page of the listing.

2. The traditional ledger consists of a number of individual accounts each of which is cumulative in nature. That is, the same account page or card is used until it is completely filled, at which time the balance is carried forward to a new page or card and the process continued.

   The computer-produced ledger is not a continuous record. Each month a new 'monthly' listing of the accounts is produced which shows: (a) the balances at the end of the previous month, (b) the debit and credit entries for the current month, and (c) the new balances at the end of the current month. Each individual listing shows the account information for a period of one month only. To examine a particular account for the entire year it is necessary to look at twelve listings.

DATE	ACCOUNT TITLE	ACCT CODE	REFERENCE	BEGINNING BALANCE	CURRENT MONTH		CLOSING BALANCE
					DEBIT	CREDIT	
AUG 31	BANK	01	BALANCE FORWARD	$5,016.25 DR			
SEPT 30		01	RECEIPTS		$9,321.16		
SEPT 30		01	DISBURSEMENTS			$10,402.16	
SEPT 30		01	JOURNAL ENTRY 65		15.00		
SEPT 30		01	BALANCE				$3,950.25 DR
AUG 31	ACCOUNTS RECEIVABLE	02	BALANCE FORWARD	$10,416.95 DR			
SEPT 30		02	SALES ON ACCOUNT		$16,402.19		
SEPT 30		02	RECEIPTS			$14,911.91	
SEPT 30		02	BALANCE				$11,907.23 DR
AUG 31	MERCHANDISE INVENTORY	03	BALANCE FORWARD	$24,117.03 DR			
SEPT 30		03	BALANCE				$24,117.03 DR
AUG 31	SUPPLIES	04	BALANCE FORWARD	$315.20 DR			
SEPT 30		04	DISBURSEMENTS		$74.20		
SEPT 30		04	PURCHASES ON ACCT		$49.15		
SEPT 30		04	BALANCE				$438.55 DR

A part of a computer-produced Ledger

Bookkeeping and Accounting Terms

Profit and Loss Statement: A financial report showing, in an orderly manner, the income, the expenses, and the net profit or the net loss of a business, that is, the operating results of the business, for a specified fiscal period.

Work Sheet: An informal columnar business paper on which is organized, in convenient form, all of the information that is required for the preparation of both the Profit and Loss Statement and the Balance Sheet.

Account Form of Balance Sheet: A horizontal or side-by-side arrangement of the Balance Sheet.

Report Form of Balance Sheet: A vertical or one-above-the-other arrangement of the Balance Sheet.

Current Assets: Cash, and assets that will be converted into cash within a period of one year in the ordinary course of business.

Fixed Assets: Assets that normally last for a number of years.

Current Liabilities: Debts of the business that are due to be paid within a period of one year.

Accounting Cycle: The total set of procedures that is required to be performed during each fiscal period.

Review Questions

1. What is the ultimate purpose of keeping a set of books?
2. Why is a Work Sheet used?
3. What are the headings of a Work Sheet?
4. What is very important about the Trial Balance columns of the Work Sheet?
5. Briefly describe the third step in the preparation of a Work Sheet.
6. How is the Work Sheet balanced?
7. If the Work Sheet does not balance, what must be done?
8. Is the balancing procedure the same for a 'profit' situation as it is for a 'loss' situation? Explain.
9. When preparing financial statements where does one look for the information?
10. Why should an accountant take the trouble to prepare the financial statements very carefully?
11. In what ways is the heading of the Profit and Loss Statement different from the heading of the Balance Sheet?
12. Explain the rules for the use of dollar signs in typewritten statements.
13. Explain the difference between the 'report' form and the 'account' form of the Balance Sheet.
14. What is meant by a 'classified' financial statement?
15. Define Current Asset.
16. Define Fixed Asset.
17. Define Current Liability.
18. Explain the accounting cycle.

Exercises

For each of the first six exercises you are required to prepare–
1. A six-column Work Sheet.
2. A Profit and Loss Statement.
3. A Balance Sheet in report form.

In working out your solutions follow carefully the samples in the textbook. After sufficient practice you should come to know the form of the financial statements.

1. The trial balance of The Arthur Company on October 31, 19—, after a fiscal period of one month, is as follows:

Cash	$1,722.16	
Jack Young	323.00	
M. H. Watson	72.00	
G. H. Clarkson	116.00	
Office Equipment	1,255.00	
Automobile	3,200.00	
Office Supply Company		$ 21.72
Local Hydro		16.42
Slick Oil Limited		31.19
M. O. Arthur		6,000.00
P. J. Arthur, Capital		1,277.50
P. J. Arthur, Drawings	1,000.00	
Sales		603.19
Automobile Expenses	65.12	
Rent Expense	70.00	
Telephone Expense	25.00	
Salaries Expense	80.00	
Miscellaneous Expense	13.74	
Advertising Expense	8.00	
	$7,950.02	$7,950.02

2. The trial balance of Morton Enterprises on February 28, 19—, after a fiscal period of three months, is as follows:

Cash	$462.12	
Arthur Ball	117.00	
K. L. Rimmer	92.55	
Supplies	150.00	
Office Equipment	741.00	
Delivery Equipment	2,840.00	
Building	17,340.00	
General Supply Co.		$ 94.80
E. S. Thomas		52.00
M. P. Morton, Capital		21,167.48
M. P. Morton, Drawings	200.00	
Sales		1,430.00
Rent Expense	120.00	
Labour Expense	510.00	
Delivery Expense	81.00	
Power Expense	54.21	
General Expense	36.40	
	$22,744.28	$22,744.28

3. The trial balance of Sturdy Insurance Agency on September 30, 19—, after a fiscal period of three months, is as follows:

Cash	$1,432.60	
P. Norman	76.00	
V. Parker	121.50	
Supplies	111.30	
Office Equipment	750.00	
Automobile	1,900.00	
Winston Motors		$ 441.00
Harper Bros.		75.00
D. K. Sandwell, Capital		3,995.80
D. K. Sandwell, Drawings	800.00	
Commissions		1,200.00
Rent Expense	110.00	
Car Expense	92.50	
Wages Expense	180.00	
Office Expense	95.00	
Miscellaneous Expense	42.90	
	$5,711.80	$5,711.80

4. The trial balance of P. C. Taylor, a lawyer, on June 30, 19—, after a fiscal period of one year, is as follows:

Cash	$ 516.20	
C. Carlisle	131.00	
G. McGregor	650.00	
Office Supplies	789.80	
Automobile	3,000.00	
Office Equipment	1,550.00	
Professional Library	1,270.00	
Bank Loan		$ 1,000.00
T. D. Goodman		1,000.00
A. E. Farrow		25.40
P. C. Taylor, Capital		8,804.60
P. C. Taylor, Drawings	12,000.00	
Fees Earned		14,721.61
Rent Expense	1,800.00	
Salaries Expense	2,645.51	
Car Expense	1,074.20	
Miscellaneous Expense	124.90	
	$25,551.61	$25,551.61

5. The trial balance of Star Delivery Company on December 31, 19—, after a fiscal period of one year, is as follows:

Cash	$ 212.00	
Chas. Green	170.00	
J. James	351.00	
V. Patterson	12.60	
Supplies	651.00	
Furniture and Fixtures	900.00	
Trucks	7,050.00	
Bank Loan		$ 3,000.00
Civic Trading Co.		746.00
R. Rankin, Capital		11,925.60
R. Rankin, Drawings	5,000.00	
Sales		8,500.00
Rent	2,000.00	
Gasoline and Oil	1,800.00	
Truck Repairs	1,000.00	
Insurance	1,000.00	
Miscellanous Expense	25.00	
Wages	4,000.00	
	$24,171.60	$24,171.60

6. The ledger of General Laundry is prepared by the owner, S. J. Travis, who is not a skilled accountant He arranges the accounts alphabetically. On November 30, 19— the trial balance of General Laundry, after a fiscal period of one month, is as follows:

Ace Supply Co.		$ 43.20
Bank Loan		1,000.00
Cash	$ 610.01	
Delivery Expense	84.00	
Delivery Truck	1,800.00	
Equipment	4,750.00	
R. Kirk	15.00	
J. Martin	92.00	
G. Leonard	12.00	
M. & S. Paint Co.		116.41
H. Phillips	157.51	
Rent Expense	100.00	
Sales		941.65
Supplies	220.90	
S. J. Travis, Capital		6,290.16
S. J. Travis, Drawings	300.00	
Wages Expense	250.00	
	$8,391.42	$8,391.42

7. You are to commence duties on November 1, 19—, at a salary of $65 per week, as accountant for J. Allan Lawson, a lawyer who has been in business for some years. In your new position you will be required to perform all the necessary accounting procedures to the point of preparing the financial statements at the end of each month.

The Chart of Accounts for this exercise appears on the facing page.

Assets	No.	Capital and Drawings	No.
Bank	1	J. Allen Lawson, Capital	31
Superior Cut Stone	2	L. Allen Lawson, Drawings	32
Briggs Pharmacy	3		
Arnold's Paving	4	*Income*	
Warren Real Estate	5	Fees Earned	41
Leyton and Leyton	6		
Barter's Service Station	7	*Expenses*	
Weston Printing Co.	8	Electricity Expense	51
J. C. Carmen	9	Insurance Expense	52
Office Supplies	10	Loss on Sale of Equipment	53
Professional Library	11	Miscellaneous Expense	54
Office Equipment	12	Rent	55
Automobile	13	Salaries Expense	56
		Travelling and Car Expense	57

Liabilities

C. H. C. Canadian Ltd.	21
Grande Oil Co.	22
Toronado Furniture Co.	23
Typewriters Limited	24

On October 31, 19— the trial balance of the business is as shown below.

J. Allen Lawson
Trial Balance
October 31, 19—

	Debits	Credits
Bank	$1,062.54	
Superior Cut Stone	450.00	
Briggs Pharmacy	120.00	
Arnold's Paving	75.00	
Office Supplies	49.00	
Professional Library	330.75	
Office Equipment	501.60	
Automobile	2,475.00	
C. H. C. Canadian Ltd.		$ 75.00
Grande Oil Co.		26.82
Toronado Furniture Co.		125.00
J. Allen Lawson, Capital		4,837.07
	$5,063.89	$5,063.89

INSTRUCTION 1.

Set up the ledger and the account balances as of October 31, 19—. If you are using the account paper that accompanies the text, it will be necessary to leave four accounts for Bank. Since this exercise involves a 'going concern', one that is continuing in business rather than just beginning, no opening entry is necessary. The technique for starting an exercise of this type is discussed in a special note on page 44.

INSTRUCTION 2.

The business transactions for the month of November are listed below. These transactions are to be journalized on journal page number 62. In recording the transactions, you are to assume that all money received is deposited daily in the bank account.

Transactions

November

3 Received $200 on account from Superior Cut Stone.

3 Issued Invoice No. 76 to Warren Real Estate for services rendered; amount, $100.

5 Purchased $5 of postage stamps; cheque No. 71 was issued.

6 Paid the Grande Oil Co. account in full; cheque No. 72 was issued.

7 Mr. Lawson withdrew $100 for his personal use; cheque No. 73 was issued.

7 Paid the accountant's salary; cheque No. 74 was issued.

7 Paid $45 for professional books purchased for the office library; cheque No. 75 was issued to the Provincial Law Association.

10 Purchased $36 of office supplies from Wilkins Brothers and issued cheque No. 76 in payment.

10 Issued invoice No. 77 to Leyton and Leyton for services rendered; amount, $375.

12 Received $120 on account from Briggs Pharmacy.

12 Purchased a new typewriter from Typewriters Limited on account. The price of the new typewriter was $315. As a downpayment on the new machine, Typewriters Limited agreed to accept an old typewriter as a trade-in and gave an allowance of $75 on it. The old machine had originally cost $225 and was included in the Office Equipment account at that figure.

Note:

At first glance, this transaction appears to be a difficult one. But it and all other transactions can be worked out if you follow the rules that have been developed. Do not give up easily.

13 Paid $37.25 to the Local Garage for car repairs; cheque No. 77 was issued.

13 Received $10 cash from G. Frankland for services rendered.

14 Mr. Lawson withdrew $90 for his personal use; cheque No. 78 was issued.

14 Paid the accountant's salary; cheque No. 79 was issued.

17 Paid C. H. C. Canadian Ltd. account in full; cheque No. 80 was issued.

18 Received a phone call from Toronado Furniture Co. requesting payment of their account claimed to be $225. This phone call brought to light an error of $100 made by the previous accountant in recording the purchase of an office desk. After correcting the error, the Toronado Furniture Co. account was paid in full. Cheque No. 81 was issued.

Note:

Think carefully here; all the information that you need is available.

19 Issued invoice No. 78 in the amount of $125 to Arnold's Paving for services rendered.

20 Received $20 cash from P. Morgan for services rendered.

20 Purchased $55 worth of office supplies from Dean's Stationery; cheque No. 82 was issued.

21 Mr. Lawson withdrew $100 for his personal use; cheque No. 83 was issued.

21 Paid the accountant's salary; cheque No. 84 was issued.

24 Paid the monthly insurance premium of $7.20. Cheque No. 85 was issued to Consumer's Insurance Company.

25 Issued Invoice No. 79 for $100 to Barter's Service Station for services rendered.

25 Issued invoice No. 80 for $150 to Weston Printing Co. for services rendered.

26 Purchased $5 of postage stamps; cheque No. 86 was issued.

26 Received a cheque from Superior Cut Stone for the balance of their account.

26 Received $75 on account from Arnold's Paving.

27 Issued invoice No. 81 for $275 to J. C. Carmen for services rendered.

27 Paid the monthly telephone bill; cheque No. 87 in the amount of $16.50 was issued to the local telephone company.

27 Paid the electricity bill for the month; cheque No. 88 in the amount of $8.27 was issued to the local hydro-electric company.

28 Received an invoice from Grande Oil Co. for the gasoline and oil used in the automobile during the month; amount, $18.60.

28 Paid the rent for the month; cheque No. 89 in the amount of $125 was issued to E. French.

28 The proprietor withdrew $110 for his personal use; cheque No. 90 was issued.

28 Paid the accountant's salary for the week; cheque No. 91 was issued.

Remember that you are to perform all the accounting functions required to the point of completing the financial statements.

Chapter 7

SUBSIDIARY LEDGER ACCOUNTING

Growth of a Business

Businessmen are of a special breed. Because their personal prosperity, and to a considerable extent their social status, depend on the success of their businesses, they are anxious that their businesses succeed. Most do achieve success and growth; they would not be in business for long otherwise.

As a business grows, a point is quickly reached at which one person is no longer able to handle all of the required accounting and office duties. At this point, the owner is forced to hire additional office staff. In so doing, keeping one eye on the profit of the business, he will normally try to hire as 'low-priced' help as he can; that is, persons whose skills and training are just enough to do the jobs that he has in mind for them.

Division of Labour

The pressure to keep costs down has been responsible for the development of a technique that permits the bulk of the office duties to be handled by a number of junior employees under the direction of a few senior persons.

Subsidiary Ledgers and Control Accounts, the topic of this chapter, is one such universally used accounting technique that permits an efficient and economical division of duties in a business office.

Growth of a Ledger

As a business grows, its ledger grows, too, but in a special way. In a ledger, most of the growth takes place in respect to the accounts of customers and creditors—as new customers and suppliers are sought out by an aggressive management. The other ledger accounts remain fairly stationary in number; they seem to change only in respect to the size of their balances.

The way in which a ledger grows may be illustrated by the following diagram. It shows most of the expansion taking place in the accounts of customers and creditors, the other accounts remaining fairly stationary in number.

Observe that once a business gets beyond the small stage, its ledger may be dominated by the accounts of customers and creditors. In many large companies the number of customers' accounts is phenomenal; for example, consider the accounts of The Bell Telephone Company.

Subsidiary Ledgers and Control Accounts

It has already been pointed out that in a mature business the office work will be divided–so that the bulk of it can be performed by less highly trained junior personnel under the guidance of a few senior persons. This is an economical way to run an office.

The recording of customers' and creditors' accounts is ideally suited to a division of duties. You have already seen that a large part of the ledger consists of **customers' and creditors' accounts**. Too, you may have guessed that these accounts involve a great deal of accounting activity.

To begin the study of Subsidiary Ledgers, examine the ledger shown in Illustration 'A' on page 80. This ledger is typical except for the fact that the number of customers' and creditors' accounts is small.

Note:
The theory of Subsidiary Ledgers holds true for any number of customers' and creditors' accounts. It is easier, but just as correct, for the author to explain the system using only a few such accounts. Remember, though, that the practical advantage of the system is in situations where the number of such accounts is large.

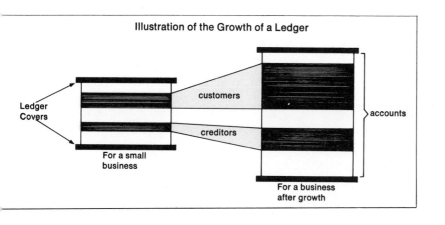

Illustration of the Growth of a Ledger

Ledger Covers

customers

creditors

accounts

For a small business

For a business after growth

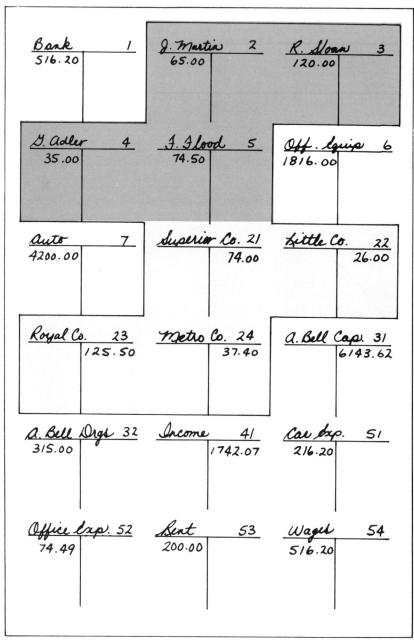

Illustration 'A'
A Simple Ledger

From this ledger extract all of the accounts of customers and creditors and set them aside in two separate groups.

In each new group, delete the account numbers, arrange the accounts in alphabetical order, and place the customers' and creditors' addresses on their account pages.

By definition, a group of accounts constitutes a ledger. Each of the two new groups of accounts conforms to this definition and is, therefore, itself a ledger. The two new ledgers, arranged alphabetically for greater convenience in handling, are shown in Illustration 'B' on page 81. They are known as Subsidiary Ledgers.

The ledger of customers' accounts, representing amounts receivable from customers, is known as the Accounts Receivable Ledger or sometimes as the Customers' Ledger. The accounts in it usually have debit balances. Occasionally, a credit balance may occur; for example, when a customer overpays his account. The ledger of creditors' accounts, representing amounts payable to creditors, is known as the Accounts Payable Ledger. These accounts usually have credit balances. Both of the new ledgers are called Subsidiary Ledgers, a term that will be specifically defined later in this chapter.

Now that there are three ledgers in the system it is necessary to be able to identify each one individually in order to avoid any possible confusion. For this reason, the main ledger, the one you are accustomed to using, is given the name 'General Ledger'.

The changeover to the three-ledger system is not yet completed. Since certain accounts were removed from it, the General Ledger in Illustration 'B' is no longer in balance; that is, it no longer balances within itself. For two reasons it cannot be left in this state. First, the concept of the ledger 'balancing' is fundamentally important. Second, the General Ledger, from which the financial statements are derived, must include the complete financial picture.

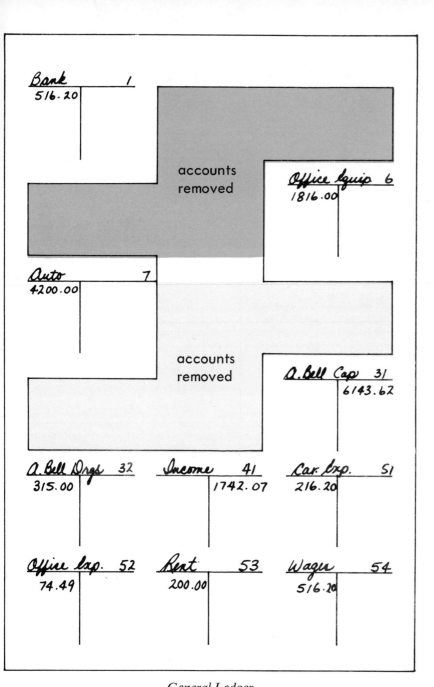

General Ledger

Bank   1
516.20

accounts removed

Office Equip   6
1816.00

Auto   7
4200.00

accounts removed

A. Bell Cap   31
6143.62

A. Bell Drgs   32   Income   41   Car. Exp.   51
315.00   1742.07   216.20

Office Exp.   52   Rent   53   Wages   54
74.49   200.00   516.20

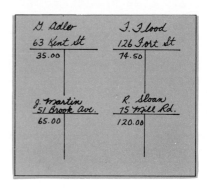

G. Adler
63 Kent St
35.00

J. Flood
126 Fort St
74.50

J. Martin
51 Brook Ave.
65.00

R. Sloan
15 Mill Rd.
120.00

Accounts Receivable Ledger
(a Subsidiary Ledger)

Little Co.
150 Doan St.
26.00

Metro Co.
27 Auld St.
37.40

Royal Co.
1250 Young St
125.50

Superior Co.
19 Hazel Ave.
74.00

Accounts Payable Ledger
(a Subsidiary Ledger)

Illustration 'B'
Partially Developed Three-Ledger System

The next step, therefore, is to open two new accounts in the General Ledger to replace all of those accounts that were previously taken out and set up in separate ledgers. The two new accounts, given the names Accounts Receivable and Accounts Payable, are shown in Illustration 'C' on page 82. Notice that the Accounts Receivable account in the General Ledger is given a balance of $294.50 Dr. which is equal to the total value of all the customers' accounts that it replaced. Similarly, the Accounts Payable account in the General Ledger is given a balance of $262.90 Cr. which is equal to the total value of all the creditors' accounts that it replaced.

Each of the two new accounts in the General Ledger is called a 'Control' account or 'Controlling' account, a term that will be defined later in this chapter.

The final appearance of the three-ledger system is shown in illustration 'C'.

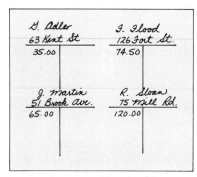

Accounts Receivable
Subsidiary Ledger
(Equal in Value to its Control Account)

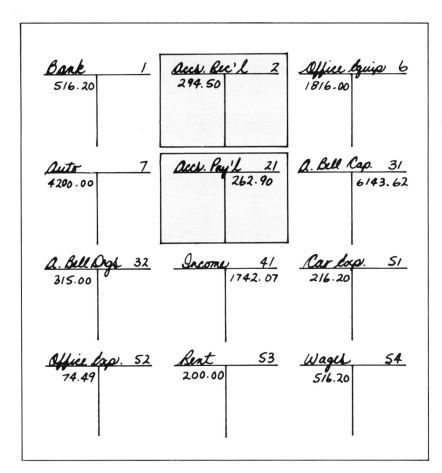

General Ledger
(In Balance)

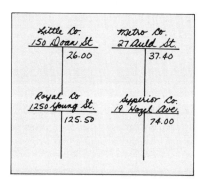

Accounts Payable
Subsidiary Ledger
(Equal in Value to its Control Account)

Illustration C
The Simple Three-Ledger System

Subsidiary Ledger Defined

A **Subsidiary Ledger** is a separate ledger that contains a number of accounts of a similar nature; these several accounts make up the detailed information in respect to one particular control account in the General Ledger.

Control Account Defined

A **Control Account** is a General Ledger account that shows the total value of a particular financial item, the details of which are maintained in a separate supporting subsidiary ledger.

Accounts Receivable and Payable on the Balance Sheet

The person responsible for the preparation of the financial statements should wait until after the three ledgers are balanced before attempting them. Only then can he be sure that the books of account are mechanically correct.

With the three-ledger system, it is no longer necessary to list the individual customers and creditors on the Balance Sheet. In fact, these individual accounts will not even appear on the Work Sheet, the source of information for statement preparation. Now the Balance Sheet will show the total of Accounts Receivable and the total of Accounts Payable as illustrated by the partial Balance Sheet shown below.

Dr. P. R. Proctor
Balance Sheet
March 31, 19–3

ASSETS

Current Assets

Bank	$1,650.21	
Accounts Receivable	7,086.14	
Supplies	1,276.00	$10,012.35

Fixed Assets

Equipment	$3,040.00	
Automobile	5,075.00	8,115.00
		$18,127.35

LIABILITIES

Current Liabilities

| Accounts Payable | | $ 4,072.16 |

Flowcharts

You should now have in mind a picture of the three-ledger system, although you do not as yet know how to operate it.

Unfortunately, the operation of the three-ledger system cannot be explained in a few words. It cannot be separated from the rather involved matters of office procedures and clerical routines. It is only within the context of the whole office system that the operation of the three-ledger system can be adequately described.

One of the purposes of this textbook is to acquaint you with the important fundamental aspects of accounting systems, routines, and procedures. It has been found that the most suitable method of describing these accounting systems is by means of flowcharts and accompanying explanatory notes (sample on page 84). Flowcharts are used extensively for this purpose throughout the remainder of this text. Before continuing with the study of subsidiary ledgers, let us break off briefly in order to examine the basic techniques of flowcharting. Then, having accomplished this, we can take immediate advantage of this very useful accounting tool.

FLOWCHARTING

'Flowcharting' is a technique ideally suited to the describing of office routines, systems, and procedures by means of diagrams and accompanying explanatory notes. Flowcharting has become an extremely important concept in modern business analysis.

The basic characteristics of flowcharting as used in this text are as follows:

1. Various business documents, books, ledgers, forms, lists, etc., are represented by certain geometric symbols such as rectangles, squares, and triangles. To assist in drawing the flowcharting symbols, a person usually has a flowcharting template such as the one illustrated on page 84.

2. Solid lines with arrows indicate the actual movement or flow of the documents through the various stages of processing to their ultimate place of permanent storage (file). The chart is usually drawn so that the flow moves from left to right and from top to bottom.

3. Broken lines with arrows indicate that information is taken from one document and is used to prepare another document, or to carry out an action (i.e. make a telephone call).

4. A permanent storage file is represented by an inverted triangle such as that shown below. Within the triangle, there appears the letter 'N', 'A', or 'D' which indicates respectively that the file is kept numerically, alphabetically, or by date.

5. The work locations (desks) of office employees are indicated by shaded ovals. (This is a technique adopted by the author and is not necessarily a standard flowcharting practice.)

6. The circled numerals refer to accompanying explanatory notes that provide the detailed information in respect to the various aspects of the business system being described.

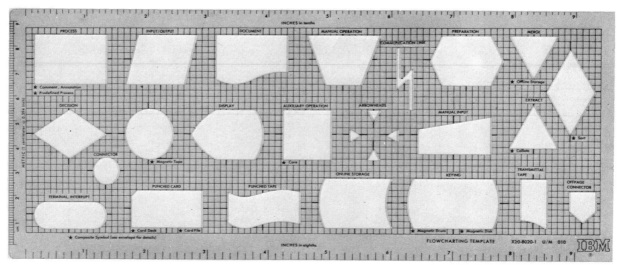

Flowchart Template (Courtesy IBM Canada Ltd.)

Basic Procedures for Accounts Receivable and Accounts Payable

On the next few pages, you will find flowcharts describing a basic accounts receivable procedure and a basic accounts payable procedure. It is your job to study these flowcharts together with the accompanying explanatory notes in order to acquire an understanding of these two important procedures. Do not presume that the procedures described here are followed precisely in every business office; this is not the case. An office manager may vary the basic procedure to suit his own special needs.

Primarily, the simple flowchart at right illustrates the following:

(a) Certain business documents, known as **source documents**, play an important role in the accounting process and are the source of the accounting entries. In this particular accounting situation the source documents are the copies of the Sales Invoices and the copies of the Daily Lists of Cash Receipts. These source documents move from desk to desk during the accounting process; eventually, they are stored in permanent files.

(b) A division of duties exists in a business office. In this particular case one employee maintains the Accounts Receivable Ledger whereas a second employee prepares the General Journal.

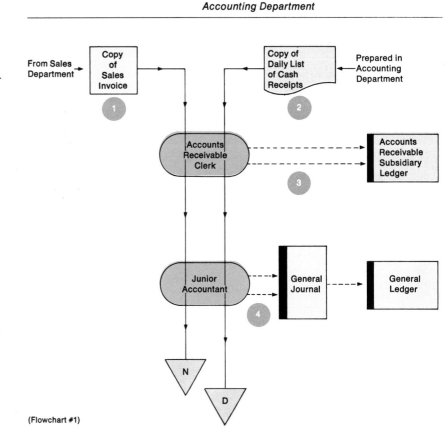

Flowchart for a Basic Accounts Receivable Procedure

Accounting Department

(Flowchart #1)

(1) A multi-part Sales Invoice (see illustration on page 52) is prepared for each sale on account. (A full sales procedure flowchart is shown in chapter 12.)

(2) Cheques received from customers are deposited in the bank each day. Before depositing them it is necessary to prepare a listing (in duplicate) as a permanent record of the pertinent information.

(3) **Posting.** It is the job of the accounts receivable clerk to keep the Accounts Receivable Ledger up to date. She accomplishes this by posting daily to the accounts in the ledger directly from the source documents that arrive on her desk.

Posting, which was previously defined as the transferring of information to the ledger from the journal, must now be considered in a broader light to include also the transferring of information to the ledger directly from the source documents.

Sales Invoices. For each Sales Invoice a debit entry must be made to a customer's account. Once or twice each day a quantity of numbered Sales Invoices arrive at the desk of the accounts receivable clerk. She places the pile of invoices in front of her and posts each one in turn to the appropriate customer's account. She records (a) the date, (b) the invoice number (in the Particulars column), (c) the debit amount, and (d) the new balance. To indicate that the posting of an invoice has been completed, the clerk places a checkmark or her initials on the Sales Invoice as a final step. No cross-referencing is done, as it is for General Ledger posting.

Cash Receipts. Each receipt from a customer represents a credit to the customer's account. On each business day, a copy of the Daily List of Cash Receipts is forwarded to the desk of the accounts receivable clerk. She posts each receipt from a customer to the appropriate customer's account, showing the date, the credit amount, and the new balance. As each receipt is posted, it is checked off on the listing. No cross-referencing is necessary.

(4) The junior accountant journalizes the routine transactions of the business in the General Journal. A number of source documents arrive at his desk each day. Among these source documents are the copies of the Sales Invoices and the Daily Lists of Cash Receipts.

Journalizing is done as before except that transactions affecting customers' accounts must now be written in terms of the General Ledger account for customers; namely, Accounts Receivable. For example, a sale on account is journalized as follows:

16	Accounts Receivable		164	—		
	Income				164	—
	Invoice #216 to P Norris					

Similarly, a receipt on account is journalized as follows:

19	Bank		75	42		
	Accounts Receivable				75	42
	Payment received from C. Watson					

Accounting Department

(Flowchart #2)

Primarily, this simple flowchart
illustrates the following:

1. The business **source documents**
in respect to the basic accounts
payable procedure are (a) the
matched sets of Purchase Orders,
Receiving Reports, and Purchase
Invoices, (b) the cheque copies.
These source documents move
from desk to desk during the accounting process. Eventually,
they are filed in permanent storage.

2. The main division of duties is
such that one employee maintains the Accounts Payable Ledger and another employee
prepares the General Journal.

ACCOMPANYING NOTES TO FLOWCHART

(1) **Purchase Order.** The Purchasing Department is responsible
for the purchasing of goods and
services. To order goods and
services, a Purchase Order form
showing all the pertinent details of the order is sent to the
supplier. One copy is sent to the
Accounting Department. (A
full description of the purchasing function is described in
the flowchart on page 211.)

Receiving Report. As goods
are received by the business,
they are counted and inspected
by members of the Receiving
Department. A Receiving Report is prepared which shows
all of the important data in respect to the goods received. A
copy of the Receiving Report is
sent to the Accounting Department. (The receiving function
is described in detail by means

of the flowchart on page 211.)
Purchase Invoice. Whenever a
business makes a sale on account it sends to the purchaser
a Sales Invoice which shows the
details of the transaction and
requests payment. In the Accounting Department of the
purchaser these suppliers' Sales
Invoices are referred to as
Purchase Invoices in order to
distinguish them from the business' own Sales Invoices.

The first step in processing
Purchase Invoices is to match
the Purchase Order, the Receiving Report, and the Purchase Invoice. (These matched
sets are then put through additional verifying steps which are
described by the flowchart on
page 223.)

(2) Cheques are prepared and issued to the supplier a few days
before payment is due.
(Cheque preparation is described by means of the flowchart on page 225.)

(3) **Posting.** The accounts payable clerk keeps the Accounts
Payable Ledger up to date by
posting daily from the source
documents that arrive at her
desk.

Purchase Invoices. Each
matched Purchase Invoice set
requires that a credit entry be
made to a supplier's account.
The clerk posts from the
matched set to the appropriate
account recording the date, the
credit amount, and the new
balance. After completing each
posting she initials or places a
checkmark on the Purchase Invoice. No cross-referencing is
done.

Cheque Copies. Each cheque
copy (if it is paying an account
payable) requires a debit entry
to a supplier's account. The
clerk posts the date, the debit
amount, and records the new
balance. She then initials or
places a checkmark on the

cheque copy. No cross-referencing is done.

(4) The junior accountant journalizes the routine transactions of the business in the General Journal. A number of source documents arrive at his desk each day. Among these source documents are the Purchase Invoice matched sets and the cheque copies.

Journalizing is done as before except that transactions affecting creditors' accounts must now be written in terms of the General Ledger Account for creditors; namely, Accounts Payable. For example, a purchase of merchandise on account is journalized as follows:

12	Purchases		275	–		
	Accounts Payable				275	–
	Merch. purchased from C. Stanby; P.I. 1406					

Similarly, a payment on account is journalized as follows:

29	Accounts Payable		64	20		
	Bank				64	20
	Cheque #156 issued to Warner's Hardware					

Posting to the General Ledger

The General Ledger is posted in the usual manner with one exception. It is no longer necessary to keep it always up to date. Only the customers' and creditors' accounts must be posted daily.

Now that the customers' and creditors' accounts are kept separately, it is general practice to refrain from posting to the General Ledger until the end of the month and then to do the posting in one concentrated effort. This is a far more efficient way of posting.

If it is found necessary to know the daily bank balance, it can be maintained in various ways other than by posting to the General Ledger.

Balancing The Ledgers

It is standard practice to balance all of the ledgers at the end of every

month, after all postings have been completed.

To balance the General Ledger, there is no change in the procedure already described. The most common method is to use an adding machine to total all of the account balances. The accounts with debit balances are entered as additions and the accounts with credit balances are entered as subtractions. If the ledger is in balance, the total of the tape will be zero.

The procedure for balancing a subsidiary ledger is quite different and is described by means of the block flowchart on page 88. The balancing of a subsidiary ledger is usually the responsibility of the clerk in charge of the ledger. You must remember not to try to balance a subsidiary ledger until both the subsidiary ledger and the General Ledger are posted up to date. (See flowchart on facing page.)

Locating Errors When A Subsidiary Ledger Does Not Balance

As indicated by the loop in the top half of the flowchart, the state of the subsidiary ledger is not acceptable until it is balanced with the control account. To be balanced, the sum of all its accounts must agree with the balance of its control account. Only then can the balancing procedure be brought to a conclusion.

When it is found that a subsidiary ledger does not balance, a search for the errors must be made. In conducting the search, let your guiding principle be this: Whenever an amount is entered in any account in the subsidiary ledger, there must be an equivalent amount entered in the control account—and vice versa.

In your search for errors, there is no need to go back in the ledgers beyond the current month. The ledgers will have been balanced at the end of the previous month. The ledgers are balanced at the end of every month and there will be trial balance tapes on file as evidence. If errors exist in the accounts, you may rest assured that they were made in the current month.

Statement of Account

A Statement of Account is a record of a customer's account for a period of one month. It is standard practice to send a Statement of Account to each customer once a month. This informs him of the entries made to his account during the month and also of the balance owed. The customer can compare the statement with his own records to see if they are in agreement. A Statement of Account also serves as a subtle reminder to the customer that prompt payment of his account is expected.

In systems where the posting is done by machines, it is usual to use collated (partially matched) ledger accounts and statement. In this way,

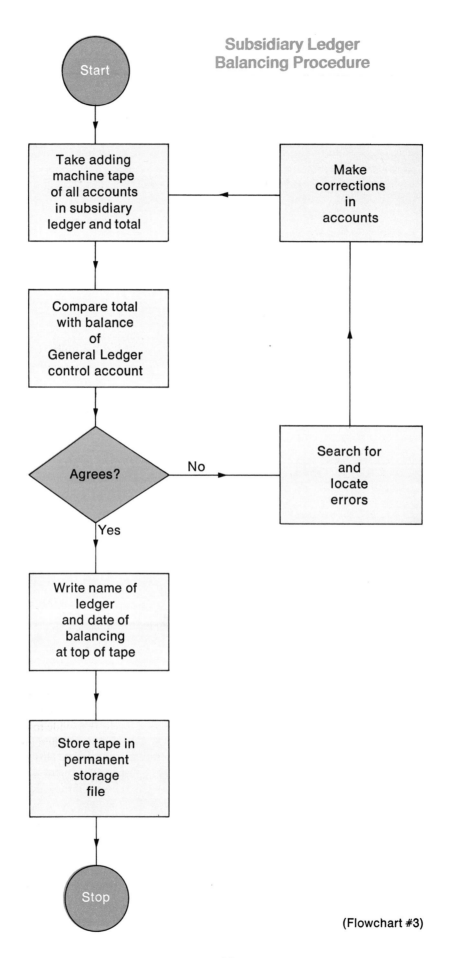

Subsidiary Ledger
Balancing Procedure

Start

Take adding
machine tape
of all accounts
in subsidiary
ledger and total

Make
corrections
in
accounts

Compare total
with balance
of
General Ledger
control account

Agrees?

No

Search for
and
locate
errors

Yes

Write name of
ledger
and date of
balancing
at top of tape

Store tape in
permanent
storage
file

Stop

(Flowchart #3)

the ledger account and the statement
can be prepared simultaneously.

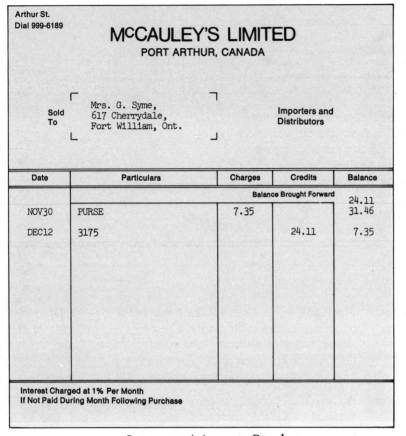

Statement of Account–Regular

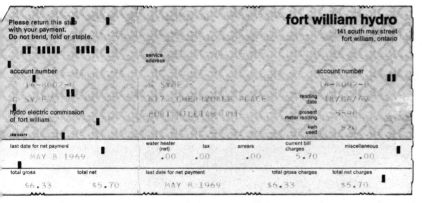

Statement of Account–Computer
(Courtesy of Hydro Electric Commission of Fort William)

14	E. Falls Drawings				4	80			
	Accounts Receivable (J. Wiggins)	✓						4	80
	To write off the account of J. Wiggins,								
	deceased, as instructed by E. Falls								

Non-Routine Entries to Subsidiary Ledgers

You have seen that accounting systems are designed so that the information flows to the office clerks by means of business source documents or vouchers. However, there are some transactions for which there are no source documents and which do not fit into the regular accounting routine. Transactions of this nature are not usually made known to the office clerks.

Consider the following.

J. Wiggins, a well-known and popular gentleman in a small community owes a small disputed balance of $4.80 to Falls & Co. Quite suddenly Mr. Wiggins dies. The owner of Falls & Co., E. Falls, decides that it would be wise to pay the disputed bill himself rather than to risk the chance of being a nuisance to the bereaved family and of possibly obtaining a bad reputation in the town. Accordingly, he instructs his accountant to write off the Wiggins balance and to charge it to his own (E. Falls) Drawings account.

Non-routine transactions are usually the full responsibility of the accountant alone. In addition to making the journal entry, he will also make any necessary postings to a subsidiary ledger. And he will do so promptly because the subsidiary ledger must be kept up to date.

The journal entry to write off the J. Wiggins account, after completing the posting of the subsidiary ledger is as shown below, left.

Observe that completion of the posting to the subsidiary ledger is indicated by drawing a diagonal line through the Posting Reference column of the journal and placing a checkmark in one of the halves. There is no source document to initial.

At the end of the month, this journal entry, along with all of the

others for the month, is posted to
the General Ledger and cross-
referenced in the usual manner.

14	*e. Talls Drawings*	32		4 80			
	Accounts Receivable (J Wiggins)	2 ✓			4 80		
	To write off the account of J. Wiggins,						
	deceased, as instructed by e. Talls						

Observe that the $4.80 credit re-
quires a double posting. The checkmark indicates the posting to the
subsidiary ledger; the numeral 2
indicates the posting to the Accounts
Receivable account in the General
Ledger.

Bookkeeping and Accounting Terms

Subsidiary Ledger: A separate ledger that contains a number of accounts of a similar nature. These several accounts make up the detailed information in respect to one particular control account in the General Ledger.

Control Account: A General Ledger account that shows the total value of a particular financial item, the details of which are maintained in a separate supporting subsidiary ledger.

Accounts Receivable Ledger: A book or file containing all the accounts of debtors (usually customers).

Accounts Payable Ledger: A book or file containing all the accounts of creditors (usually suppliers).

General Ledger: A book or file containing all the accounts of the business (other than those in subsidiary ledgers). It is these accounts that represent the complete financial position of the business or organization.

Flowchart: A diagram or pictorial representation of a system or procedure.

Cash Receipts: Cheques or cash received by the business, most commonly from customers paying their bills or from sales paid for in cash. Cash receipts are usually deposited in the bank on a daily basis.

Customer's Statement of Account:	A copy or duplicate record of the customer's account for a one-month period. Statements of account are sent to customers every month.
Purchase Order:	A business document prepared by the Purchasing Department detailing all pertinent information about an agreement to purchase goods or services.
Receiving Slip:	A business document prepared by the Receiving Department detailing all pertinent information in respect to a shipment of goods received into the business.
Purchase Invoice:	The manner of describing the supplier's Sales Invoice in the office of the purchaser to distingush it from the purchaser's own Sales Invoice.
Source Document:	Any business form or paper of the type that gives rise to an accounting entry. (The source document will be the supporting voucher for the accounting entry.)

Review Questions

1. Explain why only a few highly skilled persons are needed in an office.
2. What is meant by division of labour?
3. Describe briefly the way in which the accounts of a business grow.
4. In what ledger are the accounts of creditors kept? of debtors?
5. Give the names of the three ledgers in the three-ledger system.
6. Briefly describe flowcharting.
7. On a flowchart, what technique is used to indicate the flow of documents? of information?
8. Explain the purpose of the notes that accompany a flowchart.
9. Describe a sales invoice.
10. Explain what is meant by 'cash receipts'.
11. Posting is ordinarily performed by two methods. What are they?
12. What is a source document?
13. When posting directly from source documents, how does the clerk indicate that the posting has been completed?
14. In the Accounts Payable Ledger, are Purchase Invoices posted as debits or credits?
15. Define control account.
16. Define subsidiary ledger.
17. Before attempting to balance the three ledgers, what must one be sure of?
18. When a subsidiary ledger does not balance with its control account, what procedure is followed?
19. In searching for errors, how far back in the records must one investigate?
20. What is a Statement of Account?
21. What is a Purchase Order?
22. Describe what is meant by 'matching'.
23. Explain why non-routine transactions have to be handled differently.

Exercises

1. INSTRUCTION 1.

F. Bragg is a Public Accountant. On March 31, 19— his General Ledger trial balance is as follows:

F. Bragg
General Ledger Trial Balance
March 31, 19—

No.			
No. 1	Bank	$ 516.20	
2	Accounts Receivable	262.50	
3	Supplies	375.00	
4	Office Equipment	852.90	
5	Automobile	4,751.65	
21	Accounts Payable		$1,319.46
31	F. Bragg, Capital		3,181.23
32	F. Bragg, Drawings	400.00	
41	Fees Income		4,075.62
51	Car Expenses	196.50	
52	Light and Heat	62.75	
53	Miscellaneous Expense	47.51	
54	Rent	375.00	
55	Telephone	62.05	
56	Wages	674.25	
		$8,576.31	$8,576.31

Set up the General Ledger accounts for F. Bragg as of March 31, 19—.

INSTRUCTION 2.

The Accounts Receivable Ledger on March 31, 19— contains the following accounts:

Blue Cab Company	16 Fox Street	Inv. No. 74	$110.00
Champion Store	175 Main Street	75	37.50
Oasis Restaurant	325 Second Street	76	75.00
Village Restaurant	400 Main Street	77	40.00
			$262.50

Set up the Accounts Receivable Ledger as of March 31, 19—. Observe that the total of the four accounts is equal to the balance of the control account in the General Ledger.

INSTRUCTION 3.

The Accounts Payable Ledger on March 31, 19— contains the following accounts:

M. Ball, Consultant	430 Red Road, Bigtown	$ 200.00
Queen Finance	151 King Street	1,047.21
Stirling Company	46 River Road	42.65
Tom's Garage	705 Victoria Street	29.60
		$1,319.46

Set up the Accounts Payable Ledger as of March 31, 19—. Observe that the total of the four accounts is equal to the balance of the control account in the General Ledger.

INSTRUCTION 4.

Each day you are to perform the duties of both the Accounts Receivable clerk and the Accounts Payable clerk. From the list of business transactions shown below, you are to post daily to any customers' or creditors' accounts affected. Although it will be necessary for you to post directly from the list of transactions, try to imagine that you are posting directly from the source documents themselves. Also, remember that not all business transactions affect the accounts of customers and creditors.

INSTRUCTION 5.

Each day you are to perform the duties of the junior accountant. Journalize each transaction in the two-column General Journal. Do not post to the General Ledger accounts until the end of April.

Transactions

April

1 *Cheque Copy*
    —No. 105, to P. Walters, $125, monthly rent.

3 *Sales Invoice*
    —No. 78, to Blue Cab Company, $100.

5 *Cash Receipt*
    —From Oasis Restaurant, $75, on account.

8 *Purchase Invoice*
    —From Tom's Garage, $40.20, gasoline and oil.

9 *Cheque Copy*
    —No. 106, to Queen Finance, $90, regular monthly payment.

12 *Sales Invoices*
    —No. 79, to Champion Store, $175.
    —No. 80, to Village Restaurant, $50.

15 *Cheque Copy*
    —No. 107, to Municipal Telephone, $20.50, telephone for month.

15 *Cash Receipt*

    –From Blue Cab Company, $110, on ac-
    count.

19 *Sales Invoice*

    –No. 81, to Oasis Restaurant, $75.

22 *Purchase Invoice*

    –From Stirling Company, $35, for sup-
    plies.

24 *Cheque Copies*

    –No. 108, to M. Ball, $200, on account.
    –No. 109, to Stirling Company, $42.65,
    on account.

30 *Cheque Copies*

    –No. 110, to Municipal Hydro, $15,
    electricity for month.
    –No. 111, to R. Carter, $215, wages for
    month.

INSTRUCTION 6.

As the junior accountant, at the end of the month you are to post the General Journal to the General Ledger, after which you are to take off a General Ledger trial balance. It is your responsibility to see that the ledger balances.

INSTRUCTION 7.

As the Accounts Receivable clerk, you are to take off a trial balance of the Accounts Receivable Ledger as of April 30, 19—. It is your responsibility to see that the Accounts Receivable Ledger balances with the control account.

INSTRUCTION 8.

As the Accounts Payable clerk, you are to take off a trial balance of the Accounts Payable Ledger as of April 30, 19—. See that this ledger balances with the control account.

---

2.   INSTRUCTION 1.

On June 30, 19—, the General Ledger trial balance of United Rental and Repair Service is as follows:

United Rental and Repair Service
General Ledger Trial Balance
June 30, 19—

No.	1	Bank	$	647.20		
	2	Accounts Receivable		519.50		
	3	Supplies		312.92		
	4	Equipment		3,040.50		
	5	Delivery Truck		3,500.00		
	21	Accounts Payable			$	665.50
	31	R. B. Jones, Capital				5,107.04
	32	R. B. Jones, Drawings		3,600.00		
	41	Sales				7,500.00
	51	Light and Heat Expense		275.00		
	52	Miscellaneous Expense		135.00		
	53	Rent Expense		600.00		
	54	Telephone Expense		75.40		
	55	Truck Expense		567.02		
				$13,272.54		$13,272.54

Set up the General Ledger accounts as of June 30, 19—.

INSTRUCTION 2.

The Accounts Receivable Ledger on June 30, 19— is as follows:

A. Barrett	184 Jones Avenue	Inv. No. 50	$142.50
C. French	314 Chestnut Street	51	33.50
J. Twiddle	41 Guest Avenue	52	125.90
T. Walters	90 Brooks Street	53	217.60
			$519.50

Set up the Accounts Receivable Ledger as of June 30, 19—.

INSTRUCTION 3.

The Accounts Payable Ledger as of June 30, 19— is as follows:

Able Finance Company	3000 Belleview Ave	$512.50
General Supply Company	50 James Street	153.00
		$665.50

Set up the Accounts Payable Ledger as of June 30, 19-—.

INSTRUCTION 4.

Each day you are to perform the duties of both the Accounts Receivable clerk and the Accounts Payable clerk. From the list of business transactions that follows, you are to post daily to the accounts of customers and creditors affected by the transactions. Remember that not all of the business transactions affect the accounts of customers and creditors.

INSTRUCTION 5.

Each day you are to perform the duties of the junior accountant. Each source document is the source of a journal entry in the two-column General Journal. Do not post to the General Ledger accounts until the end of each month.

Transactions

July
 1 *Sales Invoice*
   –No. 54, to J. Twiddle, $39.
 3 *Cheque Copies*
   –No. 151, to Royal Realty, $100, for the rent for the month.
   –No. 152, to Able Finance, $56, monthly payment on the truck.
 5 *Cheque Copy*
   –No. 153, to R. B. Jones, $100, personal withdrawal.
 9 *Cash Receipt*
   –From J. Twiddle, $125.90, on account.
11 *Cheque Copy*
   –No. 154, to General Supply Company, $153, on account.
12 *Purchase Invoice*
   –From West Wind Oil, 1,000 Bay Street, $67.50, for gas and oil used in the delivery truck.
16 *Purchase Invoice*
   –From General Supply Company, $350, for supplies.
19 *Sales Invoices*
   –No. 55, to C. French, $55.
   –No. 56, to T. Walters, $100.

20 *Cheque Copy*
   –No. 155, to Len's Hardware, $13.50, for miscellaneous items.
23 *Cash Receipt*
   –From A. Barrett, $100, on account.
24 *Cheque Copies*
   –No. 156, to City Telephone Co., $20, monthly telephone bill.
   –No. 157, to West Wind Oil, $67.50 on account.
25 *Cheque Copy*
   –No. 158, to R. B. Jones, $150, personal withdrawal.
   Sales Invoice
   –No. 57, to A. Barrett, $70.
   Cash Receipt
   –From C. French, $33.50, on account.
30 *Cheque Copy*
   –No. 159, to City Electric, $18, monthly hydro bill.
31 *Sales Invoice*
   –No. 58, to J. Twiddle, $40.

INSTRUCTION 6.

Acting as the junior accountant, post the General Journal to the General Ledger at the end of July. Then balance the General Ledger.

INSTRUCTION 7.

Acting as the Accounts Receivable clerk take off a trial balance of the Accounts Receivable Ledger as of July 31. Balance the Accounts Receivable Ledger with the control account.

INSTRUCTION 8.

Acting as the Accounts Payable clerk, take off a trial balance of the Accounts Payable Ledger as of July 31. Balance the Accounts Payable Ledger with the control account.

---

3. Among your office duties with the Quick Distributing Co., are those of the Accounts Receivable clerk. From business documents arriving on your desk you are to post daily to the customers' accounts.

On the morning of each working day, there arrive on your desk the following business documents:

(a) Copies of all Sales Invoices issued on the previous working day by the Sales Department.

(b) A listing of the day's Cash Receipts, prepared first thing each morning by the clerk who opens the mail.

INSTRUCTION 1.

Set up the Accounts Receivable Ledger as of June 30, 19— from the following detailed trial balance.

Adams Bros., 12 Mountain Avenue	Inv. No. 480	$ 67.20
	507	94.20
Defoe & Son, 620 Main Street	512	75.65
A. G. Farmer, 120A Blackwell Ave.	514	315.62
S. P. Handy, Ltd., 75 Porter Ave.	484	216.25
	511	200.22
R. Mortimer, 60 Hawley Crescent	470	516.25
	496	621.90
	505	608.36
Renforth Sales, 192 Dale Place	510	137.62
Vista Limited, 2001 Central Ave.	515	50.00
		$2,903.27

INSTRUCTION 2.

From the following business papers, post to the customers' accounts daily.

July 2	*Invoices*	No. 516 Adams Bros.		$59.24
		No. 517 Renforth Sales		$145.50
	Receipts	A. G. Farmer	No. 514	$315.62
		S. P. Handy, Ltd.	No. 484	$216.25
3	*Invoice*	No. 518 Defoe & Son		$75.85
	Receipts	Nil		
4	*Invoices*	No. 519 A. G. Farmer		$217.90
		No. 520 The Williams Company		
		417 Lake Street		$150.00
	Receipts	Adams Bros.	No. 480	$67.20
		R. Mortimer No. 470 & No. 496		$1,138.15
5	*Invoices*	No. 521 Vista Limited		$94.95
		No. 522 S. P. Handy, Ltd.		$104.16
		No. 523 R. Mortimer		$56.00
	Receipt	Renforth Sales	No. 510	$137.62
6	*Invoices*	No. 524 Adams Bros.		$167.07
		No. 525 The Williams Company		$75.00
	Receipts	Defoe & Son	No. 512	$75.65
		Vista Limited	No. 515	$50.00

INSTRUCTION 3.

Take off a trial balance of the Subsidiary Ledger as of July 6 and balance the Subsidiary Ledger with the Control Account. The senior accountant has arrived at a Control Account figure of $2,048.45.

4. On September 30, 19—, the detailed Accounts Payable Trial Balance of Magnetic Controls Company was as follows:

Magnetic Controls Company
Accounts Payable Trial Balance
September 30, 19—

Daiton Enterprises	106 Fleet Street, Barbary	516	$ 430.74
Gordon & Associates	7400 King Street, Oak City	B7407	216.92
Henderson Bros.	Box 65, Welton	16421	507.00
		16907	615.00
Kohler, R. M.	141 Nixon Avenue, Barbary	615	104.70
North State Packaging	1500 Middle Road, Lennox	901	74.87
Orenson & Sons	560 The Eastway, Dayson	1604	1,046.26
		1809	516.15
Riggs, J. B.	75 Baxter Road, Estwing	74621	502.00
Smithers, P. R.	106 Farr Street, Wibbling	74	57.05
Union Advertising	1900 Primeau Avenue,		
	Marks	16352	436.21
		17201	702.16
		17306	518.90
			$5,727.96

INSTRUCTION 1.

Set up the Accounts Payable Ledger of Magnetic Controls Company.

INSTRUCTION 2.

From the business documents listed below, perform the duties of the Accounts Payable clerk by posting daily to the Accounts Payable Ledger.

Transactions

October
1 *Purchase Invoices*
 –Smithers, P. R., No. 104, $151.89.
 –North State Packaging, No. 1046, $57.25.
 Cheque Copies
 –No. 65720, Union Advertising, on account, $800.
 –No. 65721, Henderson Bros., Inv. 16421, $507.
2 *Purchase Invoices*
 –Prouse & Reid, 14 Kay Street, Saxton, No. 597G, $316.29.
 –Union Advertising, No. 18002, $505.
 –Orenson & Sons, No. 1856, $216.
 Cheque Copies
 –No. 65722, Daiton Enterprises, Inv. 516, $430.74.
 –No. 65723, Orenson & Sons, on account, $500.

5 *Purchase Invoices*
 –Gordon & Associates, No. B7502, $315.20.
 –Kohler, R. M., No. 719, $174.90.
 –Riggs, J. B. No. 74998, $472.47.
 Cheque Copies
 –No. 65734, North State Packaging, Inv. 901, $74.87.
 –No. 65735, Union Advertising, balance of Inv. 17201, $338.37.
6 *Purchase Invoices*
 –Daiton Enterprises, No. 702, $375.62.
 –Henderson Bros., No. 17436, $1,746.21.
 Cheque Copies
 –No. 65739, Gordon & Associates, Inv. B7407, $216.92.
7 *Purchase Invoices*
 –Henderson Bros., No. 17807, $65.25.
 –Kohler, R. M., No. 792, $107.64.

7 *Purchase Invoices (Cont'd.)*

–Prouse & Reid, No. 602B, $392.61.
Cheque Copies
–No. 65744, Henderson Bros., Inv. 16907, $615.

7 No. 65745, Orenson & Sons, balance of Inv. 1604, $546.26.
–No. 65746, Prouse & Reid, Inv. 597G, $316.29.
–No. 65747, Smithers, P. R., Inv. 74, $57.05.

INSTRUCTION 3.

Take off an Accounts Payable Ledger trial balance and see that it agrees with the balance of the control account. The correct control account figure is $6,221.79.

---

5. As the accountant for Willowvale Cartage, it is your responsibility to perform the accounting functions of a small business owned by B. G. Cook. Willowvale Cartage offers a cartage service on a cash basis as well as to a number of regular customers on a credit basis.

INSTRUCTION 1.

Set up the three ledgers of Willowvale Cartage from the following information:

(a)   *Willowvale Cartage*
        Chart of Accounts

Bank	No.	1
Accounts Receivable		2
Office Supplies		3
Warehouse Supplies		4
Trucks		5
Bank Loan		21
Accounts Payable		22
B. G. Cook, Capital		31
B. G. Cook, Drawings		32
Sales		41
Gasoline and Oil		51
Insurance		52
Light and Heat		53
Miscellaneous Expense		54
Rent		55
Telephone		56
Truck Expense		57
Wages		58

(b)

Willowvale Cartage
General Ledger Trial Balance
June 30, 19—

Bank	$ 316.00	
Accounts Receivable	1,246.50	
Office Supplies	275.00	
Warehouse Supplies	114.00	
Trucks and Equipment	7,540.00	
Bank Loan		$1,000.00
Accounts Payable		3,416.40
B. G. Cook, Capital		5,075.10
	$9,491.50	$9,491.50

(c)

Willowvale Cartage
Accounts Receivable Trial Balance
June 30, 19—

Adelaide Sports	65 Brody St.	No. 204	$ 212.00
Best Drug Store	1210 Van Horne Ave.	No. 209	174.50
Friday's Pharmacy	Century Plaza	No. 186	319.20
Murray's Auto Supply	100 William Street	No. 210	196.40
Ward Millwork Ltd.	565 William Street	No. 201	344.40
			$1,246.50

(d)

Willowvale Cartage
Accounts Payable Trial Balance
June 30, 19—

Credit Finance Corp.	44 Rankin Street	Instalments	$2,986.55
Hatley Equipment	12 Rupert Avenue	No. 375	363.70
Westown Garage	Century Plaza	No. 1047	66.15
			$3,416.40

INSTRUCTION 2.

From the following list of business documents, journalize the transactions in the General Journal; post to the Subsidiary Ledgers daily; post to the General Ledger at the end of the month.

Transactions

July

1 *Sales Invoices*
  –No. 211, Murray's Auto Supply, $56.
  –No. 212, Ward Millwork Ltd., $35.
  Purchase Invoice
  –Hatley Equipment, No. 392, for warehouse supplies, $42.
  Cash Sales Ticket
  –No. 57, $25.

Cash Receipt
  –Friday's Pharmacy, re No. 186, $319.20.
Cheque Copy
  –No. 402, Credit Finance Corp., monthly instalment, $200.

2 *Sales Invoices*
  –No. 213, Best Drug Store, $104.
  –No. 214, Friday's Pharmacy, $74.

2 *Purchase Invoice*
   —Westown Garage, No. 1094, for truck
    repairs, $56.
   Cash Receipts
   —Ward Millwork Ltd., re No. 201,
    $344.40.
   —Adelaide Sports, re No. 204, $212.
   Cheque Copy
   —No. 403, to the accountant (you), for
    wages, $75.
5. *Sales Invoices*
   —No. 215, Adelaide Sports, $25.
   —No. 216, Ward Millwork Ltd., $16.
   —No. 217, Best Drug Store, $37.
   Cash Receipt
   —Murray's Auto Supply, re No. 210,
    $196.40.
   Cheque Copy
   —No. 404, Civic Hydro-Electric, for
    monthly electricity, $12.57.
6 *Sales Invoices*
   —No. 218, Friday's Pharmacy, $65.
   —No. 219, Murray's Auto Supply, $35.
   Cash Receipts
   —Best Drug Store, re No. 209, $174.50.
   —Murray's Auto Supply, re No. 211,
    $56.
   Cheque Copy
   —No. 405, Hatley Equipment, on account
    re No. 375, $200.
7 *Sales Invoice*
   —No. 220, Adelaide Sports, $19.
   Purchase Invoices
   —Mercury Sales, 19 Brent Ave., No. 74,
    for office supplies, $27.50.
   —Westown Garage, No. 1103, for gasoline
    and oil, $114.16.
   Cash Sales Ticket
   —No. 58, $40.
   Cash Receipt
   —Ward Millwork Ltd., re No. 212, $35.
   Cheque Copy
   —No. 406, B. G. Cook, personal draw-
    ings, $100.
8 *Sales Invoices*
   —No. 221, Best Drug Store, $24.
   —No. 222, Ward Millwork Ltd., $32.
   —No. 223, Murray's Auto Supply, $12.
9 *Sales Invoice*
   —No. 224, Friday's Pharmacy, $23.
   Cash Receipts
   —Adelaide Sports, re No. 215, $25.
   —Friday's Pharmacy, re No. 214, $74.
   Cheque Copy
   —No. 407, to the bookkeeper, for wages,
    $75.

12 *Sales Invoices*
   —No. 226, Best Drug Store, $36.
   —No. 227, Adelaide Sports, $14.
   Cash Receipt
   —Best Drug Store, re No. 213, $104.
13 *Sales Invoices*
   —No. 227, Ward Millwork Ltd., $15.
   —No. 228, Friday's Pharmacy, $62.
   —No. 229, Adelaide Sports, $75.
   Cash Receipt
   —Murray's Auto Supply, re No. 219,
    $35.
   Cheque Copy
   —No. 408, Westown Garage, re No. 1047,
    $66.15.
14 *Sales Invoices*
   —No. 230, Murray's Auto Supply, $41.
   —No. 231, Best Drug Store, $28.
   —No. 232, Ward Millwork Ltd., $5.
   Purchase Invoice
   —Westown Garage, No. 1127, for gasoline
    and oil, $75.05.
   Cash Sales Ticket
   —No. 59, $36.
   Cash Receipts
   —Best Drug Store, re No. 217, $37.
   —Ward Millwork Ltd., re No. 216, $16.
15 *Sales Invoice*
   —No. 233, Adelaide Sports, $17.
   Cash Receipts
   —Adelaide Sports, re No. 220, $19.
   —Friday's Pharmacy, re No. 218, $65.
   Cheque Copies
   —No. 409, Buff Insurance Agency,
    monthly insurance payment, $20.
   —No. 410, Hatley Equipment, re balance
    of No. 375, $163.70.
   Miscellaneous
   —A debit memorandum was received from
    the bank stating that $7.54 had been
    deducted from the business bank account
    to pay for bank service charges.
16 *Sales Invoice*
   —No. 234, Best Drug Store, $46.
   Cheque Copy
   —No. 411, to the accountant, for wages,
    $75.
19 *Sales Invoices*
   —No. 235, Ward Millwork Ltd., $115.
   —No. 236, Murray's Auto Supply, $201.
   Purchase Invoice
   —Westown Garage, No. 1174, for gasoline
    and oil, $75.16.
   Cash Receipts
   —Best Drug Store, re No. 221, $24.
   —Murray's Auto Supply, re No. 223, $12.

20 *Sales Invoices*
   –No. 237, Friday's Pharmacy, $47.
   –No. 238, Ward Millwork Ltd., $41.
   Cash Sales Ticket
   –No. 60, $15.
   Cash Receipt
   –Adelaide Sports, re No. 226, $14.
   Cheque Copy
   –No. 412, B. G. Cook, for personal drawings, $150.

21 *Sales Invoice*
   –No. 239, Adelaide Sports, $51.
   Cash Receipts
   –Ward Millwork Ltd., re No. 222, $32.
   –Friday's Pharmacy, re No. 224, $23.
   Cheque Copy
   –No. 413, Receiver General of Canada, for postage stamps, $40.

22 *Sales Invoices*
   –No. 240, Friday's Pharmacy, $18.
   –No. 241, Best Drug Store, $43.
   Cheque Copy
   –No. 414, Magill's Office Supplies, for the cash purchase of office supplies, $16.20.

23 *Sales Invoice*
   –No. 242, Ward Millwork Ltd., $19.
   Purchase Invoices
   –Westown Garage, No. 1204, for gasoline and oil, $74, for truck repairs, $116, total $190.
   –Hatley Equipment, No. 419, for warehouse supplies, $59.
   Cash Sales Ticket
   –No. 61, $41.
   Cash Receipts
   –Best Drug Store, re No. 225, $36.
   –Ward Millwork Ltd., re No. 227, $15.
   Cheque Copies
   –No. 415, Mercury Sales, re No. 74, $27.50.
   –No. 416, to the accountant for wages, $75.
   –No. 417, A.P.M. Telephone Co., monthly bill, $15.25.

26 *Sales Invoices*
   –No. 243 Murray's Auto Supply, $25.
   –No. 244 Adelaide Sports, $29.
   –No. 245 Ward Millwork Ltd., $10.

26 *Cash Receipts*
   –Best Drug Store, re No. 231 and No. 234, $74.
   –Ward Millwork Ltd., re No. 232, $5.
   Cash Sales Ticket
   No. 62, $20.
   Cheque Copies
   –No. 418, Westown Garage, re No. 1094 and No. 1103, $170.16.
   –No. 419, Hatley Equipment, re No. 392, $42.

27 *Sales Invoice*
   –No. 246, Best Drug Store, $53.
   Cash Receipt
   –Ward Millwork Ltd., re No. 235 and No. 238, $156.

28 *Sales Invoices*
   –No. 247, Adelaide Sports, $16.
   –No. 248, Friday's Pharmacy, $40.
   –No. 249, Murray's Auto Supply, $31.
   –No. 250, Ward Millwork Ltd., $21.
   Purchase Invoice
   –Mercury Sales, No. 96, for office supplies, $114.20.
   Cash Receipts
   –Adelaide Sports, re No. 229 and No. 233, $92.
   –Friday's Pharmacy, re No. 228, $62.
   –Murray's Auto Supply, re No. 230, $41.

29 *Sales Invoice*
   –No. 251, Adelaide Sports, $24.
   Purchase Invoice
   –Westown Garage, No. 1250, for gasoline and oil, $92.
   Cash Sales Ticket
   –No. 63, $56.
   Cash Receipt
   –Murray's Auto Supply, re No. 236, $201.

30 *Cash Receipt*
   –Friday's Pharmacy, re No. 237, $47.
   Cheque Copy
   –Westown Garage, re No. 1127, $75.05.

31 *Sales Invoices*
   –No. 252, Best Drug Store, $156.
   –No. 253, Ward Millwork Ltd., $75.

INSTRUCTION 3.

By means of Trial Balances:
(a) Balance the General Ledger.

(b) Balance the Subsidiary Ledgers with their respective Control Accounts.

6. Mr. E. W. Terry, an engineer, begins a small consulting business on a spare-time basis. He officially begins operations on July 1, 19— with the following business assets: Bank Balance, $2,000; Office Furniture, $565; Automobile, $2,750; Equipment, $1,250. He has no business liabilities.

INSTRUCTION 1.

From the preceding information and the following Chart of Accounts set up the General Ledger for E. W. Terry as of July 1, 19—. Journalize and post the opening entry.

E. W. Terry
Chart of Accounts

Account	Number
Bank	1
Accounts Receivable	2
Office Supplies	3
Office Furniture	4
Automobile	5
Equipment	6
Accounts Payable	21
E. W. Terry, Capital	31
E. W. Terry, Drawings	32
Fees Earned	41
Car Expense	51
Rent Expense	52
Miscellaneous Expense	53
Telephone Expense	54

INSTRUCTION 2.

Record the following transactions of the business in the General Journal. Open Subsidiary Ledger accounts as necessary and post to them on a daily basis. Postings to the General Ledger accounts are left until the end of the month.

July

1 *Cheque*
–No. 1, Chambers Bros., advance payment for monthly rent, $140.

2 *Purchase Invoice*
–Glen Printing, No. 651, for office supplies, $86.50.

4 *Sales Invoice*
–No. 1, J. R. Greenley, for services rendered, $150.

5 *Sales Invoices*
–No. 2, R. Grieve, for services rendered, $50.
–No. 3, P. Webb, for services rendered, $35.

7 *Purchase Invoice*
–Star Blueprinting, No. 370, for the printing of plans, $15.

8 *Purchase Invoice*
–Dynamic Engineering, No. B126, for consultation, $26.

9 *Purchase Invoice*
–McKay's Garage, No. B64, for gasoline and oil, $12.50.

10 *Sales Invoice*
–No. 4, M. Page, for services rendered, $50.
Purchase Invoice
–Star Blueprinting, No. 397, for printing of plans, $26.
Cheque Copies
–No. 2, Glen Printing, re No. 651, $86.50.
–No. 3, Star Blueprinting, re No. 370, $15.
–No. 4, Dynamic Engineering, re No. B126, $26.
–No. 5, McKay's Garage, re No. B64, $12.50.

11 *Cash Receipt*
–J. R. Greenley, re No. 1, $150.

14 *Sales Invoice*
–No. 5, R. Grieve, for services rendered, $20.

15 *Sales Invoice*
–No. 6, J. R. Greenley, for services rendered, $40.
Purchase Invoice
–Automotive Electrical, No. 702, for repair to generator on car, $22.50.

16 *Sales Invoice*
–No. 7, P. Webb, for services rendered, $16.

17 *Purchase Invoice*
–Dynamic Engineering, No. B306, for consultation, $75.

18 *Cash Receipt*
–R. Grieve, re No. 2, $50.

22 *Sales Invoice*
–No. 8, M. Page, for services rendered, $18.

23 *Cash Receipt*
–M. Page, re No. 4, $50.
Purchase Invoice
–McKay's Garage, No. B96, for gasoline and oil, $9.50.

24 *Cheque Copy*
–No. 6, E. W. Terry, for personal drawings, $100.

25 *Cash Receipt*
–J. R. Greenley, re No. 6, $40.

29 *Sales Invoice*
–No. 9, J. R. Greenley, for services rendered, $20.

30 *Cheque Copies*
–No. 7, Automotive Electrical, re No. 702, $22.50.
–No. 8, Star Blueprinting, re No. 397, $26.

31 *Cash Receipt*
–P. Webb, re No. 3, $35.
Cheque Copies
–No. 9, Township Hydro, for cash payment of hydro bill, $10.40.
–No. 10, Municipal Telephone, for cash payment of telephone bill, $16.50.
–No. 11, E. W. Terry, for personal drawings, $100.

INSTRUCTION 3.

Post and balance the General Ledger.

INSTRUCTION 4.

Take off Subsidiary Ledger trial balances and agree them with their respective Control Accounts.

Chapter 8

The Trading Business

You may have noticed that none of the examples or exercises used so far in this text have involved the buying or selling of merchandise. This omission has not been accidental. The author has intentionally used only service businesses–businesses that sell a service, not a commodity. The reason for this is to avoid, during the early stages of study, a certain minor accounting difficulty connected with the buying and selling of merchandise.

However, you are now ready to study the special accounting problems of 'trading businesses', that is, businesses that deal in merchandise. As you know, businesses of this type make up a large percentage of the business community.

Merchandise Inventory

Businesses that buy goods for the purpose of selling them at a profit are known as trading businesses or merchandisers. The goods that they deal in are commonly called merchandise inventory, merchandise, stock-in-trade, or just stock.

The merchandise inventories of different businesses will consist of different types of goods. For instance, the merchandise inventory of a lumber company will consist of lumber and building materials; the merchandise inventory of a food retailer will consist of the food commodities that are ordinarily seen on the store shelves; the merchandise inventory of an automobile dealer will consist of new and used cars as well as replacement parts.

There are two common methods of accounting for merchandise inventory. Of the two, the more complex method is the 'perpetual inventory method'. Under this method a record of all items in stock is kept up to date. This method is used by businesses that have a special need for such information. In many cases, these businesses are forced to purchase expensive automated equipment in order to produce the required information.

A simpler method of accounting for merchandise inventory is the 'periodic inventory method'. With this method, the up-to-date inventory figures are known only at the end of an accounting period. At that time, they are found by 'taking the inventory', that is, by actually counting and valuing the items in detail. This method is still used by many businesses today. The routines that are described in this chapter are based on the periodic inventory method.

Balance Sheet Presentation

Because it usually must have the goods available to sell to the customer upon request, a trading business is obliged to keep a considerable inventory on hand. This inventory has a monetary value to the business and must, therefore, be included as an asset on the Balance Sheet. In particular, it will be listed as a current asset because in the ordinary course of business activity the inventory items will usually be sold and converted into cash within a year. An illustration of Merchandise Inventory on the Balance Sheet is to be found below.

The Merchandise Inventory Account

Under the periodic inventory method, the merchandise of a business is kept in two accounts. One of these,

---

Hardy's Hardware
Balance Sheet
June 30, 19—

ASSETS

Current Assets

Bank	$1,205.60	
Accounts Receivable	2,961.70	
Merchandise Inventory	8,059.00	
Supplies	316.00	$12,542.30

Fixed Assets

Store Equipment	$3,964.00	
Delivery Equipment	4,050.00	8,014.00
		$20,556.30

LIABILITIES AND CAPITAL

A Partial Balance Sheet

the Merchandise Inventory account, is used only to show the correct inventory figure at the end of an accounting period. At that time, after 'taking the inventory', the account is adjusted to reflect the correct inventory figure. This periodic adjustment is the only accounting entry made to the Merchandise Inventory account and is the responsibility of a senior person in the office. More will be said of this 'adjustment' in Chapters 14 and 15.

You may find a Merchandise Inventory account appearing in many of your exercises. Do not be confused by this account. Just remember that the balance in the account represents the adjusted inventory figure at the end of the preceding fiscal period; or, what amounts to the same thing, at the beginning of the present fiscal period.

Accounting For A Trading Business

Do not expect to learn everything about merchandise accounting in this chapter. You are not ready for it yet. At the present time, you will be given just enough of the theory to enable you to do that which is important for you now; namely, the handling of the day-to-day transactions of a trading business. The whole problem of merchandise inventory accounting will be clarified in Chapters 14 and 15.

In order to handle the day-to-day transactions of a trading business, you must become familiar with the accounting entries for two important aspects of the business; namely, **Merchandise Buying** and **Merchandise Selling.**

1. *Purchase of Merchandise.* During an accounting period, whenever merchandise intended for resale is purchased, the cost of the goods is debited to a new account called 'Purchases'. The name given to this new account is short for 'Purchases of Merchandise for Resale'.

If cash is paid for the merchandise, the accounting entry is:

Dr. Purchases	$xxxx.xx
Cr. Bank	$xxxx.xx

If the merchandise is bought on account, say from Victor Bros., the accounting entry is:

Dr. Purchases	$xxxx.xx
Cr. Accounts Payable (Victor Bros.)	$xxxx.xx

Not every item purchased is debited to the Purchases account. The Purchases account is used only for items of merchandise purchased with the intention of their being sold. For example, if a hardware store purchases a new delivery truck, the account to be debited is Delivery Truck. If the same hardware store purchases a shipment of hardware items to be put on sale, the account to be debited is Purchases. Similarly, if a tire dealer purchases some office supplies, the account to be debited is Office Supplies. But, if the same tire dealer purchases a shipment of tires to be sold to the public, the account to be debited is Purchases.

2. *Sale of Merchandise.* Whenever merchandise is sold, the selling price of the goods is credited to an income account called 'Sales'.

When goods are sold for cash the accounting entry is:

Dr. Bank	$xxxx.xx
Cr. Sales	$xxxx.xx

When goods are sold on account, say to J. Fields, the accounting entry is:

Dr. Accounts Receivable (J. Fields)	$xxxx.xx
Cr. Sales	$xxxx.xx

During the accounting period, nothing is done to record the decrease in merchandise inventory that accompanies a sale. Whenever a sale is made the goods are eventually taken or delivered from the premises of the vendor. But under the periodic inventory method of inventory accounting, this decrease is not accounted for during the accounting period. This is another bookkeeping situation where it is more expedient to allow certain records to become incorrect during the accounting period and to correct them at the end of the period. But more about that later.

Freight-in
Delivery Expense

The accounting for a trading business usually involves two additional transactions that are new to you. These involve the accounts 'Freight-in' and 'Delivery Expense'. These two new accounts are debited with the costs of transporting or delivering the goods that a business deals in.

The '**Freight-in**' account is used to accumulate transportation charges pertaining to incoming merchandise. The **'Delivery Expense'** account is used to accumulate transportation charges pertaining to outgoing merchandise.

The charges for Freight-in or Delivery Expense may originate from invoices of trucking companies, railway companies, or shipping companies. If a business has its own delivery equipment, these charges will originate from bills related to the running of the equipment, such as garage bills, repair bills, and bills for gasoline and oil.

You may wonder why two accounts so similar in nature are kept separately. The reason is that one of the accounts–Freight-in–has to do with the 'cost' of merchandise, and the other–Delivery Equipment–has to do with the 'sale' of merchandise. Owners, managers, and other senior officials are able to utilize this type of information in conducting the affairs of the business.

The Synoptic Journal

You now have acquired a reasonably good appreciation of the accounting process. But it still needs to be refined and specialized to make it even more functional and more in tune with the real business world.

The **Synoptic Journal**, the topic of this section, is a many-columned journal that differs considerably from the two-column journal that you have been using. The new concept of 'having many columns' is an extremely important one. The principle is universally accepted, and many mechanical and electronic devices have been developed to take advantage of it.

This does not mean that the two-column journal is of no further use. On the contrary, it is still widely used today but usually not for ordinary routine transactions handled by office clerks. Routine transactions are usually recorded in a many-columned type of journal of which the Synoptic Journal is one.

SYNOPTIC JOURNAL   MONTH OF_____

Date	Customer or Supplier or Explanation	#	Bank Dr.	Bank Cr.	√	Accounts Rec'l Dr.	Accounts Rec'l Cr.	√	Accounts Pay'l Dr.	Accounts Pay'l Cr.	Salesor Income Cr.	Purch's Dr.		Other Accounts Account	PR	Dr.	Cr.

The Synoptic Journal

An illustration of one style of Synoptic Journal appears on page 109. Observe the special money columns for Bank Dr., Bank Cr., Accounts Receivable Dr., Accounts Receivable Cr., Accounts Payable Dr., Accounts Payable Cr.. Sales or Income Cr., Purchases Dr., and the blank column to be named by the accountant.

The theory of the Synoptic Journal is to accumulate similar items in special columns during the journalizing process. Later, when posting to the General Ledger, it is the 'totals' of the special columns that are posted rather than the individual items contained within the columns. For each of the special columns, one posting is sufficient.

Theoretically, one could have a special column for every General Ledger account. But in practice, it is common to have special columns only for the items that occur frequently, and a general section for the remaining items. Otherwise, the Journal page would be too wide.

Journalizing in the Synoptic Journal is easy. Obtain a sheet of 'synoptic' paper and try the following sample entries.

TRANSACTION 1

May 4: Sold $56 of merchandise for cash; Sales Ticket No. 57.

According to a recently learned rule, the accounting entry for this transaction is Dr. Bank, $56; Cr. Sales, $56. In the Synoptic Journal this entry is recorded as follows:

SYNOPTIC JOURNAL   MONTH OF _May, 19—_   P. 42

Date 19—	Customer or Supplier or Explanation	#	Bank Dr.	Bank Cr.	√	Accounts Rec'l Dr.	Accounts Rec'l Cr.	√	Accounts Pay'l Dr.	Accounts Pay'l Cr.	Sales or Income Cr.	Purch's Dr.		Other Accounts Account	PR	Dr.	Cr.
May 4	Cash Sale	57	56 —								56 —						

TRANSACTION 2

May 5: Sold $112 of merchandise to Paul Boxer on account. Invoice No. 165 was issued.

The accounting entry for this transaction is Dr. Accounts Receivable (Paul Boxer), $112; Cr. Sales, $112. This entry follows the previous entry in the Synoptic Journal in the manner shown below. In respect to simple routine entries such as this, no explanations need to be written in.

SYNOPTIC JOURNAL   MONTH OF _May, 19—_   P. 42

Date 19—	Customer or Supplier or Explanation	#	Bank Dr.	Bank Cr.	√	Accounts Rec'l Dr.	Accounts Rec'l Cr.	√	Accounts Pay'l Dr.	Accounts Pay'l Cr.	Sales or Income Cr.	Purch's Dr.		Other Accounts Account	PR	Dr.	Cr.
May 4	Cash Sale	57	56 —								56 —						
5	Paul Boxer	165				112 —					112 —						

Observe that in this particular design of Synoptic Journal there is only one column provided for reference numbers. Consequently, all reference numbers, whether for cheques issued, cash sales slips, sales invoices, or other source documents, are recorded in this single column.

Observe also that no checkmark was placed in the '√' column beside Accounts Receivable to indicate that a posting to the Subsidiary Ledger was completed. This is because the system adopted here for posting to Subsidiary Ledgers is the one described in the previous chapter. You will recall that the postings to the customers' and creditors' accounts are made directly from the source documents. If the system used happens to be one in which the posting to the customers' and creditors' accounts is taken directly from the journal, then the '√' column is used to indicate that the postings are completed.

TRANSACTION 3

May 6: Purchased $316 of merchandise on account from Empire Wholesale; received their invoice.

The recently learned accounting entry for this transaction is Dr. Purchases, $316; Cr. Accounts Payable (Empire Wholesale), $316. The recording of this entry in the Synoptic Journal is shown below:

Date 19-	Customer or Supplier or Explanation	#	Bank Dr.	Bank Cr.	V	Accounts Rec'l Dr.	Accounts Rec'l Cr.	V	Accounts Pay'l Dr.	Accounts Pay'l Cr.	Sales or Income Cr.	Purch's Dr.		Other Accounts Account	PR	Dr.	Cr.
May 4	Cash Sale	57	56 —								56 —						
5	Paul Boxer	165				112 —					112 —						
6	Empire Wholesale									316 —		316 —					

SYNOPTIC JOURNAL — MONTH OF May, 19— — P. 42

TRANSACTION 4

May 7: $37.20 of Supplies is purchased and paid for with cheque No. 74 issued to Deluxe Stationers.

The accounting entry for this transaction is Dr. Supplies, $37.20; Cr. Bank, $37.20. It is recorded in the Synoptic Journal in the manner shown below:

ate 19-	Customer or Supplier or Explanation	#	Bank Dr.	Bank Cr.	V	Accounts Rec'l Dr.	Accounts Rec'l Cr.	V	Accounts Pay'l Dr.	Accounts Pay'l Cr.	Sales or Income Cr.	Purch's Dr.	Supplies Dr.	Other Accounts Account	PR	Dr.	Cr.
ay 4	Cash Sale	57	56 —								56 —						
5	Paul Boxer	165				112 —					112 —						
6	Empire Wholesale									316 —		316 —					
7	Deluxe Stationers	74		37 20									37 20				

SYNOPTIC JOURNAL — MONTH OF May, 19— — P. 42

Notice that the accountant has used the blank column for 'Supplies'. It can be assumed from this that, for this business, Supplies is a frequently occurring item.

May 7: Issued cheque No. 75 in the amount of $200 to Arrow Realty in payment of the monthly rent.

This accounting entry–Dr. Rent Expense, $200; Cr. Bank, $200–is recorded in the Synoptic Journal as shown below:

SYNOPTIC JOURNAL   MONTH OF *May, 19—*   P. 42

Date 19—	Customer or Supplier or Explanation	#	Bank Dr.	Bank Cr.	√	Accounts Rec'l Dr.	Accounts Rec'l Cr.	√	Accounts Pay'l Dr.	Accounts Pay'l Cr.	Sales or Income Cr.	Purch's Dr.	Supplies Dr.	Other Accounts Account	PR	Other Accounts Dr.	Other Accounts Cr.
May 4	Cash Sale	57	56 —								56 —						
5	Paul Boxer	165				112 —					112 —						
6	Empire Wholesale									316 —		316 —					
7	Deluxe Stationers	74		37 20									37 20				
7	Arrow Realty	75		200 —										Rent Expense		200 —	

Notice that there is not a special column for Rent Expense. The payment of the rent is a transaction that occurs only once a month and for that reason is recorded in the section headed 'Other Accounts'. Observe in this case that the amount is placed in the Debit column.

ADDITIONAL TRANSACTIONS

A number of additional transactions of a routine nature are listed below. Try to journalize them on your own before comparing your work with the Synoptic Journal entries on page 113.

No. 6 May 10: Issued cheque No. 76 in the amount of $13.50 to A. Baldwin–a payment on account.

No. 7 May 10: Issued cheque No. 77 in the amount of $46.20 to G. English & Co.–a payment on account.

No. 8 May 11: Received a cheque for $16 from R. Smith on account.

No. 9 May 11: Received a cheque for $375 from F. Jones on account.

No. 10 May 13: Issued cheque No. 78 in the amount of $112 to M. Field in payment of his wages.

No. 11 May 13: Issued cheque No. 79 in the amount of $135 to R. French in payment of his wages.

No. 12 May 14: Issued Sales Invoice No. 166 for $250 to M. Birch.

No. 13 May 14: Issued Sales Invoice No. 167 for $170 to Y. Ash.

No. 14 May 17: Received an invoice from Continental Railway in the amount of $87.50 for freight charges on incoming merchandise.

No. 15 May 18: Received an invoice from Budget Oil in the amount of $64.72.

This invoice was for gasoline and oil used in the delivery truck.

No. 16 May 19: Issued cheque No. 80 for $50 to G. Ripley, the proprietor, for his personal use.

No. 17 May 20: Issued cheque No. 81 for $300 to Ideal Supply in payment of merchandise which was purchased for cash.

No. 18 May 21: Received an invoice from Circle Supplies in the amount of $46; this invoice was in respect to the purchase of supplies on account.

No. 19   May 21: Received an invoice from Deluxe Stationers in the amount of $420; this invoice was in respect to the purchase of a new office desk at a cost of $350 and some supplies at a cost of $70.

No. 20   May 24: The owner of the business, G. Ripley, made an agreement with Crescent Bank to borrow $1,000. As a result of this agreement Crescent Bank deposited $1,000 in the business bank account and sent the business a notice to this effect.

No. 21   May 25: Received a cheque for $62 from E. McRae on account.

No. 22   May 26: Issued cheque No. 82 in the amount of $200 to Empire Wholesale on account.

No. 23   May 26: Received an invoice from Prairie Manufacturing in respect to the purchase of merchandise on account; $160.

No. 24   May 26: Received a cheque for $100 from R. Stoddard on account.

No. 25   May 27: Issued cheque No. 83 for $112 to M. Field in payment of his wages.

No. 26   May 27: Issued cheque No. 84 for $135 to R. French in payment of his wages.

No. 27   May 31: Issued Sales Invoice No. 168 for $96 to Purity Company.

No. 28   May 31: G. Ripley, the owner, brought $500 of his personal funds into the business for the purpose of increasing his equity.

SYNOPTIC JOURNAL   MONTH OF *May, 19—*   P. 42

Date 19—	Customer or Supplier or Explanation	#	Bank Dr.	Bank Cr.	V	Accounts Rec'l Dr.	Accounts Rec'l Cr.	V	Accounts Pay'l Dr.	Accounts Pay'l Cr.	Sales or Income Cr.	Purch's Dr.	Supplies Dr.	Other Accounts Account	PR	Other Accounts Dr.	Other Accounts Cr.
May 4	Cash Sale	51	56 —								56 —						
5	Paul Boxer	165				112 —					112 —						
6	Empire Wholesale									316 —		316 —					
7	Deluxe Stationers	74		37 20									37 20				
7	Arrow Realty	75		200 —										Rent Expense		200 —	
10	A. Baldwin	76		13 50					13 50								
10	B. English + Co.	77		46 20					46 20								
11	R. Smith		16 —				16 —										
11	F. Jones		375 —				375 —										
13	M. Field	78		112 —										Wages Expense		112 —	
13	R. French	79		135 —										Wages Expense		135 —	
14	M. Birch	166				250 —					250 —						
14	U. Ash	167				170 —					170 —						
17	Continental Rlwy									87 50				Freight-in		87 50	
18	Budget Oil									64 72				Delivery Exp.		64 72	
19	G. Ripley	80		50 —										G. Ripley, Drawings		50 —	
20	Ideal Supply	81		300 —								300 —					
21	Circle Supplies									46 —			46 —				
21	Deluxe Stationers									420 —			70 —	Office Equip.		350 —	
24	Crescent Bank		1 000 —											Bank Loan			1 000 —
25	E. McRae		62 —				62 —										
26	Empire Wholesale	82		200 —					200 —								
26	Prairie Manufacturing									160 —		160 —					
26	R. Stoddard		100 —				100 —										
27	M. Field	83		112 —										Wages Expense		112 —	
27	R. French	84		135 —										Wages Expense		135 —	
31	Purity Company	168				96 —					96 —						
31	G. Ripley		500 —											G. Ripley, Capital			500 —
			2 109 —	1 340 90		628 —	553 —		259 70	1 094 22	684 —	776 —	153 20			1 246 22	1 500 —

Synoptic Journal with Entries for Transactions 1 to 28

113

At the bottom of every page, and at the end of every month, a procedure called 'cross balancing' is performed on the Synoptic Journal or any columnar journal. This procedure is often referred to as just 'balancing' the journal.

The steps in cross balancing a journal are described below. As you study these steps, refer to the illustration of the Synoptic Journal on page 113.

Step 1. **Immediately beneath the last entry on the page, and in ink, draw a single ruled line across all money columns of the journal.**

Step 2. **Separately, total (foot) each money column and write in the total in small pencil figures just beneath the single ruled line.** You will recall that these small pencil figures are known as 'pencil footings' or 'pin totals'.

Step 3. **Using an adding machine or a pencil and paper, separately add all of the pin totals of the debit columns and all of the pin totals of the credit columns; include all columns of the journal.** These two additions should produce the same grand total (i.e., a total of several totals). If the two sums are the same, the journal is 'in balance'. If the two sums are not the same, the journal is 'out of balance' or 'not in balance'.

A journal out of balance indicates that one or more errors have been made in its preparation. You may not proceed to the posting of the journal until the errors have been located and corrected.

Step 4. **If step 3 indicates that the journal is in balance, write in the column totals in ink immediately beneath the pin totals.**

Step 5. **In ink, draw a double ruled line across all money columns.**

ACCOUNTING MACHINES

The same type of journal can also be produced by machine. If a business is large enough to warrant its use and is able to justify the cost, it may purchase a 'Sensimatic' accounting machine. With this machine, an operator is able to record the journal entries faster, more accurately, and, because it is printed, more neatly. A special feature of the 'Sensimatic' is its ability to accumulate automatically each of the columns as the entries are made, and to print the column totals in balanced form by activating a special switch.

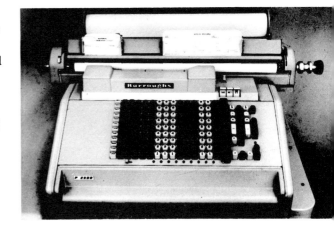

(Courtesy of Burroughs Business Machines Ltd.)

'FORWARDING' IN THE COLUMNAR JOURNAL

Whenever a new journal page is started, and it is not the beginning of a month, it is customary to start the new page with the totals from the previous page. The totals at the end of one page are 'forwarded' to the beginning of the next.

At the end of a page, after balancing it in the manner already discussed in this chapter, it is merely necessary to write in 'Carried Forward' or just 'Forwarded' in the Explanation column. This is illustrated at the top of p. 115. Remember that the journal is not posted until the end of the month.

Date 19—	Customer or Supplier or Explanation	#	Bank Dr.	Bank Cr.	V	Accounts Rec'l Dr.	Accounts Rec'l Cr.	V	Accounts Pay'l Dr.	Accounts Pay'l Cr.	Salesor Income Cr.	Purch's Dr.	Wages Dr.	Drawings Dr.	Other Accounts Account	PR	Other Accounts Dr.	Other Accounts Cr.
14	C. Palmer		131 62				131 62											
15	D. Clarke	106				85 —				85 —								
	Carried Forward		2 706 49	3 659 07		4 091 07	3 967 02		2 787 54	5 276 29	5 069 04	3 649 01	1 261 41	1 900 —			1 620 90	45 —
			2 706 49	3 659 07		4 091 07	3 967 02		2 787 54	5 276 29	5 069 04	3 649 01	1 261 41	1 900 —			1 620 90	45 —

On the first line of the next page it is then necessary to—

1. Write in the date of the last entry made on the preceding page.
2. Write in 'Brought Forward' or just 'Forwarded' in the Explanation column.
3. Write in the column totals from the previous page.

These steps are illustrated below.

Date 19—	Customer or Supplier or Explanation	#	Bank Dr.	Bank Cr.	V	Accounts Rec'l Dr.	Accounts Rec'l Cr.	V	Accounts Pay'l Dr.	Accounts Pay'l Cr.	Salesor Income Cr.	Purch's Dr.	Wages Dr.	Drawings Dr.	Other Accounts Account	PR	Other Accounts Dr.	Other Accounts Cr.
June 15	Brought Forward		2 706 49	3 659 07		4 091 07	3 967 02		2 787 54	5 276 29	5 069 04	3 649 01	1 261 41	1 900 —			1 620 90	45 —

After these steps have been carried out the journalizing process may be continued.

Posting to the General Ledger

The procedure for posting from a columnar journal is different than that used to post from the Two-column General Journal. This new posting procedure can be nicely demonstrated by means of the Synoptic Journal.

In respect to the special columns of the Synoptic Journal, it is the 'column totals' that are posted and not the individual items contained in the columns. This is true for all columns except the two general columns in the Other Accounts section of the journal. Because these two general columns usually contain several items relating to a number of different General Ledger accounts, the items in these two columns must be posted individually.

In detail, the procedure for posting a columnar journal is as follows:

1. Post the total of each special column to the account indicated in the column heading.
   (a) Post to the debit or credit side of the account according to the column heading.
   (b) In the account, date the entry with the last day of the month being posted.
   (c) When cross referencing in the account, use Sn and the number of the journal page from which the postings are taken.
   (d) When cross referencing in the journal, use the number of the account and place it in brackets beneath the column total.

2. Post each item individually in the two general columns of the Other Accounts section.
   (a) Post the amount that appears in either of the two money columns.
   (b) Post to the account named.
   (c) Post to the debit or credit side of the account according to the heading of the column in which the amount appears.
   (d) In the account, date the entry either with the last day of the month being posted, or with the day of the transaction.
   (e) When cross referencing in the account, use Sn and the number of the journal page from which the postings are taken.
   (f) When cross referencing in the journal, use the number of the account and place it in the Posting Reference (PR) column, on the same lines as the amount being posted.

Examples

In the following examples observe
that each posting being studied is
written on a white background
for purposes of highlighting.

1. *Post the 'Bank Dr.' column–*
   (a) In the account:

   (Notice that the account balance
   is not calculated at this time. Only
   after all postings are completed are
   the account balances usually determined. As a rule, they are found at
   that time with the help of an adding
   machine.)

   (b) In the Synoptic Journal:

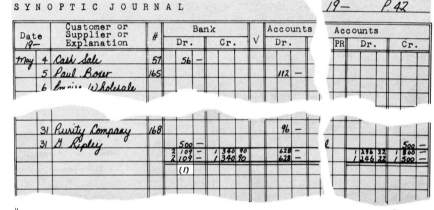

2. *Post the 'Bank Cr.' column–*
   (a) In the account:

   (b) In the Synoptic Journal:

3. *Post the item 'Rent Expense,
   $200'–*
   (a) In the account:

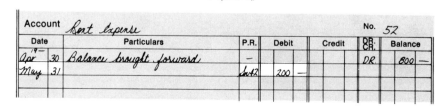

(b) In the Synoptic Journal:

Date 19—	Customer or Supplier or Explanation	#	urch's Dr.	Supplies Dr.	Other Accounts Account	PR	Dr.	Cr.
May 4	Cash Sale	5						
5	Paul Boxer	16						
6	Empire Wholesale							
7	Deluxe Stationers	7		37 20				
7	Arrow Realty	7.			Rent Expense	52	200 —	
10	A. Baldwin	76						

SYNOPTIC JOURNAL ... NTH OF May, 19— P.42

---

4. Post the item 'G. Ripley, Capital, $500'—

(a) In the account:

Account	G. Ripley, Capital					No. 31	
Date	Particulars	P.R.	Debit	Credit	DR. CR.	Balance	
19— Apr 30	Balance brought forward	—			CR	812 —	
May 31		Sn 42		500 —			

(b) In the Synoptic Journal:

Date 19—	Customer or Supplier or Explanation	#	Bank Dr.	Bank Cr.	h's	Other Accounts Account	PR	Dr.	Cr.
May 4	Cash Sale	57	56 —						
31	Purity Company	168							
31	G. Ripley		500 —			G. Ripley, Capital	31		500 —
			2 109 —	1 340 90				1 246 22	1 500 —
			2 109 —	1 340 90				1 246 22	1 500 —
			(1)	(1)					

SYNOPTIC JOURNAL ... H OF May, 19— P.42

After being posted entirely, the Synoptic Journal appears as shown below:

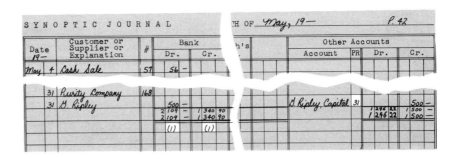

SYNOPTIC JOURNAL   MONTH OF May, 19—   P.42

Date 19—	Customer or Supplier or Explanation	#	Bank Dr.	Bank Cr.	V	Accounts Rec'l Dr.	Accounts Rec'l Cr.	V	Accounts Pay'l Dr.	Accounts Pay'l Cr.	Sales or Income Cr.	Purch's Dr.	Supplies Dr.	Other Accounts Account	PR	Dr.	Cr.
May 4	Cash Sale	51	56 —								56 —						
5	Paul Boxer	165				112 —					112 —						
6	Empire Wholesale									316 —		316 —					
7	Deluxe Stationers	74		37 20									37 20				
7	Arrow Realty	75		200 —										Rent Expense	58	200 —	
10	A. Baldwin	76		13 50						13 50							
10	G. English + Co.	77		46 20						46 20							
11	R. Smith		16 —							16 —							
11	F. Jones		375 —							375 —							
13	M. Field	78		112 —										Wages Expense	59	112 —	
13	R. French	79		135 —										Wages Expense	59	135 —	
14	M. Birch	166				250 —					250 —						
14	J. Ash	167				170 —					170 —						
17	Continental Rlwy.									87 50				Freight-in	54	87 50	
18	Budget Oil									64 72				Delivery Exp.	52	64 72	
19	G. Ripley	80		50 —										G. Ripley, Drawings	32	50 —	
20	Ideal Supply	81		300 —								300 —					
21	Circle Supplies									46 —		46 —					
21	Deluxe Stationers									420 —			70 —	Office Equip.	5	350 —	
24	Crescent Bank		1 000 —											Bank Loan	22		1 000 —
25	L. McRae			62 —			62 —										
26	Empire Wholesale	82		200 —						200 —							
26	Prairie Manufacturing									160 —		160 —					
26	R. Stoddard		100 —				100 —										
27	M. Field	83		112 —										Wages Expense	59	112 —	
27	R. French	84		135 —										Wages Expense	59	135 —	
31	Purity Company	168				96 —					96 —						
31	G. Ripley		500 —											G. Ripley, Capital	31		500 —
			2 109 —	1 340 90		628 —	553 —		259 70	1 094 22	684 —	776 —	153 20			1 246 22	1 500 —
			2 109 —	1 340 90		628 —	553 —		259 70	1 094 22	684 —	776 —	153 20			1 246 22	1 500 —
			(1)	(1)		(2)	(2)		(21)	(21)	(41)	(51)	(4)				

1. Occasionally, you may want to record a transaction of a non-routine nature in the Synoptic Journal. It is permissible to do this provided that, if the accounting entry is not self-explanatory, an explanation is written (usually in brackets). When writing explanations, it is permissible to write through the money columns. (See all three transactions illustrated below.)

2. Debit entries may be written in Credit columns or credit entries in Debit columns, provided that they are circled or written in red. This special designation of an entry indicates that its effect on the account is the opposite to that specified in the column head-ing. When the column is totaled, the designated item must be subtracted in order that the column total, when posted, will have the proper effect on the account. (See the second transaction illustrated below.)

3. Although most accounting entries require only one line in the Synoptic Journal, there are times when two or more lines may be required. This situation arises when at least two of the accounts affected by a transaction need to be recorded in the Other Accounts section of the journal, or when an explanation is written on a separate line. (See the second and third transactions illustrated below.)

SYNOPTIC JOURNAL   MONTH OF *Aug, 19—*   P.

Date 19—	Customer or Supplier or Explanation	#	Bank Dr.	Bank Cr.	Accounts Rec'l Dr.	Accounts Rec'l Cr.	Accounts Pay'l Dr.	Accounts Pay'l Cr.	Sales or Income Cr.	Purch's Dr.	Supplies Dr.	Wages Expense Dr.	Other Accounts Account	PR	Other Accounts Dr.	C
Aug 3	J. R. Proctor	902		150 —	*(Painting of office building)*								Bldg. Maintenance		150 —	
4	M. Hicks	903		27 50												
	(To refund amount overcharged on Sales Slip 174)								(27 50)							
5	Midwest Oil Co.	904		216 75									Heat Expense		195 60	
	(Heating fuel; part for oil delivered to home of proprietor)												J. Roe, Drawings		21 15	

Two Journal System

Frequently, the Synoptic Journal and the Two-Column General Journal are both used in a business. The Synoptic Journal is used to record the type of transaction for which it is most suitable; namely, routine transactions. Its preparation usually presents no difficulty for a junior employee. On the other hand, the Two-Column General Journal is used by a senior accounting person to record entries of a non-routine and usually more complex nature. The basic structure of a two-journal system is illustrated on page 119 by means of a flowchart.

In a two-journal system, each journal is prepared independently of the other, and at the end of every month each of the journals is posted individually to the General Ledger. If the General Ledger is found to be out of balance after the postings have been completed, it is necessary to consider the possibility of errors existing in two journals. The procedure for finding errors when a trial balance does not balance (page 53) must be amended to include two separate journals.

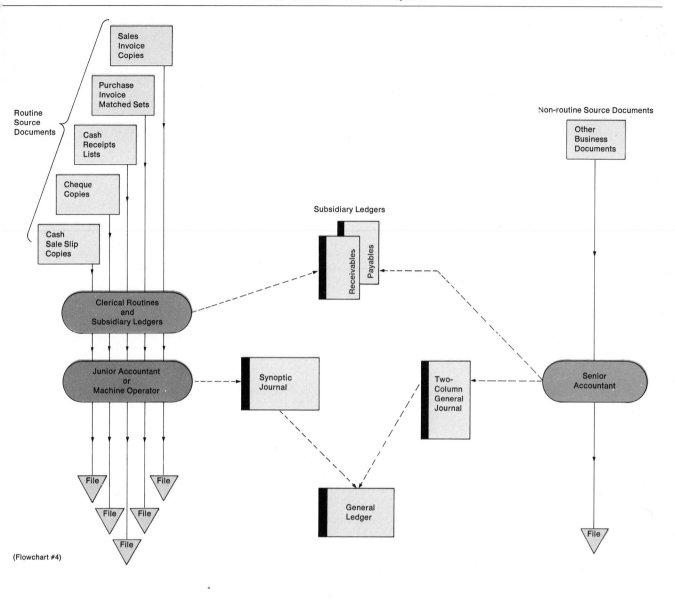

(Flowchart #4)

General Journal Vouchers

A popular alternative to the General Journal in the form of a book is the file of General Journal Vouchers. An example of a completed General Journal Voucher is shown on page 120.

Unused Journal Vouchers are kept in the form of a pad at the desk of the person who is responsible for their preparation. As circumstances warrant, the General Journal entries are written (usually one to a page),

and the vouchers are filed in numerical order on a type of ring binder. The vouchers are numbered consecutively as they are written.

At the end of each month, the General Journal Vouchers for the month are posted to the General Ledger. A minor difference in procedure is the use of the Journal Voucher number in cross referencing the journal entry in the account.

GENERAL JOURNAL VOUCHER

DATE: June 14   19 —   VOUCHER NO. 146

Account	V	Subsidiary Ledger	PR	General Ledger Debit	General Ledger Credit
Sales			41	230 95	
Accounts Receivable			2		230 95
Farrow Brothers	✓	84 75			
N. Robertson	✓	90 00			
S. Laing	✓	56 20			
		230 95			

EXPLANATION:

To cancel three Sales Invoices issued
in error: #615; #616; #617.

Bookkeeping and Accounting Terms

Trading Business: A business that deals in the buying and selling of merchandise. It buys the merchandise for the express purpose of selling it at a profit.

Merchandise Inventory:
Stock-In-Trade: The goods that a trading business deals in.

Purchases Account: The account that is charged with the cost of merchandise purchased for resale. 'Purchases' (the account name) is a short way of saying 'Purchases of Merchandise for Resale'.

Freight-In: Transportation charges on incoming merchandise.

Delivery Expense: Transportation charges on outgoing merchandise.

Synoptic Journal: A multi-columned journal having a number of selected special columns and two general columns. The special columns are used to record the more frequently occurring items; the two general columns are used to record the less frequently occurring items. Each of the special columns is reserved for a specific type of entry as indicated in the column heading; no other type of entry may be recorded in the column. At posting time, it is the totals of the special columns that are posted to the General Ledger, not the individual items contained in the columns.

Cross Balancing:
Balancing the Journal: A procedure carried out in respect to columnar journals to find out if the journalizing is arithmetically correct. After totaling separately all of the columns of the journal, the sum of the Debit column totals should equal the sum of the Credit column totals.

Review Questions

1. Explain what is meant by a 'trading business'.
2. What is 'Merchandise Inventory'? Give examples of different types of Merchandise Inventory.
3. What is 'Stock-in-Trade'?
4. Where is Merchandise Inventory shown on the Balance Sheet?
5. At the beginning of an accounting period, what does the balance in the Merchandise Inventory account represent?
6. Describe briefly what the Purchases account is used for.
7. Give the accounting entry for the purchase of merchandise, (a) for cash; (b) on account.
8. Give the accounting entry for the sale of merchandise, (a) for cash; (b) on account.
9. "Not every item purchased is debited to the Purchases account." Explain.
10. Explain the difference between Freight-in and Delivery Expense.
11. What is the principal difference between the Synoptic Journal and the Two-Column General Journal?
12. For what type of transaction is the Synoptic Journal best suited?
13. In the Synoptic Journal, what is the purpose of the special columns?
14. In the Synoptic Journal, what is the purpose of the two general columns?
15. Why is it necessary to cross balance a columnar journal?
16. What is the major advantage of the Synoptic Journal?
17. When are explanations necessary in a Synoptic Journal?
18. Briefly describe the use of General Journal Vouchers.

Exercises

1. At the end of July 19— the totals in a Synoptic Journal are as follows:

SYNOPTIC JOURNAL MONTH OF July, 19—

Date	Customer or Supplier or Explanation	#	Bank Dr.	Bank Cr.	V	Accounts Rec'l Dr.	Accounts Rec'l Cr.	V	Accounts Pay'l Dr.	Accounts Pay'l Cr.	Sales or Income Cr.	Purch's Dr.	Supplies Dr.	Wages Dr.	Other Accounts Account	PR	Other Accounts Dr.	Other Accounts Cr.
			2 694 62	3 016 21		3 096 17	2 546 21		1 596 12	1 842 94	3 309 42	1 706 40	156 97	746 02			729 74	11 26

INSTRUCTION.

Cross balance the Synoptic Journal.

2. At the end of June 19— the pin totals in a Synoptic Journal are as follows:

SYNOPTIC JOURNAL MONTH OF June, 19—

Date	Customer or Supplier or Explanation	#	Bank Dr.	Bank Cr.	V	Accounts Rec'l Dr.	Accounts Rec'l Cr.	V	Accounts Pay'l Dr.	Accounts Pay'l Cr.	Sales or Income Cr.	Purch's Dr.	Supplies Dr.	Wages Dr.	Other Accounts Account	PR	Other Accounts Dr.	Other Accounts Cr.
			6 092 10	5 961 02		10 060 22	6 142 10		4 092 17	9 402 19	10 104 11	7 574 80	356 51	3 023 65			409 97	

INSTRUCTION.

Cross balance the Synoptic Journal.

3. In the Synoptic Journal of P. D. R. Distributing Co., record the transactions listed below for the month of August, 19—. Use the spare column for 'Wages'. The Chart of Accounts for the business is as follows:

Account:

No. 1 Bank
2 Accounts Receivable
3 Merchandise Inventory
4 Supplies
5 Building
6 Furniture and Equipment
21 Accounts Payable
22 Bank Loan
23 Mortgage Payable
31 A. Orlando, Capital
32 A. Orlando, Drawings
41 Sales
51 Advertising
52 Building Repairs and Maintenance
53 Freight-in
54 Heat and Electricity
55 Miscellaneous Expense
56 Postage
57 Purchases
58 Telephone Expense
59 Wages

Transactions

August

2 *Cheque Copy*
–No. 702, to D. Macdonald, $310, cash payment for painting the building occupied by the business.

3 *Invoice*
–No. 210, to N. Rae, $34, for sale of goods.
Cash Receipt
–From B. Page, $100, on account.

5 *Cheque Copy*
–No. 703, to E. Pickard, $90, for wages.
Cash Sales
–$151.75.

8 *Cheque Copy*
–No. 704, to Receiver General of Canada, $20, for postage stamps.
Note:
Cheques to the Government of Canada are made out to the Receiver General of Canada.
Invoice
–No. 211, to Atlas Stores, $502, for sale of goods.

9 *Purchase Invoice*
–From Diamond Wholesalers, $325, for purchase of merchandise.

10 *Purchase Invoice*
–From Continental Railway, $165, for freight charges on incoming merchandise.

11 *Cash Sales*
–$74.

12 *Cheque Copies*
–No. 705, to Vance Brothers, $300, on account.
–No. 706, to E. Pickard, $90, for wages.

15 *Cheque Copies*
–No. 707, to Century '21', $10, for newspaper advertising.
–No. 708, to A. Orlando, $100, for proprietor's personal use.

18 *Cash Sales*
–$210.

19 *Cheque Copies*
–No. 709, to Merry Manufacturing, $500, on account.
–No. 710, to E. Pickard, $90, for wages.
Cash Receipt
–From G. Price, $140.25, on account.

22 *Cheque Copy*
–No. 711, to Price-Vincent Ltd., $350, for mortgage instalment.
Sales Invoice
–No. 212, to T. Schmidt, $170, for sale of goods.

23 *Purchase Invoice*
–From Deluxe Oil Company, $75, for gasoline used in the proprietor's automobile–$50 for business purposes, $25 for personal use.

24 *Bank Debit Slip*
–From General Bank, $12, for bank service charges.

25 *Cheque Copy*
—No. 712, to A. Orlando, $50, for proprietor's personal use.

26 *Cash Sales*
—$70.
Cheque Copy
—No. 713, to E. Pickard, $90, for wages.

29 *Purchase Invoice*
—From Federated Supply, $1,240, for the purchase of merchandise.

30 *Cheque Copy*
—No. 714, to Public Utilities Commission, $45, electricity charges for light and heat.

31 *Sales Invoice*
—No. 213, to R. Snell, $19, for sale of goods.
Cash Receipt
—From U. Stewart, $106, on account.
After completing the journalizing of the above transactions, cross balance and rule off the journal.

4. From exercise 3 above, summarize the postings that would be made to the General Ledger. List the information in three columns: Account, Debit Amount, Credit Amount. Show that the postings are 'balanced' by totaling the two money columns.

5. Record the following selected transactions in the Synoptic Journal of Howard Houghton Wholesaler. Use the spare column of the journal for Supplies, Dr. Since no chart of accounts is given for this exercise it will be necessary for you to make your own decisions in respect to the selection of accounts.

Transactions

November
1 *Sales Invoice*
—Issued to O. Tyler, $84.50, for sale of goods.
9 *Purchase Invoice*
—From O.K. Office Supplies, $173.25, for new office chair, $68.95, and office supplies, $104.30.
15 *Correcting Entry*
—Sales Invoice No. 50, which was issued to M. Stephens in the amount of $90, was journalized twice in error last month. Make the necessary correcting entry.
19 Howard Houghton, the owner, collected an account receivable from P. Anderson in the amount of $75. He did not turn the money into the business but kept it for his own personal use. However, he did inform you, the accountant, of the transaction and requested that you make the appropriate accounting entries.
22 Howard Houghton, the owner, purchased a first-aid kit for the business and paid for it out of his own pocket. He submitted the 'paid' bill for $15 to you and requested that you issue a cheque to reimburse him. Cheque No. 296 was issued by you.
26 Because of a period of heavy expenditures the business became short of funds. This necessitated that the owner arrange a bank loan of $1,000 from The People's Bank. You were given a memo from the bank showing that the loan had been granted and that the $1,000 had been placed in the business bank account.

INSTRUCTION.
Balance the Synoptic Journal.

6. F. Dunn is the sole proprietor of Crest Hardware. He operates the store with the assistance of his wife and some occasional part-time help. Mrs. Dunn works in the store as well as being responsible for all direct aspects of accounting. The financial statements are prepared annually from her records by a professional accountant.

The books of account are very simple and consist of a General Ledger, an Accounts Receivable Ledger, an Accounts Payable Ledger, and a Synoptic Journal. The last page used in the Synoptic Journal is page 72 and it shows that the spare column is used for General Expense.

Most of the sales of the business are cash sales or C.O.D. sales. The cash receipts are deposited in the bank on a daily basis. All payments are made by cheque.

The number of accounts in both Subsidiary Ledgers is very small. Mr. Dunn grants credit to only a few customers and buys his stock from only a few suppliers. Because of the small number of debtors and creditors the subsidiary ledger routine is very simple. All transactions are recorded in the Synoptic Journal and the postings to the Subsidiary Ledgers are made directly from the information in the journal and not from the source documents themselves. A check-mark is placed in the '√' column in the journal to indicate that a subsidiary ledger posting has been completed.

INSTRUCTION 1.

Set up the three ledgers of Crest Hardware from the following trial balances.

Crest Hardware
General Ledger Trial Balance
January 31, 19—

1	Bank	$ 1,500.00	
2	Accounts Receivable	365.25	
3	Merchandise Inventory	8,090.20	
4	Supplies	395.00	
5	Store Equipment	4,906.21	
6	Delivery Equipment	3,500.00	
21	Accounts Payable		$ 1,404.00
22	Federal Finance Co.		5,261.00
31	F. Dunn, Capital		11,739.12
32	F. Dunn, Drawings	860.00	
41	Sales		5,507.40
51	Delivery Expense	417.06	
52	Freight-in	269.50	
53	General Expense	164.10	
54	Purchases	3,064.20	
55	Rent Expense	300.00	
56	Wages Expense	80.00	
		$23,911.52	$23,911.52

R. Dunlop (Invoice 1407)	$112.76
G. Langford (Invoice 1431)	157.06
R. Potts (Invoice 1436)	95.43
	$365.25

Crest Hardware
Accounts Payable Trial Balance
January 31, 19—

City Hardware Supply (Their Invoice No. 17421)	$ 746.21
Special Steel Products (Their Invoice No. 147A)	657.79
	$1,404.00

INSTRUCTION 2.

In the Synoptic Journal, record the journal entries from the transactions listed below. Post to the Subsidiary Ledgers on a daily basis.

Transactions

February

2 *Cash Sales*
–$86.01. Sales Invoice No. 1475, to R. Dunlop, $26.40, for sale of goods.
Purchase Invoice
–No. 18021, from City Hardware Supply, $264.25, for purchase of merchandise.

3 *Cash Sales*
–$102.51.
Cash Receipt
–From R. Dunlop, $112.76, on account.

5 *Cash Sales*
–$56.42.

6 *Cash Sales*
–$109.75
Cheque Copy
–No. 316, to R. Gamble, $8, wages for part-time help.

7 *Cash Sales*
–$245.90.
Purchase Invoice
–No. 18340, from City Hardware Supply, $316.25, for purchase of merchandise.
Cheque Copies
–No. 317, Special Steel Products, $500, on account.

7 –No. 318, City Hardware Supply, $746.21, for No. 17421.
–No. 319, F. Dunn, $150, drawings.

9 *Cash Sales*
–$24.09.

10 *Cash Sales*
–$47.98.
Sales Invoice
–No. 1476, to G. Langford, $59, sale of merchandise.

12 *Cash Sales*
–$75.87.
Purchase Invoice
–No. 192A, Special Steel Products, $375.00, for purchase of merchandise.
Cheque Copy
–No. 320, to J. Moffat, $5, wages for part-time help.

13 *Cash Sales*
–$152.06.
Cheque Copy
–No. 321, to Special Steel Products, $157.79, balance of 147A.

14 *Cash Sales*
–$310.02.

14 *Sales Invoice*
   –No. 1477, to R. Potts, $243.67, sale of goods.
   Purchase Invoice
   –No. 1244, from Clix Oil Company, $23.75, for gasoline and oil used in the delivery truck.
   Cheque Copy
   –No. 322, F. Dunn, $150, drawings.

16 *Cash Sales*
   –$32.86.
   Cash Receipt
   –From G. Langford, $157.06, in payment of invoice No. 1431.

17 *Cash Sales*
   –$44.
   Purchase Invoice
   –No. 344, Joe Jay Transport, $76.45, charges for transportation on incoming merchandise.

19 *Cash Sales*
   –$129.65.
   Cheque Copy
   –No. 323, to Oak Investments, $300, for the rent for the month.

20 *Cash Sales*
   –$142.92.

21 *Cash Sales*
   –$264.08.
   Cheque Copy
   –No. 324, to F. Dunn, $150, drawings.

23 *Cash Sales*
   –$39.87.
   Sales Invoice
   –No. 1478, to R. Dunlop, $64.20, sale of goods.
   Cheque Copies
   –No. 325, to D. Parker, $9, part-time wages.
   –No. 326, to Public Utilities Commission, $25.08, cash payment of electricity and water bills.
   –No. 327, to City Telephone Company, $19.05, cash payment of telephone bill.

24 *Cash Sales*
   –$44.60.
   Cash Receipt
   –From R. Dunlop, $26.40, invoice No. 1475.

26 *Cash Sales*
   –$55.11.
   Cheque Copy
   –No. 328, to City Hardware Supply, $264.25, for invoice No. 18021.

27 *Cash Sales*
   –$74.23.

28 *Cash Sales*
   –$343.24.
   Cheque Copy
   –No. 329, to F. Dunn, $250, drawings.
   Purchase Invoice
   –No. 18472, from City Hardware Supply, $47.49, for store supplies.

INSTRUCTION 3.

(a) Balance the Synoptic Journal.
(b) Post the Synoptic Journal to the General Ledger.
(c) Balance the General Ledger.
(d) Balance the Subsidiary Ledgers.

7. The General Ledger trial balance
of Super Building Supplies on
September 30, 19— is as follows:

Super Building Supplies
General Ledger Trial Balance
September 30, 19—

1	Bank	$ 1,276.41	
2	Accounts Receivable	3,561.85	
3	Merchandise Inventory	8,487.64	
4	Office Supplies	950.00	
5	Delivery Equipment	4,640.00	
6	Office Equipment	1,065.00	
21	Accounts Payable		$10,840.20
31	D. K. Warren, Capital		9,395.88
32	D. K. Warren, Drawings	1,509.56	
41	Sales		4,709.00
51	Delivery Expense	354.00	
52	Miscellaneous Expense	75.62	
53	Purchases	2,905.00	
54	Rent Expense	120.00	
		$24,945.08	$24,945.08

The Subsidiary Ledger trial balances on September 30, 19— are as follows:

Accounts Receivable

Spartan Builders,	141 Wilson Avenue,	$ 814.16
Aurora Builders,	815 Keele Street,	900.00
Consumers' Homes,	51 Albionville Road,	100.00
Arnprior Estates,	14 Brown's Place	1,483.60
Westwood Acres,	88 Finchwood Avenue,	264.09
		$3,561.85

Accounts Payable

Mapleton Sand & Gravel,	Mapleton,	$ 2,658.19
King Crushed Stone,	King,	3,161.10
Marris Cement,	Marris,	1,851.00
General Tile Co.,	383 Hurst Street,	1,516.80
Whyte's Hardware,	Rexton,	1,653.11
		$10,840.20

INSTRUCTION 1.

Set up the three ledgers of Super Building Materials.

INSTRUCTION 2.

On page 19 of the Synoptic Journal, record the transactions for the month of October. Post to the Subsidiary Ledgers daily from the entries in the Synoptic Journal. Use the spare column of the journal for Office Supplies.

Transactions

October

2 *Cash Sale*
   –To P. Marshall, $35.

5 *Cheque Copy*
   –No. 175, to Mapleton Sand & Gravel, $100, on account.

6 *Sales Invoice*
   –No. 151, to Consumers' Homes, $955, for sale of merchandise.

9 *Cash Receipt*
   –From Arnprior Estates, $1,000, on account.

11 *Purchase Invoice*
   –From Westing Stationers, Westing, $83.60, for office supplies.

15 *Cheque Copies*
   –No. 176, to C. O. Prentice, $120, for the rent for the month.
   –No. 177, to Grand & Son, $310, cash purchase of new office desk.

18 *Sales Invoice*
   –No. 152, to Spartan Builders, $152, for sale of merchandise.

20 *Cheque Copy*
   –No. 178, to Marris Cement, $750, on account.

21 The proprietor took home merchandise for his personal use, value $125.
   Note:
   The proprietor must be charged with the value of the merchandise; furthermore, the decrease in merchandise is considered to be a decrease in 'purchases'.

25 *Cheque Copy*
   –No. 179, to Office Suppliers, $18, for cash purchase of stationery.
   Purchase Invoice
   –From General Tile, $432, purchase of tile.

28 *Cheque Copy*
   –No. 180, to Gray Lumber Co., $312, for the cash purchase of merchandise.
   Sales Invoice
   –No. 153, to Westwood Acres, $516, sale of goods.

29 *Purchase Invoice*
   –From Corgan Oil Limited, 40 Union Street, $157.50, for gas and oil used in the delivery truck.

30 *Cash Receipt*
   –From Spartan Builders, $500, on account.
   Cash Sale
   –To P. Percival, $50.

31 *Purchase Invoice*
   –From Marris Cement, $175, for cement.
   Cheque Copy
   –To Local Telephone Co., $8.50, telephone bill.

INSTRUCTION 3.

(a) Balance the Synoptic Journal and post to the General Ledger.
(b) Balance the General Ledger at October 31, 19—.
(c) Balance the Subsidiary Ledgers at October 31, 19—.

Chapter 9

THE FIVE-JOURNAL SYSTEM

Bank Debit and Credit Advices

The relationship between a bank and one of its depositors is basically this: The bank owes money to the depositor.

Suppose that Barrett Bros. has money on deposit with a bank. Both Barrett Bros. and the bank are obliged to keep track of this money. From Barrett Bros.' point of view the bank balance represents an asset but from the bank's point of view it represents a liability.

Consider the following transactions.

1. Barrett Bros. makes a deposit of $100.
   (a) Barrett Bros. will **Debit** 'Bank' (to increase an asset).
   (b) The bank will **Credit** 'Barrett Bros.' (to increase a liability).
2. Barrett Bros. makes a withdrawal of $50.
   (a) Barrett Bros. will **Credit** 'Bank' (to decrease an asset).
   (b) The bank will **Debit** 'Barrett Bros.' (to decrease a liability).

Although both the bank and the depositor are following the same rules of debit and credit, it appears to some that they are directly opposed. New students of accounting are often troubled by this aspect of banking but only because they have had no light shed on the problem.

It is important that a business be able to calculate its bank balance at any time so that it does not issue cheques for more than the amount of its bank balance. To have this facility, a business must be aware of all entries affecting the bank balance. The entries that the business itself originates present no problem, but it must be notified by the bank of any entries that the bank originates.

When a bank initiates a change to a depositor's bank balance, it notifies him immediately by means of a Bank Debit Advice or a Bank Credit Advice (may be called Bank Debit Memorandum or Bank Credit Memorandum). The Bank Debit Advice is associated with decreases to the account and the Bank Credit Advice is associated with increases to the account. Example of both forms are shown below.

The first form, the Bank Debit Advice, informs the depositor that a bank service charge has been deducted from his account. When the depositor receives this notice he must make an appropriate accounting entry in his books of account. In this case the entry will probably be a

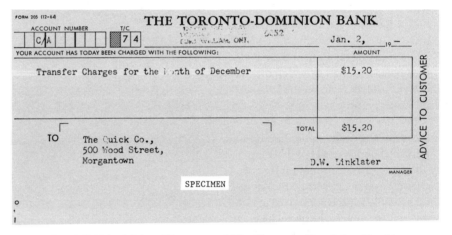

A Bank Debit Advice (Courtesy of The Toronto-Dominion Bank)

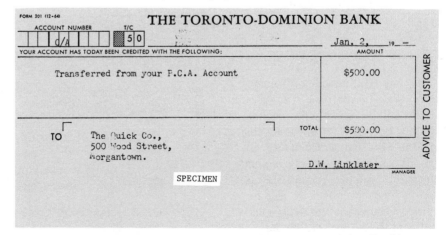

A Bank Credit Advice (Courtesy of The Toronto-Dominion Bank)

129

debit to Bank Charges and a credit to Bank.

The Bank Credit Advice shown on page 129 informs the depositor that a sum of money from his personal bank account has been transferred to the business bank account. The accounting entry that is appropriate for this transaction is a debit to Bank and a credit to the owner's Capital account.

Sales Tax

You are probably well acquainted with sales tax. It is a popular method by means of which governments raise tax revenues. It is a tax related to the sale of goods and is calculated as a certain per cent of the selling price of the goods. The seller of the goods is obliged to be the collector of the sales tax; he collects it from his customers and periodically makes a remittance to the government.

Both the rates of tax and the various types of goods on which the tax is levied will depend on the laws of the country, province, or state in which the goods are sold. In every business, someone should be well informed about sales tax. He may obtain detailed information free of charge from the government offices responsible for the administering of the tax. In Canada, businessmen must be concerned with both federal sales tax and provincial sales tax.

Accounting for Sales Tax

The simplest transaction involving sales tax is the cash sale. The seller of the goods calculates the amount of the tax or finds it from a tax table, adds the tax to the price of the goods, and collects the total amount from the customer. Because the tax portion must eventually be paid to the government, it represents a liability of the seller. Consider the following transaction.

$40 of taxable merchandise is sold to R. Brown for cash. The rate of sales tax is 5 per cent.

The accounting entry to record the transaction is:

```
Dr. Bank                    42.00
    Cr. Sales                       40.00
    Cr. Sales Tax Payable            2.00
```

'Sales Tax Payable' is a liability account set up specially to accumulate sales tax. In an accounting system using a columnar journal, there will probably be a special column for Sales Tax Payable because it is a frequently occurring item.

Goods sold on account also involve sales tax. Consider the following sales invoice on which a five per cent sales tax is charged.

SPORTS EQUIPMENT of Toronto Limited 490 Adelaide Street West / Toronto 2B, Ontario / Telephone 366-9666			SALES INVOICE NO. 9621	
Sold to: G. E. Syme, 617 Cherrydale Place, Fort William, Ontario.		Date: Nov. 16, 19-- P.O. No.: 4321 Terms: Net-30 Days		
Shipped by C.P. Express	Via Rail	F.O.B. Toronto		
Quantity	Description		Unit Price	Amount
1 pr	O. H. A. Nets- Special		18.00	18.00
1 only	P. B. M. Playball		2.75	2.75
6 only	Hockey Sticks		1.40	8.40
6 only	Bantam Hockey Sticks		.50	3.00
				32.15
ITEMS NOT EXTENDED OR SHIPPED WILL BE FORWARDED AS SOON AS POSSIBLE. NO GOODS RETURNABLE WITHOUT OUR WRITTEN PERMISSION. ALL CLAIMS FOR DAMAGES OR DEFICIENCY MUST BE MADE WITHIN FIVE DAYS FROM RECEIPT OF GOODS.		5% TAX		1.61
		SHIPPING CHARGES		
		TOTAL		33.76

(Courtesy of Sports Equipment of Toronto Limited)

The accounting entry to record this sales invoice is:

```
Dr. Accounts Receivable (G. E. Syme)   33.76
    Cr. Sales                                  32.15
    Cr. Sales Tax Payable                       1.61
```

Periodically, the seller must remit the accumulated sales tax to the government. This is usually done once a month. For example, the federal government of Canada requires that the sales tax collected during one month be sent to the government (to the Receiver General of Canada) by the fifteenth day of the following month. Taxes collected in January are due by the fifteenth of February, Taxes collected in February are due by the fifteenth of March, and so on. Government auditors make periodic visits to businesses to ensure correctness of collections and remittances.

The accounting entry to record the cheque of remittance of sales tax to the government is:

Dr. Sales Tax Payable   xx.xx
    Cr. Bank   xx.xx

The Five-Journal System

The Synoptic Journal described in the previous chapter is suitable for only a very small business or organization. The fact that only one person at a time can work on it is a big disadvantage. Most businesses soon require more than one person to be independently involved in the journalizing process. To make this possible, systems using more than one journal have been developed. One such system is the Five-Journal System.

A system such as the Five-Journal System has two main advantages. First, it provides the conditions whereby five journals may be prepared independently. Secondly, it strongly influences the accounting system towards greater specialization

of duties. The degree of specialization that develops will depend on the type of business, the volume of transactions, and other factors but, certainly, some specialization will take place.

The basic structure of the Five-Journal System is illustrated below. The illustration shows that the accounting entries are channeled from the various source documents into the five separate journals, each of which is restricted to a particular type of transaction. Each of the special journals is posted individually to the three ledgers.

It should be apparent from the illustration how a number of specialists (or department heads) may come into existence in an accounting

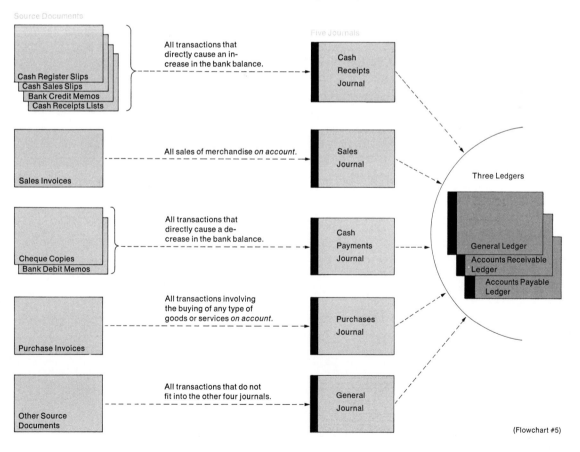

Basic Structure of the Five-journal System

Source Documents

Cash Register Slips
Cash Sales Slips
Bank Credit Memos
Cash Receipts Lists

All transactions that directly cause an increase in the bank balance.

Five Journals

Cash Receipts Journal

Sales Invoices

All sales of merchandise *on account*.

Sales Journal

Three Ledgers

General Ledger
Accounts Receivable Ledger
Accounts Payable Ledger

Cheque Copies
Bank Debit Memos

All transactions that directly cause a decrease in the bank balance.

Cash Payments Journal

Purchase Invoices

All transactions involving the buying of any type of goods or services *on account*.

Purchases Journal

Other Source Documents

All transactions that do not fit into the other four journals.

General Journal

(Flowchart #5)

system. Large offices may require a specialist for each journal. Smaller offices often find that one man can specialize in the operation of two journals. For instance, there is a natural relationship between 'Sales' and 'Cash Receipts', and another natural relationship between 'Purchases' and 'Cash Payments'. Each of these pairs offers the possibility of making very effective combinations within the accounting department.

Learning to operate the Five-Journal System is not going to be difficult for you. You will find that the General Journal, whether in the form of a book or journal vouchers, is used no differently than before.

And each of the new journals is a columnar journal that follows very closely the procedures for using the Synoptic Journal. The only significant difference is that all of the routine transactions do not go into one journal; they must be directed to one of four special journals according to their type.

Cash Receipts Journal

In the Cash Receipts Journal are recorded the accounting entries for all transactions that directly cause an increase in the bank balance. Every accounting entry in the Cash Receipts Journal involves a debit to 'Bank'. The two most common transactions affecting the Cash Receipts Journal are cash sales, and receipts on account from customers.

Illustrated below is a partially completed page from a typical Cash Receipts Journal. It was prepared from the source documents listed at right.

February
4 *Cash Sales Slip*
   —No. 64, to R. Smith, $47.50 plus sales tax of $2.38.
4 *Cash Sales Slip*
   —No. 65, to P. Wylie, $26.37 plus sales tax of $1.32.
4 *Cash Receipts*
   —D. Denison, $65.29, on account.
   —W. Scott, $146.25, on account.
5 *Cash Sales Slip*
   —No. 66, to O. Miles, $27.90 plus sales tax of $1.40.
5 *Cash Receipts*
   —J. Kelly, $52.10, on account.
   —S. Bruno, $19.02, on account.
5 *Bank Credit Advice*
   —From Centennial Bank, $34.20, for interest earned.

Date	Customer or explanation	Others Accounts Cr. Account	P.R.	Amount				Sales Tax Pay'l Cr.	Sales Cr.	Acc'ts Rec'l Cr.	√	Bank Dr.		Amount of Deposit
Feb 4	R. Smith #64							2 38	47 50			49 88		
4	P. Wylie #65							1 32	26 37			27 69		
4	D. Denison									65 29	✓	65 29		
4	W. Scott									146 25	✓	146 25		289 11
5	O. Miles #66							1 40	27 90			29 30		
5	J. Kelly									52 10	✓	52 10		
5	S. Bruno									19 02	✓	19 02		100 42
5	Centennial Bk. Cr. Memo	Interest Inc.		34 20								34 20		34 20

Cash Receipts Journal   Month of February, 19—

A Partially Completed Cash Receipts Journal

Notes:

1. Special columns are used for frequently occurring items; the 'Other Accounts Cr' section is used for infrequently occurring items.
2. There are extra columns provided for use as necessary.

3. The √ column is used to indicate that postings to the Accounts Receivable Ledger have been completed. All such postings from this journal will be credits to Accounts Receivable.
4. The little column to the right of the Bank Dr. column is not used in this journal.

5. Because it is a columnar journal, the rules for columnar journals apply to the Cash Receipts Journal. The column labeled 'Amount of Deposit' (explained below) does not form part of the balanced journal.
6. The 'Amount of Deposit' column is not a compulsory column. The

Cash Receipts Journal can be prepared without it. It is included only as a convenient way of tying in cash receipts with the record prepared by the bank. As you will see in a later chapter it is not always easy to agree the records of the business with those of the bank. For this reason only, the 'Amount of Deposit' column has been included. This column does not form a part of the balanced accounting entries and must not be included when balancing or when posting the journal. The total of the 'Amount of Deposit' column will equal the total of the 'Bank' column.

Sales Journal

In the Sales Journal are recorded the accounting entries for all sales of merchandise on account. Only one type of entry and one source document, the Sales Invoice, are involved with this journal.

Illustrated below is an example of a partially completed Sales Journal. The illustration shows how our one style of columnar paper may be used as a Sales Journal. In the example, it is assumed that the rate of sales tax is five per cent.

Date	Customer						Sales Cr.	Sales Tax Payable Cr.	Inv #	Acc'ts Rec'l Dr.	√	
19— Feb 3	G. Barber						141 —	7 05	161	148 05	√	
3	F. Lees						70 —	3 50	162	73 50	√	
4	H. Meek						37 50	1 88	163	39 38	√	
4	S. King						14 19	71	164	14 90	√	
4	W. Inglis						25 —	1 25	165	26 25	√	
5	P. Sommerville						59 —	2 95	166	61 95	√	
5	D. Ward						120 —	6 —	167	126 —	√	

Sales Journal — Month of February, 19—

A Partially Completed Sales Journal

Notes:
1. Only special columns are used in the Sales Journal. No provision is made for a general section.
2. There are extra columns provided for use as necessary in the future.
3. The √ column is used to indicate that postings to the Accounts Receivable Ledger have been completed. All such postings from this journal will be debits to Accounts Receivable.
4. Because it is a columnar journal, the rules for columnar journals apply to the Cash Receipts journal.
5. All of the money columns must be included when balancing the journal.

In the Cash Payments Journal are recorded the accounting entries for all transactions that directly cause a decrease in the bank balance. Every accounting entry in the Cash Payments Journal involves a credit to 'Bank'. The most common type of transaction affecting the Cash Payments Journal is the issuing of a cheque either as a payment on account or for a cash purchase of goods or services.

Shown below is an example of a partially completed Cash Payments Journal. The illustration shows how our one style of columnar paper may be used as a Cash Payments Journal. The journal was prepared from the source documents on the right.

February

3 *Cheque Copies*
   –No. 72, G. Collins Co., $56, on account.
   –No. 73, Taylor Bros., $75, on account.
4 *Bank Debit Advice*
   –$14.10, for bank service charges.
   Cheque Copies
   –No. 74, F. Downes, $150, for wages.
   –No. 75, K. Frost, $170, for wages.
5 *Cheque Copies*
   –No. 76, R. G. Hall, $120, for proprietor's personal use.
   –No. 77, Janson Trade Centre, $26.50, for cash purchase of merchandise.
   –No. 78, Lumley's Ltd., $50, for cash purchase of supplies.

Cash Payments Journal — Month of February, 19—

Date	Creditor or Supplier	Other Accounts Dr. Account	P.R.	Amount	Wages Dr.	Drawings Dr.	Supplies Dr.	Purchases Dr.	✓	Acc'ts Payable Dr.	Chq #	Bank Cr.
Feb 3	G. Collins Co.								✓	56 —	72	56 —
3	Taylor Bros.								✓	75 —	73	75 —
4	Centennial Bk. Dr. Memo	Bank Charges		14 10								14 10
4	F. Downes				150 —						74	150 —
4	K. Frost				170 —						75	170 —
5	R. G. Hall					120 —					76	120 —
5	Janson Trade Center							26 50			77	26 50
5	Lumley's Ltd.						50 —				78	50 —

A Partially Completed Cash Payments Journal

Notes:

1. The Cash Payments Journal is also commonly known as the Cash Disbursements Journal.
2. Special columns are used for frequently occurring items; the general section is used for infrequently occurring items.
3. The √ column is used to indicate that the postings to the Accounts Payable Ledger have been completed. All such postings from this journal will be debits to Accounts Payable.
4. Because it is a columnar journal, the rules for columnar journals apply to the Cash Payments Journal.
5. All of the money columns must be included when balancing the journal.

In the Purchases Journal are recorded the accounting entries for all transactions involving the buying of any type of goods or services on account. Every accounting entry in the Purchases Journal involves a credit to 'Accounts Payable'. The source documents for these entries are the matched sets of Purchase Invoices.

There is shown below an example of a partially completed Purchases Journal. The illustration shows how our one style of columnar paper may be used as a Purchases Journal. The journal was prepared from the source documents on the right.

February

3 *Purchase Invoices*
   –Ref. No. 602, Williams' Equipment, $156, for repairs to equipment.
   –Ref. No. 603, P. R. Trotter, $15.80, for supplies.

4 *Purchase Invoices*
   –Ref. No. 604, Pascoe's, $6.40, miscellaneous expense.
   –Ref. No. 605, Reliable Trading, $171, for merchandise.

5 *Purchase Invoices*
   –Ref. No. 606, Mason & Mason, $12.04, for supplies.
   –Ref. No. 607, A,B,C, Supply, $57, for merchandise.
   –Ref. No. 608, N.S.E.W. Railway, $74, for transportation charges on incoming goods.
   –Ref. No. 609, Hector Oil Co., $19.60; gas and oil for delivery truck.

Date	Creditor or explanation	Other Accounts Dr. Account	P.R.	Amount	Freight-In Dr.	Delivery Exp. Dr.	Misc. Exp. Dr.	Supplies Dr.	Ref. #	Purchases Dr.	√	Acc'ts Payable Cr.
Feb 3	Williams' Equip	Equip Repairs		156 —					602		√	156 —
3	P. R. Trotter							15 80	603		√	15 80
4	Pascoe's						6 40		604		√	6 40
4	Reliable Trading								605	171 —	√	171 —
5	Mason + Mason							12 04	606		√	12 04
5	A, B,C, Supply								607	57 —	√	57 —
5	N.S.E.W. Railway				74 —				608		√	74 —
5	Hector Oil Co.					19 60			609		√	19 60

Purchases Journal — Month of February, 19—

A Partially Completed Purchases Journal

Notes:

1. Special columns are used for frequently occurring items; the 'Other Accounts Dr' section is used for infrequently occurring items.
2. The √ column is used to indicate that the postings to the Accounts Payable Ledger have been completed. All such postings from this journal will be credits.
3. Because it is a columnar journal, the rules for columnar journals apply to the Purchases Journal.
4. All of the money columns must be included when balancing the Purchases Journal.
5. Purchase Invoice Reference numbers are not used in all accounting systems. An accountant setting up a purchasing system has a choice of filing the purchase documents in either numeric or alphabetic order. If he chooses alphabetic order, no reference numbers are necessary. If he chooses numeric order, a reference number must be placed on each of the purchase document sets. It is usually easier and faster to locate Purchase Invoices that are filed in numeric order.

Posting in the Five-Journal System

When the Five-Journal System is used, four of the journals are of the columnar type and must be 'balanced' before posting is started. The 'balancing' of these four journals is done in the same manner as that described on page 114 for the Synoptic Journal. Just remember to balance each of the journals separately.

You have known for some time how to post the General Journal and have recently learned (page 115) how to post a columnar journal. This is practically all that you need to know in order to post in the Five-Journal System. Each journal is posted individually but the order in which they are posted does not matter. Only after all five of the journals have been posted, should any attempt be made to balance the ledgers.

Long ago, on page 34, when discussing the topic of 'posting references in the accounts', you were told to record the journal page number from which the entry is taken and to prefix it with a code letter; for example, J14. It was stated at that time that the journal code is necessary because several journals may be used simultaneously and the code is a means of identifying the specific journal with which the page number is associated. Now, perhaps, you can appreciate more fully the advantages of coding the posting references in the accounts and the need for additional codes for the four new journals. The new codes are as follows:

Journal	Code
Cash Receipts Journal	CR
Cash Payments Journal	CP
Sales Journal	S
Purchases Journal	P

The two sample accounts shown top right illustrate the way in which the new coded posting references might appear.

Account *Accounts Payable*   No. *21*

Date		Particulars	P.R.	Debit	Credit	DR. CR.	Balance
19— June	24	Balance Forwarded	—			CR	24 375 63
	30		P106		12 970 49		
	30		CP57	15 906 26		CR	22 039 86

Account *Accounts Receivable*   No. *2*

Date		Particulars	P.R.	Debit	Credit	DR. CR.	Balance
19— Mar.	31	Balance Forwarded	—			DR	6 474 07
	31		S67	13 047 25			
	31		CR74		12 096 40		
	31		J19		42 42	DR	7 382 50

Mechanical Aids to Accounting

There are available a number of mechanical aids to accounting. Two mechanical aids that are widely used are: (1) the bookkeeping or accounting machine; and (2) the accounting peg-board or one-write system.

These two devices are illustrated below and on the facing page.

Bookkeeping or Accounting Machine
(Courtesy of Monroe International, Division of Litton Industries)

Business forms are held firmly in place by machine pressure. Information is printed by the machine onto the business form.

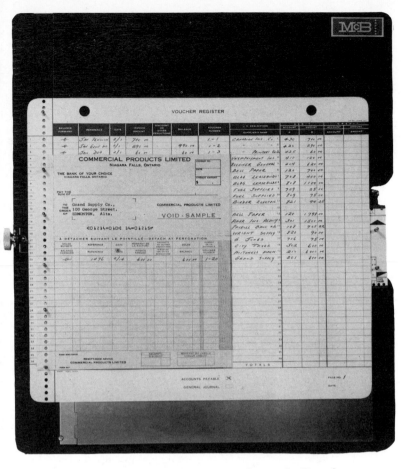

Accounting Peg-board or One-write Board.
(Courtesy of the McBee Company)

Business forms are held in place by inserting the holes in the forms over the pegs on the board. Information is handwritten onto the business form.

Both the accounting machine and the accounting peg-boards are designed to permit the simultaneous preparation by an operator of more than one business form, document, or record. This is achieved most commonly by the use of carbon paper and collated business forms. The concept of collated business forms is illustrated by means of the simple example shown below.

Purchases Journal

Account Number	Old Balance	Date	Invoice No.	Amount of Invoice	Payments and Deductions	Balance	Proof Pick-up	Distribution					.00* Proof
								1	2	3	4	5	

Accounts Payable Ledger

Date	Invoice No.	Amount of Invoice	Payments and Deductions	Balance

Collated Business Forms,
Purchase Routine

In this particular example, the two forms are made so that the five columns of the ledger card correspond exactly to five specific columns of the Purchases Journal. You can see that by placing the ledger card on top of the Purchases Journal with carbon paper interleaved and the forms properly aligned, anything that is written onto the ledger card will also come through onto the Purchases Journal page. This is the principle of 'one-write' systems.

Other common 'one-write' applications may be seen from the following illustrations:

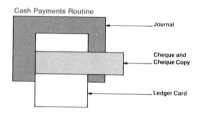

Cash Payments Routine

- Journal
- Cheque and Cheque Copy
- Ledger Card

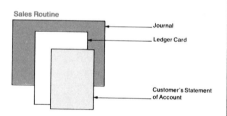

Sales Routine

- Journal
- Ledger Card
- Customer's Statement of Account

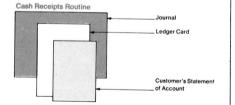

Cash Receipts Routine

- Journal
- Ledger Card
- Customer's Statement of Account

Except for retail stores and their dealings with the general public, most goods and services are bought on account and paid for later by cheque. As a result, the use of cheques in our business economy is extensive. A cheque, however, is not 'cash'. Ordinarily, the recipient of a cheque cannot be certain that it is valid. Usually, he must deposit it with his own bank and wait until it is cleared through to the bank of the issuer. The decision as to whether a cheque is good or not is made by the bank of the issuer. The decision hinges on whether or not there is a sufficient balance in the issuer's bank account to cover the cheque.

A cheque received into your business will probably progress through the following stages:

1. Because most cheques are good ones, your actions whenever you receive a cheque are based on the optimistic assumption that all cheques are good. Therefore, you will (a) record the receipt of the cheque in the Cash Receipts Journal as a debit to 'Bank' and credit to some other account, and (b) deposit the cheque in your bank account. If the cheque happens to be a good one, that is probably the last that you will hear of it.

2. Your bank, also acting on the assumption that all cheques are good, increases the balance of your account accordingly. The cheque is then sent on, through the clearing house, to the bank of the person who wrote (or issued) the cheque.

3. The issuer's bank attempts to deduct the amount of the cheque from the issuer's account. If the balance of the account is large enough to cover the cheque, the deduction will be made. However, if the balance of the account is not large enough to cover the cheque, no deduction will be made. Instead, the bank will mark on the cheque 'Not Sufficient Funds' and will send it back to your bank. It is at this point that the cheque becomes 'dishonoured' or 'N.S.F.' meaning 'not sufficient funds'. It is also referred to by many as having 'bounced'.

4. The dishonoured cheque is then received by your bank. Since your bank account was previously increased by the amount of what has turned out to be a worthless cheque, your bank exercises its right to even things out by making an offsetting deduction in the account. It does this promptly and then sends to you the dishonoured cheque together with an explanatory Debit Advice. You will be informed as quickly as possible.

5. After receiving the 'bad news' from the bank, it is necessary for you to do two things:

   (a) Immediately try to contact the person who wrote the bad cheque, in an attempt to obtain proper payment. This may not be an easy matter.

   (b) In the Cash Payments Journal, reverse the accounting entry that was previously made at the time of receiving the cheque. The required entry will be a credit to bank and a debit to some other account.

Bookkeeping and Accounting Terms

Bank Debit Advice:
Bank Credit Advice:
Bank Debit Memorandum:
Bank Credit Memorandum:
A notice sent by the bank to the depositor informing the depositor that the bank has initiated an entry to his bank account. The debit 'advice' is associated with a decrease to the account. The credit 'advice' is associated with an increase to the account.

Sales Tax: A tax related to the sale of goods and calculated as a per cent of the selling price of the goods.

Cash Receipts Journal: A special columnar journal in which are recorded the accounting entries for all transactions that directly cause an increase in the bank balance.

Cash Payments Journal:
Cash Disbursements Journal:
A special columnar journal in which are recorded the accounting entries for all transactions that directly cause a decrease in the bank balance.

Sales Journal: A special columnar journal in which are recorded the accounting entries for all sales of merchandise on account.

Purchases Journal: A special columnar journal in which are recorded the accounting entries for all transactions involving the buying of any type of goods or services on account.

One-Write System: An accounting technique that, by the use of collated business forms and carbon paper, permits the simultaneous preparation of more than one business paper.

N.S.F. Cheque:
Dishonoured Cheque:
A cheque which was not cashed when presented to the issuer's bank because there were not sufficient funds in the bank account to cover the amount of the cheque.

Review Questions

1. Explain the relationship between a bank and one of its depositors.
2. If both the bank and the depositor follow the same set of accounting rules, why does the bank's record of the depositor's money appear to be the opposite of the depositor's own record?
3. Why is it important that a business be able to calculate its bank balance at any time?
4. How is a depositor notified of changes in his bank balance that are initiated by the bank?
5. When a business receives a Bank Debit Advice or a Bank Credit Advice, what must be done in the books of account?
6. Briefly describe how sales tax works.
7. Where does one obtain information about sales tax?
8. Give three transactions that involve the account 'Sales Tax Payable'.
9. Why will there probably be a special column for Sales Tax Payable in a columnar journal?
10. When must sales tax be remitted to the government?
11. Name the five journals of the five-journal system.
12. What are the advantages of the five-journal system?

13. Name the two most common transactions recorded in a Cash Receipts Journal.
14. In the Cash Receipts Journal, what is the purpose of the column headed 'Amount of Deposit'?
15. What is the source document for entries recorded in the Sales Journal?
16. What type of entries are recorded in the Cash Payments Journal?
17. Are the postings from the Cash Payments Journal to the Accounts Payable Subsidiary Ledger debit postings or credit postings?
18. In what order are the five journals posted to the General Ledger?
19. Give the abbreviation codes for the four special journals.
20. Describe what is meant by 'collated' business forms.
21. How does a 'one-write' system work?
22. Explain what is meant by an N. S. F. cheque.
23. How does a business learn of an N. S. F. cheque?
24. What two things must be done by an accountant who learns of an N. S. F. cheque?

Exercises

1. For each of the transactions listed below, state in which of the five journals it would be recorded.

Transactions

1. A cheque is issued to a supplier on account.
2. A Purchase Invoice is received from a supplier of merchandise.
3. A cheque is received on account from a customer.
4. A cash sale is made to a customer.
5. A sale on account is made to a customer.
6. A cheque is issued to the owner for his personal use.
7. A cheque is issued to pay the wages for the period.
8. A Sales Invoice is issued.
9. A correcting entry is made to transfer a debit amount from the Supplies account to the Miscellaneous Expense account.
10. A cheque is issued to pay for a cash purchase of merchandise.
11. A bank debit advice for service charge is received.
12. A cheque is issued to a supplier on account.
13. A cheque is issued to pay for the monthly rent.
14. A bank debit advice is received with respect to an N. S. F. cheque.
15. A bank credit advice is received with respect to interest earned.
16. A new typewriter is purchased and a down-payment is required. A cheque is issued.
17. The owner collects a debt from a customer but keeps the money for his personal use.
18. The owner spends a sum of money out of his own pocket for business purposes and is reimbursed by means of a cheque.

2. INSTRUCTIONS

(a) For each of the selected transactions listed below write down the accounting entry that is necessary. Use General Journal form. Make your own choice of accounts.

(b) Beside each entry, to the right, indicate in which journal the entry would be recorded if a five-journal system is used.

Transactions

1. Issued cheque No. 65 to Morris and Hannah in payment of the rent for the month. $220.
2. Received a Purchase Invoice for $540 from Grinnelco Ltd. for merchandise.
3. Received a cheque from R. Jones, a customer, in part payment of his account. $60.
4. A cash sale of $70 was made to A. Green. Add sales tax of 5 per cent.
5. A withdrawal of $800, by means of cheque No. 76 made out to 'Cash', in order to pay the wages for the week.
6. The proprietor, C. Jones, withdrew $100 cash for his personal use. Cheque No. 91.
7. Issued Sales Invoice No. 867 for $34.78 to C. Perry. Add sales tax of 5 per cent.
8. The proprietor, C. Jones, took home merchandise valued at $48.39 for his personal use. Charge sales tax of 5 per cent.
9. An error was discovered in the General Ledger. An amount of $30 which had been debited to Miscellaneous Expense should have been debited to Supplies.
10. Sold merchandise on account to Mercer & Company. Invoice No. 911, $45. Add sales tax of 5 per cent.
11. Issued cheque No. 105 for $120 to General Supply Company on account.
12. Issued cheque No. 114 for $350.24 to the Receiver General in payment of the sales tax for the previous month.
13. Made a cash purchase of merchandise in the amount of $100 from Pressed Fittings. Cheque No. 121.
14. Received a Purchase Invoice from Office Suppliers for an office desk. $350.
15. Paid the telephone bill for the month. $10.75, cheque No. 139.
16. An error was detected in the Accounts Receivable Ledger. An amount of $12 which should have been credited to J. C. Walker's account was credited in error to P. M. Walker's account.
17. Received a Purchase Invoice from J. R. Paulson for merchandise. $200.
18. Purchased $35 of supplies from Baldwin's. Cheque No. 154.
19. Sold merchandise to P. Leonard for $150, Invoice No. 946. Add sales tax of 5 per cent. Mr. Leonard made a down-payment of $50.

Note:

An entry such as for this transaction is a combination of a sale for cash and a sale on account. As such, it theoretically fits two journals. However, it is customary to enter the whole entry in one journal, the Cash Journal.

20. S. T. Anthony, a customer, came personally to the office to pay his account of $25. While he was there he also made a cash purchase of $15. Add sales tax of 5 per cent.

3. INSTRUCTIONS

(a) For each of the selected transactions listed below write down the accounting entry that is necessary. Use General Journal form. Make your own choice of accounts. Add 5 per cent sales tax on all sales.

(b) Beside each entry, to the right, indicate in which journal the entry would be recorded if a Five-Journal System is used.

Transactions

1. Received an invoice from Continental Railway for transportation on purchases of merchandise. $96.40.
2. Received a bank Debit Advice from Royalty Bank in the amount of $19 for bank service charges.
3. The proprietor, A. Harvey, withdrew $250 for his personal use. Cheque No. 204.
4. Cheque No. 215 was issued to C. Pearce on account. $84.
5. Invoice No. 86A was issued to Jenkins & Williams. $65.75.
6. Issued cheque No. 224 for $22.50 to the local telephone company in payment of the bill for the month.
7. Received a bank Debit Advice from Royalty Bank. The amount of the charge was $52 and was with respect to a cheque from W. Patterson which had been dishonoured. The cheque had been given as payment for a cash sale.
8. The wages for the week amounted to $750. Cheque No. 231 for this amount was issued to C. Worth, the company paymaster, who took it to the bank and cashed it. He brought the money back to the office and gave it in turn to the proper employees.
9. Issued cheque No. 240 to Parker Investments in payment of the rent for the month. Amount, $300.
10. A cash sale of $42 was made to C. Donovan. Cash Sales Slip No. 92.
11. Received a cheque for $75 from R. Grant, on account.
12. Received a Purchase Invoice from Jimpson's Garage for $157. Of the $157 charge, $124.70 was for gas, oil, and repairs for the delivery truck, and $32.30 was for gas and oil delivered to A. Harvey's (the proprietor's) summer cottage for use in a motor boat.
13. A. Harvey, the proprietor, collected a debt from a customer, E. Spence, in the amount of $40. He kept the money and used it for his own purposes. He requested the accountant to record the collection.
14. Received a Purchase Invoice for $25 for office supplies from Lailey & Co. Lailey & Co. is a customer of ours and has an account balance of $271.56, debit. The $25 is to be deducted from the amount owed to us by Lailey & Co.
15. Purchased a new typewriter from Embassy Typewriter Company at a cost of $325. A down-payment of $150 was made. Cheque No. 257.
16. Received a Purchase Invoice from O.K. Fabricators in the amount of $176. The invoice was with respect to the repair of the company building.
17. Issued cheque No. 260 to P. Lundy on account. $65.
18. Issued cheque No. 265 to Paramount Loan Company in payment of the monthly instalment on the automotive equipment. $310.
19. Sales Invoice No. 114A was issued to Provincial Processors. $23.45.
20. Issued cheque No. 271 to Imperial Office Supplies for the cash purchase of office supplies. $43.23.

---

4. INSTRUCTION 1.

Set up the General Ledger of Bristol Appliances Company as of December 31, 19—.

On December 31, 19—, the combined Chart of Accounts and General Ledger trial balance of Bristol Appliances Company was as follows:

1	Bank Cash	$ 813.12	
2	Accounts Receivable	2,471.49	
3	Supplies	312.50	
4	Merchandise Inventory	7,416.40	
5	Store Equipment	800.00	
6	Delivery Truck	2,200.00	
21	Accounts Payable		$1,941.60
22	Bank Loan		8,000.00
23	Sales Tax Payable		60.00
31	S. C. Scales, Capital		4,011.91
32	S. C. Scales, Drawings		*300*
41	Sales		
51	Purchases		*9370 219*
52	Rent		
53	Salaries		
54	Delivery Expense		
55	Miscellaneous Expense		

INSTRUCTION 2.

Set up the Subsidiary Ledgers of Bristol Appliances
Company as of December 31, 19—.
On December 31, 19—, the Subsidiary Ledger
trial balances appeared as follows:

Accounts Receivable Trial Balance
December 31, 19—

C. Booth, 129 James Street	Inv. No. 325	$ 316.10
M. Howard, 881 Wilson Avenue	296	95.00
J. Hudson, 14 Brook Drive	306	912.75
O. Langley, 65 Finch Avenue	315	163.87
T. Miles, 110 Church Street	326	50.00
S. Thorpe, 375 Beckett Drive	217	135.00
D. Wilkins, 70 Dixon Avenue	331	500.00
	346	298.77
		$2,471.49

Accounts Payable Trial Balance
December 31, 19—

Stirling Company, 20 River Street	Inv. No. B245	$ 560.20
Triangle Electric, Roxborough	4701	316.47
Universal Vacuums, 20 Dexter Street	6508	1,000.00
Western Electric, 1,000 Fleet Street	246R	64.93
		$1,941.60

INSTRUCTION 3.

In the journal of Bristol Appliances Company, record the
transactions shown below.
Bristol Appliances uses a Five-
Journal System. The journals
and the page numbers to be
used are:

The Subsidiary Ledgers of Bristol Appliances are posted daily, directly from the source documents.

A 5 per cent sales tax is to be applied on all sales of merchandise.

Transactions

January

2 *Cash Sales Slip*
—No. 401, to T. Arthur, $125 plus sales tax.
Cash Receipt
—From C. Booth, $116.10, on account.
Cheque Copy
—No. 376, to J. C. Brown, $37.42, for the cash purchase of supplies.

3 *Purchase Invoice*
—No. 1212, from Smith's Service Station, 3 Cary Street, $63.50, for gasoline and oil used in the delivery truck.
Cash Sales Slip
—No. 402, to R. Malone, $475 plus sales tax.

4 *Sales Invoice*
—No. 347, to M. Howard, $310 plus sales tax.

5 *Cheque Copies*
—No. 377, to Universal Vacuums, $500, on account.
—No. 378, to 'Cash', $285, for the salaries for the week.

8 *Cash Receipt*
—From T. Miles, $50, in full payment of account.
Correcting Entry
—An error was discovered in an entry made in December. An amount of $16.10 was debited incorrectly to Delivery Expense; it should have been debited to Miscellaneous Expense.

9 *Cash Sales Slip*
—No. 403, to H. McPhee, $800 plus sales tax.

10 *Purchase Invoice*
—No. 306R, from Western Electric, $630, for the purchase of merchandise.

10 *Cheque Copy*
—No. 379, to Stirling Company, $712, for the cash purchase of merchandise.

11 *Sales Invoices*
—No. 348, to O. Langley, $137.50 plus sales tax.
—No. 349, to T. Miles, $200 plus sales tax.
—No. 350, to S. Thorpe, $475.12 plus sales tax.

12 *Cash Receipt*
—From Clover Stores, $105; because of a recent change in the system, certain supplies on hand were not usable and were sold for cash at a price of $105.
Cheque Copy
—No. 380, to 'Cash', $310, for the salaries for the week.

15 *Cheque Copies*
—No. 381, to S. C. Scales, $300, for his personal use.
—No. 382, to the Provincial Government, $60, for sales tax for the previous month.
Cash Receipts
—From C. Booth, $100; on account.
—From J. Hudson, $512.75, on account.
—From S. Thorpe, $135, invoice No. 217.
—From D. Wilkins, $798.77, invoices No. 331 and No. 346.
Cash Sales Slips
—No. 404, to F. Lang, $480 plus sales tax.
—No. 405, to K. Klein, $750 plus sales tax.

16 *Purchase Invoice*
—No. 406, from Ritz Furniture, Melody Road, $150, for the purchase of merchandise.

17 *Purchase Invoice*
—No. 708, from Super Stationers, $76.40, for supplies.

17 *Non-routine Transaction*
-The proprietor took an office typewriter home for his permanent personal use. The typewriter was included in the accounts at a value of $150. The transaction is subject to a 5 per cent sales tax.

18 *Cheque Copies*
-No. 383, to Triangle Electric, $316.47, paying invoice No. 4701.
-No. 384, to Stirling Company, $560.20, paying invoice No. B245.
-No. 385, to Western Electric, $64.93, paying invoice No. 246R.
-No. 386, to Smith's Service Station, $63.50; paying invoice No. 1212.

19 *Cheque Copy*
-No. 387, to 'Cash' $290, in payment of the weekly salaries.

22 *Sales Invoices*
-No. 351, to D. Wilkins, $300 plus sales tax.
-No. 352, to C. Booth, $281.63 plus sales tax.
-No. 353, to S. Thorpe, $31.12 plus sales tax.

23 *Purchase Invoice*
-No. 4912, from Triangle Electric, $65, for purchase of merchandise.

24 *Purchase Invoice*
-No. 842, from Super Stationers, $30, for supplies.

25 *Cheque Copy*
-No. 388, to local telephone company, $16.50, for monthly telephone bill.

26 *Cheque Copies*
-No. 389, to Boston Television Co., $112.60, for the cash purchase of merchandise.
-No. 390, to Admirable Company, $83, for the cash purchase of merchandise.
-No. 391, to 'Cash', $275, for the weekly salaries.
-No. 392, to Grayson Brothers, $250, for the rent for the month.

30 *Purchase Invoice*
-No. 864, from Super Stationers, $100, for supplies.

31 *Purchase Invoices*
-No. B319, from Stirling Company, $300, for merchandise.
-No. 6722, from Universal Vacuums, $261.81, for merchandise.
-No. 512, from Ritz Furniture, $86.40, for merchandise.

Cash Sales Slip
-No. 406, to M. Morse, $906.50 plus sales tax.

Sales Invoices
-No. 354, to J. Hudson, $1,200 plus sales tax.
-No. 355, to M. Howard, $12.08 plus sales tax.
-No. 356, to S. Thorpe, $19.65 plus sales tax.

Cheque Copy
-No. 393, to local hydro, $16.40, for hydro for the month.

INSTRUCTION 4.

(a) Balance the special journals and post the five journals to the General Ledger.
(b) Balance the General Ledger as of January 31.
(c) Balance the Subsidiary Ledgers as of January 31.

5. C. D. Mould is the proprietor of Husky Hardware. He uses five journals and three ledgers in his accounting system. He posts the Subsidiary Ledgers daily, directly from the source documents. In his locality there is a 3 per cent sales tax on all sales.

The Chart of Accounts for Husky Hardware is shown below:

Husky Hardware
Chart of Accounts

1. Bank
2. Accounts Receivable
3. Merchandise Inventory
4. Supplies
5. Store Equipment
6. Delivery Equipment
21. Accounts Payable
22. Sales Tax Payable
31. C. D. Mould, Capital
32. C. D. Mould, Drawings
41. Sales
51. Purchases
52. Rent
53. Miscellaneous Expense
54. Wages

The General Ledger trial balance of Husky Hardware as of June 30, 19— is as follows:

Husky Hardware
General Ledger Trial Balance
June 30, 19—

Bank	$ 1,614.20	
Accounts Receivable	412.50	
Merchandise Inventory	4,095.12	
Supplies	300.00	
Store Equipment	2,675.00	
Delivery Equipment	3,500.00	
Accounts Payable		$ 5,063.94
Sales Tax Payable		108.52
C. D. Mould, Capital		6,864.36
C. D. Mould, Drawings	5,876.34	
Sales		19,800.00
Purchases	9,500.00	
Rent	1,800.00	
Miscellaneous Expense	216.41	
Wages	1,847.25	
	$31,836.82	$31,836.82

The Subsidiary Ledger trial balances are as follows:

Husky Hardware
Accounts Receivable Trial Balance
June 30, 19—

J. Barkley, 260 Western Avenue	No. 490	$92.46	
	496	15.02	
	503	60.10	$167.58
T. Fairley, 300 Center Road	501		56.42
S. Harvey, 466 Keeley Street	502		76.50
R. Taylor, 588 Truway Drive	498		112.00
			$412.50

Husky Hardware
Accounts Payable Trial Balance
June 30, 19—

Household Utensils Company 487 Faith Avenue	Inv. No. 52	$1,067.50
J. & A. Hardware Supply 600 Young Street	596	505.25
Learner Bros. 5012 Direct Avenue	141	3,067.20
Specialty Manufacturing Co. Barbary	163	423.99
		$5,063.94

INSTRUCTION 1.

Set up the three ledgers of Husky Hardware as of June 30, 19—.

INSTRUCTION 2.

Journalize the transactions listed below in the five journals of Husky Hardware. Use the following page numbers:

Cash Receipts Journal	Page 42
Cash Payments Journal	Page 93
Sales Journal	Page 56
Purchases Journal	Page 85
General Journal	Page 16

July

2 *Cheque Copy*

–No. 187, to D. C. Harper, $300, for the rent for July.

Purchase Invoice

–From Household Utensils Company, No. 87, $184.50, for the purchase of merchandise.

3 *Sales Invoices*

–No. 504, to S. Harvey, $50 plus sales tax.

–No. 505, to R. Taylor, $26.85 plus sales tax.

–No. 506, to T. Fairley, $12.85 plus sales tax.

–No. 507, to J. Barkley, $64 plus sales tax.

4 *Cash Receipt*

–From the owner C. D. Mould, $1,000, for the purpose of increasing his investment in the business.

5 *Purchase Invoice*

–From Learner Brothers, No. 206, $35.60, for supplies.

Cheque Copy

–No. 188, to Federal A–1 Supply House, $146, for the cash purchase of merchandise.

Cash Register Slips

–$846.81. The cash sales for the week amounted to $822.15 plus sales tax of $24.66.

8 *Cash Receipt*

–From T. Fairley, $56.42, paying invoice No. 501.

9 *Sales Invoices*

–No. 508, to L. Peck, $41 plus sales tax.

–No. 509, to S. Harvey, $18 plus sales tax.

–No. 510, to T. Fairley, $25.50 plus sales tax.

10 *Purchase Invoice*

–From J. & A. Hardware Supply, $312, for a shipment of hammers saws and other tools.

12 *Cash Register Slips*

–$964.08. The cash sales for the week amounted to $936 plus sales tax of $28.08.

Bank Debit Memo

–From Sovereign Bank, $10.20, bank account decreased because of bank service charge.

12 *Cheque Copy*

–No. 189, to Modern Manufacturing Company, $265, for the cash purchase of merchandise.

13 *Cash Receipts*

–From S. Harvey, $128, paying invoices No. 502 and No. 504.

–From J. Barkley, $107.48, paying invoices No. 490 and No. 496.

15 *Cheque Copies*

–No. 190, to Learner Brothers, $1,500, on account.

–No. 191, to Household Utensils Company, $500, on account.

–No. 192, to B. Wiley, $150, wages for the first half of the month.

–No. 193, to W. Brown, $170, wages for the first half of the month.

–No. 194, to C. D. Mould, $300, personal withdrawal by proprietor.

–No. 195, to the Provincial Government, $108.52, sales tax for the previous month.

17 *Sales Invoices*

–No. 511, to V. Parker, 466 Janes Road, $75 plus sales tax.

–No. 512, to L. Peck, $45 plus sales tax.

–No. 513, to S. Harvey, $19.50 plus sales tax.

Cash Receipt

–From R. Taylor, $112, paying invoice No. 498.

18 *Non-routine Transaction*

–The proprietor submits bills amounting to $24.08 for miscellaneous expenses which he has paid out of his own pocket. He asks that his Drawings accounts be credited.

19 *Cash Register Slips*

–$881.68. The cash sales for the week amounted to $856 plus $25.68 sales tax.

Cash Receipts

–From S. Harvey, $38.63, paying his acount in full.

–From T. Fairley, $13.24; paying invoice No. 506.

–From L. Peck, $42.23, paying invoice No. 508.

22 *Purchase Invoice*

–From Maple Feed Company, Maple, No. 996, $600, for the purchase of merchandise.

23 *Purchase Invoice*
   –From Household Utensils Company, No. 156, $412.65, for the purchase of merchandise.

26 *Cash Register Slips*
   –$1,096.95. The cash sales for the week amounted to $1,065 plus sales tax of $31.95.

   Cheque Copy
   –No. 196, to Learner Brothers, $263, for the cash purchase of merchandise.

29 *Cheque Copies*
   –No. 197, to Household Utensils Company, $567.50, paying the balance of invoice No. 52.
   –No. 198, to J. & A. Hardware Supply, $505.25, paying invoice No. 596.
   –No. 199, to Specialty Manufacturing Company, $423.99, paying invoice No. 163.

31 *Cheque Copies*
   –No. 200, to B. Wiley, $150, wages for the last half of the month.
   –No. 201, to W. Brown, $170, wages for the last half of the month.
   –No. 202, to C.D. Mould, $300, for his personal use.

INSTRUCTION 3.

(a) Balance and post the journals to the General Ledger.
(b) Balance the General Ledger.
(c) Balance the Subsidiary Ledgers.

---

6.   Travel Trailers is a business owned and operated by Charles Fowler. The business earns its income from the selling and servicing of mobile homes and trailers. All sales and service transactions are subject to a five per cent sales tax.

Because of a special arrangement with an independent finance company, Travel Trailers is able to treat every trailer sale as a cash transaction. This is possible because the finance company pays Travel Trailers in full for any trailer sold and then collects from the customer on an instalment basis including interest charges.

INSTRUCTION 1.

From the following combined Chart of Accounts and General Ledger Trial Balance, set up the General Ledger of Travel Trailers as of May 31, 19—.

Travel Trailers
General Ledger Trial Balance
May 31, 19—

1	Bank	$ 751.75	
2	Accounts Receivable	1,166.97	
3	Supplies	151.00	
4	Inventory-Trailers	19,476.42	
5	Inventory-Parts	5,946.90	
6	Equipment	8,472.94	
7	Delivery Truck	3,000.00	
21	Accounts Payable		$ 4,987.50
22	Bank Loan		20,000.00
23	Sales Tax Payable		517.40
31	C. Fowler, Capital		8,253.37
32	C. Fowler, Drawings	4,074.00	
41	Sales		49,373.51
51	Purchases-Trailers	29,940.70	
52	Purchases-Parts	2,641.05	
53	Bank Interest Expense	516.50	
54	Delivery Expense	174.72	
55	Miscellaneous Expense	94.72	
56	Rent Expense	1,000.00	
57	Wages Expense	5,724.11	
		$83,131.78	$83,131.78

INSTRUCTION 2.

From the information shown below set up the Accounts Receivable Ledger of Travel Trailers as of May 31, 19—.

Customer	Address	Invoice	Amount
B. Fraser	15 Gay Street	Re. Invoice No. 634	$ 330.75
W. Hoyle	49 First Street	635	77.70
A. Newman	250 Fort Road	629	225.75
Schell Brothers	96 Garrison Avenue	633	204.75
N. Thompson	20 Wilson Avenue	630	315.00
L. Walker	4 Dennis Avenue	631	13.02
		Total	$1,166.97

INSTRUCTION 3.

From the following information set up the Accounts Payable Ledger of Travel Trailers as of May 31, 19—.

Supplier	Address	Invoice	Amount
Double-G Industries	Manortown	Inv. No. 420	$1,575.00
Modern Mobile Homes	West City	2213	2,100.00
National Hardware	64 Venture St.	2309	787.50
Windsor Manufacturing Co.	Windsor	404	525.00
		Total	$4,987.50

INSTRUCTION 4.

Travel Trailers uses five journals in its accounting system. Set up the five journals for the month of June as shown on facing page.

Date	Name					INV. No.	Accounts Rec'l DR.	✓	Sales Tax Pay'l CR	Sales CR

Sales Journal — Page 19

Date	Name	Other Accounts DR				Delivery Expense DR	Supplies DR	Purch's Parts DR	Purch's Trailers DR	✓	Acc'ts Pay'l CR
		Account	PR	Amount							

Purchases Journal — Page 74

Date	Name	Other Accounts CR				Sales Tax Payable CR	Sales CR	Acc'ts Rec'l CR	Bank DR		
		Account	PR	Amount							

Cash Receipts Journal — Page 37

Date	Name	Other Accounts DR			Wages DR	Drawings DR	Supplies DR	Purch's Parts DR	Purch's Trailers DR	Acc't's Pay'l DR	CH #	Bank CR
		Account	PR	Amount								

Cash Payments Journal — Page 84

Date	Particulars	PR.	Debit	Credit

General Journal — Page 5

INSTRUCTION 5.

Journalize the following transactions for the month of June. Post to the Subsidiary Ledgers daily.

Transactions

June

1 *Sales Invoice*

–No. 636, to A. Newman, $190 plus 5 per cent sales tax, for repairs to trailer.

Cheque Copy

–No. 755, issued to General Real Estate, $200, for the monthly rent.

2 *Sales Invoice*

–No. 637, to L. Walker, $300 plus 5 per cent sales tax, for sale of trailer parts.

Cheque Copy

–No. 756, issued to Double-G Industries, $300, on account.

3 *Purchase Invoices*

–From Parker Manufacturing, 10 Bergen Street, No. 40, $35, for Supplies.

–From Double-G Industries, No. 472, $351.20, for trailer parts.

4 *Cash Receipts*

–Received from W. Hoyle, $77.70, in payment of account.

–Received from Federated Finance Company, $2,835 cash, for sale of trailer, selling price $2,700, sales tax $135.

Bank Debit Advice

–From Central Bank, $120, for interest charged on bank loan.

5 *Cheque Copies*

–No. 757, issued to C. Fowler, $200, owner's personal use.

–No. 758, made out to Cash, $275 for the wages for the week.

Sales Invoice

–No. 638, to N. Thompson, $370 plus sales tax, for trailer repairs and parts.

8 *Cheque Copy*

–No. 759, to J. C. Pat Supply, $16.62, for cash purchase of supplies, $13.50, and miscellaneous expense, $3.12.

8 *Non-Routine Item*
   –Correction required. $12.50 item was charged incorrectly to Delivery Expense; it should be charged to Miscellaneous Expense.

9 *Cash Receipt*
   –From A. Newman, $225.75, on account.
   Purchase Invoices
   –From Windsor Manufacturing, No. 452, $420, for trailer parts.
   –Maynard's Garage, 49 Larry's Lane, No. 64; $37.50, for gasoline and oil used in delivery truck.

10 *Bank Debit Advice*
   –From Central Bank, $1,000, to reduce the bank loan.
   Sales Invoice
   –No. 639, to B. Fraser, $150 plus 5 per cent sales tax, for trailer parts.
   Cheque Copies
   –No. 760, to Modern Mobile Homes, $1,000, on account.
   –No. 761, to Double-G Industries, $500, on account.
   Purchase Invoice
   –From Windsor Manufacturing Co., No. 481, $1,575, for one new trailer.

11 *Sales Invoice*
   –No. 640, to Schell Brothers, $575 plus 5 per cent sales tax, for trailer parts and service.
   Cheque Copy
   –No. 762, to C. Fowler, $200, owner's personal use.

12 *Cash Receipts*
   –From Schell Brothers, $204.75, on account.
   –From B. Fraser, $330.75; on account.
   –From N. Thompson, $315; on account.
   Cheque Copy
   –No. 763, made out to Cash, $301, weekly wages.

15 *Cash Receipt*
   –From Federated Finance Company, $3,255, cash for sale of trailer, selling price, $3,100, sales tax $155.
   Cheque Copies
   –No. 764, to Provincial Government, $517.40, paying sales tax collected in month of May.
   –No. 765, to Double-G Industries, $775, paying the balance of invoice No. 420.

15 *Purchase Invoice*
   –From Maynard's Garage, No. 82, $42, for repairs to delivery truck.

16 *Purchase Invoices*
   –From National Hardware, No. 2412, $12.50, for supplies.
   –From Double-G Industries, No. 515, $1,680, for one new trailer.
   –From Windsor Manufacturing Co., No. 499, $170, for trailer parts.

17 *Sales Invoice*
   –No. 641, to W. Hoyle, $110 plus sales tax, for trailer service.
   Cheque Copy
   –No. 766, to Emerald Store, $10.50, for the cash purchase of miscellaneous items.

18 *Cheque Copies*
   –No. 767, to C. Fowler, $200, owner's drawings.
   –No. 768, to National Hardware, $787.50 on account.
   –No. 769, to Modern Mobile Homes, $1,000, on account.

19 *Purchase Invoice*
   –From National Hardware, No. 2480, $409.50, for trailer parts.
   Cheque Copy
   –No. 770, made out to Cash, $260, for the wages for the week.

22 *Sales Invoice*
   –No. 642, to L. Walker, $290 plus sales tax of 5 per cent, for trailer parts and service.
   Purchase Invoice
   –From Parker Manufacturing, No. 90, $56, for supplies.
   Non-routine Transaction
   –The owner collected $13.02 from L. Walker (for invoice No. 631) but he kept the money for his own use. (Debit his Drawings account.)

24 *Cash Receipt*
   –Received from Federal Finance Company, $2,047.50 cash, for sale of trailer, selling price $1,950, sales tax $97.50.

25 *Cheque Copy*
   –No. 771, to C. Fowler, $200, personal drawings.

26 *Sales Invoice*
   –No. 643, to A. Newman, $236 plus sales tax, for trailer repairs.

26 *Cheque Copies*
   –No. 772, to Windsor Manufacturing,
   $945.00, on account.
   –No. 773, made out to Cash, $298, for the
   wages for the week.

29 *Cash Receipts*
   –From B. Fraser, $157.50, on account.
   –From Schell Brothers, $603.75; on ac-
   count.

29 *Purchase Invoices*
   –From Modern Mobile Homes, No. 2409,
   $1,050, for new trailer unit.
   –From National Hardware, No. 2561,
   $53, for supplies.

30 *Sales Invoice*
   –No. 644, to W. Hoyle, $230 plus sales
   tax, for trailer servicing.

INSTRUCTION 6.

(a) Balance the special journals.
(b) Post the five journals to the
     General Ledger.
(c) Balance the General Ledger
     as of June 30.
(d) Balance the Subsidiary
     Ledgers as of June 30.

Chapter 10

SPECIAL TRANSACTIONS

Certain transactions, although not as simple as those that you have already studied, are still classed as being 'routine'. Because they occur with considerable frequency, they are considered to be 'everyday' transactions and as such require your close attention.

Cash Discounts

Perhaps you are already acquainted with 'cash discounts'. They are usually offered on all water, hydro, and similar bills that come into the home from the offices of municipalities.

A cash discount is a reduction that may be taken in the amount of a bill, provided that it is paid before a certain date stipulated on the bill. The purpose of a cash discount is to encourage the customer to pay promptly. Many businesses, as well as municipalities, offer cash discounts to their customers.

Terms of Sale

Every seller of goods or services makes certain arrangements with his customers as to when the goods or services are to be paid for and whether a cash discount is to be offered. These arrangements are commonly known as the 'terms of sale'.

The terms of sale can be anything that the seller and buyer agree to but most often the terms are standard ones such as those listed above right.

The terms of sale to a customer will depend on his reputation for reliability in paying, particularly as evidenced by past experience with him. A reliable customer of long standing will probably be granted very favourable terms, whereas a new customer about whom there is little information available will probably be required to pay cash on delivery, at least for a short time.

The terms of every sale are recorded on the Sales Invoice (see Illustration page 156). Each time the customer makes a purchase he is, therefore, reminded of the arrangements for making payment.

Once the terms of sale for a particular customer have been decided on, they will likely remain unchanged for some time. It is, therefore, a simple matter to record the customer's usual terms on his account card as illustrated below. This provides very helpful information to the credit manager, the man who is responsible for collecting the debts.

	STANDARD TERMS OF SALE	
Terms	*Explanation*	
1. C.O.D.	The goods must be paid for at the time they are delivered.	
2. On Account or Charge	The full amount of the invoice is due at the time the invoice is received but usually a brief time, 10 to 15 days, is given to make payment.	
3. 30 Days or Net 30	The full amount of the invoice is due 30 days after the date of the invoice.	
60 Days or Net 60 Days	The full amount of the invoice is due 60 days after the date of the invoice.	
4. 2/10,n/30	This is read as '2 per cent, 10; net, 30'. If the bill is paid within 10 days from the invoice date, a cash discount of 2 per cent may be taken. Otherwise, the full amount of the invoice is due 30 days after the invoice date.	
1/15,n/60	If the bill is paid within 15 days from the invoice date, a cash discount of 1 per cent may be taken. Otherwise, the full amount of the invoice is due 60 days after the invoice date.	

Account Card, Showing 'Terms of Sale'

ACCOUNT					
Customer's Name *Baxter + Son*			Account No. —		
Customers Address *15 Deacon Street*			Terms of Sale 2/10, *n*/30		
Mayville			Credit Limit *$600.*		
Date	Reference	Debit	Credit	Balance	
June 10 '68	429	50.00		DR. 50.00	

Accounting For Cash Discount

Accounting for cash discount begins at the time a credit sale is made to a customer and an invoice offering a cash discount is issued. Examine the invoice at right.

STAR SUPPLY

419 Mill's Gate, Oak City

SOLD TO W. Hay,
16 Mark's Road,
Oak City.

INVOICE NUMBER 971

DATE March 15, 19--

TERMS 3/10,N/30

Quantity	Description	Unit Price	Amount
6 Pkg.	Typewriting paper 8 1/2 X 11	$7.50	$45.00
	5% Federal Sales Tax		2.25
			$47.25

IN THE BOOKS OF STAR SUPPLY (THE SELLER)

From a copy of the Sales Invoice the seller makes the following accounting entry in the Sales Journal:

SALES JOURNAL

DATE	CUSTOMER	SALES CR	SALES TAX PAY'L CR	ACC'S REC'L DR
Mar 15	W. Hay	45.00	2.25	47.25

One or more copies of the Sales Invoice will be sent by mail to the buyer, W. Hay.

The theoretical effect of the transaction is shown below:

Acc's Rec'l (W. Hay)		Sales		Sales Tax Payable	
47.25			45.00		2.25

IN THE BOOKS OF W. HAY (THE BUYER)

The accounting entries in the books of the buyer will depend on his accounting system. Assuming that he records the Purchase Invoice (Star Supply's Sales Invoice) in his Purchases Journal as soon as it arrives in the mail (say March 17), the accounting entry will appear as follows:

PURCHASES JOURNAL

DATE	CREDITOR	SUPPLIES DR	PURCHASES DR	ACC'S PAY'L CR
Mar 17	Star Supply	47.25		47.25

Observe that it is not necessary for a buyer of goods to do any accounting for sales tax on the goods purchased. The theoretical effect of the transaction is shown below:

Supplies		Acc's Pay'l (Star Supply)	
47.25			47.25

In the accounting department of the buyer, someone will have the responsibility of checking each Purchase Invoice to see if a discount is offered. Where discounts are offered special treatment is necessary to ensure that payment is made within the allotted time. This special treatment may take several forms. Assume in this case that a cheque to pay the invoice is prepared immediately, but is dated March 25 (10 days after the invoice date), and is held in the office for release one day before the date on the cheque. The cheque will be made out for $45.83. This amount is arrived at by deducting the 3 per cent discount ($1.42) from the amount of the invoice ($47.25). The cheque will carry an explanation that it is in payment of Invoice No. 971.

On March 25 an accounting entry will be recorded in the Cash Payments Journal from the details shown on the copy of the cheque now released. The effect of the entry is to–

1. Decrease Bank by $45.83, the amount of the cheque.
2. Eliminate the debt of $47.25 to Star Supply. (It was agreed between the two parties that a cheque of $45.83 within 10 days would be sufficient to pay off the full debt of $47.25.)
3. Record the discount of $1.42 that was earned on the transaction.

The accounting entry as it appears in the Cash Payments Journal is shown below:

CASH PAYMENTS JOURNAL

DATE	CREDITOR	ACC'S PAY'L DR	DISCOUNTS EARNED CR	BANK CR
Mar 25	Star Supply	47.25	1.42	45.83

The theoretical effect of the two transactions is shown below:

Supplies	Acc's Pay'l (Star Supply)	Discounts Earned	Bank
47.25	47.25		
	47.25	1.42	45.83

Take note that the Discounts Earned account is an Income account.

IN THE BOOKS OF STAR SUPPLY (THE SELLER)

When Mr. Hay's cheque is received by Star Supply, it will be absorbed into the system. Of special interest to us now is the fact that the details of the cheque will be included on the daily Cash Receipts Listing which is forwarded to the Accounts Receivable clerk for posting to the Subsidiary Ledger. As part of her regular duties, this clerk will be required to verify any cash discounts that have been taken and to write on the listing the amount of any discount as well as the gross amount of the payment (i.e., the amount before the deduction for discount). In cases where there are discounts, the clerk will post the *gross amount* to the customer's account.

After being journalized in the Cash Receipts Journal by a second clerk, the accounting entry recording the cheque of W. Hay appears as follows:

CASH RECEIPTS JOURNAL

DATE	CUSTOMER	DISCOUNTS ALLOWED DR	ACC'S REC'L CR	BANK DR
Mar 26	W. Hay	1.42	47.25	45.83

The effect of the above accounting entry is to–

1. Increase Bank by the amount of the cheque, $45.83.
2. Eliminate the $47.25 debt of W. Hay.

3. Record the discount of $1.42 that was allowed on the transaction.

The theoretical effect of the two transactions is shown below:

Acc's Rec'l (W. Hay)	Sales	Sales Tax Payable	Discounts Allowed	Bank
47.25				
47.25	45.00	2.25	1.42	45.83

Take note that the Discounts Allowed account is an Expense account.

There are still a few facts to learn about Cash Discounts.

1. You have probably wondered what is done when a customer takes a late discount. In other words, what is done when a customer still takes the discount after the discount period has expired. A wise businessman will be reasonable in his handling of such situations, remembering that there may be postal or other legitimate delays. He wants to avoid acquiring a reputation for being niggardly, but at the same time, he does not want to let his customers take advantage of him.

   If it is decided to disallow a late discount, the usual practice is to: cash the customer's deficient cheque; credit the customer's account by the amount of the deficient cheque; write to the customer requesting politely that he make up the deficiency in the payment.

2. The Discounts Earned account is often referred to as the Discount off Purchases account. The Discounts Allowed account is ofen referred to as the Discount off Sales account.

3. Every business will try to take advantage of cash discounts offered by its suppliers. Therefore, entries to Discounts Earned account can be ex-

pected to occur frequently and will normally require a special column in the Cash Payments Journal of every business.

   Not all businesses will require a Discounts Allowed account—only those that offer cash discounts to customers. Businesses that do offer cash discounts will need to set up a special column for Discounts Allowed in the Cash Receipts Journal.

Returns and Allowances

You have probably had the experience of purchasing an item only to find out later that there is something wrong with it. Do you recall how anxious and impatient you were for the store to make matters right?

This same kind of transaction occurs time and time again in business and gives rise to a number of different accounting situations each requiring special treatment. Consider the following cases (pages 158 to 163).

Case 1.   *Replacement of Goods*

Star Supply issues the following invoice as a result of a sale to J. Morris:

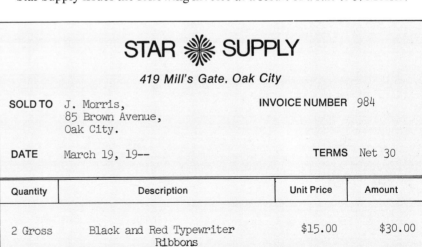

STAR ✳ SUPPLY

419 Mill's Gate. Oak City

SOLD TO	J. Morris, 85 Brown Avenue, Oak City.	INVOICE NUMBER	984
DATE	March 19, 19--	TERMS	Net 30

Quantity	Description	Unit Price	Amount
2 Gross	Black and Red Typewriter Ribbons	$15.00	$30.00
	5% Federal Sales Tax		1.50
			$31.50

IN THE BOOKS OF STAR SUPPLY (THE SELLER)

The journal entry is:

SALES JOURNAL

DATE	CUSTOMER	SALES CR	SALES TAX PAY'L CR	ACC'S REC'L DR
Mar 19	J. Morris	30.00	1.50	31.50

The theoretical effect of the transaction is:

ACC'S REC'L (J. MORRIS)		SALES		SALES TAX PAYABLE	
31.50			30.00		1.50

Provided that the returned goods are put back in stock, no accounting entries are necessary for the exchange. However, because of the delay, through no fault of the purchaser, it is understood that payment will not be expected until 30 days after the delivery of the proper goods.

IN THE BOOKS OF J. MORRIS (THE BUYER)

Upon receipt of the invoice and the goods which appear to be satisfactory, the journal entry is:

PURCHASES JOURNAL

DATE	CREDITOR	SUP-PLIES DR	PUR-CHASES DR	ACC'S PAY'L CR
Mar 20	Star Supply	31.50		31.50

The theoretical effect of the transaction is:

SUPPLIES		ACC'S PAY'L (STAR SUPPLY)	
31.50			31.50

When the package of typewriting ribbons is opened by the employees of J. Morris, it is found that the ribbons are all black, and not red and black as ordered. A phone call is put through to the office of Star Supply and a complaint registered. Star Supply agrees to make good on the order. A short time later, the correct goods are delivered and the incorrect goods are picked up.

No accounting entries are necessary for this exchange.

Case 2.
Return of Goods

Star Supply issues the invoice on the right as a result of a sale to Super Stationery.

STAR ✳ SUPPLY

419 Mill's Gate, Oak City

SOLD TO Super Stationery, 51 McLeod Avenue, Oak City,		**INVOICE NUMBER** 997
DATE March 22, 19—		**TERMS** Net 30

Quantity	Description	Unit Price	Amount
8 Doz.	"Fabulous" Ball Pens	$1.50	$12.00
	5% Federal Sales Tax		.60
			$12.60

The journal entry and the theoretical effect of the transaction are:

SALES JOURNAL

DATE	CUSTOMER	SALES CR	SALES TAX PAY'L CR	ACC'S REC'L DR
Mar 22	Super Stationery	12.00	.60	12.60

ACC'S REC'L (SUPER STATIONERY)	SALES	SALES TAX PAYABLE
12.60	12.00	.60

Upon receipt of the invoice and the goods, the journal entry and the theoretical effect in the accounts are as shown below. Because Super Stationery purchased the ball pens for resale, the debit entry is to Purchases account.

PURCHASES JOURNAL

DATE	SUPPLIER	SUP-PLIES DR	PUR-CHASES DR	ACC'S PAY'L CR
Mar 23	Star Supply		12.60	12.60

PURCHASES	ACC'S PAY'L (STAR SUPPLY)
12.60	12.60

When the ball pens are used, Super Stationery discovers that they are defective. Contact is made with Star Supply and a complaint is registered. The outcome of the discussion is that the goods are to be returned (picked up by the vendor) and not to be replaced. Of course, Super Stationery is not expected to pay for them.

No accounting entry is made at this time.

IN THE BOOKS OF STAR SUPPLY

When the goods are received back from Super Stationery, the sale has in fact been canceled and action must be taken by Star Supply to correct the accounts. Of prime concern is the customer; his account must be reduced by a **Credit** entry and he must be informed that the reduction has been made.

The accounting entry to record the return of goods, and the **Credit** to the customer's account in particular, is begun by the issuing of a **Credit Invoice** by the vendor. A Credit Invoice (also known by the names **Credit Note** and **Credit Memo**) is in reality a minus invoice having precisely the opposite effect to a regular invoice.

Star Supply's Credit Invoice crediting the account of Super Stationery for the return of the ball pens is shown on the right and is a typical example of a Credit Invoice.

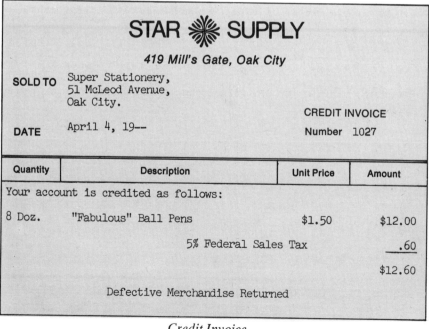

STAR ✱ SUPPLY

419 Mill's Gate, Oak City

SOLD TO Super Stationery,
51 McLeod Avenue,
Oak City.

CREDIT INVOICE

DATE April 4, 19—

Number 1027

Quantity	Description	Unit Price	Amount
	Your account is credited as follows:		
8 Doz.	"Fabulous" Ball Pens	$1.50	$12.00
	5% Federal Sales Tax		.60
			$12.60
	Defective Merchandise Returned		

Credit Invoice

160

1. In the accounts, the effect of a Credit Invoice is opposite to that of a regular Sales Invoice.
2. The Credit Invoice is also known by the names Credit Note and Credit Memo.
3. For any one business, the Credit Invoice is usually of the same

basic design and appearance as the regular Sales Invoice form.
4. The word 'Credit' is prominently displayed on the form.
5. The Credit Invoice form is usually either (i) printed on pink paper, or (ii) printed on white paper using red ink.

6. Credit Invoices may be numbered in sequence with the regular invoices or they may be given their own sequence of numbers.
7. The path of a Credit Invoice is the same as that of a regular Sales Invoice. See page 84.

IN THE BOOKS OF STAR SUPPLY

Credit Invoices are most efficiently recorded through the Sales Journal (although they may be handled through the General Journal). However, since a Credit Invoice has the opposite effect to a regular Sales Invoice, the amounts entered from the Credit Invoice must be individually circled in the journal. For a review of this technique, refer to page 118.

The way in which the Credit Invoice is recorded in the Sales Journal is illustrated below (fifth line):

SALES JOURNAL

DATE	CUSTOMER	SALES CR	SALES TAX PAY'L CR	INV. NO.	ACC'S REC'L DR
r 3	Delsey's	24.00	1.20	1023	25.20
3	R. Brown	10.00	.50	1024	10.50
4	J. Jones	18.00	.90	1025	18.90
4	A & A Printing	15.00	.75	1026	15.75
4	Super Stationery	(12.00)	(.60)	1027	(12.60)
4	Heart Hair	20.00	1.00	1028	20.10

If written in General Journal form, the entry would be:

Dr. Sales 12.00
Dr. Sales Tax Payable .60
  Cr. Accounts Receivable
  (Super Stationery) 12.60

The theoretical effect of the two transactions is:

ACC'S REC'L (SUPER STATIONERY)		SALES		SALES TAX PAYABLE	
12.60			12.00		.60
	12.60	12.00		.60	

At this point, Star Supply has completed its accounting for the sale of and the return of the defective merchandise.

IN THE BOOKS OF SUPER STATIONERY

When received by Super Stationery, the Credit Invoice of Star Supply will follow the routine established for Purchase Invoices. However, since the effect of a Credit Invoice is opposite to that of a regular Sales Invoice, care must be taken to circle individually the amounts entered in the Purchases Journal from the Credit Invoice. The accounting entry to record the Credit Invoice in the Purchases Journal is shown below. Observe that the credit entry is to Purchases account since that is the account that was previously debited.

PURCHASES JOURNAL

DATE	SUPPLIER	SUP-PLIES DR	PUR-CHASES DR	ACC'S PAY'L CR
Apr 6	Star Supply		(12.60)	(12.60)

The theoretical effect of the two transactions is:

PURCHASES		ACC'S PAY'L (STAR SUPPLY)	
12.60			12.60
	12.60	12.60	

At this point, Super Stationery has completed its accounting for the purchase of and the return of the defective merchandise.

Case 3.
Allowance for Goods

Star Supply issues the invoice on the right as a result of a sale to P. & Q. Garage.

419 Mill's Gate, Oak City

SOLD TO P. & Q. Garage, 95 Sentinel Street, Tidings Corner.	**INVOICE NUMBER** 1008	
DATE March 24, 19--	**TERMS** 2/10,N/30	

Quantity	Description	Unit Price	Amount
4 Pkgs.	Invoice Forms	$12.00	$48.0
	5% Federal Sales Tax		2.4
			$50.4

IN THE BOOKS OF STAR SUPPLY (THE SELLER)

The journal entry is recorded as for the two previous cases.
    The theoretical effect of the transaction is:

IN THE BOOKS OF P. & Q. GARAGE (THE BUYER)

The journal entry is recorded as for the two previous cases with Supplies being the account debited.
    The theoretical effect of the transaction is:

SUPPLIES	ACC'S PAY'L (STAR SUPPLY)
50.40	50.40

    At the time the goods are inspected, it is found that the four packages of invoice forms are not printed according to the instructions given to Star Supply. A complaint is made to Star Supply and a compromise is made between the two companies as follows: P. & Q. Garage is persuaded to keep and use the invoice forms, and Star Supply agrees to give an allowance of 50 per cent off the price of the goods.

STAR ✸ SUPPLY

419 Mill's Gate, Oak City

SOLD TO P. & Q Garage,
P. O. Box 10,
Ormsby.

CREDIT INVOICE

DATE April 7, 19--

Number 1036

Quantity	Description	Unit Price	Amount
	Your account is credited as follows:		
	50% Allowance for merchandise on invoice #1008, goods incorrectly printed:		
4 Pkgs.	Invoice Forms	$6.00	$24.00
	5% Federal Tax		1.20
			$25.20

IN THE BOOKS OF STAR SUPPLY

As was shown in Case 2, the making right of the accounting for such a situation is begun by the vendor company who issues a Credit Invoice. Accordingly, Star Supply issues the Credit Invoice shown on the right.

The journal entry recording the Credit Invoice is:

SALES JOURNAL

DATE	CUSTOMER		SALES CR	SALES TAX CR	ACC'S REC'L DR
Apr 7	P & Q Garage		24.00	1.20	25.20

The theoretical effect of the two transactions is:

```
ACC'S REC'L
(P. & Q. GARAGE)          SALES                    SALES TAX
50.40                        | 48.00                 PAYABLE
      | 25.20        24.00 |                              | 2.40
                                              1.20 |
```

At this point, Star Supply has completed its accounting for the sale of and the allowance for the defective merchandise.

IN THE BOOKS OF P. & Q. GARAGE

The Credit Invoice is accepted and processed in the normal way. The journal entry recording the transaction is:

PURCHASES JOURNAL

DATE	SUPPLIER		SUP-PLIES DR	PUR-CHASES DR	ACC'S PAY'L CR
Apr 9	P & Q Garage		25.20		25.20

The theoretical effect of the two transactions is:

```
                            ACC'S PAY'L
   SUPPLIES               (STAR SUPPLY)
50.40 |                              | 50.40
      | 25.20          25.20 |
```

At this point, the accounting for the sale of and the allowance for the defective merchandise is complete.

163

Cash Refund

The cash sale is a very common business transaction. But dissatisfaction can occur with cash sales as well as with sales on account. When a buyer pays cash for goods and later finds them to be unsatisfactory, he usually demands and gets his money back– in other words, he obtains a **Cash Refund**. The accounting for cash refunds takes place as follows:

TRANSACTION

On May 16, 19—, Star Supply makes a cash purchase of a new battery from Cut-Rate Auto Parts. The cost of the battery is $25 plus sales tax of 5 per cent. A cheque is issued by Star Supply to pay for the goods.

BOOKS OF SELLER

Journal entry is:

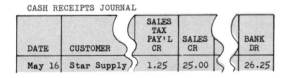

CASH RECEIPTS JOURNAL

DATE	CUSTOMER	SALES TAX PAY'L CR	SALES CR	BANK DR
May 16	Star Supply	1.25	25.00	26.25

The theoretical effect is:

BANK	SALES	SALES TAX PAYABLE
26.25	25.00	1.25

BOOKS OF BUYER

Journal entry is:

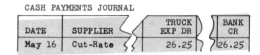

CASH PAYMENTS JOURNAL

DATE	SUPPLIER	TRUCK EXP DR	BANK CR
May 16	Cut-Rate	26.25	26.25

The theoretical effect is:

TRUCK EXPENSE	BANK
26.25	26.25

TRANSACTION

On May 18, 19—, at the time the battery is being installed, the mechanic finds that it is cracked. It is, therefore, returned to Cut-Rate Auto Parts and a refund cheque for the full amount is obtained. The refund cheque is included in the day's cash receipts.

BOOKS OF SELLER

Journal entry is:

CASH PAYMENTS JOURNAL

DATE	SUPPLIER	OTHER ACCOUNTS DR		BANK CR
		ACCOUNT	AMOUNT	
May 18	Star Supp	Sales	25.00	26.25
		S. Tax Pay'l	1.25	

The cumulative effect is:

BANK		SALES		SALES TAX PAYABLE	
26.25	26.25		25.00		1.25
		25.00		1.25	

BOOKS OF BUYER

Journal entry is:

CASH RECEIPTS JOURNAL

DATE	CUSTOMER	OTHER ACCOUNTS CR		BANK DR
		ACCOUNT	AMOUNT	
May 18	Cut-Rate	Truck Exp	26.25	26.25

The cumulative effect is:

TRUCK EXPENSE		BANK	
26.25	26.25		26.25
		26.25	

Note:

Rather than give a refund to a cash customer, many businesses prefer to issue a Credit Note. The issuing of a Credit Note sets up an account for the customer in which there is a credit balance. The customer is thus encouraged to make purchases from the business which are to be paid for out of the credit balance. He is also discouraged from spending the refund at another place of business.

Cash Discount Combined With A Return or Allowance

If an invoice is received on which there is a cash discount, and some time before the discount date a portion of the goods is returned or an allowance is obtained, the discount may be taken only on the net cost of the goods. The net cost is found by deducting the amount of the Credit Note from the amount of the Sales Invoice. In such cases, it is wise to make certain of the discount date by discussing it with the vendor. Because of the circumstances, the discount date will probably be moved ahead, perhaps to the date of the Credit Note.

Sales Returns and Allowances Account

The previous sections indicated that the accounts involved in the accounting for returns, allowances, or cash refunds are the same (except used in reverse) as those used for the original sale. This is correct accounting practice and is adopted extensively in the business community.

However, there are some businesses, large department stores for example, that require more specific information in respect to returns, allowances, and refunds. They want to know what proportion of the goods sold is returned to them. They obtain this information by using a separate account in which to accumulate sales returns and allowances.

Consider the following transactions.

TRANSACTION

Simplex Co. sells $50 of goods to A. Moss. An invoice is issued for the sale on November 12, 19—.

The journal entry for the transaction in the books of Simplex Co. is:

SALES JOURNAL

DATE	CUSTOMER	SALES RETURNS ALLOW'S DR	SALES CR	SALES TAX PAY'L CR	ACC'S REC'L DR
Nov 12	A. Moss		50.00	2.50	52.50

The effect in the accounts is:

ACC'S REC'L (A. MOSS)	SALES TAX PAYABLE	SALES
52.50	2.50	50.00

TRANSACTION

Because a portion of the goods sold to A. Moss is defective and returned, Simplex Co. issues a Credit Invoice for $18 plus tax on November 18, 19—. (Simplex Co. uses a Sales Returns and Allowances account.)

The journal entry for the transaction in the books of Simplex Co. is:

SALES JOURNAL

DATE	CUSTOMER	SALES RETURNS ALLOW'S DR	SALES CR	SALES TAX PAY'L CR	ACC'S REC'L DR
Nov 18	A. Moss	18.00		.90	18.90

Observe that—
1. Because Simplex Co. accumulates returns and allowances separately, there is a special column provided for a Sales Returns and Allowances account in the Sales Journal.
2. The Sales Returns and Allowances column is a Debit column because entries to the Sales Returns and Allowances account are normally debits.

The cumulative effect in the accounts is:

ACC'S REC'L (A. MOSS)		SALES TAX PAYABLE		SALES RETURNS & ALLOWANCES	SALES
52.50	18.90	.90	2.50	18.00	50.00

These two accounts together will show the true 'Sales' figure, called 'Net Sales'. In this case the Net Sales figure is $32.

165

There are certain businesses that consider it necessary to know the total amount of returns and allowances for merchandise purchased. They want to know what proportion of the merchandise purchased by them is returned to their suppliers. They obtain this information by using a separate account in which to accumulate purchases returns and allowances. (Note that this includes only items of merchandise inventory that are purchased and later returned. It does not include items such as supplies or items expense such as truck parts. These latter items are handled by means of a direct credit to the account involved.)

Consider the following transactions.

TRANSACTION

On June 12, 19—, Baytown Drug Market receives a shipment of drugs and the Sales Invoice for them from Drug Wholesale Company. The total of the invoice is $147.

The journal entry for the transaction in the books of Baytown Drug Market is:

PURCHASES JOURNAL

DATE	SUPPLIER	PURCH RETURNS ALLOW'S CR	PUR- CHASES DR	ACC'S PAY'L CR
Jun 12	Drug Whols		147.00	147.00

The effect in the accounts is:

TRANSACTION

On June 14, Baytown Drug Market notices that a number of the packages received from Drug Wholesale Company are damaged. The damaged goods are returned for credit and a Credit Note for $48.30 is received on June 16. (Baytown Drug Market uses a Purchases Returns and Allowances account.)

The journal entry for the transaction in the books of Baytown Drug Market is:

PURCHASES JOURNAL

DATE	SUPPLIER	PURCH RETURNS ALLOW'S CR	PUR- CHASES DR	ACC'S PAY'L CR
June 16	Drug Whols	48.30		48.30

Observe the use of a Purchases Returns and Allowances credit column in the Purchases Journal.

The cumulative effect in the accounts is:

These two accounts together will show the true 'Purchases' figure, called 'Net Purchases'. In this case, the Net Purchases figure is $98.70.

Petty Cash — Imprest Method

The most common method of making payment for expenditures is by cheque. However, every business must continually face the situation where it is not convenient to issue a cheque and where 'cash' is the expected thing. Consider the following transactions:

1. The janitor requires some electrical fuses and during his lunch period he purchases with his own money a quantity of fuses from the local hardware store. He then submits the cash register slip for 60¢ to the accounting department so that he may be reimbursed.

2. Two salaried employees are asked to work overtime in order to complete a special job. As a favour, they are each given $3 for supper money.

3. A parcel is delivered by an express company for which express charges of $2.50 must be paid immediately.

The most efficient way to pay for small expenditures of this type is with cash. For this reason a small quantity of cash, usually no more than $100, is kept in the office. It is called the Petty Cash Fund.

Establishing A Petty Cash Fund

To establish a Petty Cash fund it is merely necessary to withdraw a sum of money from the bank account and to put it in the care of some person in the office. More precisely, a cheque is issued (made out to Petty Cash usually) and given to the person chosen to be in charge of Petty Cash; this person cashes the cheque and brings the money (in the form of small bills and coins) back to the office. The Petty Cash Fund is usually kept in a metal cash box (with lock) and, outside of office hours, the box is usually kept in the com-

pany safe or vault. Naturally, the keeper of the Petty Cash is instructed as to the type of expenditure that may be made out of Petty Cash funds.

The accounting entry to establish a Petty Cash Fund is shown by the following.

TRANSACTION

It is decided to establish a Petty Cash Fund of $50. A cheque, dated September 20, 19— in the amount of $50 is made out to Petty Cash and is given to the person chosen to keep the Petty Cash.

The journal entry to record the transaction is:

The effect in the accounts is:

At this time, after the cheque is cashed, the Petty Cash box will contain $50 in cash.

Operating The Petty Cash Fund

The keeper of the Petty Cash Fund is authorized to make small payments out of the fund from time to time. But for every amount paid out of the fund, a bill for the expenditure (submitted by the recipient of the money) must be put in. If a bill is not available, the recipient of the money must fill out a **Petty Cash Voucher** such as the one on page 168. The Petty Cash Voucher is then placed in the box. A supply of unused Petty Cash Vouchers (also known as Petty Cash Slips) is kept with the Petty Cash Fund.

Can you see that at any time the total of the bills, vouchers, and cash in the Petty Cash box should be equal to the Petty Cash Fund? The keeper of the fund is responsible for seeing that this is so.

The accounting for this aspect of Petty Cash is easy because, under the Imprest system, no entry is made. It is one of those accounting situations where it is advantageous to allow the records to become temporarily incorrect.

PETTY CASH
VOUCHER

DATE _March 15, 19—_

AMOUNT _4.30_

PAID TO _Holmes Hardware_

EXPLANATION _2 extension_
cords for janitors

SIGNATURE _PWatts_
Received by

CHARGE TO A/C _#59_

Miscellaneous Exp.

A Petty Cash Voucher

Replenishing Petty Cash

As time passes, of course, the cash in the Petty Cash box will diminish as the bills and vouchers are paid. A point will be reached where there may not be enough cash in the fund to pay the next bill or voucher. To prevent this, a lower limit is usually placed on the fund. When this point is reached, the fund must be replenished.

To show the accounting for replenishing Petty Cash, let us continue the example begun previously.

TRANSACTION

On October 2, the contents of the Petty Cash box are as follows:

Cash	$ 4.15
Bills and Vouchers	45.85
Total	$50.00

The breakdown of the bills and vouchers by account charged is as follows:

Vouchers

1.	Miscellaneous Expense	$ 2.59
2.	Postage	4.00
3.	Miscellaneous Expense	3.75
4.	Building Maintenance	1.56
5.	Donations	5.00
6.	Building Maintenance	4.75
7.	Truck Expense	5.15
8.	Miscellaneous Expense	6.00
9.	Postage	4.00
10.	Supplies	9.05
	Total	$45.85

The lower limit of the Petty Cash Fund is set at $5.

Because the amount of cash in the Petty Cash box is less than the lower limit of $5, it is necessary to replenish the Petty Cash Fund. The first step is for the keeper of the fund to prepare a summary of the charges from the bills and vouchers in the box. There is no definite form in which the summary must be prepared. The summary might appear as shown below.

Petty Cash Fund Summary of Charges October 2, 19—		
Building Maintenance	6	31
Donations	5	00
Miscellaneous Expense	12	34
Postage	8	00
Supplies	9	05
Truck Expense	5	15
	45	85

To this summary, are attached the bills and vouchers from which the summary was prepared.

The second step in replenishing the Petty Cash Fund is for the keeper of the fund to obtain a cheque with which to replace the cash that has been expended out of the fund. He does this by submitting the bills, vouchers, and the summary to the department that issues cheques, and by receiving a cheque, made out to Petty Cash, for an amount equal to the total shown on the summary (in this example, $45.85). The summary and the supporting papers are accepted as the source document for the cheque.

When the cheque is cashed and the money placed in the Petty Cash box (along with the $4.15 already there), the fund is restored to its original amount of $50 cash. It is then ready to begin another cycle.

Under the Imprest method of handling Petty Cash, the accounting entry to record the issuing of the replenishing cheque is as follows:

CASH PAYMENTS JOURNAL

| DATE | NAME | OTHER ACC'S DR | | BANK CR |
		ACCOUNT	AMOUNT	
Oct 2	Petty Cash	Bldg Mntc	6.31	45.85
		Donations	5.00	
		Misc. Exp	12.34	
		Postage	8.00	
		Supplies	9.05	
		Truck Exp	5.15	

Observe that the accounting entry is one that—

1. Debits a number of accounts in exact accordance with the Petty Cash Summary of Charges,

2. Credits Bank with the amount of the replenishing cheque.

Note:

The above entry is in effect a consolidation of more than one entry; namely, (a) those that re-

quire a charge to an expense or asset account and a decrease to Petty Cash, and (b) the one that requires an increase to Petty Cash and a decrease to Bank.

In the accounts, the cumulative effect of the two entries, i.e. (1) the entry to establish the fund, and (2) the replenishing entry, is:

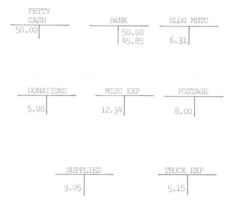

The above accounts reflect the two usual types of accounting entries that are necessary when the Imprest method of Petty Cash is used. These are—

1. The entry to establish the fund, or what amounts to the same thing, to increase the fund.

2. The replenishing entry that records the credit to Bank and distributes the charges to the various accounts.

It is worth noting that the many ins and outs of the Petty Cash account have been completely bypassed.

169

Cash Discount: A reduction that may be taken in the amount of a bill provided that the bill is paid within the discount period shown on the bill.

Terms of Sale: The conditions agreed to at the time of sale, between the buyer and the seller, in respect to the length of time allowed for payment and whether a cash discount may be taken.

Discounts Earned:
Discount off Purchases: Income acquired by a business that takes advantage of cash discounts offered by its suppliers.

Discounts Allowed:
Discount off Sales: Expense incurred by a business that offers a cash discount to its customers who take advantage of the offer.

Sales Return:
Purchase Return: The result of the buyer of goods returning them to the seller either for a Credit Note or for replacement, the goods being returned because in some way they were deficient. From the seller's position, this is a 'Sales Return'; from the buyer's position, this is a 'Purchase Return'.

Sales Allowance:
Purchase Allowance: The result of an agreement between the buyer and the seller of 'deficient' goods to the effect that the goods will not be returned but that the price will be decreased by means of a Credit Note. From the seller's position, this is a 'Sales Allowance'; from the buyer's position, this is a 'Purchase Allowance'.

Cash Refund: The result of the buyer of goods having his money returned by the seller in respect to 'deficient' goods that had been paid for.

Credit Invoice:
Credit Note:
Credit Memo: A business document, the purpose of which is to initiate a reduction in a customer's account. The reason for the reduction is explained in detail on the Credit Invoice form. A Credit Invoice is really a negative Sales Invoice.

Net Sales: The figure obtained by subtracting the balance of the Sales Returns and Allowances account from the balance of the Sales account.

Net Purchases: The figure obtained by subtracting the balance of the Purchases Returns and Allowances account from the balance of the Purchases account.

Petty Cash: A small amount of money, usually $100 or less, kept in the office for the convenience of paying cash for small bills and expenditures.

Review Questions

1. What is a cash discount?
2. What is the purpose of a cash discount?
3. Explain the meaning of 'Terms of Sale'.
4. Explain the meaning of C.O.D.; Net 30; 2/15,n/30.
5. Where may the Terms of Sale be seen?
6. Under what circumstances might a customer be requested to pay C.O.D.?
7. Of what value is it to record a customer's usual terms of sale on his account card?
8. In the office of the buyer, what is done with a Purchase Invoice on which a cash discount is offered?
9. Calculate the discount and the net amount of an invoice for $52.50 if the rate of discount is 3 per cent.
10. If J. Jones pays a bill of $50 by means of a cheque for $49 because he was entitled to a 2 per cent discount, what is the amount of the entry made to his account in the books of the seller?
11. Are discounts earned associated with the buyer or the seller?
12. What is usually done when a customer takes a late discount?
13. What is another name for Discounts Allowed? for Discounts Earned?
14. Nearly all businesses have a Discounts Earned account but not all business have a Discounts Allowed account. Explain.
15. Explain the difference between a 'sales return' and a 'sales allowance'.
16. When goods are purchased and later returned for credit, under what circumstances in the books of the buyer will the credit entry be to Purchases account (or Purchase Returns and Allowances account)?
17. In your own words, explain why you think the term Credit Invoice was chosen.
18. How can you usually distinguish between a regular Sales Invoice and a Credit Invoice?
19. When you journalize a Credit Invoice in the Sales Journal, what must you be careful to do?
20. Under what circumstances would a buyer want a cash refund?
21. Explain how a cash discount is calculated when a return or allowance is involved in the transaction.
22. Under what circumstances does a business maintain a separate account for Sales Returns and Allowances?
23. Why is it necessary to have a Petty Cash Fund in a business office?
24. State the rule that the keeper of the fund must follow when expenditures from the fund are made.
25. How often is the Petty Cash Fund replenished?

Exercises

1. Complete the following schedule by calculating the amount of the payment that is necessary in each case. Where Credit Notes are involved assume that the discount period is adjusted to start from the date on the Credit Note.

Date of Invoice	Amount of Invoice	Terms of Sales	Amount of Credit Note	Date of Credit Note	Date Payment is Made	Amount of Payment Required
Mar 12	$52.50	2/10,N/30	-	-	Mar 20	
May 18	47.25	Net 30	-	-	May 27	
Sep 4	115.50	3/15,N/60	-	-	Oct 10	
Feb 6	1,050.00	1/20,N/60	$126.00	Feb 18	Mar 6	
Oct 19	588.00	2/10,N/30	42.00	Nov 5	Nov 27	
Aug 27	882.00	2/15,N/60	168.00	Sep 7	Sep 10	

2. On March 16, 19–, after a bill of $12.16 is paid, the contents of a Petty Cash Fund having a lower limit of $5 are as follows:

Cash	$1.68
Bills and Vouchers	
Miscellaneous Expense	6.04
Miscellaneous Expense	1.25
Sales Promotion	3.17
Building Expense	10.50
Miscellaneous Expense	2.05
Postage	9.00
Miscellaneous Expense	4.15
Building Expense	12.16

INSTRUCTION 1.

Prepare the Summary of Charges necessary to replenish the fund.

INSTRUCTION 2.

In General Journal form, write out the accounting entry necessary to replenish the fund.

3. On June 10, 19–, a $25 Petty Cash Fund, having a lower limit of $2, is in the following condition:

Cash	$ .54
Bills and Vouchers	
Office Expense	5.02
Office Supplies	.75
Advertising	2.00
Office Expense	2.14
P. Martin, Drawings	10.00
Office Expense	1.20
Office Expense	2.00
Office Supplies	1.35

INSTRUCTION 1.

Prepare the Summary of Charges necessary to replenish the fund.

INSTRUCTION 2.

In General Journal form, write out the required accounting entry to replenish the fund.

4. Record the following 'selected' transactions of the Canadian Copper Company in General Journal Form.

Transactions

October

1 *Purchase Invoice*
   —No. 6457, from Dominion Nickel Company, dated September 29, amount, $11,760, terms, Net 30 days, for a shipment of copper.

3 *Cheque Copy*
   —No. 750, to Petty Cash, $25, to increase Petty Cash fund from $25 to $50.

7 *Purchase Invoice*
   —No. 354, from Continental Railway Company, $762.12, in respect to the shipment of copper from Dominion Nickel Company.

8 *Cheque Copy*
   —No. 765, to Mallory & Co., $353.99, in payment of their Sales Invoice No.6421 for $361.21 less a 2 per cent discount.

11 *Cheque Copy*
   —No. 784, to Ewing & Barlock, $51.62; cash refund for defective copper bars returned. (Canadian Copper Company does not keep seperate accounts for Returns and Allowances.)

12 *Cash Receipt*
   —Cheque from Kirby Brothers, $116.62, in payment of Sales Invoice No. 692, dated September 30, having terms of 2/15,n/30.

17 *Cheque Copy*
   —No. 801, to Petty Cash, $48.68; replenishing cheque for the following charges: Office Supplies, $17.14; Miscellaneous Expense, $23.22; Delivery Expense, $1.35; Freight-in, $6.97.

25 *Cheque Copy*
   —No. 814, to Pearson Bros., $12.14; for the cash purchase of office supplies.

26 *Sales Invoice*
   —No. 751, to Toro Fixtures, $643; sale of goods on account; terms of sale, Net 30 days; sales tax 3 per cent to be added.

27 *Cheque Copy*
   —No. 827, to Commercial Cartage, $412; cash payment for delivery service for the month of September.

30 *Credit Note Received*
   —No. 6529, from Dominion Nickel Company, $900; allowance for defective goods on invoice No. 6457.

---

5. Record the following 'selected' transactions of Wholesale Food Distributors in General Journal Form. In working out your answers, bear in mind the following:
   (a) A few of the transactions are dependent on previous ones.
   (b) Wholesale Food Distributors maintains separate accounts for both Purchase Returns and Allowances and Sales Returns and Allowances.
   (c) The amounts of certain cheques (receipts and expenditures) have been left for you to decide.

November

3 *Sales Invoices*
–No. 962, Palmer's Grocery, $496.26; terms, 2/10,n/30; 5 per cent sales tax.
–No. 963, Grey's Market, $376.14; terms, 2/10,n/30; 5 per cent sales tax.
–No. 964, Alec's Groceteria, $197.26; terms, 2/10,n/30; 5 per cent sales tax.

4 *Cheque Copy*
–No. 404, to D. K. Knight, $100, loan to an employee to help him overcome a personal hardship.

5 *Purchase Invoice*
–No. 213, from Gordon Canners, $1,260, dated Nov. 2; terms 3/20,n/60, for merchandise purchased.

5 *Bank Debit Note*
–From City Bank, $75.10, cheque returned N.S.F. from Doyle's Grocery.

7 *Cheque Copy*
–No. 412, to Outboard Motor Sales, $425; instructions from J. D. Doan, the owner, to pay for a new outboard motor delivered to his cottage for his personal use.

8 *Purchase Invoice*
–No. 5698, from Elmer Canners, $1,050; for merchandise purchased; terms, Net 60 days, dated Nov. 6.

10 *Credit Note Received*
–No. 445, from Gordon Canners, $147, dated Nov. 9; allowance granted on invoice No. 213 for incorrect goods.

10 *Cheque Copy*
–No. 443, to Petty Cash, to replenish Petty Cash as per the following Summary of Charges:

Travelling Expenses	$12.92
Delivery Expense	40.89
Building Maintenance	26.14
Miscellaneous Expense	16.19

11 *Cheque Copy*
–No. 447, to Brown Brothers, $275, to pay for C.O.D. delivery of new office desk.

12 *Cash Receipt*
–Cheque of Grey's Market, paying Sales Invoice No. 963.

12 *Credit Note Issued*
–No. 1007, to Palmer's Grocery, $56.70, for defective merchandise returned; discount period adjusted to begin on November 12.

14 *Credit Note Received*
–No. 565, from Burlington Fruit Growers Association, $2,332.80; correcting their invoice No. 412, which was issued incorrectly in the amount of $2,592 instead of $259.20. (**Note:** This is neither a 'Return' nor an 'Allowance'.)

18 *Cheque Copy*
–No. 474, to G. Simcoe, $47.25; cash refund for defective merchandise that had been returned.

22 *Cash Receipt*
–Cheque from Palmer's Grocery, paying invoice No. 962 and Credit Note No. 1007 less discount.

25 *Cheque Copy*
–No. 491, to Gordon Canners, paying Sales Invoice No. 213 and Credit Note No. 445 less discount.

26 *Cheque Copy*
–No. 497, to Elmer Canners, paying invoice No. 5698.

30 *Cash Receipt*
–Cheque from Alec's Groceteria, paying Sales Invoice No. 964.

---

6. T. O. Sprague is the sole proprietor of Best Wholesale Confectionery, a business that has been in operation for a number of years.

The combined General Ledger Trial Balance and Chart of Accounts of Best Wholesale Confectionery as of August 31, 19— is shown on page 175.

Best Wholesale Confectionery
General Ledger Trial Balance
August 31, 19—

1	Petty Cash	$ 50.00	
2	Bank	1,562.50	
3	Accounts Receivable	514.50	
4	Merchandise Inventory	5,100.00	
5	Supplies	125.00	
6	Delivery Equipment	6,040.00	
7	Warehouse Equipment	2,984.00	
101	Accounts Payable		$3,318.00
102	Sales Tax Payable		201.00
201	T. O. Sprague, Capital		10,953.63
202	T. O. Sprague, Drawings	6,425.00	
301	Sales		28,875.00
401	Bank Charges	36.70	
402	Delivery Expense	516.90	
403	Discounts Allowed	572.00	
404	Discounts Earned		119.12
405	Light and Heat	275.00	
406	Maintenance Expense	174.50	
407	Office Expense	151.20	
408	Purchases	14,975.25	
409	Rent	2,100.00	
410	Telephone	184.20	
411	Wages	1,680.00	
		$43,466.75	$43,466.75

On August 31, 19— the Accounts Receivable Ledger contains the following accounts:

Customer Name	Address	Invoice Number	Invoice Date	Amount
Dick's Confectionery	16 Brown Street	703	Aug. 27	$ 57.75
G.E.S. Smoke & Gift Shop	702 Dan Avenue	704	Aug. 27	73.50
Haddy's Variety Store	49 Porterfield Road	700	Aug. 27	94.50
Harry's Cigarette Store	156 Main Street	690	Aug. 15	42.00
Howie's Sweets	27 Lake Street	696	Aug. 20	157.50
Jim's Snack Bar	35 College Street	701	Aug. 27	26.25
M. D. Sundries	516 Franklin Avenue	702	Aug. 27	63.00
				$514.50

All sales made by Best Wholesale Confectionery are on terms of 2/10,n/30. It is a policy of the business to allow its customers to be one day late in respect to discounts; the customer's cheque must arrive by the eleventh day to be eligible for the discount.

Sales tax in this locality is at the rate of 5 per cent.

On August 31, 19— the Accounts Payable Ledger contains the following accounts:

Supplier Name	Address	Invoice Number	Invoice Date	Terms	Amount
City Confections	65 Monarch Drive	492	July 30	Net 60	$1,060.50
Famous Candy Co.	72 Queen's Place	565	Aug 4	Net 30	1,312.50
Memory Novelties	100 Regal Lane	209	Aug 22	3/20,n/60	525.00
Paramount Tobacco	46 Park Street	1756	July 30	Net 60	236.25
Winner Supplies	52 River Drive	974	Aug 29	2/15,n/30	183.75
					$3,318.00

Best Wholesale Confectionery tries to take advantage of discounts offered by its suppliers. Its policy is to pay invoices having discounts on the day before the discount expires— provided, of course, that there is a sufficient balance in the bank account to cover the cheques. To avoid the possible embarrassment of issuing a bad cheque, the accountant is responsible for calculating the bank balance at the end of each day. He does this by adding the day's cash receipts and subtracting the day's cash payments from the calculated bank balance of the previous day.

Best Wholesale Confectionery uses a Five-Journal System. The journals and the next unused page numbers are:

Cash Receipts Journal	Page 76
Cash Disbursements Journal	Page 94
Sales Journal	Page 67
Purchases Journal	Page 85
General Journal	Page 24

The owner of the business, T. O. Sprague, does not consider it worthwhile to have separate accounts for returns and allowances, and consequently he does not have them.

The Subsidiary Ledgers of the business are posted directly from the source documents rather than from the journals themselves. Mr. Sprague finds this method to be more efficient.

INSTRUCTION 1.
(a) Set up the three ledgers of Best Wholesale Confectionery as of August 31, 19—.
(b) Prepare the five journals of Best Wholesale Confectionery for the September transactions.

INSTRUCTION 2.
Journalize the transactions for the month of September listed below. Post to the Subsidiary Ledgers daily.

Transactions

September
3 *Sales Invoices*
—No. 705, to Jim's Snack Bar, $620 plus $31 sales tax, for sale of goods.

—No. 706, to Howie's Sweets, $400 plus $20 sales tax, for sale of goods.

3 *Cheque Copy*

—No. 442, to Amber & Green, $300, rent for September.

4 *Cash Receipts*

—Cheque of Harry's Cigarette Store, $42, in full of account.

—Cheque of P. Watson, $63, cash sale $60 plus 5 per cent sales tax.

Purchase Invoices

—From Famous Candy Co., No. 615, $262.50, dated Sept. 2; terms, Net 30, for merchandise.

—From Winner Supplies, No. 1004, $52.50, dated Sept. 1; terms, 2/15,n/30, for supplies (assume goods are satisfactory).

5 *Bank Credit Note*

—From Cliffside Bank, $1,000; because Famous Candy Co.'s invoice of August 4 was overdue, Mr. Sprague borrowed $1,000 from the bank.

Cheque Copies

—No. 443, to Famous Candy Co., $1,312.50; paying invoice No. 565.

—No. 444, to Petty Cash, $47.20; replenishing cheque for the following Summary of Charges:

Office Expense	$24.02
Delivery Expense	8.18
Drawings	15.00

Credit Note Issued

—No. 707, to Dick's Confectionery, $8 plus 40¢ sales tax; allowance for defective merchandise; discount date adjusted to date of Credit Note.

6 *Cash Receipts*

—Cheque of G.E.S. Smoke & Gift Shop, $72.03, in payment of invoice No. 704 less $1.47 cash discount.

—Cheque of Haddy's Variety Store, $92.61, in payment of invoice No. 700 less $1.89 cash discount.

—Cheque of Jim's Snack Bar, $25.72; in payment of invoice No. 701 less 53¢ cash discount.

Credit Note Received

—From City Confections, No. 540, $94.50; dated Sept. 4; no discount date adjustment; correction in price charged for goods.

7 *Purchase Invoice*

—From Wonderful Cartage Co., 8 Elm Street, No. 402, $64.15; terms Net 30; dated Sept. 6; for delivery services performed for the month of August.

7 *Cheque Copy*

—No. 445, to 'Cash', $250, for the wages of employees for the week just ended.

10 *Sales Invoices*

—No. 708, to G.E.S. Smoke & Gift Shop, $640 plus $32 sales tax; of merchandise.

—No. 709, to M. D. Sundries, $765 plus $38.25 sales tax; sale of merchandise.

11 *Cash Receipts*

—Cheque of Howie's Sweets. $157.50, paying invoice No. 696.

—Cheque of M. D. Sundries, $61.74, paying invoice No. 702 less $1.26 cash discount.

Cheque Copy

—No. 446, to Memory Novelties, $509.25, paying invoice No. 209 less $15.75 cash discount.

Purchase Invoice

—From Paramount Tobacco, No. 1803, $157.50, dated Sept. 10; terms, Net 60; for merchandise.

12 *Cheque Copy*

—No. 447, to Municipal Telephone Co., $16.15, cash payment of telephone bill for September.

Purchase Invoice

—From Memory Novelties, No. 305, $325.50, dated Sept. 11; terms 3/20, n/60; for merchandise.

13 *Cash Receipts*

—Cheque of Howie's Sweets, $411.60, paying invoice No. 706 less $8.40 cash discount.

—Cheque of Jim's Snack Bar, $637.98, paying invoice No. 705 less $13.02 cash discount.

Purchase Invoice

—From Winner Supplies, No. 1111, $152.25, dated Sept. 12; terms, 2/15, n/30; for supplies.

Cheque Copy

—No. 448, to Winner Supplies, $180.07, paying invoice No. 974 less $3.68 cash discount.

14 *Cheque Copies*

—No. 449, to 'Cash', $270; for the wages for the week.

—No. 450, to T. O. Sprague, $500; drawings for personal use.

—No. 451, to Federal Government, $201; paying the sales tax collected for the previous month.

—No. 452, to Municipal Electric, $15.02; cash payment for electricity used for the month of August.

17 *Cash Receipts*

–Cheque of Dick's Confectionery, $48.36, paying invoice No. 703 and Credit Note No. 707 less 99¢ cash discount.

–Cheque of W. Symons, $183.75, cash sale of $175 plus $8.75 sales tax.

Sales Invoices

–No. 710, to Haddy's Variety Store, $310 plus $15.50 sales tax, sale of merchandise.

–No. 711, to Harry's Cigarette Store, $307 plus $15.35 sales tax, sale of merchandise.

–No. 712, to Jim's Snack Bar, $767 plus $38.35 sales tax, sale of merchandise.

Credit Note Received

–From Paramount Tobacco, No. 1851, $52.50, dated Sept. 16; terms, adjusted to start from date of Credit Note; allowance on invoice No. 1756 for inferior merchandise.

Cheque Copy

–No. 453, to Winner Supplies, $51.45, paying invoice No. 1004 less $1.05 cash discount.

18 *Cash Receipts*

–Cheque of G.E.S. Smoke & Gift Shop, $658.56, paying invoice No. 708 less $13.44 cash discount.

–Cheque of M. D. Sundries, $787.18 paying invoice No. 709 less $16.07 cash discount.

Cheque Copies

–No. 454, to City Confections, $966, paying invoice No. 492 and Credit Note No. 540.

19 *Purchase Invoices*

–From Famous Candy Co., No. 719, $588, dated Sept. 18; terms, Net 30; for purchase of merchandise.

–From City Confections, No. 588, $105, dated Sept. 17; terms, Net 60; for purchase of merchandise.

–From Memory Novelties, No. 351, $210, dated Sept. 18; terms, 3/20,n/60; for purchase of merchandise.

19 *Cheque Copy*

–No. 455, to W. Symons, $15.75, cash refund for inferior goods, $15 plus 75¢ sales tax.

20 *Bank Debit Memo*

–From Cliffside Bank, $12.50, bank service charge.

21 *Cheque Copies*

–No. 456, to 'Cash', $256, wages for the week.

–No. 457, to T. O. Sprague, $200, personal drawings.

24 *Sales Invoices*

–No. 713, to Dick's Confectionery, $240 plus $12 sales tax, sale of merchandise.

–No. 714, to Howie's Sweets, $147 plus $7.35 sales tax, sale of merchandise.

25 No transactions.

26 *Purchase Invoice*

–From Winner Supplies, No. 1190, 78.75, dated Sept. 25; terms, 2/15,n/30; purchase of supplies.

27 *Cheque Copy*

–No. 458, to Winner Supplies, $149.20, paying invoice No. 1111 less $3.05 cash discount.

Cash Receipts

–Cheque of Jim's Snack Bar, $789.24, paying invoice No. 712 less $16.11 cash discount.

–Cheque of Harry's Cigarette Store, $315.90, paying invoice No. 711 less $6.45 cash discount.

28 *Purchase Invoice*

–From Paramount Tobacco, No. 1892, $199.50, dated Sept. 26; terms, Net 60; for merchandise purchased.

Cheque Copies

–No. 459, to 'Cash', $290, wages for the week.

–No. 460, to T. O. Sprague, $200, personal drawings.

–No. 461, to Petty Cash, $47.51; to replenish the fund for the following Summary of Charges:

Office Expense	$15.00
Maintenance Expense	18.42
Delivery Expense	14.09

INSTRUCTION 3.

(a) Balance the journals as necessary.

(b) Post the journals to the General Ledger.

(c) Balance the General Ledger and the two Subsidiary Ledgers.

Chapter 11

CASH AND BANKING ACTIVITIES

The word 'cash' is used in both a narrow and a broad sense. In its narrow sense, 'cash' means dollar bills and coins. In its broad sense, 'cash' includes not only dollar bills and coins but also cheques, bank balances, and certain other items such as money orders. In most cases, the context of the sentence will tell which of the two meanings is intended.

The acquisition of cash is a major pursuit of a business. The principal objective of a business is to earn a profit. But it is equally important to have this profit available in the form of cash. It is only in the form of cash that a business can use its profits to pay its bills, to meet its expenses, to give to the owners, and so on.

Because of its importance in business, there is usually a quantity of cash (in addition to Petty Cash) on hand in the office each day. For the most part, this cash is received from customers—either in the form of cheques sent through the mails to pay their accounts, or in the form of cash collected in a store or other retail outlet.

Internal Control

Cash is the single item most likely to be stolen outright by employees or to tempt employees to embezzle; that is, to steal money and to try to cover up the theft by falsifying the accounting records. This characteristic of cash leads us to another aspect of accounting called **Internal Control.**

Internal control has to do with the ability of the accounting system to compel the employees to be correct and to be honest. In very small businesses where the owner is able to exercise control personally, no internal control is necessary. But as soon as employees are brought into the business, internal control becomes a factor to be considered. And where there are numerous employees, internal control is essential. No matter that most employees are honest; it takes only one rogue or incompetent to give a business a serious headache, and sometimes one that leads to the death of the business through insolvency (inability of a business to pay its debts). It is too great a risk for a businessman to rely solely on the honesty and the ability of his employees. He is forced to administer accounting controls. A wise businessman will establish the best internal control that is practicable in his business.

The most important elements of good internal control are—
1. In preparing accounting records and documents the system, where possible, should be designed so that the work of one person must agree with the work of another person whose work is created independently.
2. The person whose function it is to record transactions or prepare accounting records should not also have the function of handling or controlling assets.
3. All assets should physically be kept in a safe place. For negotiable assets (those that can be easily converted into cash) it should be required that two authorized persons be present before access to the assets is allowed.
4. Powers of approval and authorization should be restricted to a few key employees.
5. Periodically, there should be an audit to ensure that the accounting system is being followed in the prescribed manner.

In this and future chapters, you will see various aspects of the total accounting system. Be alert to the elements of good internal control that are present.

Cash Registers

No doubt you are familiar with businesses that have a cash register. You are probably also aware that these are businesses that take in considerable amounts of cash, usually from the general public through retail outlets. However, unless you have had the opportunity to use a cash register, you probably know no more about it than the average customer. Let us then look at what a cash register can do for an owner or manager.

By visiting any sales office of a manufacturer of cash registers, you will quickly learn that there is a wide selection of cash registers to choose from. They are manufactured in a variety of models with capabilities ranging from simple to complex. They will not all be studied here. Only the basic features of an intermediate level machine will be considered.

A National Cash Register machine is shown on page 180; it is an intermediate level machine. For an owner or a manager it can do the following:

1. It provides a cash drawer in which money may be conveniently stored in an orderly way and in relative safety.
2. It displays the type and amount of the transaction in the glass window at the top of the machine. This is called the **Indication.** The displaying of this information in full view of the customer has the effect of discouraging dishonesty on the part of the cashier.
3. It provides for the customer an itemized receipt, often referred to as the Cash Register Slip.
4. If required, it prints the details of transactions on the customer's bill or sales slip which may be inserted in an opening in the machine.
5. It provides a detailed record of all transactions, stored internally on a continuous paper tape. This record is usually referred to as the 'Audit Strip' or in some cases the 'Sales Journal'. At the end of each day, the used portion of the paper tape audit strip is torn off, to be used for accounting purposes.
    A sample audit strip is shown above right. Observe the detailed information and the coding provided by the machine.

The audit strip may be locked inside the machine. A key, usually kept by the manager, is required to unlock the machine and gain access to the audit strip. This is an important control feature of the cash register.

6. At the end of each business day, as a result of certain cash register keys being depressed, it prints a summary of the totals for the day on the audit strip. As the total for each type of transaction is printed by the machine it is also displayed visibly in the Indication window. In this way the clerk operating the cash register can obtain the summary totals without gaining access to the audit strip.
    An example of an audit strip 'summary' is shown on the right.
    A very important control feature provided by the machine is that the summarizing operation cannot be performed unless a special key (Proprietor's Reset Key) is inserted into the machine. This key is usually kept in the custody of the manager, and as a result the totals are locked in the mechanism of the register until the manager wishes them to be released.
7. By means of 'activity counters', it provides a count of such things as the number of sales made by each clerk, the number of sales made by each department, and the total number of sales.
8. It permits the operator to sub-total the purchases for any one customer so that the sales tax may be ascertained from a tax schedule (attached to the machine using a piece of tape.) The amount of the sales tax may then be entered into the cash register and added on to the amount of the customer's purchases.

Using the Cash Register

It is not a purpose of this book to teach you the detailed operation of a cash register. That information may

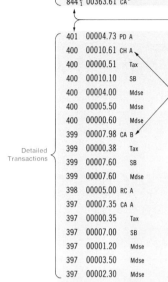

Cash Register Audit Slip

be obtained from the manufacturer. The objective here is to acquaint you with certain features of the machine that are essential to an understanding of cash register accounting.

At the beginning of each day, a quantity of money, called a **Change Fund**, is placed in the cash drawer of the cash register. This change fund is made up of a mixture of bills and coins and usually is in the amount of twenty or twenty-five dollars. It is customary to make it the same each day.

The simplest and most common type of transaction is the **Cash Sale**. With the cash sale, it is merely necessary for the clerk to record into the cash register the amounts of the individual items purchased, take a sub-total, add in the sales tax, code the transaction 'cash' by depressing the 'cash' key, and take a final total. (**Note:** When some of the items are taxable and some are non-taxable, a variation of this procedure is necessary.) The cash received from the customer is placed in the cash drawer. Transaction No. 397 on the audit strip shown on page 180 is a good example of this type of transaction. (Observe that the audit strip must be read from bottom to top.)

In addition to recording the transaction through the cash register, a **Charge Sale** requires the preparation of a sales slip similar to the one directly below. The sales slip is made out in duplicate; the original is for the customer; the copy is used as the source document for a debit entry to the Accounts Receivable Ledger. The procedure, which may vary from system to system, is approximately as follows:

1. Prepare the sales slip in duplicate.
2. Enter each of the items purchased in the cash register.
3. Take a subtotal.
4. Add on the sales tax.
5. Place the sales slip in the slip printer device of the machine.
6. Take a total, using the 'charge' key; details of the transaction are printed at the top of the sales slip (see example below).
7. Give original of sales slip to customer.

8. Place copy of sales slip in cash drawer for posting to customer's account.

Note:

No money is received as a part of a charge sale transaction. On the audit strip on page 180 transaction No. 400 illustrates a charge sale.

The procedure for recording a **Receipt on Account** is approximately as follows:

1. Prepare a sales slip such as the one directly below in duplicate.
2. Place the sales slip in the slip printer, so that it will be register printed.
3. Enter the amount of the transaction in the cash register; code the transaction 'received'; press the 'Total' key.
4. Give the Original of the sales slip to the customer.
5. Place the copy of the sales slip in the cash register drawer for posting to the customer's account.
6. Place the money received in the cash drawer.

See transaction No. 398 on the audit strip shown on page 180.

In stores having a cash register it is generally not customary to have a Petty Cash Fund. Small expenditures that would normally be paid out of a Petty Cash Fund can be paid out of the cash register. The procedure for recording a **Paid Out** is approximately as follows:

1. Obtain a bill or voucher for the expenditure to be made. If the expenditure is for goods or services, the supplier's sales invoice must be obtained. However, if the expenditure is for a sales refund, it will be necessary to prepare a sales slip form in the manner shown directly below.
   Observe that it is necessary to show the amount of the sales tax.
2. Place the bill or sales slip in the printer so that it will be register printed.
3. Enter the amount of the transaction in the cash register; code it 'Paid Out'; press the 'Total' key.
4. Pay out the required sum of money.
5. Place the bill or sales slip in the cash register drawer to be used later for accounting purposes.

See transaction No. 401 on the audit strip.

---

16 SEP 68   400   10.61   CH A

OXFORD DRUG STORE

Date _March 5, 19—_

Name _a. Klein_

Address _55 Lamb Avenue_

1	Roué marker		60
1	P40 film	5	50
1	Ace Salve	4	00
		10	10
	Tax		51
		10	61

---

16 SEP 68   398   05.00   RC A

OXFORD DRUG STORE

Date _March 7, 19—_

Name _Mrs. J. Watson_

Address _37 Kirkdale Road_

Received on a/c	5	—

---

16 SEP 68   401   04.73   PD A

OXFORD DRUG STORE

Date _March 17, 19—_

Name _Mr. P. Carlisle_

Address _85 Birch Place_

	Cash Refund for		
1	Pair Sunglasses	4	50
	Tax		23
		4	73

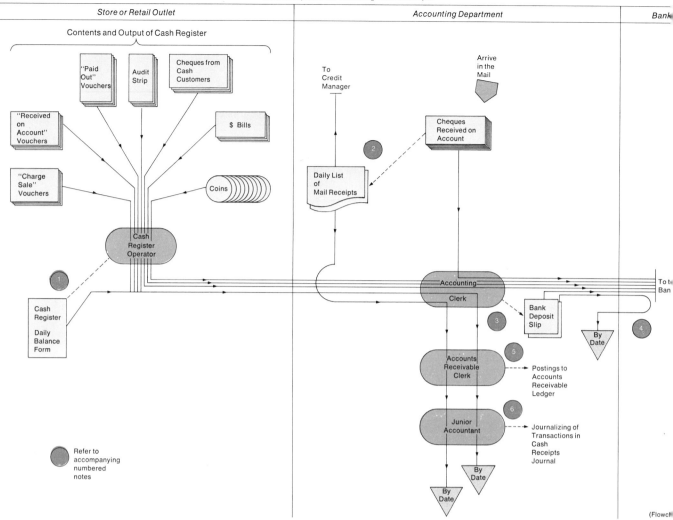

Basic Cash Receipts System

The flowchart above and its explanatory notes describe a basic system for handling and recording cash register receipts and mail receipts.

this text. In actual practice, you will find a variety of designs and form names in use.

The steps required to prepare this form are as follows:
(a) Obtain the cash register summary totals from the cash register using the

Proprietor's Reset Key. The cash Register system used here produces the type of summary shown on page 180 and explained below:
(b) On the Cash Register Daily Balance Form, write

NOTES TO FLOWCHART #6

(1) **End-of-Day Procedure–Cash Register Operator**. At the end of each business day, the operator of each cash register must count the cash in the register and prepare a summary of the day's activity on a form to be used by the accounting department. In this text, the form shown on page 183 is used; it is called a Cash Register Daily Balance Form and is designed especially for students using

SUMMARY FIGURES		EXPLANATION
34.29	TAX	The total sales tax on all sales.
688.86	MDSE	The total sales figure, for both charge sales and cash sales, but not including sales tax.
16.90	PO	The total cash paid out, for which there should be equivalent vouchers in the cash register drawer.
91.50	RC	The total cash received on account from customers for which there should be equivalent vouchers in the drawer.
359.54	CH	The total charge sales including sales tax, for which there should be equivalent vouchers in the drawer.
363.61	CA	The total cash sales including sales tax.

in the six totals from the audit strip summary. The appropriate places on the Daily Balance Form are marked with an asterisk, (*). It is not difficult to decide where each total goes.

(c) (i) Remove the cash and vouchers from the cash register drawer;

(ii) Separate the cash from the vouchers and sort the vouchers into three groups: PO's; RC's; and CH's. For each of these three groups, see that the total of the vouchers agrees with the figure shown on the audit strip summary;

(iii) Count out (in the desired mixture) the amount of the change fund with which the day was started. Put it in a safe place overnight. It will be used to begin business on the next business day.

(iv) Count the remaining cash (be sure to double check) and record the amount on line 6 of the Daily Balance Form.

(v) Complete the 'Summary of Cash' portion of the form.

Note:

If line 5 is greater than line 6, there will be a cash shortage; if line 5 is less than line 6, there will be a cash overage; if line 5 is equal to line 6, there will be neither an overage nor a shortage.

(d) Analyse the Paid Out vouchers and complete the 'Breakdown of Paid Outs' portion of the Daily Balance Form.

CASH REGISTER   DAILY BALANCE FORM   DATE *September 16* 19—

SUMMARY OF CASH

Cash Sales Total *	363 61'	1
Received on Account Total *	91 50	2
Add	455 11	3
Less: Paid Out Total *	16 90	4
Total Cash Called For	438 21	5
Actual Cash in Drawer	435 21	6
Cash Short	3 00	7
Cash Over		8

BREAKDOWN OF PAID OUTS

Cash Refunds - Merchandise	4 50	9
- Sales Tax	23	10
Total Refunds	4 73	11
Other a/c's - *Misc. Exp.*	7 50	12
- *Supplies*	4 67	13
-		14
Paid Out Total 4	16 90	15

SUMMARY OF SALES

Merchandise Total *	688 86	16
Less: Merchandise Refunded 9	4 50	17
Net Sales	684 36	18

SUMMARY OF SALES TAX PAYABLE

Sales Tax Total *	34 29	19
Less: Sales Tax on Refunds 10	23	20
Net Sales Tax Payable	34 06	21

ACCOUNTING SUMMARY

		DEBIT	CREDIT
DEBITS: Bank	6	435 21	
Acc's Rec'l (Charge Sales) *		359 54	
Other a/c's - *Misc. Exp.* 12		7 50	
- *Supplies* 13		4 67	
- 14			
Cash Short and Over	7	3 00	
CREDITS: Accounts Receivable	2		91 50
Sales	18		684 36
Sales Tax Payable	21		34 06
Cash Short and Over	8		
BALANCING TOTALS		809 92	809 92

* Pick up from Audit Strip Summary

Clerk *M Fowler*

(e) Complete the 'Summary of Sales' portion and the 'Summary of Sales Tax Payable' portion of the Daily Balance Form. Observe that the figure to be entered on line 17 is obtained from line 9, and the figure to be entered on line 20 is obtained from line 10 and so on. This is a technique used throughout the form.

(f) Complete the 'Accounting Summary' portion of the Daily Balance Form. The two balancing totals must agree if the work has been done correctly.

(g) Date and sign the Cash Register Daily Balance Form and deliver it to the accounting department together with the money and the three groups of vouchers.

CASH SHORT AND OVER. Businesses that deal with the general public for cash are subject to cash shortages and overages due to errors made by their clerks. The way in which a shortage or overage is calculated has just been shown to you in the preceding section.

It is the policy of some businesses to hold their clerks responsible for shortages and overages. That is, the clerks may keep any overages, but must make up any shortages out of their own pockets. In such a business, it is not necessary to record the shortages or overages in the books of account.

Other businesses take a more liberal attitude and accept the shortages and overages themselves. In this type of business, it is necessary to record the overages and shortages in the books of account. During the accounting period, they are accumulated in an account called 'Cash Short and Over'. The shortages go into the account as debits since they are losses or decreases in equity. The overages go in as credits since they are gains or increases in equity. At any particular time the balance in the account will represent either expense or income depending on whether it has a debit balance or a credit balance. A debit balance means that the shortages have exceeded the overages and a credit balance means that the overages have exceeded the shortages.

(2) Each day a list is prepared of the cheques that arrive in the day's mail. It is necessary to prepare the list because the cheques themselves cannot be kept but must be deposited in the bank. The listing is illustrated below.

arrived this clerk will prepare the bank deposit by performing the steps below. As you read these steps, refer to the sample deposit slip shown below.

(Courtesy of The Toronto-Dominion Bank)

(a) Obtain a bank deposit slip form (to be prepared in duplicate by using carbon paper). A supply of these forms is usually kept in the office.

(b) Count the currency by the various denominations and write the number of each type of bill and the corresponding value on the bank deposit slip in the appropriate spaces.

(c) Count the coin and write the total amount in the proper space on the bank deposit slip. Coins should be wrapped in coin wrappers if there are sufficient quantities. (50 pennies; 40 nickels; 50 dimes; 40 quarters.)

(d) Examine the cheques from customers to ensure that they have been made out properly. Then endorse each cheque on the reverse side.

Oxford Drug Store
Cash Receipts
Sept. 16, 19—

Customer	Cheque Date	Invoice Number	Amount
P. Bourne	Sept. 14	3154	$ 64.10
R. Walsh	Sept. 15	—	75.00
			$139.10

Daily List of Cash Receipts

(3) The preparation of the bank deposit is an important duty in a business office and is entrusted to an experienced employee. The flowchart on page 182 shows the cash, cheques, and the supporting documents being channeled to the desk of this clerk. After they have all

Note:
Although there are a number of different ways to endorse a cheque, businesses usually just rubber stamp them in the manner shown below.

FOR DEPOSIT ONLY
TO THE CREDIT OF
WILBY SALES LIMITED

FOR DEPOSIT ONLY
TO THE CREDIT OF
DR. J. P. SMITH

When the depositor deposits a cheque, he gets money (in the form of an increase in his bank balance) in return from the bank. By endorsing the cheque he is guaranteeing it. If for any reason the cheque is not good, the depositor has agreed to repay the bank.

(e) List the cheques by name and amount in the appropriate section of the deposit slip. Total the cheques and transfer the totals as indicated on the slip. Complete the deposit slip except for the exchange calculation which is best left to the teller at the bank. Ask him to collect the exchange once a month by means of a Bank Debit Memo; this is the simplest way.

(f) See that the deposit slip total is equal to the sum of (1) the Daily List of Mail Receipts, plus (2) the Cash Register Daily Balance Form (line 6).

(4) The cash, cheques, and the deposit slip are placed in an envelope or cloth bag to be taken to the bank. This is done daily, as it is dangerous to keep any sizable sum of money on the premises. Deposits may now be taken to the bank even after banking hours by using what is called 'night depository'.

The bank's clerk will check the accuracy of the deposit slip preparation. If he finds it in order he will place the bank's stamp on all copies of the deposit slip. One copy will be returned to the business where it is filed in the accounting department.

If all is not found to be in order the bank will not process the deposit until the matter is discussed and corrected.

(5) From the listing of mail receipts and the cash register vouchers that arrive on her desk the accounts receivable clerk posts to the Accounts Receivable Ledger as necessary.

(a) Each cash register 'Charge Sale' voucher requires a debit posting to a customer's account.

(b) Each cash register 'Received on Account' voucher requires a credit posting to a customer's account.

(c) Each receipt from a customer listed on the Daily List of Mail Receipts requires a credit posting to a customer's account.

As each posting is completed a checkmark or the clerk's initials must be placed on the voucher or list, usually beside the amount that was posted. The cash register vouchers are then stapled to the Cash Register Daily Balance Form.

(6) It is the responsibility of the junior accountant to record the accounting entries for each of the two types of cash receipts.

(a) *Mail Receipts.* The source document for mail receipts is the Daily List of Mail Receipts. The necessary accounting entry is recorded in the Cash Receipts Journal. This entry may be written in detail, showing the receipt from each customer separately, as in Example A shown below, or it may be written in summary form showing only the totals, as in Example B below. When the latter method is used and it is found necessary to check back on a transaction, one must refer to the mail receipts lists for the detailed information. These are kept on file.

(b) *Cash Register Receipts.* The accounting entry to record the cash register receipts is picked up directly from the 'Accounting Summary' section of the Cash Register Daily Balance Form. The data is merely transferred from the Daily Balance form to the Cash Receipts Journal as shown in the following illustration of the journalizing required for the Daily Balance Form on page 183.

Example A—Detailed Entry

Example B—Summary Entry

Cash Receipts Journal

Observe:

1. The circled amounts in Credit columns are treated as debits when totaling a column or when posting.
2. The amount of deposit, $574.31 includes both the mail receipts and the cash register receipts.
3. If it is necessary to check back on any individual receipt, it will have to be done by referring back to the individual vouchers attached to the Daily Balance form.
4. Postings to customers' accounts will be made directly from the cash register vouchers.

The Banking Relationship

The relationship between a bank and a business (depositor) was explained in a previous chapter (see page 129). Several important facts about this relationship were pointed out. You were told that both the bank and the business are obliged to keep track of the business' money kept on deposit at the bank. You were also told that the record prepared by the bank appears to be the opposite of the record prepared by the business. This is so because the business considers the money to be an asset whereas the bank considers it to be a liability. Also, you have learned that most of the transactions affecting the bank balance are originated by the business—through the making of deposits and the issuing of cheques. And, whenever the bank finds it necessary to originate an entry to its customer's account, it informs him promptly by sending a debit memo or a credit memo.

Current Bank Account

A bank provides various types of deposit accounts to meet the special needs of its customers. Especially for businesses, it provides the 'current' bank account. The special features of a current bank account are—

1. No interest is allowed on the account balance (as there is on a 'savings' account).
2. Once a month the bank sends to the depositor a copy of all Debit and Credit Memos issued during the month and all of the cheques cashed during the month. These cheques are known as the 'paid' cheques.
3. Once a month, also, the bank sends to the depositor a carbon copy of its ledger account for

him. This form is known as the Bank Statement and is illustrated below.

4. The service charge required for the cashing and handling of cheques is left to the discretion of the bank manager. His decision is affected by such things as the number of cheques cashed, the average bank balance, the amount of any bank loan, and so on.

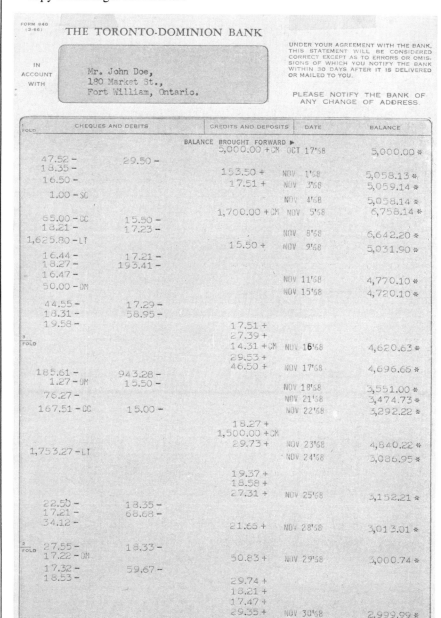

Bank Statement (Courtesy of The Toronto-Dominion Bank)

Bank Reconciliation

Since both the bank and the business keep track of the same funds, you might expect that the month-end balance shown by the Bank Statement would agree with the month-end balance shown by the General Ledger bank account. However, this is rarely the case. Usually, when the Bank Statement is received, it is found to have a different 'balance' than the General Ledger Bank account.

Since the Bank Statement usually shows a balance that is different from the Bank account in the General Ledger, how can the accountant be certain that either record is correct? He accomplishes this by 'reconciling the bank account'. At the end of each month, he conducts a thorough investigation of the two sets of records in order to ascertain precisely the reasons for the difference. When this is done, he then formally documents the evidence by preparing a Bank Reconciliation Statement.

An example of a Bank Reconciliation Statement is as shown on the right.

STEPS IN RECONCILING A BANK ACCOUNT

The steps in reconciling a bank account are:

(1) Have the following records available: (a) the Bank Statement and related vouchers received from the bank; (b) the Bank Reconciliation Statement for the previous month end; (c) the General Ledger, the Cash Receipts Journal, the Cash Payments Journal, and the General Journal.

(2) On proper paper, write the heading of the Bank Reconciliation Statement.

(3) On one side of the page, enter the Balance per Bank Statement figure, which will be the final amount in the 'balance' column of the Bank Statement.

Coxwell and Company Bank Reconciliation Statement March 31, 19—					
Balance per Bank Statement	1 204	90	Balance per General Ledger	1 147	76
Add:			Deduct:		
Outstanding Deposit	300	51	Amount of error in		
	1 505	41	recording cheque #697		
			Was recorded as $5.60		
Deduct:			Should have been $6.50		
Outstanding Cheques			Difference 90¢		90
#702 $60.00				1 146	86
#705 72.40					
#709 51.90			Deduct:		
#710 175.00			Bank Service Charges		
#711 2.75	362	05	deducted on bank		
			statement but not		
			recorded in company		
			books in same month		3 50
True Balance	1 143	36	True Balance	1 143	36

On the other side of the page, enter the Balance per General Ledger figure, which will be the final balance in the Bank account (after the General Ledger is posted and balanced).

(4) Search for the items causing the difference between the two balances. This is the most difficult and most important part of a reconciliation. It involves comparing in detail the bank's record against the business' record. You are looking for items that are not recorded equally in both records. Techniques for doing this are explained more fully below in the section headed 'Locating the Items of Disagreement'.

(5) Record the items of disagreement on the Reconciliation Statement, adding or subtracting them as is necessary until the two balances are shown to be equal. This step is explained in detail on page 188 in the section headed 'Recording the Items of Disagreement'. You cannot consider the job completed until the point of balance is reached.

(6) Record in the books of the business the items of disagreement that are listed on the General Ledger side of the Reconciliation Statement. These represent items that have already been recorded by the bank and which must also be recorded by the business.

LOCATING THE ITEMS OF DISAGREEMENT

Locating the items of disagreement usually requires a well-organized and skilful approach. Truly, experience is the best teacher. The general suggestions given below will be of help to you but the actual experience of solving the problems at the end of the chapter will benefit you the most.

1. When comparing the two sets of records, it is never necessary to go back in the books beyond one month. Any differences that occurred before then will be listed on the previous Reconciliation Statement.

2. The bank's record must be compared in detail against the business' record. When items are found to correspond exactly, they are marked in some way with a coloured pencil. After the comparison is over, the items without

the coloured marks are the significant ones. They are the items of disagreement.

3. The most common source of disagreement between the two sets of records is the quantity of uncashed cheques commonly known as the 'outstanding cheques'. When a cheques is issued by a business, it is recorded promptly in the books of the business, but it is not recorded in the records of the bank until the time it is cashed. In many cases, this is after some time has elapsed.

4. A less frequently occurring but fairly common source of disagreement between the two records is the 'outstanding deposit'. An outstanding deposit is one that is recorded in the books of the business during a certain month but which is not deposited in the bank until the following month. This usually occurs on the last day of the month in businesses that have a one-day delay in the depositing of cash receipts. (The outstanding deposit will appear on the bank statement of the following month, usually as the first item in the Deposit column.)

5. There are numerous other possible items of disagreement. One of these would be an error made by either a bank employee or a company employee. Another would be a bank service charge that has not yet been recorded in the books of the company.

6. When comparing the records, it is important not to forget the items of disagreement that appear on the previous Reconciliation Statement. During the current month, most of these items will cease to be items of disagreement. For example, an outstanding cheque on the April 30 Reconciliation Statement, if cashed during the month of May, will not be an item of disagreement on the May 31 Reconciliation Statement.

Some items, however, may not be cleared up in the current month and will have to be carried forward to the new reconciliation. For example, an outstanding cheque appearing on the April reconciliation, if not cashed during the month of May, will continue to be outstanding and must appear also on the May reconciliation.

RECORDING THE ITEMS OF DISAGREEMENT

The items of disagreement must be recorded on the Bank Reconciliation Statement.

1. All items of disagreement must be included. It is often advisable to group items of a similar nature, e.g., outstanding cheques.

2. Each item must be recorded on one side of the Reconciliation Statement only; that is, either on the Bank Statement side or on the General Ledger side. You must follow this rule: Choose the side where the item has not been seen or recorded as of the reconciliation date. For example, an outstanding cheque, because it represents an item not seen by the bank, would be recorded on the Bank Statement side. Similarly, an outstanding bank service charge, because it represents an item not recorded in the company records, would be entered on the General Ledger side.

3. Each item represents either an increase or a decrease to the balance. Your common sense should tell you which it is. Just decide what effect the item has on the bank balance and act accordingly. For example, cheques and service charges represent decreases to the bank balance and are therefore treated as deductions on the reconciliation. Similarly, deposits increase the bank balance and are therefore treated as additions on the reconciliation.

4. If all of the items of disagreement are found and entered correctly, the two sides of the Reconciliation Statement should balance. If not, then it will be necessary for you to repeat the process. The differences must be found.

Bookkeeping and Accounting Terms

Internal Control: An accounting technique of designing the accounting system in a way that fosters the accuracy of the records and the honesty of the employees. This is achieved primarily by the agreement of one person's work with the work prepared independently by another person.

Current Bank Account: A type of deposit account and related service provided by the bank specifically to meet the needs of businesses.

Bank Reconciliation: A routine procedure to ascertain the reasons for the difference between the balance on deposit as shown by the bank and the balance on deposit as shown by the business or individual.

1. The word 'cash' is used in both a narrow and a broad sense. Explain.
2. Briefly, what is 'internal control'?
3. In very small businesses, why are accounting controls usually not necessary?
4. At what stage in the development of a business, is it necessary to introduce some accounting controls?
5. Name the first element of internal control.
6. What is the purpose of the cash register 'indication' window?
7. Explain the purpose of the cash register slip.
8. Briefly, what is the 'audit strip'?
9. What accounting controls are provided by the cash register?
10. How does a cash register assist the operator in the calculating of sales tax?
11. What information is printed on the 'daily summary' section of the audit strip?
12. List four types of transactions that can be handled by means of a cash register.
13. Briefly describe the balancing procedure of the cash register operator.
14. What is the purpose of the Cash Receipts Daily Balance Form?
15. Explain how the cash register change fund works.
16. Give the accounting entry for a cash shortage of $5.
17. Who prepares the bank deposit slip?
18. Give an example of the most common type of endorsement used by businesses.
19. What is the purpose of endorsing a cheque?
20. What are the source documents for the accounting entries for cash receipts?
21. Name a special feature of a current bank account.
22. Explain briefly the need for reconciling a bank account.
23. What is an outstanding cheque? an outstanding deposit?
24. Why is it necessary to prepare a bank reconciliation statement?

Exercises

1. Miss Murphy is a cash register operator at Loew's Book Supply. At the end of the March 20 business day the contents of her cash register are as follows:

(a) *Dollar Bills* – $20 × 6
   – $10 × 14
   – $5 × 6
   – $2 × 14
   – $1 × 78
(b) *Coin* – $8.19
(c) *'Paid Out' Vouchers*
   (i) A bill for the cash purchase of supplies, $6.90,
   (ii) A cash refund for $10.50, including 50¢ sales tax,

(d) *'Received' Vouchers*
   (i) R. B. Morrow– $75.00
   (ii) J. N. Perroux– $50.00
   (iii) M. Rogers–$50.00
(e) *'Charge' Vouchers*
   (i) B. Anderson–$57.75
   (ii) M. N. Brown– $18.38
   (iii) C. Carter–$97.60
   (iv) O. Orville–$78.54
   (v) A. Farrow–$52.45

The summary of the day's transactions as shown by the cash register audit strip is as follows:

Tax	$ 25.32
Mdse	506.24
PO	17.40
RC	175.00
CH	304.72
CA	226.84

The amount of the change fund given to Miss Murphy at the beginning of each day is $20. At the end of each day, $20 is taken out of the contents of the cash drawer to be used to start with on the next business day. On this particular day Miss Murphy removes $8 in coin and 12 one-dollar bills.

INSTRUCTION.

Prepare the Cash Register Daily Balance Form.

---

2. You are a clerk at Loew's Book Supply. One of your duties is the preparation of the bank deposit. Each day you receive (a) a copy of the Daily List of Mail Receipts together with the customers' cheques, and (b) the Cash Register Daily Balance Form together with the related vouchers.

On March 20, you receive the Cash Register Daily Balance Form and the related vouchers of exercise 1. You also receive the Daily List of Mail Receipts shown below together with the accompanying cheques.

Loew's Book Supply
Daily List of Mail Receipts
March 20, 19—

J. Stinson	on account	$ 50.00
W. Walker	on account	100.00
		$150.00

INSTRUCTION.

Prepare the deposit slip for the cash receipts of Loew's Book Supply for March 20.

---

3. As the junior accountant for Loew's Book Supply, record the accounting entries for exercises 1 and 2 in the Cash Receipts Journal.

---

4. On the next business day the contents of Miss Murphy's cash register are:

(a) *Currency*

$20 × 10	
$10 × 9	
$5 × 11	
$2 × 31	
$1 × 5	

Cheque from J. Gorman $10.00

(b) *Coin* $19.38

(c) *'Paid Out' Vouchers*

(i)	Cash Purchase of Supplies	$ 4.50
(ii)	Cash Payment for delivery charges	2.50
(iii)	Cash Refund including 30¢ sales tax	6.25
(iv)	Cash Refund including 78¢ sales tax	16.28
		$29.53

(d) *'Received' Vouchers*

(i)	P. Tilson	$37.50
(ii)	D. Wilson	19.25
		$56.75

(e) *'Charge' Vouchers*

(i)	C. Cox	$ 63.00
(ii)	T. Franks	147.00
(iii)	M. Nelson	26.25
(iv)	G. Tutt	73.50
		$309.75

The summary of the day's transactions as shown by the audit strip is:

Tax	$ 33.46
Mdse	669.20
PO	29.53
RC	56.75
CH	309.75
CA	392.91

INSTRUCTION.

Prepare the Cash Register Daily Balance Form.

5. If Miss Murphy keeps $10 in coin, 4 two-dollar bills, and 2 one-dollar bills to make up her change fund for the next day, and if there are no mail receipts, prepare the bank deposit slip for March 21.

6. Journalize the cash receipts for March 21.

7. The following is a summary of the Accounts Receivable Ledger of Select Sales Company on June 1, 19—.

Customer	Address	Sales Slip	Amount	Balance
P. J. Carey	88 Kenneth Ave.	141		$ 48.30
M. P. Dewar	94 Belair Drive	151		105.00
D. E. Gale	400 Brewster Street	147		89.25
R. B. Hancock	41 Bisher Avenue	146		31.50
F. Lipton	900 Mandor Drive	99		42.00
G. McDonald	102 Mid-Land Blvd.	96	$21.00	
		157	52.50	73.50
W. Pimm	16 Brent Road	132		63.00
F. Slater	12 Hastings Avenue	104	$15.75	
		125	26.25	
		162	94.50	136.50
				$589.05

INSTRUCTION 1.

Set up the Accounts Receivable Ledger of Select Sales Company as of June 1.

INSTRUCTION 2.

From the following transactions post to the Subsidiary Ledger accounts as required. The system adopted by Select Sales Company is that of posting directly from the source documents to the Subsidiary Ledgers.

Transactions

June
2 *Partial Cash Register Daily Balance Form*

ACCOUNTING SUMMARY		DEBIT	CREDIT
DEBITS:Bank	6	641 15	
Acc's Rec'l (Charge Sales)*		347 55	
Other a/c's -	12		
-	13		
-	14		
Cash Short and Over	7	1 00	
CREDITS:Accounts Receivable	2		195 30
Sales	18		756 50
Sales Tax Payable	21		37 90
Cash Short and Over	8		
BALANCING TOTALS		989 70	989 70

'Charge' Vouchers

Sales Slip 163	P. J. Carey		$ 47.25
Sales Slip 164	W. Pimm		65.10
Sales Slip 165	D. E. Gale		119.70
Sales Slip 166	M. P. Dewar		115.50
			$347.55

'Received' Vouchers

On Sales Slip 167 from P. J. Carey	Re 141	$ 48.30
On Sales Slip 168 from F. Slater	Re 104, 125	42.00
On Sales Slip 169 from M. P. Dewar	Re 151	105.00
		$195.30

2 *Daily List of Mail Receipts*

Cheque from R. B. Hancock Paying Sales Slip 146 $31.50

3 *Partial Cash Register Daily Balance Form*

ACCOUNTING SUMMARY		DEBIT		CREDIT	
DEBITS:Bank	6	373	25		
Acc's Rec'l (Charge Sales)*		194	25		
Other a/c's -	12	10	00		
-	13				
-	14				
Cash Short and Over	7				
CREDITS:Accounts Receivable	2			94	50
Sales	18			460	00
Sales Tax Payable	21			23	00
Cash Short and Over	8				
BALANCING TOTALS		577	50	577	50

'Charge' Vouchers

Sales Slip 170	F. Lipton	$78.75
Sales Slip 171	G. McDonald	115.50
		$194.25

'Received' Vouchers

On Sales Slip 172   from F. Slater   Re 162 $94.50

4 *Partial Cash Register Daily Balance Form*

ACCOUNTING SUMMARY		DEBIT		CREDIT	
DEBITS:Bank	6	466	35		
Acc's Rec'l (Charge Sales)*		135	50		
Other a/c's -	12				
-	13				
-	14				
Cash Short and Over	7				
CREDITS:Accounts Receivable	2			63	00
Sales	18			512	00
Sales Tax Payable	21			25	60
Cash Short and Over	8			1	25
BALANCING TOTALS		601	85	601	85

'Charge' Vouchers

Sales Slip 173	F. Slater	$ 52.50
Sales Slip 174	W. Pimm	83.00
		$135.50

'Received' Vouchers

On Sales Slip 175   from W. Pimm   re 132 $63.00

4 *Daily List of Mail Receipts*

Cheque From F. Lipton	Paying Sales Slip 99	$42.00
Cheque from G. McDonald	Paying Sales Slip 96	21.00
		$63.00

INSTRUCTION 3.

Prepare a Subsidiary Ledger trial balance as of June 4.

---

8. The Bank account in the General Ledger of J. C. Waters shows a balance of $1,267.91 DR. at March 31, 19—. On that same date, the bank statement shows a balance of $672.88 CR. The following items were found to be the items of difference.

(a) Outstanding deposit of $516.13.

(b) Outstanding cheques of $112.40, $70.23, $16.21, and $19.40.

(c) A cheque of $166.20 which had been cashed by the bank but which had mistakenly not been recorded in the Cash Payments Journal.

(d) A cheque of $29.06 which had been cashed by the bank for $29.60 and charged by them as $29.60.

(e) Bank Service charge of $1.40 recorded on the bank statement on the last day of the month.

(f) An N. S. F. cheque for $129 shown on the bank statement on the last day of the month.

INSTRUCTION 1.

Prepare a bank reconciliation statement.

INSTRUCTION 2.

In General Journal Form, show the journal entries required in the books of the company.

9. Shown below, are all of the records that you will need to reconcile the current bank account of Proctor & Kemp at July 31, 19—.

Note:
Normally the bank returns the 'paid' cheques to the customer along with the Bank Statement. It is not feasible to do this in a textbook. Instead, an explanation is given on the Bank Statement in brackets beside the amount of each cheque.

(a) Bank Reconciliation Statement for the previous month end.

Proctor & Kemp
Bank Reconciliation Statement
June 30, 19—

Balance per Bank Statement		1 406 03	Balance per General Ledger		773 28
Add: Outstanding Deposit		551 00	Deduct: Bank Charges		
		1 957 03	not entered in books		
Deduct: Outstanding Cheques			of company		
#83	$5.10		(1) Service Charge $16.50		
780	71.03		(2) Loan Interest 33.50		50 00
828	400.00				
846	96.02				
852	123.50				
860	15.00				
871	16.01				
873	17.50				
881	33.60				
886	121.47				
889	60.00				
890	170.00				
891	31.94				
892	27.61				
894	13.82				
898	12.50				
899	18.65	1 233 75			
True Balance		723 28	True Balance		723 28

(b) 'Amount of Deposits' column of Cash Receipts Journal for July, Page 14.

262.75
312.70
274.19
161.40
700.20
265.92
400.61
396.21
316.40
_____
3,090.38
=======

194

(c) Excerpts from Cash Payments Journal for July, Page 18.

Explanation	Chq. No.	Bank Credit
	900	100.00
	901	171.31
	902	142.19
Loan Interest June		33.50
Service Charge June		16.50
	903	16.41
	904	17.50
	905	10.00
	906	12.40
	907	19.61
	908	31.40
	909	76.39
	910	65.20
	911	500.00
	912	216.75
	914	8.21
	915	2.60
	916	9.40
	917	50.00
	918	50.00
	919	33.19
	920	29.33
	921	65.00
	922	25.00
	923	25.00
	924	419.63
	925	372.60
	926	900.00
		3,419.12

(d) July General Journal entry affecting 'Bank', Page 9.

Bank	5.10	
Miscellaneous Income		5.10
To cancel outstanding cheque		
No. 83 issued June 19—		

(e) Partial General Ledger 'Bank' account.

	BANK					No.1	
DATE	PARTICULARS	P.R.	DEBIT	CREDIT	BALANCE	DR CR
19--						
June 30					773.28	DR
July 31		CR14	3090.38			
31		CP18		3419.12		
31		J9	5.10		449.64	DR

CHEQUES				DEPOSITS	DATE	BALANCE
					June 30	1,406.03
18.65	(899)	31.94	(891)	551.00	July 2	1,906.44
121.47	(886)				3	1,784.97
100.00	(900)	96.02	(846)	262.75	5	1,851.70
12.50	(898)				5	1,839.20
71.03	(780)	27.61	(892)		6	1,740.56
142.19	(902)				6	1,598.37
400.00	(828)			312.70	8	1,511.07
15.00	(860)	13.82	(894)		9	1,482.25
16.01	(871)	171.31	(901)		10	1,294.93
17.50	(904)				10	1,277.43
10.00	(905)			274.19	11	1,541.62
500.00	(911)				12	1,041.62
33.60	(N.S.F. cheque of R.C. Jones)			161.40	15	1,169.42
50.00	(913)				16	1,119.42
170.00	(890)	12.40	(906)		17	937.02
76.39	(909)				19	860.63
31.40	(908)			700.20	22	1,529.43
9.40	(916)	19.61	(907)		23	1,500.42
2.60	(915)				23	1,497.82
				265.92	25	1,763.74
				400.61	26	2,131.16
33.19	(919)				27	2,113.66
17.50	(873)			396.21	30	2,459.87
50.00	(917)				31	2,015.24
25.00	(922)	419.63	(924)		31	1,850.24
165.00	(Promissory Note paid to Arno Bros.)				31	1,850.24
29.00	(Interest on Loan)				31	1,821.24
12.60	(Service Charge)				31	1,808.64

(f) July Bank Statement.

INSTRUCTION.

Reconcile the bank and make the necessary accounting entries in the books of the company

---

10. From the following records, reconcile the bank account of Baker and Baker as of April 30, 19—.

Baker and Baker
Bank Reconciliation Statement
March 31, 19—

			Balance per General Ledger		305 08
Balance per Bank Statement	943 80				
Add: Outstanding Deposit	216 50				
	1 160 30				
Deduct: Outstanding Cheques					
#1207 $23.01					
#1361 14.16					
#1390 17.50					
#1406 36.71					
#1409 19.40					
#1415 141.72					
#1420 13.16					
#1425 51.61					
#1426 36.44					
#1428 18.19					
#1431 76.42					
#1432 19.36					
#1433 14.40					
#1434 85.19					
#1435 19.65					
#1436 116.40					
#1438 78.90					
#1439 25.00					
#1440 50.00	857 22				
	303 08				
Add: Correction of bank error					
Cheque #1416 for $10.00 was cashed for $12.00 and charged to account for $12.00	2 00				
True Balance	305 08		True Balance		305 08

(a) Previous Bank Reconciliation Statement.

Date		Chq. No.				Bank CR
19-- APRIL	1	1441				75.92
	2	1442				80.00
	2	1443				120.00
	4	1444				33.71
	5	1445				10.00
	8	1446				17.50
	9	1447				20.10
	9	1448				10.00
	9	1449				125.00
	10	1450				300.00
	11	1451				14.77
	12	1452				84.33
	15	1453				19.06
	15	1454				69.50
	15	1455				20.00
	16	1456				5.61
	18	1457				3.20
	19	1458				42.75
	20	1459				41.00
	20	1460				18.30
	23	1461				19.00
	23	1462				80.00
	24	1463				100.00
	24	1464				64.70
	25	1465				30.00
	26	1466				10.00
	27	1467				4.50
	27	1468				3.50
	27	1469				12.00
	30	1470				19.00
	30	1471				36.00
	30	1472				7.85
						1497.30

(b) Partial Cash Payments Journal for April, Page 17.

April	4	216.50
	10	171.41
	15	94.80
	20	156.80
	24	363.85
	27	410.00
	30	94.00
		1507.36

(c) 'Amount of Deposit' column of Cash Receipts Journal for April, Page 8.

(d) April General Journal entry affecting 'Bank', Page 9.

Bank	42.75	
Accounts Payable–C. Brown		42.75

To cancel cheque No. 1458 which was issued in error

	BANK								No.1		
DATE		PARTICULARS	P.R.	DEBIT			CREDIT			BALANCE		DR CR
March	31									305	08	DR
April	30		CR8	1	507	36						
	30		CP17				1	497	30			
	30		J9		42	75				357	89	DR

(e) Partial General Ledger 'Bank' account.

CHEQUES				DEPOSITS	DATE	BALANCE
					Mar 31	943.80
				216.50	Apr 1	1160.30
116.40	(#1436)	13.16	(#1420)		2	1030.74
75.92	(#1441)	17.50	(#1390)	216.50	4	
76.42	(#1431)				4	1077.40
19.40	(#1409)	85.19	(#1434)		5	
10.00	(#1445)				5	962.81
18.19	(#1428)				8	944.62
36.71	(#1406)	50.00	(#1440)	171.41	10	
25.00	(#1439)	120.00	(#1443)		10	
300.00	(#1450)				10	584.32
14.40	(#1433)				11	569.92
78.90	(#1438)	80.00	(#1442)		15	
20.00	(#1455)	20.10	(#1447)		15	370.92
141.72	(#1415)			94.80	16	324.00
51.61	(#1425)	125.00	(#1449)		18	147.39
			(Correct March Error)	2.00	19	149.39
				156.80	20	306.19
36.44	(#1426)	84.33	(#1452)		23	
18.30	(#1460)				23	167.12
100.00	(#1463)			363.85	24	430.97
19.65	(#1435)	16.09	(#1453)		25	395.23
				410.00	27	805.23
DM	5.60	(Service Charge)			27	799.63
NT	36.00	(Interest on Loan)			30	763.63
DM	250.00	(Loan Reduction)			30	513.63
		(Note Collected, R.Smith)		100.00	30	613.63
3.20	(#1457)	4.50	(#1467)			
					30	605.93

(f) April Bank Statement.

INSTRUCTION.

Record the necessary accounting entries in the books of the business.

---

11. From the following records, prepare the Bank Reconciliation Statement
for Madison Company as of October 31, 19—.

Madison Company
Bank Reconciliation Statement
September 30, 19—

Bal. per Bk. Statement		2 102 69	Bal. per General Ledger		1 652 95
Deduct: Outstanding Chqs.			Deduct:		
#519	$20.00		Service Charge $12.50		
#526	37.50 ✓		Loan Interest 36.25		48 75
#528	105.00 ✓				
#529	2.70 ✓				
#531	5.19 ✓				
#532	74.10 ✓				
#533	112.02 ✓				
#534	56.94 ✓				
#535	85.04 ✓	498 49			
True Balance		1 604 20	True Balance		1 604 20

(a) Previous Bank Reconciliation Statement.

General Journal   Page 64

Date	Particulars	P.R.	Debit	Credit
Oct 4	Bank Charges	54	12 50	
	Bank Interest	56	36 25	
	Bank	1		48 75
	To record charges picked up			
	from September bank statement			

(b) October General Journal entry affecting 'Bank'.

(c) Partial Cash Payments Journal

Date	Chq No	Bank Cr	
19— Oct 1	536	✓	19 05
1	537	✓	164 02
2	538	✓	73 74
3	539	✓	27 60
3	540	✓	1 95
4	541	✓	365 12
5	542		92 06
8	543	✓	74 09
8	544	✓	19 65
10	545		74 02
11	546	✓	76 75
12	547		56 21
12	548	✓	42 96
15	549	✓	33 21
17	550		24 02
19	551	✓	88 61
22	552	✓	58 36
22	553		19 05
23	554	✓	91 50
24	555	✓	13 30
24	556		17 50
26	557	✓	8 61
29	558	✓	1 047 65
29	559		319 02
30	560		1 75
31	561		2 50
31	562		19 41
			2 831 71

(d) Partial Cash Receipts Journal

Date	Bank Dr	Amount Deposit	
19— Oct 3	16 50		
3	25 02		
3	576 95	558 47	✓
8	104 20		
8	756 12		
8	56 12		
8	96 02	1 012 46	✓
11	33 40	33 40	✓
15	17 50		
15	12 09	29 59	✓
22	19 06		
22	502 00	521 06	✓
24	12 06		
24	13 50		
24	91 02		
24	16 51	133 09	✓
29	56 93		
29	83 16		
29	102 52		
29	127 06		
29	31 50	401 17	✓
31	167 75		
31	138 44	306 19	
	2 995 43	2 995 43	
	(1)		

(c) Partial Cash Payments Journal (d) Partial Cash Receipts Journal

(e) Bank Statement for October.

CHEQUES				DEPOSITS	DATE	BALANCE
37.50	(526) ✓				Sep 30	2,102.69
					Oct 2	2,065.19
				558.47	3	2,623.66
2.70	(529) ✓	85.04	(535) ✓		4	2,535.92
19.05	(536) ✓				5	2,516.87
74.10	(532) ✓	105.00	(528) ✓		8	2,337.77
73.74	(538) ✓			1,012.46	9	3,276.49
5.19	(531) ✓	27.60	(539) ✓		10	3,243.70
56.94	(534) ✓				11	3,186.76
74.09	(543) ✓	112.02	(533) ✓	33.40	15	3,034.05
96.02	(N.S.F. cheque of J. Marble) ✓				15	2,938.03
164.02	(537) ✓				16	2,774.01
33.21	(549) ✓	19.65	(544) ✓	29.59	17	2,750.74
365.12	(541) ✓				18	2,385.62
76.75	(546) ✓			521.06	22	2,829.93
1.95	(540) ✓	58.36	(552) ✓		23	2,769.62
42.96	(548) ✓				24	2,726.66
				133.09	25	2,859.75
88.61	(551) ✓				26	2,771.14
91.50	(554) ✓				29	2,679.64
13.30	(555) ✓			401.17	30	3,067.51
8.61	(557) ✓	1,047.65	(558) ✓		31	2,011.25
15.20	(Int)	30.20	(Service Charges)		31	1,965.85

(f) General Ledger account showing October figures.

Account	Bank					No.	1		
Date	Particulars	P.R.	Debit		Credit		DR. CR.	Balance	
19— Sept 30		—					DR	1 652	95
Oct 4		J 64			48	75			
31		CP174			2 831	71			
31		CR147	2 995	43			DR	1 767	92

199

Supplement to Chapter 11

GREEN THUMB GARDEN CENTER EXERCISE

INTRODUCTORY INFORMATION

The Green Thumb Garden Center is a business owned and operated by Mr. G. O. Emms. It is a seasonal business which the owner closes down each year from November 1 to March 31. During the season that the business is open, it is operated seven days a week. The most profitable business days are Saturdays and Sundays.

The Green Thumb Garden Center sells a variety of goods and services. Among these are the following: shrubs, bushes, trees, plants, fertilizers, seeds, bulbs, insecticides, sod, loam, soil, concrete products, and landscaping. All goods and services sold by the business are subject to a five per cent government sales tax.

Mr. Emms employs a number of workers to assist him. Most of these are hired on a part-time basis as they are needed. Once each week Mr. Emms withdraws from the bank (by means of a cheque made out to Cash) sufficient cash to pay the employees.

Most of the sales of the business are on a cash basis. As a result, the accounting system of the business is geared towards the cash register. In addition to the cash sales, all charge sales and receipts from customers are processed through the cash register. There are relatively few charge customers.

At the close of each day's business, a cash register balancing procedure is performed and an accounting summary prepared. A bank deposit is made each day by using a night depository service.

Small expense items are not paid for out of the cash register funds. Mr. Emms maintains a petty cash fund of $100 for this purpose.

The business accounting system utilizes three special journals as follows:

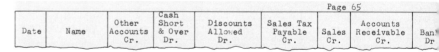

					Page 77		
Date	Name	Other Accounts Dr.	Truck Expense Dr.	Soil Prep. & Mtce. Dr.	Equipment Expense Dr.	Purchases Dr.	Accounts Payable Cr.

Purchases Journal

						Page 47		
Date	Name	Other Accounts Dr.	Wages Dr.	G.O.E. Drawings Dr.	Soil Prep. & Mtce. Dr.	Discounts Earned Cr.	Accounts Payable Dr.	Bank Cr.

Cash Payments Journal

						Page 65		
Date	Name	Other Accounts Cr.	Cash Short & Over Dr.	Discounts Allowed Dr.	Sales Tax Payable Cr.	Sales Cr.	Accounts Receivable Cr.	Bank Dr.

Cash Receipts Journal

The business does not keep perpetual inventory records.

Green Thumb Garden Center
General Ledger Trial Balance   May 31, 19—

NO.	ACCOUNT	DR	CR
1.	Petty Cash	$ 100.00	
2.	Bank	1,527.24	
3.	Accounts Receivable	2,469.91	
4.	Inventory–Merchandise and Nursery Stock	10,746.53	
5.	Supplies	595.00	
6.	Land	8,000.00	
7.	Buildings	3,500.00	
8.	Trucks and Tractors	17,500.00	
21.	Bank Loan		$20,000.00
22.	Mortgage Payable		2,500.00
23.	Accounts Payable		7,861.87
24.	Sales Tax Payable		160.45
31.	G. O. Emms, Capital		14,175.94
32.	G. O. Emms, Drawings	5,654.60	
41.	Sales		25,042.19
51.	Bank Charges	547.53	
52.	Building Repairs	146.51	
53.	Cash Short and Over	10.04	
54.	Discounts Allowed	95.75	
55.	Discounts Earned		316.70
56.	Equipment Expense	506.86	
57.	Freight-in	256.50	
58.	Light, Heat, and Power	306.75	
59.	Miscellaneous Expense	92.41	
60.	Purchases	10,001.05	
61.	Soil Preparation and Maintenance	2,001.15	
62.	Telephone	519.42	
63.	Truck Expense	1,104.40	
64.	Wages	4,375.50	
		$70,057.15	$70,057.15

Green Thumb Garden Center
Accounts Receivable Ledger   May 31, 19—

Customer	Address	Usual Terms	Inv. Date	Inv. No.	Amount
P. Barker	16 Ava Street	Net 30	May 16	398	$ 131.25
J. Bowen	42 Woodlawn Ave.	Net 30	May 14	394	78.75
F. Carson & Sons	165 Pleasant Road	2/10,n/30	May 30	408	541.80
N. Everist	46 Hart Street	Net 30	May 4	375	56.70
O. Harrison	96 Brock Road	Net 30	May 5	377	63.00
P. Pierce	205 Ford Street	Net 30	May 6	379	36.53
A. Renforth	90 Oak Lane	Net 30	May 12	390	178.50
C. Swinton	27 North Cr.	2/10,n/30	May 26	407	1,094.63
Varga Brothers	55 Sharp Drive	2/10,n/30	May 24	402	288.75
					$2,469.91

Supplier	Address	Terms	Inv. No.	Inv. Date	Amount	Account Balance
Acorn Seed Company	10 Lynn Road	2/15,n/30	654	May 18	$147.00	
			672	May 21	317.10	$ 464.10
Clay Ceramic Co	74 Pine Street	Net 45	1701	Apr 24		540.75
Canada Products	100 Willow Ave.	Net 30	B160	May 4	$ 58.80	
			B188	May 12	98.91	
			B249	May 30	35.91	193.62
Kemp Haulage	Summerside	1/10,n/30	747	May 23	$ 52.50	
			754	May 23	52.50	
			760	May 23	52.50	
			772	May 27	52.50	
			795	May 31	78.75	288.75
M & M Chemicals	500 Grand St.	Net 60	1046	Apr 9		1,932.00
Poplar Finance	200 Crest Rd.	Per Contract				2,560.00
Sylvester Concrete	482-4 Delta Rd.	Net 30	446	May 5		783.51
Triangle Sod	4th Side Road	Net 30	374	May 22		1,099.14
						$7,861.87

INSTRUCTION 1.

Set up the three ledgers of the Green Thumb Garden Center as of May 31, 19—.

INSTRUCTION 2.

Set up the journals for the Green Thumb Garden Center for the month of June, 19—.

INSTRUCTION 3.

Journalize the transactions listed below. Post daily to the subsidiary ledgers directly from the source documents.

Transactions

June 1 *Cash Register Summary*

ACCOUNTING SUMMARY	DEBIT	CREDIT
DEBITS: Bank	160 05	
Acc's Rec'l (Charge Sales)		
Cash Short and Over	2 00	
CREDITS: Accounts Receivable		
Sales		154 33
Sales Tax Payable		7 72
Cash Short and Over		
BALANCING TOTALS	162 05	162 05

Purchase Invoice

—From Canada Products, No. B261, $372.75, dated May 31; terms Net 30; for fertilizer for resale.

June 2 *Cash Register Summary*

ACCOUNTING SUMMARY	DEBIT	CREDIT
DEBITS: Bank	551 98	
Acc's Rec'l (Charge Sales)		
Discounts Allowed	5 78	
Cash Short and Over		
CREDITS: Accounts Receivable		288 75
Sales		256 20
Sales Tax Payable		12 81
Cash Short and Over		
BALANCING TOTALS	557 76	557 76

'Received' Voucher

—Voucher No. 416 to Varga Brothers, paying Invoice No. 402 for $288.75 less 2 per cent discount; net amount $282.97.

Purchase Invoice

–From Triangle Sod, No. 406, $312.90, dated June 1; terms Net 30; for sod for resale (Assume goods satisfactory for all purchases).

Cheque Copies

–No. 661, to Acorn Seed Company, $?, paying Invoice No. 654 less 2 per cent cash discount.

–No. 662, to Kemp Haulage, $?, paying Invoices No. 747, No. 754, No. 760 less 1 per cent cash discount.

June 3 Cash Register Summary

ACCOUNTING SUMMARY	DEBIT	CREDIT
DEBITS: Bank	247 20	
Acc's Rec'l (Charge Sales)		
Cash Short and Over		
CREDITS: Accounts Receivable		56 70
Sales		180 00
Sales Tax Payable		9 —
Cash Short and Over		1 50
BALANCING TOTALS	247 20	247 20

'Received' Voucher

–Voucher No. 417 to N. Everist, paying Invoice No. 375 for $56.70.

Cheque Copy

–No. 663, to Petty Cash, $?, to reimburse Petty Cash Fund with respect to the following summary:

Petty Cash Summary	
June 3, 19-	
Building Repairs	$14.10
Equipment Expense	2.50
Soil Preparation & Maint.	35.50
Truck Expense	17.70
Miscellaneous Expense	26.75

June 4 Cash Register Summary

ACCOUNTING SUMMARY	DEBIT	CREDIT
DEBITS: Bank	100 38	
Acc's Rec'l (Charge Sales)	330 75	
Cash Short and Over		
CREDITS: Accounts Receivable		
Sales		410 60
Sales Tax Payable		20 53
Cash Short and Over		
BALANCING TOTALS	431 13	431 13

'Charge' Voucher

–Voucher No. 418 to Varga Brothers for the sale of merchandise, $315.00 plus 5 per cent sales tax; terms, 2/10,n/30; total $330.75.

Purchase Invoices

–From Clay Ceramic Co., No. 1916, $1,003.80, dated June 3; terms, Net 45; flower pots and ornamental garden items (merchandise for resale).

–From M. & M. Chemicals, No. 1193, $84, dated June 3; terms, Net 60; for insecticides etc., for resale.

Cheque Copies

–No. 664, to Sylvester Concrete, $?, paying Invoice No. 446.

–No. 665, to Public Utilities Commission, $14.85, for electricity for month of May. (Note: As soon as this bill was received cheque No. 665 was prepared.)

Bank Statement and Vouchers

–The Bank Statement and related vouchers and paid cheques arrived from the bank. Included in the vouchers was a Debit Note for bank charges in the amount of $41.50 for the month of May; this was the first notice for these charges.

At this time, the following Bank Reconciliation Statement was prepared. You will require this statement in order to prepare the reconciliation statement at the end of June.

Green Thumb Garden Center Bank Reconciliation Statement May 31, 19—				
Balance per Bk. Statement		1 406 15	Balance per Gen. Ledger	1 527 24
Add: Outstanding Deposit		516 31	Deduct: Bank Interest	
		1 922 46	and Service Charge	41 50
Deduct: Outstanding Cheques				
#641	$74.00			
#650	36.50			
#654	29.12			
#655	116.26			
#657	37.40			
#658	42.15			
#659	95.14			
#660	6.15	436 72		
True Balance		1 485 74	True Balance	1 485 74

June 5 Cash Register Summary

ACCOUNTING SUMMARY	DEBIT	CREDIT
DEBITS: Bank	1 669 90	
Acc's Rec'l (Charge Sales)		
Discounts Allowed	21 89	
Cash Short and Over	23	
CREDITS: Accounts Receivable		1 194 16
Sales		475 10
Sales Tax Payable		23 76
Cash Short and Over		
BALANCING TOTALS	1 693 02	1 693 02

'Received' Vouchers

–Voucher No. 419, to C. Swinton, paying Invoice No. 407 in the amount of $1,094.63 less a 2 per cent cash discount; net amount $1,072.74.

–Voucher No. 420, to O. Harrison, paying Invoice No. 377 in the amount of $63.

–Voucher No. 421, to P. Pierce, paying Invoice No. 379 in the amount of $36.53.

Cheque Copies

–No. 666 to Cash, $204.16, wages for the week.

–No. 667, to G. O. Emms, $140, personal drawings of owner.

–No. 668, to Acorn Seed Company, $?, paying Invoice No. 672 less a 2 per cent cash discount.

June 6 *Cash Register Summary*

ACCOUNTING SUMMARY	DEBIT	CREDIT
DEBITS: Bank	847 44	
Acc's Rec'l (Charge Sales)	852 15	
Cash Short and Over		
CREDITS: Accounts Receivable		
Sales		1 618 66
Sales Tax Payable		80 93
Cash Short and Over		
BALANCING TOTALS	1 699 59	1 699 59

'Charge' Vouchers

–Voucher No. 422, to C. Swinton, $516.07 plus 5 per cent sales tax, for sale of merchandise; terms, 2/10,n/30; total $541.87.

–Voucher No. 423, to A. Renforth, $295.50 plus 5 per cent sales tax, for sale of merchandise; terms, Net 30; total $310.28.

Purchase Invoices

–From Equipment Repair and Supply, 16 Barr St., No. 21, $157.50, dated June 5; terms, Net 30; for repairs to equipment.

–From Canada Products, No. B295, $997.50, dated June 4; terms, Net 30; for fertilizers and chemicals for soil to be charged as follows: Purchases, $871.50; Soil Preparation & Maintenance, $126.

Cheque Copies

–No. 669, to Clay Ceramic Co., $540.75, paying Invoice No. 1701.

–No. 670, to Kemp Haulage, $?, paying Invoice No. 772 less a 1 per cent cash discount.

–No. 671, to Canada Products, $58.80, paying Invoice No. B160.

June 7 *Cash Register Summary*

ACCOUNTING SUMMARY	DEBIT	CREDIT
DEBITS: Bank	941 83	
Acc's Rec'l (Charge Sales)		
Cash Short and Over	10 00	
CREDITS: Accounts Receivable		
Sales		906 50
Sales Tax Payable		45 33
Cash Short and Over		
BALANCING TOTALS	951 83	951 83

Cheque Copy

–No. 672, to Public Utilities Commission, $17.50, cash payment of water bill (charge Soil Preparation & Maintenance).

June 8 *Cash Register Summary*

ACCOUNTING SUMMARY	DEBIT	CREDIT
DEBITS: Bank	611 18	
Acc's Rec'l (Charge Sales)		
Discounts Allowed	10 84	
Cash Short and Over		
CREDITS: Accounts Receivable		541 80
Sales		76 40
Sales Tax Payable		3 82
Cash Short and Over		
BALANCING TOTALS	622 02	622 02

'Received' Voucher

–Voucher No. 424, to F. Carson & Sons, paying Invoice No. 408 for $541.80 less a 2 per cent cash discount; net amount $530.96.

Cheque Copies

–No. 673, to M. & M. Chemicals, $1,932, paying Invoice No. 1046.

–No. 674, to Poplar Finance, $175, regular monthly payment on truck.

June 9 *Cash Register Summary*

ACCOUNTING SUMMARY	DEBIT	CREDIT
DEBITS: Bank	117 60	
Acc's Rec'l (Charge Sales)	71 40	
Cash Short and Over		
CREDITS: Accounts Receivable		
Sales		180 00
Sales Tax Payable		9 00
Cash Short and Over		
BALANCING TOTALS	189 00	189 00

'Charge' Voucher

–Voucher No. 425, to O. Harrison, $68 plus 5 per cent sales tax; terms, Net 30; for sale of merchandise; total $71.40.

Purchase Invoices

–From City Gas & Oil Co., 15 Boa Street, No. 1651, $135.68, dated June 8; terms, Net 30; for gasoline and oil used in the trucks and equipment as follows: Trucks, $94.67; Equipment, $41.01.

–From Kemp Haulage, No. 822, $231, dated June 7; terms, 1/10,n/30; topsoil for resale.

June 10 *Cash Register Summary*

ACCOUNTING SUMMARY	DEBIT	CREDIT
DEBITS: Bank	301 79	
Acc's Rec'l (Charge Sales)		
Cash Short and Over		
CREDITS: Accounts Receivable		78 75
Sales		211 76
Sales Tax Payable		10 53
Cash Short and Over		75
BALANCING TOTALS	301 79	301 79

'Received' Voucher

–Voucher No. 426, to J. Bowen; paying Invoice No. 394.

June 10 *Cheques Copies*

–No. 675, to Northwestern Telephone Company, $25.20, cash payment of telephone bill.
–No. 676, to Kemp Haulage, $?, paying Invoice No. 795 less the 1 per cent cash discount.

June 11 *Cash Register Summary*

ACCOUNTING SUMMARY	DEBIT	CREDIT
DEBITS: Bank	137 66	
Acc's Rec'l (Charge Sales)	131 25	
Cash Short and Over		
CREDITS: Accounts Receivable		
Sales		256 10
Sales Tax Payable		12 81
Cash Short and Over		
BALANCING TOTALS	268 91	268 91

'Charge' Voucher

–Voucher No. 427, to P. Pierce, for the sale of merchandise, $125 plus 5 per cent sales tax; terms, Net 30; total $131.25.

Purchase Invoice

–From M. & M. Chemicals, No. 1221, $81.90, dated June 10; terms, Net 60; to be charged to Soil Preparation & Maintenance.

Cheque Copy

–No. 677, to Canada Products, $98.91, paying Invoice No. B188.

June 12 *Cash Register Summary*

ACCOUNTING SUMMARY	DEBIT	CREDIT
DEBITS: Bank	594 2	
Acc's Rec'l (Charge Sales)	278 25	
Cash Short and Over	09	
CREDITS: Accounts Receivable		178 50
Sales		661 00
Sales Tax Payable		33 05
Cash Short and Over		
BALANCING TOTALS	872 55	872 55

'Received' Voucher

–Voucher No. 428, to A. Renforth, $178.50; paying Invoice No. 390.

'Charge' Voucher

–Voucher No. 429, to F. Carson & Sons; for the sale of merchandise; terms 2/10,n/30; $265 plus 5 per cent sales tax; total $278.25.

Cheque Copies

–No. 678, to Cash, $205.19, for the wages for the week.
–No. 679, to G. O. Emms, $150, owner's personal drawings.
–No. 680, to Foster Bros., $44.21, for the cash purchase of miscellaneous items to be charged to Miscellaneous Expense.

June 13 *Cash Register Summary*

ACCOUNTING SUMMARY	DEBIT	CREDIT
DEBITS: Bank	669 06	
Acc's Rec'l (Charge Sales)		
Cash Short and Over	21	
CREDITS: Accounts Receivable		
Sales		637 40
Sales Tax Payable		31 87
Cash Short and Over		
BALANCING TOTALS	669 27	669 27

Purchase Invoice

–From Acorn Seed Company, No. 756, $82.43, dated June 12; terms, 2/15,n/30; for merchandise for resale.

June 14 *Cash Register Summary*

ACCOUNTING SUMMARY	DEBIT	CREDIT
DEBITS: Bank	1 112 95	
Acc's Rec'l (Charge Sales)		
Discounts Allowed	6 62	
Cash Short and Over		
CREDITS: Accounts Receivable		330 75
Sales		751 26
Sales Tax Payable		37 56
Cash Short and Over		
BALANCING TOTALS	1 119 57	1 119 57

'Received' Voucher

–Voucher No. 430, to Varga Brothers, $324.13 paying Invoice No. 418 less 2 per cent cash discount.

Purchase Invoice

–From Triangle Sod, No. 452, $787.50, dated June 12; terms, Net 30; for purchase of sod for resale.

Bank Debit Advice

This Debit Note from Central Bank stated that $2,000 had been deducted from the business bank account for the purpose of reducing the bank note. Mr. Emms had instructed the bank to make the deduction.

June 15 *Cash Register Summary*

ACCOUNTING SUMMARY	DEBIT	CREDIT
DEBITS: Bank	230 21	
Acc's Rec'l (Charge Sales)		
Cash Short and Over		
CREDITS: Accounts Receivable		131 28
Sales		94 20
Sales Tax Payable		4 71
Cash Short and Over		05
BALANCING TOTALS	230 21	230 21

'Received' Voucher

–Voucher No. 431, to P. Barker, $131.25, paying Invoice No. 398.

Cheque Copies

–No. 681, to Government Treasurer, $?, paying the sales tax for the previous month.

–No. 682, to Proud Insurance Company, $78.50, regular monthly mortgage payment.

June 16 *Cash Register Summary*

ACCOUNTING SUMMARY		DEBIT	CREDIT
DEBITS: Bank		75 60	
Acc's Rec'l (Charge Sales)		26 93	
Cash Short and Over			
CREDITS: Accounts Receivable			
Sales			97 65
Sales Tax Payable			4 88
Cash Short and Over			
BALANCING TOTALS		102 53	102 53

'Charge' Voucher
–Voucher No. 432, to P. Barker, for sale of merchandise; terms, Net 30; $25.65 plus 5 per cent sales tax.

Cheque Copies
–No. 683, to Central Supply, $39.38, for the cash purchase of supplies.
–No. 684, to Mainline Express, $15.85, for the cash payment of express charges, to be charged to Freight-in.

June 17 *Cash Register Summary*

ACCOUNTING SUMMARY		DEBIT	CREDIT
DEBITS: Bank		758 50	
Acc's Rec'l (Charge Sales)			
Discounts Allowed		10 84	
Cash Short and Over			
CREDITS: Accounts Receivable			541 87
Sales			216 50
Sales Tax Payable			10 82
Cash Short and Over			15
BALANCING TOTALS		769 34	769 34

'Received' Voucher
–Voucher No. 433, to C. Swinton, $531.03, paying Invoice No. 422 less a 2 per cent cash discount. Although the payment was received after the discount period it was decided to allow the customer the discount.

Purchase Invoices
–From Equipment Repair and Supply, No. 40, $201.60, dated June 15; terms, Net 30; for truck repairs.
–From Kemp Haulage, No. 856, $211.05, dated June 16; terms, 1/10,n/30; topsoil and fertilizer to improve the condition of the soil on the business' property, to be charged to Soil Preparation & Maintenance.
Cheque Copy
–No. 685, to Kemp Haulage, $?, paying Invoice No. 822 less the cash discount.

June 18 *Cash Register Summary*

ACCOUNTING SUMMARY		DEBIT	CREDIT
DEBITS: Bank		321 57	
Acc's Rec'l (Charge Sales)		420 00	
Cash Short and Over			
CREDITS: Accounts Receivable			52 50
Sales			656 20
Sales Tax Payable			32 81
Cash Short and Over			
BALANCING TOTALS		741 57	741 51

'Charge' Voucher
–Voucher No. 434, to Varga Brothers, for the sale of merchandise; terms, 2/10,n/30; $400 plus 5 per cent sales tax; total $420.
'Credit Note' Voucher
–Voucher No. 435, to P. Pierce, to credit the customer's account for defective merchandise, $50 plus 5 per cent sales tax.

Cheque Copy
–No. 686, to The Business House, $15.75, for the cash purchase of items to be charged to Miscellaneous Expense.

June 19 *Cash Register Summary*

ACCOUNTING SUMMARY		DEBIT	CREDIT
DEBITS: Bank		332 01	
Acc's Rec'l (Charge Sales)			
Cash Short and Over			
CREDITS: Accounts Receivable			
Sales			316 20
Sales Tax Payable			15 81
Cash Short and Over			
BALANCING TOTALS		332 01	332 01

Purchase Invoice
–From Sylvester Concrete, No. 491, $236.25, dated June 17; terms, Net 30; patio stones for resale.
Cheque Copies
–No. 687, to Cash, $267.25, wages for the week.
–No. 688, to G. O. Emms, $150, owner's personal drawings.

June 20 *Cash Register Summary*

ACCOUNTING SUMMARY		DEBIT	CREDIT
DEBITS: Bank		545 03	
Acc's Rec'l (Charge Sales)			
Cash Short and Over			
CREDITS: Accounts Receivable			
Sales			519 05
Sales Tax Payable			25 98
Cash Short and Over			
BALANCING TOTALS		545 03	545 03

Purchase Invoice
–From Triangle Sod, No. 474, $558.08, dated June 19; terms, Net 30; sod for resale.

June 21   *Cash Register Summary*

ACCOUNTING SUMMARY	DEBIT	CREDIT
DEBITS: Bank	784 71	
Acc's Rec'l (Charge Sales)		
Cash Short and Over	9 40	
CREDITS: Accounts Receivable		
Sales		756 25
Sales Tax Payable		37 86
Cash Short and Over		
BALANCING TOTALS	794 11	794 11

Cheque Copies

—No. 689, to Petty Cash, $?, reimbursement with respect to following summary:

Petty Cash Summary	
June 21, 19-	
Soil Preparation & Maintenance	$26.15
Sales	35.00
Sales Tax Payable	1.75
Miscellaneous Expense	35.01

—No. 690, to Triangle Sod, $, paying Invoice No. 374.

June 22   *Cash Register Summary*

ACCOUNTING SUMMARY	DEBIT	CREDIT
DEBITS: Bank	432 78	
Acc's Rec'l (Charge Sales)	2 159 50	
Discounts Allowed	5 57	
Cash Short and Over		
CREDITS: Accounts Receivable		278 25
Sales		2 209 14
Sales Tax Payable		116 46
Cash Short and Over		
BALANCING TOTALS	2 597 85	2 597 85

'Charge' Voucher

—Voucher No. 436, to C. Swinton, for the sale of merchandise; terms, 2/10,n/30; $2,056.67 plus 5 per cent sales tax; total $2,159.50.

'Received' Voucher

—Voucher No. 437, to F. Carson & Sons, $272.68, paying Invoice No. 429 less 2 per cent cash discount.

June 23   *Cash Register Summary*

ACCOUNTING SUMMARY	DEBIT	CREDIT
DEBITS: Bank	136 77	
Acc's Rec'l (Charge Sales)		
Cash Short and Over		
CREDITS: Accounts Receivable		100 00
Sales		35 02
Sales Tax Payable		1 75
Cash Short and Over		
BALANCING TOTALS	136 77	136 77

'Received' Voucher

—Voucher No. 438, to A. Renforth, $100, on account.

June 24   *Cash Register Summary*

ACCOUNTING SUMMARY	DEBIT	CREDIT
DEBITS: Bank	107 00	
Acc's Rec'l (Charge Sales)		
Cash Short and Over	10	
CREDITS: Accounts Receivable		
Sales		102 00
Sales Tax Payable		5 10
Cash Short and Over		
BALANCING TOTALS	107 10	107 10

Purchase Invoices

—From Acorn Seed Company, No. 801, $813.75, dated June 23; terms, 2/15,n/30, merchandise for resale.

—From Clay Ceramic Co., No. 2016, $136.50, dated June 22; terms, Net 45; merchandise for resale.

June 25   *Cash Register Summary*

ACCOUNTING SUMMARY	DEBIT	CREDIT
DEBITS: Bank	126 47	
Acc's Rec'l (Charge Sales)	97 23	
Cash Short and Over		
CREDITS: Accounts Receivable		
Sales		213 05
Sales Tax Payable		10 65
Cash Short and Over		
BALANCING TOTALS	223 70	223 70

'Charge' Voucher

—Voucher No. 439, to A. Renforth, for sale of merchandise; terms, Net 30; $92.60 plus 5 per cent sales tax; total $97.23.

Cheque Copy

—No. 691, to Poplar Finance Co., $102, regular finance payment on tractor.

June 26   *Cash Register Summary*

ACCOUNTING SUMMARY	DEBIT	CREDIT
DEBITS: Bank	436 13	
Acc's Rec'l (Charge Sales)		
Cash Short and Over		
CREDITS: Accounts Receivable		
Sales		412 50
Sales Tax Payable		20 63
Cash Short and Over		3 00
BALANCING TOTALS	436 13	436 13

Cheque Copies

—No. 692, to Acorn Seed Co., $?, paying Invoice No. 756 less a 2 per cent cash discount.

—No. 693, to Cash, $205.60, wages for the week.

—No. 694, to G. O. Emms, $200, owner's personal drawings.

June 27 *Cash Register Summary*

ACCOUNTING SUMMARY	DEBIT	CREDIT
DEBITS: Bank	1 436 29	
Acc's Rec'l (Charge Sales)		
Discounts Allowed	8 41	
Cash Short and Over		
CREDITS: Accounts Receivable		491 40
Sales		907 90
Sales Tax Payable		45 39
Cash Short and Over		
BALANCING TOTALS	1 444 69	1 444 69

'Received' Vouchers

–Voucher No. 440, to O. Harrison, $71.40; paying Invoice No. 425.

–Voucher No. 441, to Varga Brothers, $411.60; paying Invoice No. 434 less a 2 per cent discount.

Purchase Invoice

–From Canada Products, No. B340, $330.75, dated June 25; terms, Net 30; for merchandise for resale.

June 28 *Cash Register Summary*

ACCOUNTING SUMMARY	DEBIT	CREDIT
DEBITS: Bank	730 00	
Acc's Rec'l (Charge Sales)		
Cash Short and Over		
CREDITS: Accounts Receivable		
Sales		695 21
Sales Tax Payable		34 76
Cash Short and Over		03
BALANCING TOTALS	730 00	730 00

June 29 *Cash Register Summary*

ACCOUNTING SUMMARY	DEBIT	CREDIT
DEBITS: Bank	59 01	
Acc's Rec'l (Charge Sales)	105 00	
Cash Short and Over		
CREDITS: Accounts Receivable		
Sales		156 20
Sales Tax Payable		7 81
Cash Short and Over		
BALANCING TOTALS	164 01	164 01

'Charge' Vouchers

–Voucher No. 442, to J. Bowen, for sale of merchandise; terms, Net 30; $30 plus 5 per cent sales tax; total $31.50.

–Voucher No. 443, to P. Pierce, for sale of merchandise; terms, Net 30; $70 plus 5 per cent sales tax; total $73.50.

Cheque Copies

–No. 695, to Canada Products, $35.91, paying Invoice No. B249.

–No. 696, to First-Rate Repair Service, $233.10, cash payment to be charged to Equipment Expense.

Credit Note Received

–From Triangle Sod, No. 509, $183.75, with respect to inferior goods shipped on Invoice No. 474.

June 30 *Cash Register Summary*

ACCOUNTING SUMMARY	DEBIT	CREDIT
DEBITS: Bank	88 20	
Acc's Rec'l (Charge Sales)		
Cash Short and Over		
CREDITS: Accounts Receivable		
Sales		84 00
Sales Tax Payable		4 20
Cash Short and Over		
BALANCING TOTALS	88 20	88 20

INSTRUCTION 4.

Balance the journals and post to the General Ledger.

INSTRUCTION 5.

Balance the General Ledger, the Accounts Receivable Ledger, and the Accounts Payable Ledger.

INSTRUCTION 6.

On July 3, the Bank Statement and related vouchers arrive from the bank. The Bank Statement appears on page 209. Reconcile the bank account of Green Thumb Garden Center as of June 30.

THE CENTRAL BANK

In
Account   Green Thumb Garden Center,
With   Concord Highway.

Cheques and Debits				Deposits	Date	Balance
				Balance Brought Forward	May 31	1,406.15
(#650)	36.50	(#660)	6.15	516.31	June 1	1,879.81
(#659)	95.14			160.05 –	June 2	1,944.72
(#661)	144.06			551.98	June 3	2,352.64
				247.20	June 4	2,599.84
(#662)	155.92	(#663)	96.55	100.38		
(#665)	14.85				June 5	2,432.90
(#657)	37.40			1,669.90		
				847.44		
				941.83	June 8	5,854.67
(#666)	204.16			611.18	June 9	6,261.69
				117.60	June 10	6,379.29
(#667)	140.00	(#668)	310.76	301.76	June 11	6,230.32
(DM)	2,000.00	(Loan Reduction)		137.66	June 12	4,367.98
(#658)	42.15	(#669)	540.75	594.21		
(#681)	160.45			669.06		
				1,112.95	June 15	6,000.85
				230.21	June 16	6,231.06
(#641)	74.00	(#670)	51.97	75.60	June 17	6,180.69
(#671)	58.80	(#677)	98.91	758.50	June 18	6,781.48
(#682)	78.50	(#685)	228.69	321.51	June 19	6,795.80
(#655)	116.26	(#686)	15.75	332.01		
				545.03		
				784.71	June 22	8,325.54
(#673)	1,932.00	(#684)	15.85	432.78	June 23	6,810.47
(#675)	25.20	(#678)	205.19	136.77	June 24	6,716.85
(#679)	150.00	(#687)	267.25	107.00	June 25	6,406.60
(#676)	77.96			126.47	June 26	6,455.11
(#654)	29.12			436.13		
				1,436.29		
				730.00	June 29	9,028.41
(#688)	150.00	(#691)	102.00			
(#690)	1,099.14			59.01		
(DM)	101.10	(Bank Interest)			June 30	7,635.18

Chapter 12

BASIC ACCOUNTING SYSTEMS AND PROCEDURES

It is important that students of accounting have an appreciation of the various activities and procedures that occur in business offices. The purpose of this chapter is to help you acquire this appreciation by describing a number of office routines by means of flowcharts and supporting notes. You must keep in mind, of course, that the routines shown here are very simple ones illustrating basic ideas. The routines found in the real business world will be variations of those shown here.

Purchasing Routine

The buying of materials, parts, and services is something that all businesses must do. In some businesses, the office of a public accountant for example, 'purchasing' is a minor function and relatively unimportant. But in other businesses, such as manufacturing companies and large department stores, the purchasing function is a matter of considerable importance and requires special attention.

The flowchart below and the accompanying explanatory notes describe a basic 'purchasing' routine.

NOTES TO FLOWCHART #7

(1) In most businesses, there are key persons who have the authority to initiate the making of purchases. These are usually department heads or other persons of authority. Under their direction, the first step in the purchase routine is taken. This first step is the preparation of a business document called a Purchase Requisition. An illustration of a Purchase Requisition appears on page 212.

A Purchase Requisition is a business form requesting the

A Basic Purchasing Procedure

(Flowchart #7)

PURCHASE REQUISITION   NO. 1354

DATE: *March 15, 19—*
DEPARTMENT: *Production*
APPROVED BY: *P. Hewitt*

Quantity	Stock Number	Description	Suggested Price
15	C-54	*Belting - 6 ft. long - 12 inches wide*	2.50 *ea.*

SPECIAL INSTRUCTIONS

Order from:	*Mercury Belting*
Date required:	*April 15*
Ship via:	*cheapest*
Destination:	*main plant*

	Purchase Order Number

Purchasing Department to order certain goods or services according to the information and instructions recorded on the form. One copy of each Purchase Requisition is sent to the Purchasing Department.

(2) It is the responsibility of the Purchasing Department (under the direction of the Purchasing Agent) to be expert in matters related to purchasing. This department keeps available the latest information in respect to such things as sources of supply, new products, latest prices, quality suppliers, means of transportation, and so on.

When the Purchasing Department receives a Purchase Requisition it proceeds to order the goods. On the basis of past experience, the instructions of the requisitioner, and the information that it has available, a supplier is selected. The order is formally placed by means of a Purchase Order form which authorizes the supplier to send the goods and to bill the purchaser. The Purchase Order form, such as the one illustrated on the right, specifies all information necessary to the purchase, including quantity, price, part number, description, de-

livery date, method of shipment, and so on.

Several copies of the Purchase Order form are prepared. The flowchart indicates the use to which each copy is put.

(3) One copy of the Purchase Order is forwarded to the Receiving Department to assist the Receiver in the checking of the goods when they arrive. The Receiver will not accept goods for which he has not received a Purchase Order nor will he accept goods that he can see are in poor condition.

After checking the goods against the supplier's Packing Slip and the Purchase Order, the Receiver writes up a Receiving Report. This business

JOHN F. GILL SUPPLY LTD.

Telephone 634-41
Telex 444-522

"Gill" Quality Industrial Supplies
347 Winona Dr. Fort William, Ontario

PURCHASE ORDER   NO. 609

TO

Mercury Belting Company Limited,
4001 Monarch Drive,
Winnipeg, Manitoba.

Quantity	Stock Number	Description	Unit Price
15	B 65	Belting - 6' long - 12" wide	$2.50

Date Ordered	Date Required	Shipping Instructions
March 16, 19--	April 15, 19--	Via Express FOB Fort William

John F. Gill Supply Ltd.

Per *P. Carson*
Purchasing Agent

form, illustrated on the right, provides all the pertinent details with respect to the goods received.

(4) A Packing Slip is enclosed with the goods by the supplier for the convenience of the buyer in identifying the goods. It is a business paper providing a description of the goods and showing the quantities but not the prices. In many instances, the Packing Slip is merely a carbon copy of the supplier's Sales Invoice with the prices blocked out.

(5) One copy of the Purchase Order and one copy of the Receiving Report are sent to the Accounting Department where they are matched with the supplier's Sales Invoice as part of the Accounts Payable routine. The Accounts Payable routine is described by means of the flowchart and explanatory notes on page 223.

RECEIVING REPORT				NO. 211
Date Goods Received *April 12, 19—*			P.O. No. *609*	
Goods Received From *Mercury Belting Co. Ltd., 4001 Monarch Drive, Winnipeg, Manitoba*				
Quantity	Stock Number	Description		Unit Price
15	*B65*	*6 ft. lengths of belting -12 inches wide*		*2.50*
No. Packages *1*			Weight *35#*	
Del'd By *Nairn Transport*			Via *Truck Express*	
Rec'd By *Parks*			Checked By *Parks*	

Bookkeeping and Accounting Terms

Purchase Requisition: A business form requesting the Purchasing Department to order certain goods or services in accordance with the information and instructions recorded on the form. Only key personnel, such as department heads, are usually authorized to issue Purchase Requisitions.

Purchase Order: A business form initiated by the Purchasing Department authorizing the supplier to ship certain goods or to perform certain services as detailed on the Purchase Order, and to send a bill for these goods or services.

Receiving Report: A business form initiated by the Purchasing Dement on which is recorded detailed information with respect to goods received by the business.

Packing Slip: A business paper providing a description of the goods and of the quantities shipped but not of prices. In many instances, the Packing Slip is merely a carbon copy of the Sales Invoice with the prices and dollar amounts blocked out. The Packing Slip is enclosed with the goods by the supplier for the convenience of the purchaser's employees in identifying the goods.

Review Questions

1. Name two specific local businesses in which 'Purchasing' is an important function. Explain the reasons for your selection.
2. Give the name of the business document that is used to initiate a purchase of goods or services.
3. What persons in a business are given the authority to initiate Purchase Requisitions? Give five specific examples from businesses in your community.
4. Only certain employees are allowed to initiate Purchase Requisitions. Why?
5. Where is the original Purchase Requisition filed? Where is the copy filed?
6. Where does the Purchasing Department obtain the information necessary to prepare the Purchase Order form? List the key items of information shown on the Purchase Order.
7. If you were required to reduce the number of copies of the Purchase Order to three (in addition to the original), which copies would you eliminate? Give reasons for your choice.
8. Where is the Receiving copy of the Purchase Order eventually filed? To what use is it put before it is filed?
9. Where is copy #4 of the Purchase Order sent?
10. Explain the purpose of the original Purchase Order.
11. Explain the purpose of the supplier's Packing Slip.
12. When goods arrive at the Receiving Department what procedure is followed? Explain in your own words.
13. Why are two copies of the Receiving Report required (in addition to the original)?
14. Both the Purchase Order forms and the Receiving Report forms are numbered in sequence. Why do you think this is done?

INDIVIDUAL PROJECTS

1. Write a brief report explaining the methods used by a Purchasing Department to keep up to date and expert in regard to the procurement of goods and services. The information for your report should be obtained from the manager of the Purchasing Department of a local business.

2. By visiting the Purchasing Department of a local business, find out what factors are taken into consideration when selecting a supplier. Write a brief report.

3. Ask the manager of the Purchasing Department of a local business to help you prepare a flowchart of the purchasing routine for his business.

CLASS PROJECT

Collect samples of Purchase Requisitions, Purchase Orders, and Receiving Reports from a number of businesses. Each member of the class should be responsible for writing a letter of request to the Purchasing Department of a large or medium-sized company.

Prepare a bulletin board display.

A Basic Sales Procedure

A basic sales routine is described by means of the flowchart shown at the top of page 215 and the accompanying explanatory notes. Again, it is necessary to explain that the system described is a basic one only and that in actual practice it would be adapted with variations to suit particular businesses.

NOTES TO FLOWCHART #8

(1) Orders from customers may be received in the following ways:
   (a) By mail, either in the form of a letter or a Purchase Order.
   (b) By telephone.
   (c) By Salesmen.
   On a multiple-copy form known as the Sales Order (or Shipping Order) the order clerk types or writes the information necessary to the sale. The Sales Order form is not completely filled in at this time. Certain items of information are supplied by other employees later in the routine. An example of a Sales Order is shown on page 215.

(2) Before any other step is taken, if the customer requires credit, the approval of the credit manager must be obtained. For regular customers of proven reliability credit approval is given easily. However, for new customers or for those whose reputation is poor, the credit manager has work to do. He must investigate the customer's credit history and credit rating and will probably discuss the terms of sale with him. Before approving credit, he must be satisfied that no difficulty will be encountered in collecting from the customer.

Eventually, on the basis of his investigation, the credit manager will either grant or refuse credit to the customer. If he refuses credit, and the customer will not agree to pay cash, then that particular sales transaction is stopped and the copies of the Sales Order are filed. If he approves credit, the Sales Order is signed by him and forwarded intact to the Shipping Department.

(3) For each Sales Order that it receives, the Shipping Depart-

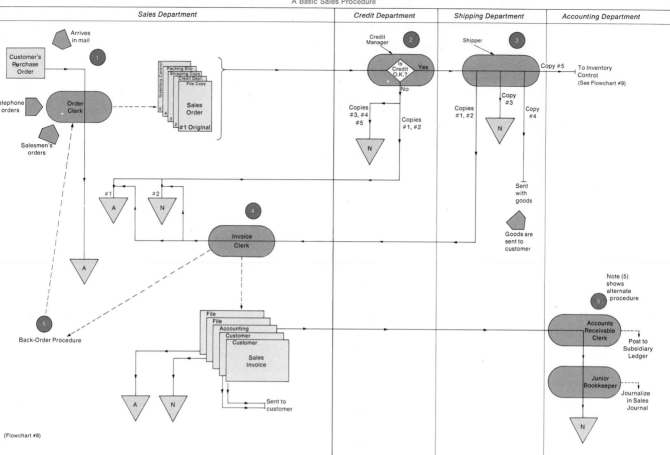

| Sales Department | Credit Department | Shipping Department | Accounting Department |

(Flowchart #8)

ment prepares the goods for shipment. This involves (a) obtaining the goods from the stockkeeper, (b) packaging and wrapping the goods if necessary, (c) addressing the goods, (d) completing the shipper's portion of the Sales Order form, separating the copies of the form and enclosing the Packing Slip copy, (e) loading the goods for delivery.

The relationship between the Shipping Department and the stockroom must of necessity be a close one and in many businesses, the stockroom comes under the jurisdiction of the Shipping Department. In most cases, the stockroom is located close to the shipping facilities. This is an efficient arrangement because it enables the shipping room employees to learn quickly what goods are in stock, and it also speeds up delivery.

The shipping room and the

THE QUICK CO.
500 Wood Street
Morgantown

SALES ORDER
NO. 1168

Date	May 12, 19—		Salesman	J. Green
Sold to	Irving Frank + Co.		Ship To	Same
Address	21 James Street		Address	
City	Morgantown		City	
P.O. No.	69	Terms Net 30 days	Date Req.	May 31

Quantity	Stock No.	Description	Unit Price	Quantity Shipped	Quantity Back Ordered
15	H96	Hammers	2.49		
24	H16	Saw Blades	.51		
3	D.40	100' ½" hose	12.75		

| Via | Our truck | F.O.B. | Frank + Co. | Shipper | |
| Credit Approved | | | | | |

stockroom are two areas of a business that require strict accounting controls. This is especially true of businesses that deal in such goods as hardware items, radios, clothing, etc., that may be tempting to steal, easy to dispose of for cash, and difficult to identify. The flowchart on page 215 describes a system that has the following accounting controls:

(a) No one except the stockkeeper and his assistants are allowed into the stockroom.

(b) No goods may be released from the stockroom for shipment unless a proper Sales Order (copy #3 in this case) is presented.

(c) The Sales Order forms are serially numbered and kept under the control of the Sales Order clerk.

(d) No goods may be shipped without there being a Packing Slip (copy #4) sent with them.

(e) Copy #5 of the Sales Order is forwarded to the Inventory Control section where the quantities of all goods are kept track of and periodically checked against the actual goods on hand.

The shipper must complete the shipper's portion of the Sales Order form. He does this by (a) writing in the quantity shipped, (b) writing in the quantity back-ordered*, (c) signing his name in the appropriate place on the form, and (d) if the method of shipment is changed from that shown on

* If the business is short of a particular item and is unable to fill the customer's order for that item entirely, the shipper ships as many of the item as he has on hand. He records this under 'Quantity Shipped'. At the same time, he finds out if the short item is in the process of being re-stocked. If the answer is 'yes', he records the quantity that was short in the section headed 'Back-Ordered'. This action initiates a new order for the quantity that was short-shipped (see Note 6).

the form, changing the information on the form. See the illustration below.

(4) The primary function of the invoice clerk is to prepare the typewritten Sales Invoice (except where the system is automated). Once prepared, the copies of the Sales Invoice are separated and started on their special ways. All the information necessary for the preparation of the Sales Invoice, except the sales tax which must be calculated, is to be found on the Sales Order copies. Only goods actually shipped are invoiced. An example of a completed Sales Invoice appears on page 217.

(5) The flowchart illustrates a simple and common method of handling the accounting entries for Sales Invoices. With this method, each invoice is used

first as the source of an entry to the Account Receivable Ledger and second as the source of an entry in the Sales Journal. However, this is not the only method available to the accountant. Two common alternatives are described below:

Alternative 1

(a) Make the postings to the Accounts Receivable Ledger from the individual invoice copies as shown in the flowchart.

(b) Do not journalize each individual invoice as shown in the flowchart. **Instead**, accumulate the Sales Invoices for each month in a binder. At the end of each month, using an adding machine, summarize these Sales Invoices to find the accounting entry for the month.

THE QUICK CO.				SALES ORDER	
500 Wood Street Morgantown				NO. 1168	

Date May 12, 19—			Salesman J. Green		
Sold to Irving Frank + Co.			Ship To Same		
Address 21 James Street			Address		
City Morgantown			City		
P.O. No. 69		Terms Net 30 days		Date Req. May 31	

Quantity	Stock No.	Description	Unit Price	Quantity Shipped	Quantity Back Ordered
15	H96	Hammers	2.49	15	
24	H16	Saw Blades	.51	20	4
3	D40	100' ½" hose	12.75	3	

Via Our truck	F.O.B. Frank + Co.	Shipper
Credit Approved R. B. Hamilton		

Journalize this accounting entry in the General Journal. With this system, the accounting entry will be the same as when a Sales Journal is used, but there will be no actual Sales Journal. The Sales Journal for any month is replaced by a binder containing all the Sales Invoices for that month.

Alternative 2

(a) Have two copies of the Sales Invoices come to the accounting department.
(b) Do not have the conventional type of subsidiary ledger for Accounts Receivable (i.e., account pages or account cards). **Instead**, let the Sales Invoice copies (one of the two copies received) form the Accounts Receivable Ledger. As the Sales Invoice copies are received they are placed in an 'Unpaid Invoices' file. As the invoices are paid they are taken out of the 'Unpaid Invoices' file and are placed in a 'Paid Invoices' file. When an invoice is partially paid the amount of the partial payment is noted on the invoice copy but the copy remains in the 'unpaid' file until it is paid in its entirety. The invoices remaining in the 'unpaid' file represent the Accounts Receivable of the business.

Although theoretically simple, this system requires strong accounting controls. Only authorized personnel may have access to the files. The difficulty lies in the danger of invoice copies being removed from the files by non-authorized persons and of the copies not being returned or of their being placed back in the wrong file.

(c) The second invoice copy is used as the source document for the journal entries. Either of the two methods shown above may be selected; that is, the method shown on the flowchart or the method described in alternative 1.

(6) *'Back-Order Procedure'*

You have already seen that when an order can be only partially filled the goods that are available are shipped and billed (i.e., an invoice is issued to the customer). This allows the customer to have immediately those goods that are available.

When the invoice clerk receives Sales Orders showing that certain items have been back-ordered, in addition to performing the normal routine, she also prepares a new Sales Order for the goods that are back-ordered. In this respect, the invoice clerk works under the control and supervision of the order clerk.

These new Sales Orders are processed in the usual manner except that when they arrive at the Shipping Department they will be set aside awaiting the arrival of the merchandise to be shipped.

THE QUICK CO.		SALES INVOICE	
500 Wood Street Morgantown		NO. 510	

Sold to: Irving Frank & Co.
21 James Street
Morgantown

Date: May 15, 19--
P.O. No.: 69
Terms: Net 30 days

Shipped by	Via	F.O.B.	
Truck	Our Truck	Frank & Co.	

Quantity		Description	Unit Price	Amount
15	H 96	Hammers	$2.49	$37.35
20	H 16	Saw Blades	.51	10.20
3	G 40	100 ft. 1/2 in. hose	12.75	38.25
				$85.80
		5 Per Cent Sales Tax		4.39
			Total	$90.09

Bookkeeping and Accounting Terms

Shipping Order:
Sales Order:
A business form originated by the Order Department (a division of the Sales Department) on which is recorded detailed information in respect to goods or services requested for purchase by customers.

Review Questions

1. Would all businesses receive orders from customers in the three ways indicated on the flowchart; i.e., by mail, by telephone, and by salesmen? Explain.
2. With what business form is the sales routine started? List the key pieces of information shown on this form.
3. Why is it important that a customer's credit be approved by the Credit Department?
4. If credit is approved, what happens next to the Sales Order set?
5. If credit is not approved, what happens to the five copies of the Sales Order set?
6. If a customer's credit is not good, what alternatives does the credit manager have?
7. Explain the function of the Shipping Department.
8. Describe the steps necessary to get goods ready for shipment.
9. Explain the purpose of copy #4 of the Sales Order.
10. Explain why the stockroom is usually close to the shipping room.
11. Why are strict controls necessary in the shipping room and the stockroom?
12. Name the five steps of internal control in the stockroom. Discuss the merits of each step.
13. Explain the meaning of 'back-ordering'.
14. How does the invoice clerk obtain the information necessary to prepare the Sales Invoices?
15. Why is there both a numerical and an alphabetical file of Sales Order copies?
16. How does the invoice clerk know when to follow the back-order procedure?
17. What key information is shown on the Sales Invoice?
18. What is the source document for debit entries to the Accounts Receivable Ledger?

INDIVIDUAL PROJECTS

1. Write a brief report explaining the methods used by a Credit Department to find out about the credit reputation of its customers and potential customers. The information for this report is best obtained by contacting directly the credit manager of a local business.
2. Ask the office manager of a local business to assist you in preparing a flowchart of the sales routine for his business.

CLASS PROJECT

Collect samples of Sales Orders and Sales Invoices from a number of businesses. Display these forms on the bulletin board.

Inventory Control (Manual Perpetual Inventory System for a Trading Company)

For many businesses, the keeping of accurate and up-to-date information about inventories is an essential requirement. Manufacturers must avoid stoppages in production due to lack of parts or materials; wholesalers must maintain adequate supplies of merchandise to meet the needs of their customers. Therefore, these and other businesses must keep on hand certain minimum quantities of all inventory items. And to be able to do this they must know what quantities they have on hand.

The most efficient way of keeping track of the many inventory items is by means of a card record called a 'perpetual inventory' file. A flowchart describing a perpetual inventory system (manual method) is shown at the top of page 219. Along with its accompanying notes it describes a typical manual system.

NOTES TO FLOWCHART #9

(1) A perpetual inventory file is made up of a number of cards such as the one shown on page 219. One card is included for each individual item kept in stock.

In the top portion of an inventory card (stock card), the following information is recorded:

(a) The Stock Number. In a handwritten system, the stock number is used for accurate and easy reference. However, in modern automated systems, the Stock Number is of far greater importance. Some manual systems include a stock number only because they expect to make a change to an automated system in the near future and by already having the stock numbers in use the transition from a 'manual' to an 'automated' system may be made more easily.

(b) A general description of the merchandise.

(c) The location of the merchandise in the warehouse.

(d) The maximum and minimum quantities to be kept in stock. The purpose of setting a 'maximum' figure is to avoid having any more funds tied up in inventory than is necessary. The purpose of setting a 'minimum' figure is to avoid running short of any item and therefore being unable to supply a customer.

These maximum and minimum quantities are decided upon by management on the basis of factors such as (1) sales statistics, (2) seasonal nature of the inventory item, (3) nearness to a source of supply, and (4) expected changes in the market. From time to time they are reviewed and changed if necessary.

For each inventory item, there is an inventory card. The main body of the card is used to keep track of the quantity of the item in stock. Changes in the quantities result from goods being shipped out to customers or being received in from suppliers or returned from customers. The inventory clerk learns of these transactions by means of the Shipping Orders (Sales Orders) and the Receiving Reports that come to his desk. Each Shipping Order represents a shipment of goods out of the plant and must

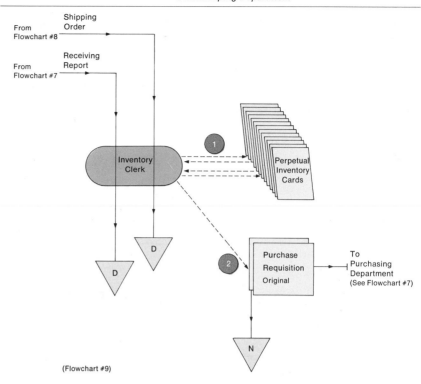

Stockkeeping Department

(Flowchart #9)

INVENTORY CONTROL CARD

Stock Number L 591
Description 200 Watt Light Bulbs
Location: Row 17 Bin 35

Maximum 500 DOZ.
Minimum 50 DOZ.

Date	Reference	Unit Cost	Quantity Received	Quantity Shipped	Balance on Hand
19— nov. 5	Balance forward				216
11	S.O. 436			100	116
14	S.O. 501			40	76
19	S.O. 530			35	41
21	S.O. 539			20	21
22	R.R. 1074	41¢	450		471
25	S.O. 561			75	396

be recorded on the appropriate card as a decrease. Each Receiving Report represents a receipt of goods into the plant and must be recorded on the appropriate card as an increase.

Observe that each time a new supply of an item is purchased the unit cost is recorded on the inventory card as well as the quantity. This unit cost is used at the end of the fiscal period when the merchandise inventory is evaluated for the financial statements.

(2) In addition to keeping the perpetual inventory cards up to date, the inventory clerk is responsible for initiating the Purchase Requisition required to order the additional goods that may be necessary. Each time a shipment is recorded he must compare the 'balance on hand' figure with the 'minimum' figure shown at the top of the card. If the balance on hand is equal to or lower than the minimum suggested, the inventory clerk must write up a Purchase Requisition ordering a sufficient quantity of the goods to bring the balance on hand up to the suggested maximum figure.

Bookkeeping and Accounting Terms

Perpetual Inventory: An inventory system in which a detailed record for each inventory item is kept showing the quantity of the item on hand and the unit cost of the item.

Review Questions

1. Name three businesses for which inventory control is essential. Give reasons for your choices.
2. Name three businesses for which inventory control is not essential. Give reasons for your choices.
3. A business should carry as small an inventory as it effectively can. Explain the disadvantage of carrying too much inventory.
4. What information is shown on a perpetual inventory card?
5. Explain the use and importance of stock numbers.

6. Name the two source documents for entries to the perpetual inventory.
7. The inventory clerk has two main responsibilities. Describe them briefly.
8. How does the inventory clerk know when it is necessary to order an inventory item?
9. How does the inventory clerk arrive at the quantity of an item to be ordered?

10. Invariably, for some of the inventory items, the physical quantity actually on hand will disagree with the quantity shown on the inventory card. Explain the factors that could cause this.
11. Periodically, the perpetual inventory cards are all made correct. How is this accomplished?
12. Explain how the maximum and the minimum figures are arrived at.
13. Explain the purpose of recording the unit cost on the inventory cards.

INDIVIDUAL PROJECT

Arrange to visit a company that has a perpetual inventory of parts and materials to be used by the business (for example, a manufacturing company). Find out how this type of perpetual inventory differs from the one described in this text for a trading company. Write a brief report.

CLASS PROJECT

Arrange to visit a business to view the shipping and stockroom facilities. Write a brief report. In your report, explain the accounting controls that are used.

Inventory Control For A Trading Company (Automated System Using Punched Cards)

In larger businesses where the number of transactions is very high and where more and faster information is demanded, inventories are usually maintained by means of automated equipment such as a computer. The flowchart on page 221 together with its accompanying notes describes such a system.

NOTES TO FLOWCHART #10

(1) As in the manual method, the Shipping Orders and the Receiving Reports are the source documents representing changes in the inventory. In an automated system, these source documents are forwarded to a keypunch operator in the Data Processing Department. For each different inventory item on each source document the keypunch operator prepares a 'punched' card that contains the essential details of the transaction in coded form (using combinations of punched holes). This card is known as the 'transaction' card. All of the transaction cards together are known as the Transaction File. A transaction card is shown in the centre of page 221.

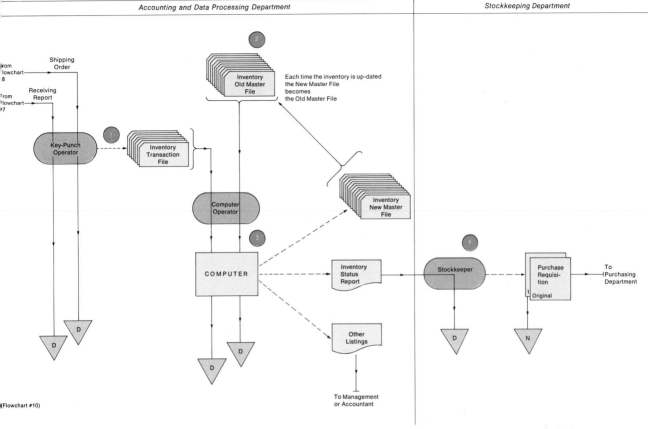

(Flowchart #10)

(2) Each week (or each day in some businesses) the entire inventory records are updated by the computer (or other automated equipment) and produced in printed and punched card form. One card is produced for each inventory item. All of the inventory cards together are known as a **Master File**. The most recent master file is called the New Master File; the next to most recent one is called the Old Master File. An example of an inventory master file card is shown lower right.

(3) The Old Master File and the Inventory Transaction File are fed into the computer which is programmed to update the inventory. Among those things produced will be a New Master File of punched cards and an Inventory Status Report. A sample page of a computer-

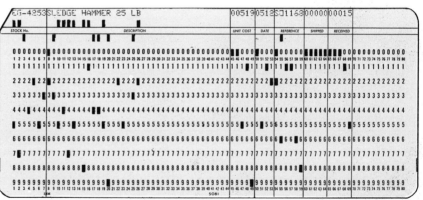

Inventory Card–Transaction File (Courtesy of IBM Canada Ltd.)

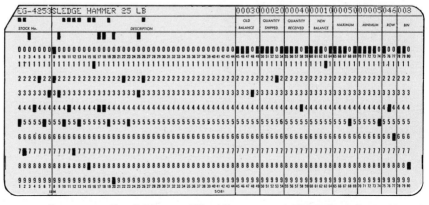

Inventory Card–Master File (Courtesy of IBM Canada Ltd.)

STOCK NUMBER	DESCRIPTION	OLD BALANCE	QUANTITY RECEIVED	QUANTITY SHIPPED	NEW BALANCE	MAXIMUM	MINIMUM
EH-3703	BALL HAMMER 8 OZ	74	0	33	41	100	40
EH-3704	BALL HAMMER 16 OZ	52	50	26	76	100	25
EH-3705	BALL HAMMER 24 OZ	24	170	19	175	200	25
EH-3707	BALL HAMMER 32 OZ	36	150	170	16	200	25
EH-3709	BALL HAMMER 40 OZ	47	0	6	41	200	25
EG-4119	CLAW HAMMER 13 OZ	12	35	1	46	50	15
EG-4126	CLAW HAMMER 16 OZ	74	0	32	42	200	50
EG-4131	CLAW HAMMER 16 OZ (STANLEY)	156	0	53	103	300	100
EG-4132	CLAW HAMMER 16 OZ (NEOPHRENE HANDLE)	13	0	5	8	25	10
EG-4135	CLAW HAMMER 16 OZ (LEATHER HANDLE)	90	200	5	285	300	100
EG-4108	TACK HAMMER 8 OZ	54	95	3	146	150	50
EH-3725	BRICK HAMMER	12	60	2	70	75	25
BE-5263	RUBBER MALLET 14 OZ	32	0	12	20	100	25
BE-5266	RUBBER MALLET 28 OZ	27	70	13	84	100	25
EH-3753	SLEDGE HAMMER 6 LB	40	0	20	20	100	25
EH-3755	SLEDGE HAMMER 8 LB	11	90	3	98	100	25
EH-3757	SLEDGE HAMMER 10 LB	5	45	3	47	50	10
EG-3203	HAND DRILL 1/4 INCH	37	0	13	24	100	25
EG-3206	HAND DRILL 1/4 INCH HEAVY DUTY	46	0	15	31	100	25
EG-3224	AUTOMATIC PUSH DRILL (8 BITS)	56	0	27	29	100	25

(Courtesy of IBM Canada Ltd.)

produced Inventory Status Report is shown above.

(4) The Inventory Status Report is designed for easy analysis by the stockkeeper. In analysing the report, he looks in particular to see which items are in short supply and therefore need to be restocked. For any item which shows a balance on hand lower than the suggested minimum, he will write up a Purchase Requisition to initiate the ordering of additional stock.

Review Questions

1. What type of businesses require automated inventory control systems?
2. Name the source document for an increase in inventory.
3. Name the source document for a decrease in inventory.
4. Explain what happens to the two source documents.
5. What does a keypunch operator do?
6. What is a transaction card?
7. How many transaction cards are prepared from the information on one Sales Order?
8. What is a transaction file?
9. Explain the difference between the new master file and the old master file.
10. What is the 'input' to the computer?
11. What is the 'output' to the computer?
12. Who receives the Inventory Status Report? For what purpose does he use it?
13. List the key information that appears on the Inventory Status Report?
14. "The master file is updated." Explain.
15. How often is a master file updated?
16. How does the new master file become the old master file?
17. What is the purpose of the Purchase Requisition?

Visit a computer installation to view an inventory updating procedure. Observe both the differences and the similarities between the system you observe and the one described in this chapter. Summarize your findings.

Basic Procedure for Accounts Payable and Cheque Preparation

Flowchart #11 below illustrates a basic procedure for the processing of Purchase Invoices and for the preparation of the cheques to pay them. Study this flowchart and the accompanying notes carefully.

NOTES TO FLOWCHART #11

(1) The Sales Invoice is a business form prepared by the seller of goods or services whenever he makes a sale on account. Two copies of the Sales Invoice are sent to the purchaser.

In the Accounting Department of the purchaser the suppliers' Sales Invoices are referred to as 'Purchase Invoices' in order to distinguish them from the business' own Sales Invoices.

(2) The 'processing of a Purchase Invoice begins at the desk of a junior clerk. As you can see from the flowchart, this clerk

receives a copy of the Purchase Order and a copy of the Purchase Invoice. Among this clerk's various duties are the following:

(a) To mark (using a rubber stamp and ink pad) the Purchase Invoice with an **Authorizations Stamp** such as the one shown below.

AUTHORIZATIONS	
AGREED WITH PURCHASE ORDER	_Jd._
EXTENSIONS AND ADDITIONS	_Jd._
GOODS RECEIVED	_O.Y._
ACCOUNTS TO BE CHARGED	51
APPROVED FOR PAYMENT	_M.M._

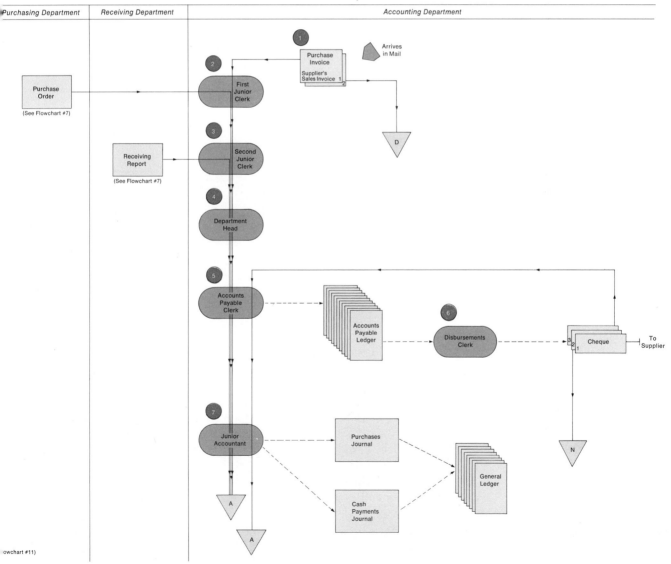

A Basic Accounts Payable Procedure

(b) To check the extensions (quantity times price) and the additions on the Purchase Invoice.

(c) To compare the Purchase Order with the Purchase Invoice to ensure that the details (quantities, prices, part numbers, etc.) are in agreement.

If everything is in order the clerk initials the Purchase Invoice in the appropriate sections of the 'Authorizations' stamp. The Purchase Invoice and the Purchase Order copy are clipped together and forwarded to another clerk for further processing. Purchase Invoices that are not correct in all respects are separated from the others and given to a senior person for investigation and clarification.

(3) All Purchase Invoice-Purchase Order combinations arrive at the desk of a second junior clerk. This clerk also receives a copy of all Receiving Reports. It is the responsibility of this clerk to match the Receiving Reports with the Purchase Invoice-Purchase Order combinations. Matched documents are attached together, initialed by the clerk in the appropriate section of the 'Authorizations' stamp, and forwarded for additional processing. Unmatched forms stay at the desk of the clerk awaiting a partner. After a reasonable period of time, those that do not match are given to a senior person for special attention.

(4) The final step in the verification of the purchase documents is the scrutiny and approval by the department head. He initials the matched set of purchase documents if he is satisfied that all aspects of the accounting routine have been carried out properly. His initials indicate that the Purchase Invoice is approved for payment.

(5) The Accounts Payable clerk posts directly from the source documents to the individual accounts in the Accounts Payable Ledger. The Purchase Invoice matched sets are posted as credits; the cheque copies, if they affect the customers' accounts, are posted as debits. The posting process may be done manually or by means of a posting machine.

(6) The Disbursements Clerk has the responsibility for preparing all cheques as required and of mailing them to the intended recipients. Most cheques issued are for goods and services received from suppliers, and consequently the information for the preparation of these cheques comes from the Accounts Payable Ledger. Periodically, the clerk examines the accounts in the ledger and decides who should be paid and how much they should receive. Then the cheques are prepared, signed by company officials, and sent on their way.

The information for every cheque is not obtained from the Accounts Payable Ledger. Many cheques are issued merely on the instructions of the Disbursement Clerk who is completely familiar with all business activities that require the issuing of cheques. For example, he knows of all contracts, loan agreements, instalment purchases, and so on entered into by the business. He will originate some cheques merely upon the receipt of a written memorandum from a senior company officer.

(7) The Purchase Invoice matched sets are the source documents for the accounting entries to the Purchases Journal. The cheque copies are the source documents for the accounting entries to the Cash Payments Journal.

Review Questions

1. Explain the difference between a Sales Invoice and a Purchase Invoice.
2. Briefly describe the duties of the first junior clerk.
3. Explain the purpose of the Authorizations stamp.
4. Explain the meaning of the term 'matching'.
5. Which documents match? Explain.
6. Briefly describe the duties of the second junior clerk.
7. Will there be a Receiving Report to match every Purchase Invoice? Explain.
8. When all of the authorizations are completed, what is the status of the Purchase Invoice?
9. Name the source document for debit entries to the Accounts Payable Ledger.
10. Name the source document for entries in the Purchases Journal.
11. Name the source document for credit entries to the Accounts Payable Ledger.
12. Name the source document for entries to the Cash Payments Journal.
13. Briefly explain the duties of the Disbursements clerk.
14. Do you think that the work of the Disbursements clerk is important? Explain.
15. How does the Disbursements clerk know what cheques should be issued?

INDIVIDUAL PROJECT

Write a report describing the aspects of internal control that are present in the Accounts Payable routine.

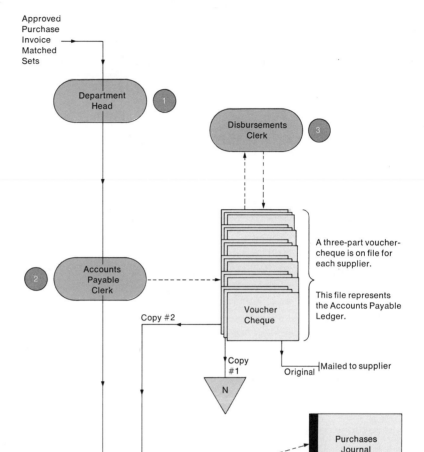

(Flowchart #12)

Cheque Preparation for Accounts Payable (Voucher Cheque System)

A second alternate method of preparing cheques is described by means of the flowchart on the right and the accompanying explanatory notes.

NOTES TO FLOWCHART #12

(1) As in the previous method, the Purchase Invoice matched sets undergo a series of veryifying steps. The final step is the authorization by the Department Head.

(2) The heart of this system is the voucher cheque such as the one at the top of page 226.

In addition to serving as the cheque with which payment is made to the supplier, the voucher cheque also serves as a form of Accounts Payable account. There is kept on file a voucher cheque for each supplier. The supplier's name is the first item of information that is placed on the cheque. The file of cheques represents the Accounts Payable Ledger. As approved Purchase Invoices

(or Credit Notes representing adjustments to previous Purchase Invoices) are received by the Accounts Payable clerk, they are recorded in the voucher section of the appropriate suppliers' cheques.

The voucher section of the cheque is designed for the accumulation of several Purchase Invoices. The cheque shown upper right has four entries on it, three charges and one credit. Although the balance owing to the supplier is not shown, it can be readily found by means of an adding machine.

(3) The Disbursements clerk has the responsibility of authorizing payments to be made to suppliers. To carry out this responsibility it is necessary for him to be thoroughly familiar with the file of voucher cheques, the suppliers' terms of sale, and the due dates and the discount dates of the invoices.

When he decides that a certain supplier should be paid, he instructs a subordinate clerk to total the Purchase Invoices listed on the voucher section of the cheque (Net Amount column) and to complete the cheque section of the form. The cheque is then signed by an officer of the company and the three parts are sent on their respective ways. Before being mailed the completed cheque appears as shown lower right.

(4) The junior accountant journalizes from the Purchase Invoices to the Purchases Journal and from the cheque copies to the Cash Payments Journal.

With this particular system, it is not necessary to use a Cash Payments Journal although one may choose to do so. Instead the following technique may be used:

(a) During each month, accumulate in a binder all the *accounting* copies of the voucher cheques.

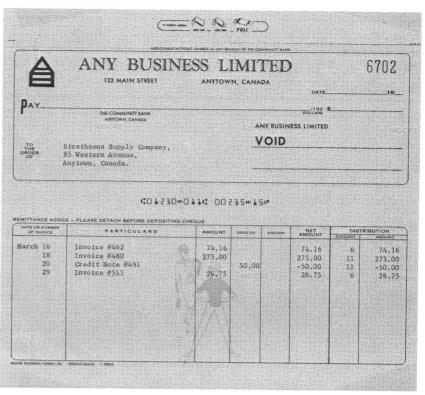

Partially Completed Voucher Cheque

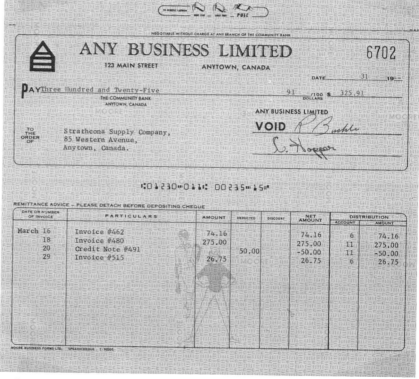

Completed Voucher Cheque (Courtesy of Moore Business Forms Ltd.)

(b) At the end of each month, summarize these voucher cheque copies to determine the required accounting entry for the month. To do this it is necessary to go through the vouchers several times using an adding machine to accumulate the total charges to each of the various accounts listed in the section of the cheque headed 'Distribution'. The credit to Bank is obtained by totaling all of the cheque amounts. The accounting entry for the month will be the same as if a Cash Payments Journal had been used. The accounting entry is journalized in the General Journal when this system is used.

Review Questions

1. The voucher cheque has two major parts. Explain what they are.
2. Explain briefly how the voucher cheque is used to accumulate the liability to a supplier.
3. Explain how the voucher cheque is used to pay a debt.
4. Explain the work of the Disbursements clerk.
5. Briefly explain the alternate procedure to using a Cash Payments Journal. What are the advantages and the disadvantages?

CLASS PROJECT

Obtain samples and literature from a manufacturer of voucher cheques. Prepare a bulletin board display.

Chapter 13

PAYROLL ACCOUNTING

The term payroll is used to refer to that portion of the accounting process which deals specifically with the salaries and wages paid to employees for a certain period of time. This certain period of time, referred to as the pay period, may be a weekly, bi-weekly (every two weeks), semi-monthly (every ½ month), or monthly pay period. The federal government, through various legislation such as the Income Tax Act, the Unemployment Insurance Act and the Canada Pension Plan Act requires the employer to keep accurate records of all salaries and wages paid to each employee for each pay period.

The following excerpt from a government publication tells what records must be kept for the Canada Pension Plan.

"You will need records sufficient to determine correct contributions. In order to prepare the annual T4 return you will need to know the total earnings, contributory earnings, if different from total earnings, and the correct contributions for the year."*

Similar information with respect to Unemployment Insurance is given in another government publication.

"Employers are required to keep a record of the remuneration paid to their employees and to have such record available for inspection by an auditor of the Commission.

"Unemployment Insurance Auditors visit all employers to ensure that

every employer is complying with the law.

"If you do not keep the records required, you are liable to prosecution and the auditor will determine contributions payable on the basis of five per cent of the actual estimated remuneration paid or payable to your insurable employees. This increases the amount of your liability. It is therefore to your advantage to keep proper records.

"The books and records . . . are required to be kept and made available at any reasonable time requested by an auditor at:

(i) your place of business or other place designated by you,

or

(ii) your residence or other place designated by the auditor if you have no place of business or have not designated one to the Commission."†

It is important that care be taken in the preparation of the payroll. All the payroll data must be collected carefully and accurately in order that calculations resulting in the proper pay for each employee may be made. Once the payroll is prepared, the data are used to record the appropriate amount of expenses to the salaries and wages accounts. Also, as previously mentioned, the government requires accurate payroll records to determine the employees' and the employer's liabilities for taxes, pension premiums, and unemployment insurance premiums.

Methods of Paying Employees

There are three basic methods of calculating the pay for an employee: Employees are paid either a salary, a wage, or a commission.

Salaries

Salaries are paid to office workers, teachers, supervisors, executives, and civil servants. Salaries are usually paid on a yearly basis with equal payments being made each pay period. For example, consider the case of Harold Evans who is employed by Viking Enterprises, a food wholesaler. Mr. Evans receives an annual salary of $7,670 and is paid every two weeks (bi-weekly). His pay for each pay period is calculated as follows:

$$\underbrace{7{,}670}_{\text{annual salary}} \div \underbrace{26}_{\substack{\text{pay periods} \\ \text{per year}}} = \underbrace{\$295}_{\text{per pay period}}$$

Wages

Wages are paid to workers in large factories and shops. A person paid on a wages basis receives a certain amount of pay for each hour worked, with payments being made some time after the completion of the pay period. In some industries, a wage-earner may be paid on a piece-work basis so that his wage is measured by how much production he turns out. Some businesses pay a certain minimum amount based on the hours worked plus a piece-work bonus for extra quantities produced over and above a stated amount per day or per week.

* Department of National Revenue, Taxation Division, *Information for Employers, The Canada Pension Plan* (Ottawa: the Queen's Printer, 1965), p. 19.

† Unemployment Insurance Commission, *Information for Employers on Unemployment Insurance* (Ottawa: the Queen's Printer, 1968), p. 17.

Time Card							
Week Ended		September 14		19			
Social INS. No.	603 456 667						
Name	Burns, Joseph						
Day	Morning In Out		Afternoon In Out		Extra In Out		Total Hours
M	7:58	12:01	12:59	5:01			8
T	7:56	12:01	12:58	5:02			8
W	8:03	12:00	12:58	5:01			7¾
T	7:58	12:01	12:59	5:01			8
F	7:59	12:01	12:57	5:00	5:57	7:02	8 / 1
S	7:59	12:02					/ 4
S							
				Hours	Rate	Earnings
Regular Time				39¾	2.48	98:58
Overtime				5	3.72	18.60
Gross Pay						117.80

Time Clock (Courtesy of Simplex International Time Equipment Co. Ltd.)

TIME-CLOCKS AND TIME CARDS

Where the amount of an employee's pay depends on the number of hours he has worked, a method is needed to record (a) the time that each employee starts work each morning, afternoon, and evening; (b) the time that each employee leaves work each morning, afternoon, and evening.

This record permits the payroll department to calculate the total hours worked by each employee for each pay period. A mechanical device that is widely used to accumulate this information is the time-clock and time cards.

When a time card is inserted into the time-clock, the mechanism of the clock automatically imprints the time at which the employee is entering or leaving the plant. Time-clocks are usually located near the employees' entrance to the plant. The time card shown above right is for a one-week period. The times are automatically recorded by the clock in either of six positions—Morning In, Morning Out, Afternoon In, Afternoon Out, Extra In, Extra Out.

COMPLETING THE TIME CARD

At the end of the payroll period the payroll clerk completes the time cards for all of the employees. To do this he must, for each card—

1. Calculate the number of hours worked each day (both regular and overtime).

Notes:

(a) For this particular business the regular work week consists of a five-day week of eight hours per day. Any time worked after 5:00 p.m., or on Saturday and Sunday, is considered to be overtime.

(b) Most business firms have some rules with respect to employees who are late coming to work. Assume that employees are penalized 15 minutes if they are late by one to 15 minutes, 30 minutes if they are late 16 to 30 mintues, and so on.

2. Total the number of regular hours.

3. Total the number of overtime hours.

4. Complete the bottom section of the card. There is space provided to multiply the regular hours by the regular rate, and the overtime hours by the overtime rate. Then, the regular earnings and the overtime earnings are added together to obtain the gross earnings for the employee.

Commission

Commission is paid to salesmen, sales clerks, and sales agents. Commission is a stated percentage of the sales made and completed by the employee. In most cases, however, a basic salary is paid to the employee in addition to the commission to provide him with at least a minimum income during difficult periods. To illustrate how this affects a particular employee, consider the following. Rod Ferguson, a salesman for Viking Enterprises, receives $70 per week with a commission equal to one half per cent of the net sales made by him. During the last two weeks Mr. Ferguson sold $29,000 worth of merchandise.

Calculation:

Basic Salary (2 weeks × $70.00)	=	$140.00
Commission (½ % of $29,000.00)	=	$145.00
Total Earnings for two weeks	=	$285.00

Payroll Deductions

You are probably aware of the factors involved in the preparation of a pay cheque. Employees are hired with the understanding that they will be paid a certain amount per hour, week, or year. You will recall that Harold Evans receives an annual salary of $7,670 payable every two weeks in equal portions of $295. When Evans received his last pay cheque, it was made out in the amount of $224.43. The difference between the $295 and the $224.43 he received is $70.57. Harold Evans was not short-changed. The $70.57 represents various deductions made. The $295 is referred to as the **Gross Pay** while the $224.43 is referred to as the **Net Pay**. The payroll equation, therefore, is as follows:

For
Harold Evans:
GROSS PAY − DEDUCTIONS = NET PAY
$295 − $70.57 = $244.43

The calculations that were necessary in order to arrive at the net pay for Harold Evans were made on a special columnar paper called a **Payroll Journal**, Payroll Summary or Payroll Register. Viking Enterprises, the wholesaling firm which employs Evans, uses the Payroll Journal illustrated below.

As was previously mentioned, the employer is required to withhold a portion of the employee's pay from his pay cheque because of government legislation. These deductions include Canada or Quebec Pension, personal income taxes, and Unemployment Insurance. Naturally, care must be taken to see that each employee is credited properly for his contributions. To assist in this respect the federal government requires each employee to apply for a Social Insurance Number as soon as he starts to work. This is his permanent identification number. With the increasing use of computers to process information, the Social Insurance Number becomes very important. Below is an illustration of the Social Insurance Card showing the Social Insurance Number.

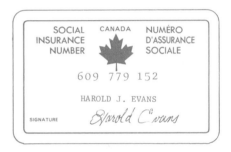

Canada Pension Plan or Quebec Pension Plan

The first deduction to be considered is the Canada Pension Plan or Quebec Pension Plan. There are many people who are unable, during their

PAYROLL JOURNAL									For the _____ ended _____ 19___						
Employee	Total Personal Exempt.	Hours		Earnings			Deductions							Net Pay	Cheque Number
		Reg.	O/T	Regular	Extra	Total	C.P.P.	Income Tax	U.I.C.	Hospital Ins.	Medical Ins	Union Dues	Group Life		

productive working years, to accumulate enough savings for those days when they will no longer be able to work. Pension plans were devised to provide an income for people after retirement or for those who have to stop working because of disabilities. They also provide an income for a wife if she is widowed.

The federal government instituted a pension plan for the Canadian worker which became effective as of January 1, 1966. This plan, which is named the Canada Pension Plan, is called the Quebec Pension Plan in the Province of Quebec and is administered there by the provincial government, but elsewhere by the federal government. Both plans are portable.

The following are extracts from a booklet on the Canada Pension Plan prepared by the Department of National Health and Welfare, Canada.

"The Plan operates in all parts of the country except where a province establishes its own comparable program. The Province of Quebec is doing so. The two Plans are to be closely co-ordinated.

"This means that if your place of employment is changed to Quebec or if as a self-employed person you move your residence to Quebec, your contributions to the Quebec Pension Plan will produce the same benefits as are described in this booklet. The reverse also applies. Anyone who is now in Quebec, but later moves to take up work in any other part of the country, will get the same benefits as if he had contributed to one Plan throughout.

"Benefits are portable. Once you have contributed to the Plan, you cannot lose the right to the retirement pension based on those years of contribution. If you change jobs in Canada, your pension rights are the same as if you had been in one job all the time. If you leave Canada, you retain your right to the pension you earned before you left. The same rules apply to the other benefits, provided that you meet the qualifying conditions. . .

BI-WEEKLY PAY PERIOD
.$.00 — $182.79

Maximum employee contribution to be withheld for the year by an employer is $82.80.
Employers are required to match their employee's contribution.

REMUNERATION	DEDUCT	REMUNERATION	DEDUCT	REMUNERATION	DEDUCT	REMUNERATION	DEDUCT
.00 — 23.08	.00	62.80 — 63.35	.72	102.80 — 103.35	1.44	142.80 — 143.35	2.16
23.09 — 23.91	.01	63.36 — 63.91	.73	103.36 — 103.91	1.45	143.36 — 143.91	2.17
23.92 — 24.46	.02	63.92 — 64.46	.74	103.92 — 104.46	1.46	143.92 — 144.46	2.18
24.47 — 25.02	.03	64.47 — 65.02	.75	104.47 — 105.02	1.47	144.47 — 145.02	2.19
25.03 — 25.57	.04	65.03 — 65.57	.76	105.03 — 105.57	1.48	145.03 — 145.57	2.20
25.58 — 26.13	.05	65.58 — 66.13	.77	105.58 — 106.13	1.49	145.58 — 146.13	2.21
26.14 — 26.68	.06	66.14 — 66.68	.78	106.14 — 106.68	1.50	146.14 — 146.68	2.22
26.69 — 27.24	.07	66.69 — 67.24	.79	106.69 — 107.24	1.51	146.69 — 147.24	2.23
27.25 — 27.79	.08	67.25 — 67.79	.80	107.25 — 107.79	1.52	147.25 — 147.79	2.24
27.80 — 28.35	.09	67.80 — 68.35	.81	107.80 — 108.35	1.53	147.80 — 148.35	2.25
28.36 — 28.91	.10	68.36 — 68.91	.82	108.36 — 108.91	1.54	148.36 — 148.91	2.26
28.92 — 29.46	.11	68.92 — 69.46	.83	108.92 — 109.46	1.55	148.92 — 149.46	2.27
29.47 — 30.02	.12	69.47 — 70.02	.84	109.47 — 110.02	1.56	149.47 — 150.02	2.28
30.03 — 30.57	.13	70.03 — 70.57	.85	110.03 — 110.57	1.57	150.03 — 150.57	2.29
30.58 — 31.13	.14	70.58 — 71.13	.86	110.58 — 111.13	1.58	150.58 — 151.13	2.30
31.14 — 31.68	.15	71.14 — 71.68	.87	111.14 — 111.68	1.59	151.14 — 151.68	2.31
31.69 — 32.24	.16	71.69 — 72.24	.88	111.69 — 112.24	1.60	151.69 — 152.24	2.32
32.25 — 32.79	.17	72.25 — 72.79	.89	112.25 — 112.79	1.61	152.25 — 152.79	2.33
32.80 — 33.35	.18	72.80 — 73.35	.90	112.80 — 113.35	1.62	152.80 — 153.35	2.34
33.36 — 33.91	.19	73.36 — 73.91	.91	113.36 — 113.91	1.63	153.36 — 153.91	2.35
33.92 — 34.46	.20	73.92 — 74.46	.92	113.92 — 114.46	1.64	153.92 — 154.46	2.36
34.47 — 35.02	.21	74.47 — 75.02	.93	114.47 — 115.02	1.65	154.47 — 155.02	2.37
35.03 — 35.57	.22	75.03 — 75.57	.94	115.03 — 115.57	1.66	155.03 — 155.57	2.38
35.58 — 36.13	.23	75.58 — 76.13	.95	115.58 — 116.13	1.67	155.58 — 156.13	2.39
36.14 — 36.68	.24	76.14 — 76.68	.96	116.14 — 116.68	1.68	156.14 — 156.68	2.40
36.69 — 37.24	.25	76.69 — 77.24	.97	116.69 — 117.24	1.69	156.69 — 157.24	2.41
37.25 — 37.79	.26	77.25 — 77.79	.98	117.25 — 117.79	1.70	157.25 — 157.79	2.42
37.80 — 38.35	.27	77.80 — 78.35	.99	117.80 — 118.35	1.71	157.80 — 158.35	2.43
38.36 — 38.91	.28	78.36 — 78.91	1.00	118.36 — 118.91	1.72	158.36 — 158.91	2.44
38.92 — 39.46	.29	78.92 — 79.46	1.01	118.92 — 119.46	1.73	158.92 — 159.46	2.45
39.47 — 40.02	.30	79.47 — 80.02	1.02	119.47 — 120.02	1.74	159.47 — 160.02	2.46
40.03 — 40.57	.31	80.03 — 80.57	1.03	120.03 — 120.57	1.75	160.03 — 160.57	2.47
40.58 — 41.13	.32	80.58 — 81.13	1.04	120.58 — 121.13	1.76	160.58 — 161.13	2.48
41.14 — 41.68	.33	81.14 — 81.68	1.05	121.14 — 121.68	1.77	161.14 — 161.68	2.49
41.69 — 42.24	.34	81.69 — 82.24	1.06	121.69 — 122.24	1.78	161.69 — 162.24	2.50
42.25 — 42.79	.35	82.25 — 82.79	1.07	122.25 — 122.79	1.79	162.25 — 162.79	2.51
42.80 — 43.35	.36	82.80 — 83.35	1.08	122.80 — 123.35	1.80	162.80 — 163.35	2.52
43.36 — 43.91	.37	83.36 — 83.91	1.09	123.36 — 123.91	1.81	163.36 — 163.91	2.53
43.92 — 44.46	.38	83.92 — 84.46	1.10	123.92 — 124.46	1.82	163.92 — 164.46	2.54
44.47 — 45.02	.39	84.47 — 85.02	1.11	124.47 — 125.02	1.83	164.47 — 165.02	2.55
45.03 — 45.57	.40	85.03 — 85.57	1.12	125.03 — 125.57	1.84	165.03 — 165.57	2.56
45.58 — 46.13	.41	85.58 — 86.13	1.13	125.58 — 126.13	1.85	165.58 — 166.13	2.57
46.14 — 46.68	.42	86.14 — 86.68	1.14	126.14 — 126.68	1.86	166.14 — 166.68	2.58
46.69 — 47.24	.43	86.69 — 87.24	1.15	126.69 — 127.24	1.87	166.69 — 167.24	2.59
47.25 — 47.79	.44	87.25 — 87.79	1.16	127.25 — 127.79	1.88	167.25 — 167.79	2.60
47.80 — 48.35	.45	87.80 — 88.35	1.17	127.80 — 128.35	1.89	167.80 — 168.35	2.61
48.36 — 48.91	.46	88.36 — 88.91	1.18	128.36 — 128.91	1.90	168.36 — 168.91	2.62
48.92 — 49.46	.47	88.92 — 89.46	1.19	128.92 — 129.46	1.91	168.92 — 169.46	2.63
49.47 — 50.02	.48	89.47 — 90.02	1.20	129.47 — 130.02	1.92	169.47 — 170.02	2.64
50.03 — 50.57	.49	90.03 — 90.57	1.21	130.03 — 130.57	1.93	170.03 — 170.57	2.65
50.58 — 51.13	.50	90.58 — 91.13	1.22	130.58 — 131.13	1.94	170.58 — 171.13	2.66
51.14 — 51.68	.51	91.14 — 91.68	1.23	131.14 — 131.68	1.95	171.14 — 171.68	2.67
51.69 — 52.24	.52	91.69 — 92.24	1.24	131.69 — 132.24	1.96	171.69 — 172.24	2.68
52.25 — 52.79	.53	92.25 — 92.79	1.25	132.25 — 132.79	1.97	172.25 — 172.79	2.69
52.80 — 53.35	.54	92.80 — 93.35	1.26	132.80 — 133.35	1.98	172.80 — 173.35	2.70
53.36 — 53.91	.55	93.36 — 93.91	1.27	133.36 — 133.91	1.99	173.36 — 173.91	2.71
53.92 — 54.46	.56	93.92 — 94.46	1.28	133.92 — 134.46	2.00	173.92 — 174.46	2.72
54.47 — 55.02	.57	94.47 — 95.02	1.29	134.47 — 135.02	2.01	174.47 — 175.02	2.73
55.03 — 55.57	.58	95.03 — 95.57	1.30	135.03 — 135.57	2.02	175.03 — 175.57	2.74
55.58 — 56.13	.59	95.58 — 96.13	1.31	135.58 — 136.13	2.03	175.58 — 176.13	2.75
56.14 — 56.68	.60	96.14 — 96.68	1.32	136.14 — 136.68	2.04	176.14 — 176.68	2.76
56.69 — 57.24	.61	96.69 — 97.24	1.33	136.69 — 137.24	2.05	176.69 — 177.24	2.77
57.25 — 57.79	.62	97.25 — 97.79	1.34	137.25 — 137.79	2.06	177.25 — 177.79	2.78
57.80 — 58.35	.63	97.80 — 98.35	1.35	137.80 — 138.35	2.07	177.80 — 178.35	2.79
58.36 — 58.91	.64	98.36 — 98.91	1.36	138.36 — 138.91	2.08	178.36 — 178.91	2.80
58.92 — 59.46	.65	98.92 — 99.46	1.37	138.92 — 139.46	2.09	178.92 — 179.46	2.81
59.47 — 60.02	.66	99.47 — 100.02	1.38	139.47 — 140.02	2.10	179.47 — 180.02	2.82
60.03 — 60.57	.67	100.03 — 100.57	1.39	140.03 — 140.57	2.11	180.03 — 180.57	2.83
60.58 — 61.13	.68	100.58 — 101.13	1.40	140.58 — 141.13	2.12	180.58 — 181.13	2.84
61.14 — 61.68	.69	101.14 — 101.68	1.41	141.14 — 141.68	2.13	181.14 — 181.68	2.85
61.69 — 62.24	.70	101.69 — 102.24	1.42	141.69 — 142.24	2.14	181.69 — 182.24	2.86
62.25 — 62.79	.71	102.25 — 102.79	1.43	142.25 — 142.79	2.15	182.25 — 182.79	2.87

"Benefit amounts are not fixed once and for all. They will be increased in line with rises in the cost of living."*

"The Plan covers on a compulsory basis all types of employment except those listed below.

"To be covered for a particular year, you must be between the ages of 18 and 70 and earn more than $600 in that year if you are an employee, or at least $800 in that year if you are self-employed.

* Department of National Health and Welfare, *The Canada Pension Plan* (Ottawa: Queen's Printer, 1965), p. 7.

Employment Not Covered

1. Employment by your spouse;

2. Employment by your father, mother or any other person who supports you but does not pay you cash wages;

3. Employment on a casual basis that is not for the purpose of your employer's business;

4. Employment as a migratory worker–in occupations like farming, fishing, trapping, hunting, logging–where you work less than 25 days a year for the same employer or where you earn less

aximum employee contribution to be withheld for
e year by an employer is $82.80.
ployers are required to match their employee's
tribution.

BI-WEEKLY PAY PERIOD
$182.80 — $342.79

Remuneration	Deduct	Remuneration	Deduct	Remuneration	Deduct	Remuneration	Deduct
182.80 — 183.35	2.88	222.80 — 223.35	3.60	262.80 — 263.35	4.32	302.80 — 303.35	5.04
183.36 — 183.91	2.89	223.36 — 223.91	3.61	263.36 — 263.91	4.33	303.36 — 303.91	5.05
183.92 — 184.46	2.90	223.92 — 224.46	3.62	263.92 — 264.46	4.34	303.92 — 304.46	5.06
184.47 — 185.02	2.91	224.47 — 225.02	3.63	264.47 — 265.02	4.35	304.47 — 305.02	5.07
185.03 — 185.57	2.92	225.03 — 225.57	3.64	265.03 — 265.57	4.36	305.03 — 305.57	5.08
185.58 — 186.13	2.93	225.58 — 226.13	3.65	265.58 — 266.13	4.37	305.58 — 306.13	5.09
186.14 — 186.68	2.94	226.14 — 226.68	3.66	266.14 — 266.68	4.38	306.14 — 306.68	5.10
186.69 — 187.24	2.95	226.69 — 227.24	3.67	266.69 — 267.24	4.39	306.69 — 307.24	5.11
187.25 — 187.79	2.96	227.25 — 227.79	3.68	267.25 — 267.79	4.40	307.25 — 307.79	5.12
187.80 — 188.35	2.97	227.80 — 228.35	3.69	267.80 — 268.35	4.41	307.80 — 308.35	5.13
188.36 — 188.91	2.98	228.36 — 228.91	3.70	268.36 — 268.91	4.42	308.36 — 308.91	5.14
188.92 — 189.46	2.99	228.92 — 229.46	3.71	268.92 — 269.46	4.43	308.92 — 309.46	5.15
189.47 — 190.02	3.00	229.47 — 230.02	3.72	269.47 — 270.02	4.44	309.47 — 310.02	5.16
190.03 — 190.57	3.01	230.03 — 230.57	3.73	270.03 — 270.57	4.45	310.03 — 310.57	5.17
190.58 — 191.13	3.02	230.58 — 231.13	3.74	270.58 — 271.13	4.46	310.58 — 311.13	5.18
191.14 — 191.68	3.03	231.14 — 231.68	3.75	271.14 — 271.68	4.47	311.14 — 311.68	5.19
191.69 — 192.24	3.04	231.69 — 232.24	3.76	271.69 — 272.24	4.48	311.69 — 312.24	5.20
192.25 — 192.79	3.05	232.25 — 232.79	3.77	272.25 — 272.79	4.49	312.25 — 312.79	5.21
192.80 — 193.35	3.06	232.80 — 233.35	3.78	272.80 — 273.35	4.50	312.80 — 313.35	5.22
193.36 — 193.91	3.07	233.36 — 233.91	3.79	273.36 — 273.91	4.51	313.36 — 313.91	5.23
193.92 — 194.46	3.08	233.92 — 234.46	3.80	273.92 — 274.46	4.52	313.92 — 314.46	5.24
194.47 — 195.02	3.09	234.47 — 235.02	3.81	274.47 — 275.02	4.53	314.47 — 315.02	5.25
195.03 — 195.57	3.10	235.03 — 235.57	3.82	275.03 — 275.57	4.54	315.03 — 315.57	5.26
195.58 — 196.13	3.11	235.58 — 236.13	3.83	275.58 — 276.13	4.55	315.58 — 316.13	5.27
196.14 — 196.68	3.12	236.14 — 236.68	3.84	276.14 — 276.68	4.56	316.14 — 316.68	5.28
196.69 — 197.24	3.13	236.69 — 237.24	3.85	276.69 — 277.24	4.57	316.69 — 317.24	5.29
197.25 — 197.79	3.14	237.25 — 237.79	3.86	277.25 — 277.79	4.58	317.25 — 317.79	5.30
197.80 — 198.35	3.15	237.80 — 238.35	3.87	277.80 — 278.35	4.59	317.80 — 318.35	5.31
198.36 — 198.91	3.16	238.36 — 238.91	3.88	278.36 — 278.91	4.60	318.36 — 318.91	5.32
198.92 — 199.46	3.17	238.92 — 239.46	3.89	278.92 — 279.46	4.61	318.92 — 319.46	5.33
199.47 — 200.02	3.18	239.47 — 240.02	3.90	279.47 — 280.02	4.62	319.47 — 320.02	5.34
200.03 — 200.57	3.19	240.03 — 240.57	3.91	280.03 — 280.57	4.63	320.03 — 320.57	5.35
200.58 — 201.13	3.20	240.58 — 241.13	3.92	280.58 — 281.13	4.64	320.58 — 321.13	5.36
201.14 — 201.68	3.21	241.14 — 241.68	3.93	281.14 — 281.68	4.65	321.14 — 321.68	5.37
201.69 — 202.24	3.22	241.69 — 242.24	3.94	281.69 — 282.24	4.66	321.69 — 322.24	5.38
202.25 — 202.79	3.23	242.25 — 242.79	3.95	282.25 — 282.79	4.67	322.25 — 322.79	5.39
202.80 — 203.35	3.24	242.80 — 243.35	3.96	282.80 — 283.35	4.68	322.80 — 323.35	5.40
203.36 — 203.91	3.25	243.36 — 243.91	3.97	283.36 — 283.91	4.69	323.36 — 323.91	5.41
203.92 — 204.46	3.26	243.92 — 244.46	3.98	283.92 — 284.46	4.70	323.92 — 324.46	5.42
204.47 — 205.02	3.27	244.47 — 245.02	3.99	284.47 — 285.02	4.71	324.47 — 325.02	5.43
205.03 — 205.57	3.28	245.03 — 245.57	4.00	285.03 — 285.57	4.72	325.03 — 325.57	5.44
205.58 — 206.13	3.29	245.58 — 246.13	4.01	285.58 — 286.13	4.73	325.58 — 326.13	5.45
206.14 — 206.68	3.30	246.14 — 246.68	4.02	286.14 — 286.68	4.74	326.14 — 326.68	5.46
206.69 — 207.24	3.31	246.69 — 247.24	4.03	286.69 — 287.24	4.75	326.69 — 327.24	5.47
207.25 — 207.79	3.32	247.25 — 247.79	4.04	287.25 — 287.79	4.76	327.25 — 327.79	5.48
207.80 — 208.35	3.33	247.80 — 248.35	4.05	287.80 — 288.35	4.77	327.80 — 328.35	5.49
208.36 — 208.91	3.34	248.36 — 248.91	4.06	288.36 — 288.91	4.78	328.36 — 328.91	5.50
208.92 — 209.46	3.35	248.92 — 249.46	4.07	288.92 — 289.46	4.79	328.92 — 329.46	5.51
209.47 — 210.02	3.36	249.47 — 250.02	4.08	289.47 — 290.02	4.80	329.47 — 330.02	5.52
210.03 — 210.57	3.37	250.03 — 250.57	4.09	290.03 — 290.57	4.81	330.03 — 330.57	5.53
210.58 — 211.13	3.38	250.58 — 251.13	4.10	290.58 — 291.13	4.82	330.58 — 331.13	5.54
211.14 — 211.68	3.39	251.14 — 251.68	4.11	291.14 — 291.68	4.83	331.14 — 331.68	5.55
211.69 — 212.24	3.40	251.69 — 252.24	4.12	291.69 — 292.24	4.84	331.69 — 332.24	5.56
212.25 — 212.79	3.41	252.25 — 252.79	4.13	292.25 — 292.79	4.85	332.25 — 332.79	5.57
212.80 — 213.35	3.42	252.80 — 253.35	4.14	292.80 — 293.35	4.86	332.80 — 333.35	5.58
213.36 — 213.91	3.43	253.36 — 253.91	4.15	293.36 — 293.91	4.87	333.36 — 333.91	5.59
213.92 — 214.46	3.44	253.92 — 254.46	4.16	293.92 — 294.46	4.88	333.92 — 334.46	5.60
214.47 — 215.02	3.45	254.47 — 255.02	4.17	294.47 — 295.02	4.89	334.47 — 335.02	5.61
215.03 — 215.57	3.46	255.03 — 255.57	4.18	295.03 — 295.57	4.90	335.03 — 335.57	5.62
215.58 — 216.13	3.47	255.58 — 256.13	4.19	295.58 — 296.13	4.91	335.58 — 336.13	5.63
216.14 — 216.68	3.48	256.14 — 256.68	4.20	296.14 — 296.68	4.92	336.14 — 336.68	5.64
216.69 — 217.24	3.49	256.69 — 257.24	4.21	296.69 — 297.24	4.93	336.69 — 337.24	5.65
217.25 — 217.79	3.50	257.25 — 257.79	4.22	297.25 — 297.79	4.94	337.25 — 337.79	5.66
217.80 — 218.35	3.51	257.80 — 258.35	4.23	297.80 — 298.35	4.95	337.80 — 338.35	5.67
218.36 — 218.91	3.52	258.36 — 258.91	4.24	298.36 — 298.91	4.96	338.36 — 338.91	5.68
218.92 — 219.46	3.53	258.92 — 259.46	4.25	298.92 — 299.46	4.97	338.92 — 339.46	5.69
219.47 — 220.02	3.54	259.47 — 260.02	4.26	299.47 — 300.02	4.98	339.47 — 340.02	5.70
220.03 — 220.57	3.55	260.03 — 260.57	4.27	300.03 — 300.57	4.99	340.03 — 340.57	5.71
220.58 — 221.13	3.56	260.58 — 261.13	4.28	300.58 — 301.13	5.00	340.58 — 341.13	5.72
221.14 — 221.68	3.57	261.14 — 261.68	4.29	301.14 — 301.68	5.01	341.14 — 341.68	5.73
221.69 — 222.24	3.58	261.69 — 262.24	4.30	301.69 — 302.24	5.02	341.69 — 342.24	5.74
222.25 — 222.79	3.59	262.25 — 262.79	4.31	302.25 — 302.79	5.03	342.25 — 342.79	5.75

Calculation:

1. $\$5,200.00 - \$600.00 = \$4,600.00$
2. $\$4,600.00 \times 1.8\% = \$82.80$

To avoid the necessity of making the above calculation for each employee, the Department of National Revenue, Taxation Division has published a book of tables for determining the amount of deduction to be made from each gross pay. There are tables for pay periods of one day, one week, two weeks, half-month, four weeks, one month, ten months and one year. Each table shows the correct deduction to be made for a wide range of gross earnings. The illustrations on these facing pages show the first two pages for the bi-weekly pay period. These show a range of earnings from $.00–$342.79.

To determine the deduction for an employee, look down the 'Remuneration' column until you find the bracket containing the employee's gross pay. You will recall that Harold Evans has a bi-weekly salary of $295. This falls in the bracket of $294.47–$295.02. The deduction of $4.89 is indicated to the immediate right of the income bracket. The amount of the deduction is then recorded in the Payroll Journal in the C.P.P. column opposite Evans' name as shown below.

At this point, it needs to be pointed out that the employer is required to contribute an amount equal to that contributed by the employee. Note also that by using the tables to determine the $4.89 as a deduction, Harold Evans will reach the maximum annual deduction of $82.80 in the 17th pay period (total number of pay periods for Harold Evans is 26).

17 pay periods × $4.89 per pay period = $83.13

than $250 a year from the same employer;

. Employment as a member of a religious Order if you have taken a vow of perpetual poverty–unless otherwise provided by regulation;

. Employment as an exchange teacher from another country."†

Ibid., p. 9.

EMPLOYEE CONTRIBUTIONS

The maximum earnings on which contributions must be made is $5,200 less an annual basic exemption of $600, or $4,600. The rate of contribution is 1.8 per cent. Therefore, the maximum deduction in a year for any of the employees is $82.80

YROLL JOURNAL   For the _2 weeks_ ended _June 19_ 19–9

Employee	Total Personal Exempt.	Hours Reg.	O/T	Earnings Regular	Extra	Total	C.P.P.	Income Tax	U.I.C.	Hospital Ins.	Medical Ins	Union Dues	Group Life	Net Pay	Cheque Number
Harold Evans	2600 00			295 00		295 00	4 89								

It is the responsibility of the employer to keep track of the accumulated contributions for each employee. Once the maximum of $82.80 is reached, no further deduction for C.P.P. or Q.P.P. is to be made in that year.

Income Taxes

According to Canadian Income Tax law, employers are required to deduct from each of the employees' earnings a certain amount for personal income taxes. The amount to be deducted from the employee depends upon two factors. The first factor is the gross pay (less the contribution for C.P.P.) and the second factor is the employee's total personal exemption.

PERSONAL EXEMPTION

Every employee is required to fill out a Form TD-1 (illustrated at right). This form is completed each time an employee starts a new job, and it is used by the employer to determine the employee's total personal exemption. The total personal exemption refers to that amount of annual earnings that a person may earn without being taxed. This amount varies with the employee's marital status and the number of dependent children and other dependants. The illustration shows the TD-1 form for Harold Evans who is married and has two children, aged ten and seven.

CALCULATING INCOME TAX DEDUCTION

Harold Evans has a total personal exemption of $2,600 as indicated by his Form TD-1. His gross pay for two weeks as recorded in the payroll journal is $295 and his contribution to C.P.P. is $4.89. This leaves a figure of $290.11 as the basis for determining the income tax deduction.

DEPARTMENT OF NATIONAL REVENUE, TAXATION

EMPLOYEE'S TAX DEDUCTION RETURN

TD 1

- Complete and file one copy of this return with your employer
  (a) when you commence employment, or
  (b) within seven days of any change affecting your personal exemptions.
- If you do not file this return, as required, income tax will be deducted as though you were a single person without dependants.
- Do not claim for any other dependant whose income for the year will exceed $950.
- Income of your spouse or dependants includes any pension or supplement under the Old Age Security Act or any similar Act of a province, and benefits under the Canada or Quebec Pension Plan.

Family or last name (Print): EVANS
Social insurance number: 609779152
Usual first name and initials: HAROLD J.
Present address (If present address is temporary, give permanent address only): 178 NORTH CLARKSON AVE.
Date of birth — Day 09 Month 02 Year 39
Name and address of spouse: PATRICIA (same as above)

Claim for Personal Exemptions

Basic Personal Exemption ► $1,000

Age Exemption—You may claim $500 if you are (a) 70 years of age or over, or (b) 65 years of age or over but under 70 and will not receive any pension under the Old Age Security Act for any month in the year. ► $

Married or Equivalent Exemption—If applicable, check ☐ and claim only one of these 5 items.
If your spouse's income, while married, will exceed $1,250 in the year, you may not claim this exemption.

Married and supporting spouse
☐ 1. whose income for the year, while married, will not be over $250. — Claim $1,000
☐ 2. whose income for the year, while married, will be over $250 but not over $1,250. — $1,250 — Less: spouse's income $ — Claim $

Single, divorced, separated or widow(er) and supporting
☐ 3. a wholly dependent child under age 21, or any age if infirm or in full-time attendance at a school or university. Provide details below and claim $1,000
☐ 4. a wholly dependent person related by blood, marriage or adoption and living in a dwelling maintained by you. Provide details below and claim $1,000
☐ 5. a relative wholly dependent on you and one or more other persons living in a dwelling maintained by you and such other persons. (You may claim here only if it has been agreed that no other person will claim for the same dependant or in respect of the same dwelling.) Provide details below and claim $1,000

► $1,000

Details of Dependant

Name and address of dependant	Relationship to you	Estimated Annual Income	If a child, state age, and if over 21, state school attended or whether infirm
		$	

Exemption for Wholly Dependent Children

Exemption may be claimed for wholly dependent son, daughter, grandchild, niece or nephew under age 21 or any age if in full-time attendance at a school or university or if infirm. A niece or nephew may be claimed only if (a) you have complete custody and control of the child or (b) the child resides in Canada and the child's mother is a widow or is separated or divorced and does not receive alimony or similar allowance for the child's maintenance or the child's father is infirm. Provide details below and claim $300 for each child who will be under age 16 on the last day of the year and $550 for each child who will be age 16 or over on the last day of the year.

A wholly dependent child for whom an exemption of $1,000 has been claimed in item 3 above may also be claimed here if the child is supported in a dwelling wherein you employ a full-time servant. If you do, state servant's name below.

Name of child (Attach list if space is insufficient)	Relationship to you	Estimated Annual Income	Year of birth	If over 21, state school attended or whether infirm	
DAVID		$ —	64		► $300
CATHERINE		—	67		► $300
					► $

Exemption for Other Dependants

(A) Parents, Grandparents, Brothers or Sisters (including in-laws)
(B) Aunts or Uncles Resident in Canada (including in-laws)

Provide details below and claim amount to be spent in support of each dependant up to a maximum of $300 for each dependant who will be under age 16 on the last day of the year or $550 for each dependant who will be age 16 or over on the last day of the year. If any other person also contributes to the support of a dependant listed here, the combined amount claimed by you and such other person must not exceed the maximum of $300 or $550 mentioned above. No claim may be made here for (a) a dependant over age 21 who is not mentally or physically infirm (unless that dependant is a brother or sister in full-time attendance at a school or university) or (b) a dependant in respect of whom you have claimed an exemption of $1,000.

Name and address of dependant (Attach list if space is insufficient)	Relationship to you	Dependant's Income in year	Year of birth	Estimated amount you will spend in support of dependant	If over 21, state school attended or whether infirm	
		$		$		► $
						► $
						► $

Total Personal Exemptions .... ► $2,600
Claim for Tuition Fees by Students Only — (Ask your District Taxation Office for further information) .... ► $
Total Claim .... ► $2,600

Exemption Claim for Casual, Seasonal or Part-time Employment — (Valid for current calendar year only)

This area must be completed by an employee who is receiving pay at a rate that is subject to tax deduction but who claims exemption because total earnings (including free board and lodging) from all sources for the full calendar year will be less than the total personal exemptions claimed. No claim may be made here by a person not resident in Canada for the whole year unless his earnings for the year in Canada will be less than his exemptions apportioned to the period of residence in Canada.

Earnings to date this year from all sources .... ► $
Estimated earnings for remainder of year from all sources .... ► $
Total estimated earnings from all sources .... ► $

Certification

I HEREBY CERTIFY that the information given in this return is true, correct and complete to the best of my knowledge and belief.
Signature: Harold Evans — Date: 7 June — 19-4
It is a serious offence to make a false return

Warning: An employer should refer a form TD1 containing doubtful statements to the District Taxation Office. Any person who knowingly accepts a form TD1 containing false or deceptive statements commits a serious offence. Employers must retain completed forms TD1 for inspection by officers of the Department of National Revenue, Taxation.
Form authorized and prescribed by the Minister of National Revenue.

Just as for C.P.P., the Department of National Revenue, Taxation Division has published a booklet of deduction tables for Income Taxes. Pages 16 and 17 of the booklet which are the first two pages for the bi-weekly pay period are shown on page 235. Looking at the tables, the shaded column along the left-hand side gives the various income brackets. At the top of each of the fifteen deduction columns are the total personal exemption brackets. To find the correct income tax deduction, it is necessary to locate the appropriate income bracket in the shaded area and to follow it to the right until you arrive at the correct exemption column. The correct deduction is found at the intersection of these two columns. For Harold Evans, whose earnings figure is $290.11 and whose personal exemption is $2600, the deduction falls in column number 7 and amounts to $42.20. This amount is then entered in the Payroll Journal as shown below the charts.

BI-WEEKLY TAX DEDUCTIONS
Basis—26 Pay Periods per Year

TABLE 155

DÉDUCTIONS D'IMPÔT DE DEUX SEMAINES
Base—26 périodes de paie par année

IF THE TOTAL OF EXEMPTIONS IS — SI LE TOTAL DES EXEMPTIONS EST DE

BI-WEEKLY PAY — DE	1	2	3	4	5	6	7	8	9	10	11	12	13	14	15

(Tax deduction table — detailed numeric values)

BI-WEEKLY TAX DEDUCTIONS
Basis—26 Pay Periods per Year

TABLE 155

DÉDUCTIONS D'IMPÔT DE DEUX SEMAINES
Base—26 périodes de paie par année

IF THE TOTAL OF EXEMPTIONS IS — SI LE TOTAL DES EXEMPTIONS EST DE

	$1,000-$1,249	$1,250-$1,499	$1,500-$1,749	$1,750-$1,999	$2,000-$2,249	$2,250-$2,499	$2,500-$2,749	$2,750-$2,999	$3,000-$3,249	$3,250-$3,499	$3,500-$3,749	$3,750-$3,999	$4,000-$4,249	$4,250-$4,499	$4,500-$4,750
	1	2	3	4	5	6	7	8	9	10	11	12	13	14	15

DEDUCT FROM EACH PAY — DÉDUISEZ SUR CHAQUE PAIE

(Tax deduction table — detailed numeric values)

EXEMPTIONS OVER $4,750
Reduce the tax in Column 15 by $1.40 for each $250 (or part) of additional exemption.

EXEMPTIONS DÉPASSANT $4,750
Réduire l'impôt dans la Colonne 15 de $1.40 pour chaque $250 (ou partie) d'exemption supplémentaire.

PAYROLL JOURNAL

For the 2 weeks ended June 19 19-9

Employee	Total Hours Personal Exempt.	Reg.	O/T	Earnings Regular	Extra	Total	Deductions C.P.P.	Income Tax	U.I.C. Ins.	Hospital Ins.	Medical Ins.	Union Dues	Group Life	Net Pay	Cheque Number
Harold Evans	2600 00			295 00		295 00	4 89	42 20							

235

Unemployment Insurance

Whenever a person both willing and able to work cannot find suitable employment, it is treated under Canadian law as a condition against which insurance is provided. While a worker is employed, he pays a portion of his earnings into an Unemployment Insurance fund. These payments are in the form of deductions made by his employer from his pay. If the worker becomes unemployed while willing and able to accept employment, he receives payments out of the fund to maintain himself and his dependants while out of work. Unemployment Insurance is described as follows in the government booklet 'Information, Worker's Benefits.'

"Unemployment Insurance is your protection against unemployment. The contributions paid by workers and their employers together with money received from the Government, go into a common fund from which benefits are paid to those who lose their jobs and who meet the conditions set out in the Act and Regulations. Unemployment Insurance is like fire insurance where many people pay small premiums so that the few who lose their property will receive compensation. It is not a savings account. The premium pays for protection during the term of the policy and, whether or not there has been a loss, there is no refund of the amount paid in. You must not expect that, simply because you have paid contributions you are, as a consequence, entitled to benefit."*

* Unemployment Insurance Commission, *Information, Worker's Benefit* (Ottawa: the Queen's Printer, 1967), unpaginated.

UNEMPLOYMENT INSURANCE COMMISSION

1968

TABLE OF CONTRIBUTIONS AND DEDUCTIONS FROM WAGES, FOR STAMP, METERING DEVICE AND BULK PAYMENT METHODS

1968

BULK PAYMENT SYMBOL	Meter Symbol-1 — Gross Earnings during ONE WEEK OR LESS — **1**	Total Weekly Contribution	Employee Deduction	Denomination of WEEKLY stamp required
1/2 or 11	Up to $19.99	$ .20	$ .10	$ .40(a)
	$ 20.00 to $ 29.99	.40	.20	.40
	30.00 to 39.99	.70	.35	.70
	40.00 to 49.99	1.00	.50	1.00
1	50.00 to 59.99	1.30	.65	1.30
OR	60.00 to 69.99	1.60	.80	1.60
12	70.00 to 79.99	1.90	.95	1.90
	80.00 to 89.99	2.20	1.10	2.20
	90.00 to 99.99	2.50	1.25	2.50
	100.00 and over	2.80	1.40	2.80

BULK PAYMENT SYMBOL	Meter Symbol -2 — Gross Earnings during TWO WEEKS — **2**	Total Contribution for the two weeks	Employee Deduction	Denomination of the two weekly stamps required
2/2 or 21	Up to $39.99	$ .40	$ .20	$ .40(b)
	$ 40.00 to $ 59.99	.80	.40	.40
	60.00 to 79.99	1.40	.70	.70
2	80.00 to 99.99	2.00	1.00	1.00
OR	100.00 to 119.99	2.60	1.30	1.30
22	120.00 to 139.99	3.20	1.60	1.60
	140.00 to 159.99	3.80	1.90	1.90
	160.00 to 179.99	4.40	2.20	2.20
	180.00 to 199.99	5.00	2.50	2.50
	200.00 and over	5.60	2.80	2.80

BULK PAYMENT SYMBOL	Meter Symbol-3 — Gross Earnings during THREE WEEKS — **3**	Total Contribution for the three weeks	Employee Deduction	Denomination of the three weekly stamps required
3/2 or 31	Up to $59.99	$ .60	$ .30	$ .40(b)
	$ 60.00 to $ 89.99	1.20	.60	.40
	90.00 to 119.99	2.10	1.05	.70
	120.00 to 149.99	3.00	1.50	1.00
3	150.00 to 179.99	3.90	1.95	1.30
OR	180.00 to 209.99	4.80	2.40	1.60
32	210.00 to 239.99	5.70	2.85	1.90
	240.00 to 269.99	6.60	3.30	2.20
	270.00 to 299.99	7.50	3.75	2.50
	300.00 and over	8.40	4.20	2.80

BULK PAYMENT SYMBOL	Meter Symbol-4 — Gross Earnings during FOUR WEEKS — **4**	Total Contribution for the four weeks	Employee Deduction	Denomination of the four weekly stamps required
4/2 or 41	Up to $79.99	$ .80	$ .40	$ .40(b)
	$ 80.00 to $119.99	1.60	.80	.40
	120.00 to 159.99	2.80	1.40	.70
	160.00 to 199.99	4.00	2.00	1.00
4	200.00 to 239.99	5.20	2.60	1.30
OR	240.00 to 279.99	6.40	3.20	1.60
42	280.00 to 319.99	7.60	3.80	1.90
	320.00 to 359.99	8.80	4.40	2.20
	360.00 to 399.99	10.00	5.00	2.50
	400.00 and over	11.20	5.60	2.80

BULK PAYMENT SYMBOL	Meter Symbol-5 — Gross Earnings during FIVE WEEKS — **5**	Total Contribution for the five weeks	Employee Deduction	Denomination of the five weekly stamps required
5/2 or 51	Up to $99.99	$ 1.00	$ .50	$ .40(b)
	$100.00 to $149.99	2.00	1.00	.40
	150.00 to 199.99	3.50	1.75	.70
	200.00 to 249.99	5.00	2.50	1.00
5	250.00 to 299.99	6.50	3.25	1.30
OR	300.00 to 349.99	8.00	4.00	1.60
52	350.00 to 399.99	9.50	4.75	1.90
	400.00 to 449.99	11.00	5.50	2.20
	450.00 to 499.99	12.50	6.25	2.50
	500.00 and over	14.00	7.00	2.80

BULK PAYMENT SYMBOL	Meter Symbol-6 — Gross Earnings during SIX WEEKS — **6**	Total Contribution for the six weeks	Employee Deduction	Denomination of the six weekly stamps required
6/2 or 61	Up to $119.99	$ 1.20	$ .60	$ .40(b)
	$120.00 to $179.99	2.40	1.20	.40
	180.00 to 239.99	4.20	2.10	.70
	240.00 to 299.99	6.00	3.00	1.00
6	300.00 to 359.99	7.80	3.90	1.30
OR	360.00 to 419.99	9.60	4.80	1.60
62	420.00 to 479.99	11.40	5.70	1.90
	480.00 to 539.99	13.20	6.60	2.20
	540.00 to 599.99	15.00	7.50	2.50
	600.00 and over	16.80	8.40	2.80

Footnotes:
(a) Use one-half of a 40 cent stamp.
(b) Place one-half of a 40 cent stamp in the space for each week concerned.
(c) Employers operating on a semi-monthly or monthly pay period refer to tables "S" "M" or "X" on the reverse side.

UIC 465 (3-68)

Everyone who earns up to $7,800 in one year pays into the Fund unless he is employed in a manner that is specifically exempted and excluded. Teachers, athletes, private nurses, and domestic servants are a few examples of such persons.

The employer is required to contribute an amount equal to that deducted from each employee. He is also required to keep accurate records on each employee as far as contributions are concerned. Shown above is a portion of the tables that are used in determining the amount of the Unemployment Insurance deduction.

To determine the contribution that Harold Evans is required to make, refer to Table 2 (table for 'Gross Earnings during Two

Weeks'). Locate the column that is headed 'Employee Deduction'. Follow this column down until you come to the income bracket which includes $295. That is the last line on the table. It shows that his deduction for U.I.C. is $2.80. This amount is then entered in the payroll journal as illustrated below.

PAYROLL JOURNAL   For the _2 weeks_ ended _June 19_ 19_–9_

| Employee | Total Personal Exempt. | Hours | | Earnings | | | Deductions | | | | | | | Net Pay | Cheque Number |
		Reg	O/T	Regular	Extra	Total	C.P.P.	Income Tax	U.I.C.	Hospital Ins.	Medical Ins	Union Dues	Group Life		
Harold Evans	2600 00			295 00		295 00	4 89	42 20	2 80						

Hospitalization and Medical Insurance

In most firms, there is some form of hospital insurance available for employees. It may be a plan which is sponsored by a provincial government or it may be a plan with a private insurance firm. It should be noted at this time that government-sponsored Medical programs are becoming more and more prominent. Employers are authorized to make deductions from the wages and remit the amounts deducted to the sponsor or administrator of the plan.

The same type of conditions exist for the medical insurances. These may be public plans (government sponsored and administered) or private plans. Just as with the hospital insurance plans, deductions for the medical insurance plans are made from wages and remitted to the plan administrators. In both types of insurance plans, the amount of the deduction generally depends upon the marital status of the employee and the number of dependants. The premiums for a single person are less than for a person who is married and has dependent children.

Example of Rates for Hospital Insurance		
1. Single person	Public ward	$ 66.00 (per year)
	Semi-private	$ 75.00 (per year)
2. Family (head and all dependants)	Public ward	$132.00 (per year)
	Semi-private	$150.00 (per year)

CALCULATING HOSPITAL INSURANCE DEDUCTION

Harold Evans pays the family rates and has semi-private coverage. His annual premium is therefore $150. To determine the premium for the two-week pay period requires the following calculation:

$150.00 (annual premium) ÷ 26 (pay periods per year) = $5.77

This amount is recorded in the Payroll Journal as shown below:

For the _2 weeks_ ended _June 19_ 19_-9_

Employee	Total Personal Exempt.	Hours Reg.	Hours O/T	Earnings Regular	Earnings Extra	Earnings Total	C.P.P.	Income Tax	U.I.C.	Hospital Ins.	Medical Ins	Union Dues	Group Life	Net Pay	Cheque Number
Harold Evans	2600 00			295 00		295 00	4 89	42 20	2 80	5 77					

Example of Rates for Medical Insurance

1. Single person	$ 70.80 per year
2. Family of two	$141.60 per year
3. Family of three or more	$177.00 per-year

CALCULATING MEDICAL INSURANCE DEDUCTION

Harold Evans pays the rate indicated
in item (3). To determine the premium that he must pay each pay
period, the following calculation is
necessary:

$$\$177.00 \div 26 = \$6.81$$

PAYROLL JOURNAL For the _2 weeks_ ended _June 19_ 19_-9_

Employee	Total Personal Exempt.	Hours Reg.	Hours O/T	Earnings Regular	Earnings Extra	Earnings Total	C.P.P.	Income Tax	U.I.C.	Hospital Ins.	Medical Ins	Union Dues	Group Life	Net Pay	Cheque Number
Harold Evans	2600 00			295 00		295 00	4 89	42 20	2 80	5 77	6 81				

Union Dues 'Check-off'

Very often the employees of
medium-sized or larger businesses
are organized into a labour union.
Dues to unions are often deductions
made by the employer who remits the
monies to the union periodically.
This obligation of the employer is
usually part of the contract negoti-
ated between the employer and the
employees.

ARTICLE II–Deduction of Union Dues

2.01 The Company will deduct each
month from the wages of each
employee in the bargaining unit an
amount equivalent to the normal
monthly Union dues and will remit
such sums deducted to the appropriate official of the Union.

This clause is taken from a contract obtained in 1965 by the
Brotherhood of Railway and Steam-
ship Clerks, Freight Handlers, Express and Station Employees, Lodge
No. 650. The amount that is deducted from the employees depends
on the union local. In the case of
Harold Evans, his union requires a
deduction of $4.50 each pay period.
The journal shows the deduction
entered.

PAYROLL JOURNAL For the _2 weeks_ ended _June 19_ 19_-9_

Employee	Total Personal Exempt.	Hours Reg.	Hours O/T	Earnings Regular	Earnings Extra	Earnings Total	C.P.P.	Income Tax	U.I.C.	Hospital Ins.	Medical Ins	Union Dues	Group Life	Net Pay	Cheque Number
Harold Evans	2600 00			295 00		295 00	4 89	42 20	2 80	5 77	6 81	4 50			

Some firms make it possible for their employees to enrol in some form of group life insurance plan. Premiums are therefore handled as a payroll deduction. Premiums are paid at a specified amount per $1,000 worth of insurance. The amount of insurance that an employee may obtain depends on his gross earnings, his marital status, and the number of his dependants.

Harold Evans has group life insurance and pays a premium of 15 cents per week per $1,000 worth of insurance. He has a total amount of $12,000 of insurance. This means that his premium is $1.80 per week or $3.60 each pay period. The Payroll Journal below shows the premium properly entered.

PAYROLL JOURNAL — For the _2 weeks_ ended _June 19_ 19_–9_

Employee	Total Personal Exempt.	Hours Reg	O/T	Earnings Regular	Extra	Total	C.P.P.	Income Tax	U.I.C.	Hospital Ins.	Medical Ins	Union Dues	Group Life	Net Pay	Cheque Number
Harold Evans	2600 00			295 00		295 00	4 89	42 20	2 80	5 77	6 81	4 50	3 60		

Other Deductions

There are other deductions that can be made from the pay cheque if authority is granted by the employee to have them made. They are handled in a manner similar to those deductions that have been discussed and illustrated so far. Some of these other deductions include charitable donations, credit union contributions, and purchases of bonds and shares of stock. Registered pension plans are also very common.

CALCULATING NET PAY

At this point, the last deduction to be made from Harold Evans' pay has been entered. There are two steps remaining. First, add all the deductions together. The answer of $70.57 is then subtracted from the gross pay of $295 giving a net pay of $224.43.

This amount is entered in the Net Pay column of the journal. If and when a cheque is issued, the cheque number is recorded in the Cheque Number column. The next illustration shows the completed calculations for Harold Evans' pay cheque.

PAYROLL JOURNAL — For the _2 weeks_ ended _June 19_ 19_–9_

Employee	Total Personal Exempt.	Hours Reg	O/T	Earnings Regular	Extra	Total	C.P.P.	Income Tax	U.I.C.	Hospital Ins.	Medical Ins	Union Dues	Group Life	Net Pay	Cheque Number
Harold Evans	2600 00			295 00		295 00	4 89	42 20	2 80	5 77	6 81	4 50	3 60	224 43	P4029

COMPLETING THE PAYROLL JOURNAL

The procedure that has been discussed and illustrated for Harold Evans is repeated for each of the employees in the company. One line of the Payroll Journal is used for each employee. When all of the details for all of the employees are entered in the journal, the amount columns are totaled as shown at the top of page 240.

For the _2 weeks_ ended _June 19_ 19–9

Employee	Total Personal Exempt.	Hours Reg	O/T	Earnings Regular	Extra	Total	Deductions C.P.P.	Income Tax	U.I.C.	Hospital Ins.	Medical Ins	Union Dues	Group Life	Net Pay	Cheque Number
Harold Evans	2600 00			295 00		295 00	4 89	42 20	2 80	5 77	6 81	4 50	3 60	224 43	P4029
Ronald Baker	2000 00			280 00		280 00	4 62	45 40	2 80	5 77	5 45	4 50	3 00	208 46	P4030
Bob Turnston	2300 00			268 00		268 00	4 41	39 20	2 80	5 77	6 81	4 50	2 40	202 11	P4031
Leo Williams	1000 00			240 00	35 00	275 00	4 53	54 15	2 80	2 89	2 72	4 50	1 50	201 91	P4032
Dennis Murray	2300 00			290 00		290 00	4 80	47 70	2 80	5 77	6 81	4 50	3 00	214 62	P4033
TOTALS				1373 00	35 00	1408 00	23 25	228 65	14 00	25 97	28 60	22 50	13 50	1051 53	

Proving the Accuracy of the Journal

The next step is a proving or checking procedure. There are two steps required to ensure the accuracy of the journal.

1. The Regular Earnings column + the Extra Earnings column = the Total Earnings column.

2. The Total Earnings column − the sum of all the deduction columns = the Net Pay column.

Recording the Payroll

When the column totals have been verified, it is necessary to record the accounting entries in the General Journal. There are three entries to be made.

1. Recording the payroll Summary Figures from the Payroll Journal.
2. Recording the employer's liability for Canada Pension.
3. Recording the employer's liability for Unemployment Insurance.

ENTRY 1. RECORDING THE PAYROLL SUMMARY FIGURES FROM THE PAYROLL JOURNAL

The information for the first payroll entry is obtained from the column totals of the Payroll Journal. In preparing this entry the accountant must be aware of the following:

(a) The total Gross Pay figure represents the Wages (or Salaries) *expense* to the business and is recorded as a debit to an expense account.

(b) Each of the deductions from the employees' earnings has been made on behalf of the government or some private agency and, until remitted, represents a *liability* of the em-

ployer. Each deduction total, therefore, is recorded as a credit to a separate liability account.

(c) The Net Pay figure represents a *liability* to the employees and is credited to a liability account called Payroll Payable.

The illustration below shows the first payroll entry completed:

Date	Particulars	P.R.	Debit	Credit
June 19	Salary Expense		1 408 00	
	Canada Pension Plan Payable			23 25
	Employees Income Taxes Payable			228 65
	Unemployment Insurance Payable			14 00
	Hospital Insurance Payable			25 97
	Medical Insurance Payable			28 60
	Union Dues Payable			22 50
	Group Life Insurance Payable			13 50
	Payroll Payable			1 051 53
	To record the payroll of June 19			

General Journal — Page 43

ENTRY 2. RECORDING THE EMPLOYER'S LIABILITY FOR CANADA PENSION

In the discussion of the Canada Pension plan, it was noted that the employer is required to contribute an amount equal to that made by the employee. The employer considers his portion as an operating expense. The entry shown at the top of page 241 records this obligation.

June	19	Canada Pension Plan Expense			23 25	
		Canada Pension Plan Payable				23 25
		To record the employer's share				

ENTRY 3. RECORDING THE EMPLOYER'S LIABILITY FOR UNEMPLOYMENT INSURANCE

June	19	Unemployment Insurance Expense			14 00	
		Unemployment Insurance Payable				14 00
		To record the employer's share				

The same type of obligation exists with Unemployment Insurance as with the Canada Pension Plan. Whatever is contributed by the employees must be matched by the employer. Therefore, the entry on the right is necessary to record the employer's obligation.

Each of the three entries is then posted to the appropriate General Ledger accounts. The 'T' accounts at right show the effect of postings.

```
                    Salary Expense
          June 19  $1,408.00
```

```
  Employees' Income              Unemployment Insurance
   Taxes Payable                        Payable
        $228.65 June 19                      $14.00 June 19
                                             $14.00 June 19

  Canada Pension                  Hospital Insurance
   Plan Payable                         Payable
        $23.25 June 19                       $25.97 June 19
        $23.25 June 19

  Medical Insurance               Union Dues Payable
     Payable
        $28.60 June 19                       $22.50 June 19

  Group Life Insurance            Payroll Payable
      Payable
        $13.50 June 19                       $1,051.53 June 19
```

Methods of Making Payment

METHOD 1. PAYING BY CASH

When employees receive their pay in cash, it is necessary to prepare each pay envelope with the correct amount of cash. In order to have the right number of bills and coins for all of the employees' envelopes, it is usual to prepare a 'currency requisition' form.

This form is taken to the bank, together with a cheque drawn on the regular bank account for the total amount shown on the form. The cheque is cashed, and the required

PAYROLL CURRENCY REQUISITION										PAY PERIOD ENDED June 19, 19-9	
Employee	NetPay	$20	$10	$5	$1	50¢	25¢	10¢	5¢	1¢
Harold Evans	224 43	11			4		1	1	1	3
Ronald Baker	208 46	10		1	3		1	2		1
Bob Funston	202 11	10			2			1		1
Les Williams	201 91	10			1	1	1	1	1	1
Dennis Murray	214 62	10	1		4	1		1		2
Number of bills or coins		51	1	1	14	2	3	6	2	8
Dollar Values	1 051 53	1 020 -	10 -	5 -	14 -	1 -	75	60	10	08

number of each of the bills and coins as shown on the form is requested from the bank. The accounting entry for this cheque is:

Dr. Payroll Payable $1,051.53
     Cr. Bank $1,051.53

The employees' pay envelopes are filled with currency and coins as shown by the currency requisition form. Included with each pay envelope is a statement showing the employee's earnings, deductions, and net pay. This statement may be printed on the outside of the envelope or may be a separate statement enclosed in the envelope. The employee's signature is obtained at the time of paying as proof of payment.

METHOD 2. PAYING BY CHEQUE

Many businesses, and in particular firms having a large number of employees, prefer to pay by cheque rather than by cash. It eliminates the problem of having large sums of money around the office. Too, the canceled cheques serve as evidence that the employees did receive their pay. The cheques that the employees receive may be drawn on the company's regular bank account or on a special bank account established to meet the payroll only.

Regular Bank Account. A separate cheque, drawn on the regular bank account, is issued to each employee for his pay. For each cheque the accounting entry, recorded in the Cash Payments Journal, is:

Dr. Payroll Payable $1,051.53
    Cr. Bank $1,051.53

The sum of all the individual cheques issued in this way will be equal to the total of the Net Pay column of the Payroll Journal. Since each of the cheques results in a debit to the Payroll Payable account, they will have the effect of eliminating the balance in this liability account.

Special Payroll Bank Account. To allow the Payroll Department to operate independently and to issue its own payroll cheques, many businesses set up a separate Payroll Bank Account.

Using this method, one cheque only is drawn on the regular bank account for the amount of the total net pay. In the Cash Payments Journal the accounting entry to record this cheque is:

Dr. Payroll Payable $1,051.53
    Cr. Bank $1,051.53

This cheque is cashed and the funds deposited in the special Payroll Bank Account, thereby providing funds for the Payroll Department to meet the payroll obligation. The Payroll Department then issues separate payroll cheques to the employees as necessary. No accounting entries are required for these cheques. When all of the cheques are cashed the balance in the Payroll bank account will be reduced to zero.

Paying Unemployment Insurance

METHOD 1

Within three days of the pay day, the employer is required to affix in each employee's Unemployment Insurance Stamp Book, stamps equal to the combined contributions of the employee and the employer. These stamps are purchased from the Post Office. When the payroll was recorded, the Unemployment Insurance Payable account was credited with $28–$14 twice (once for the employees' share and once for the employer's share). The entry to show the purchase of $28 of stamps is as follows.

June	22	Unemployment Insurance Payable			28	00		
		Bank					28	00
		To record purchase of U.I.C. stamps						

This entry, when posted, removes the liability for Unemployment Insurance. The 'T' accounts show the effect of the above entry.

Bank		Unemployment Insurance Payable	
	$ 28.00 June 22	June 22 $ 28.00	$ 14.00 June 19
			14.00 June 19

METHOD 2

The procedure developed so far is based on the fact that the business

242

purchases stamps only as they are required at the end of each pay period. Many businesses, however, purchase stamps in advance. When this method is used, usually a machine called a stamp meter is taken to the post office where it is set to record the purchase of a certain total amount of stamp registry. The entry on the right is necessary to show the purchase of $250 of stamp value in advance.

June	17	Unemployment Insurance Stamps			250	00		
		Bank					250	00
		To record purchase of U.I.C. stamps in advance						

The employees' stamp books are imprinted by the meter, which automatically deducts internally the amounts that have been registered in the books.

When the required $28 of stamps is imprinted in the employees' stamp books, the accounting entry required is as shown at right.

June	22	Unemployment Insurance Payable			28	—		
		Unemployment Insurance Stamps					28	—
		Total value of stamps affixed in U.I.C.						
		books (equal contribution of both						
		employer and employee)						

METHOD 3

A third method of paying for Unemployment Insurance is by the Bulk Payment Method. Using this method, the employees' stamp books are replaced by contribution statement forms UIC-443B as shown at right. No stamps are required as entries are made by hand. Only the employee's contribution is recorded. The illustration shows Harold Evans' contribution statement.

When the bulk payment method is used, the liability for unemployment insurance needs to be paid only once a month. The UIC-443B forms must be summarized in order to determine the total amount to be paid. Then a cheque is remitted for this amount. The accounting entry required is:

Dr Unemployment Insurance Payable $xxxx.xx
  Cr. Bank $xxxx.xx

Paying Employees' Income Taxes and Canada Pension Plan

On the fifteenth day of each month, the employer is required to remit to the Receiver-General of Canada the combined amount deducted for Employee's Income Taxes and Canada Pension Plan. The amount to be paid is equal to the deductions of the previous month. For example, on the 15th of September a cheque would be issued for the deductions made in August. This amount would be obtained by referring to the ledger accounts as of the end of August as shown at right.

On August 31, the balance in Employees' Income Taxes Payable account is $457.30 and in Canada Pension Plan Payable it is $46.50. One cheque for the combined amount is drawn to pay for both liabilities as they are both payable to the Receiver General of Canada. The entry is as shown at right.

The entry is posted, removing liabilities created the prior month.

As the other liabilities resulting from payroll deductions become due, they are handled in much the same way. A cheque is issued payable to the agency involved for the appropriate amount.

Canada Pension Plan Payable	
	$46.50 Bal. Aug. 31

Employees' Income Taxes Payable	
	$457.30 Bal. Aug. 31

Sept. 15	Employees Income Taxes Payable			457 30		
	Canada Pension Plan Payable			46 50		
	Bank				503 80	
	Issued cheque #4798 to the Receiver General					

Using the Payroll Journal as a Book of Original Entry

It should be noted at this point that it is possible to record the payroll in another way. We have been considering the Payroll Journal as a summary sheet and not as a book of original entry. As a result it was necessary to journalize the totals of the payroll into the General Journal.

Many business firms, regardless of the journal system used, treat the Payroll Journal as a book of original entry. As a result, the first payroll entry need not be recorded in the General Journal but may be posted directly to the General Ledger from the Payroll Journal. It must be pointed out at this time that the second and third accounting entries for payroll must still be recorded in the usual manner. This is necessary because the Payroll Journal only shows the employees' share of Unemployment Insurance and Canada Pension. The employer's share must be recorded also.

Basic Payroll Records

You are by now aware of the importance of written documents in the accounting process. There are three important records that are required for payroll. They are (1) the payroll journal, (2) the payroll cheque or payroll cash statement, and (3) the individual employee's earnings record.

1. Payroll Journal:

The Payroll Journal was discussed and illustrated during the discussion of the various payroll deductions. It is prepared for each pay period and is used to accumulate information about wage and salary costs.

2. Payroll Cheques or Payroll Cash Statements:

In most businesses, the employees are paid by cheque. Attached to each pay cheque is a voucher that shows the employee's gross pay, deductions, and the net pay. A payroll cheque is shown at the top of page 245.

Those businesses that prefer to pay by cash rather than by cheque use a payroll cash statement. It serves the same purpose as the voucher portion of the payroll cheque. It indicates the earnings, the various deductions and the net pay.

3. Employee's Earnings Record:

For each employee, the employer must keep an Employee's Earnings Record form on which are accumulated the details of every pay. This form is shown on page 245.

At the end of the calendar year, the columns are totaled to obtain the information necessary for the

NAME	PERIOD ENDING	REGULAR HOURS	RATE	OVER-TIME HOURS	RATE	REGULAR	EXTRA	GROSS PAY	CANADA PENSION	INCOME TAX	U.I.C.	HOSPITAL INSURANCE	MEDICAL INSURANCE	UNION DUES	CODE	MISC. AMOUNT	TOTAL DED'NS	NET
HAROLD EVANS	JUNE 19	—	—	—	—	295.00	—	295.00	4.89	42.20	2.80	5.77	6.81	4.50	A	3.60	70.57	224.43
						★ EARNINGS ★						DEDUCTIONS						

DETACH AND RETAIN THIS STATEMENT OF YOUR EARNINGS AND DEDUCTIONS

VIKING ENTERPRISES, LAKEHEAD, ONTARIO

Miscellaneous Deductions

A. GROUP LIFE INSURANCE

B. _____

C. _____

FORT WILLIAM W 6942-69
SYSTEMS "One Writing" EQUIPMENT LIMITED FORM 204P   LITHO IN CANADA

VIKING ENTERPRISES
888 Fort William Road
LAKEHEAD, ONTARIO

PAYROLL   P   4029

DATE JUNE 19 19-9

PAY TO THE ORDER OF   HAROLD EVANS $ 224.43

THE SUM OF   Two Hundred twenty-four — 43/100 DOLLARS

VIKING ENTERPRISES

VOID

NATIONAL BANK OF CANADA
1867 CONFEDERATION AVENUE
LAKEHEAD, ONTARIO

⑆94 200⑈0041⑆ 800 4⑈21369⑈

NAME EVANS, Harold

SOCIAL INSURANCE No. 609-779-152
DEPT. No. WAREHOUSE
MARITAL STATUS MARRIED
DEPENDENTS 2 CHILDREN

ADDRESS 178 N. Clarkson Ave.
Thunder Bay Ontario
PHONE 344-9506

INCOME TAX EXEMPTION 2,600.00
DATE OF BIRTH FEB. 9, 1939
DATE STARTED JUNE 4, 19-4
DATE LEFT
REASON

DATE	RATE	STANDARD EARNINGS	STANDARD DEDUCTIONS							
JAN. 2		270.00	4.44	35.30	2.80	5.77	6.81	4.50	A 3.60	63.22
MAY 8		295.00	4.89	42.20	2.80	5.77	6.81	4.50	A 3.60	70.57

NAME	DATE	1	2	3	4	5	6	7	8	9	10	11	12	13	14	15	16	17	NET PAY	CHEQUE No.	PERIOD
FORWARD																					
HAROLD EVANS	JAN 2					270.00		270.00	4.44	35.30	2.80	5.77	6.81	4.50	A 3.60		63.22	206.78	P1565	1
HAROLD EVANS	JAN 16					270.00		270.00	4.44	35.30	2.80	5.77	6.81	4.50	A 3.60		63.22	206.78	P2074	2
...LD EVANS	JAN 30					270.00		270.00	4.44	35.30	2.80	5.77	6.81	4.50	A 3.60		63.22	206.78	P2967	3
HAROLD EVANS	JUNE 5					295.00		295.00	4.89	42.20	2.80	5.77	6.81	4.50	A 3.60		70.57	224.43	P3768	12
HAROLD EVANS	JUNE 19					295.00		295.00	4.89	42.20	2.80	5.77	6.81	4.50	A 3.60		70.57	224.43	P4029	13
																				14
																				15
																		TOTAL		16
																		YEAR TO DATE		

SYSTEMATIC "One Writing"—Form 105
Manufactured by Systems Equipment Limited
LITHO IN CANADA

PROVINCE OF EMPLOYMENT	SOCIAL INSURANCE NUMBER	TOTAL EARNINGS BEFORE DEDUCTIONS	PENSION CONTRIBUTION		REGISTERED PENSION FUND CONTRIBUTION	INCOME TAX DEDUCTED	C.P.P. CONTRIBUTORY EARNINGS IF DIFFERENT FROM TOTAL EARNINGS	EXEMPTIONS PER TD1	TAXABLE ALLOWANCES AND BENEFITS INCLUDED	COMMISSIONS INCLUDED
			CANADA PLAN	QUEBEC PLAN						

EARNINGS RECORD

preparation of the annual Statement of Remuneration Paid form (T-4 slip). This form is required for income tax purposes. Copies of the T-4 slips are sent to the District Taxation Office and two copies are sent to the employee. When the employee makes out his annual income tax return, he attaches one copy to the income tax return. The illustration at the top of page 246 shows the T-4 slip of Harold Evans.

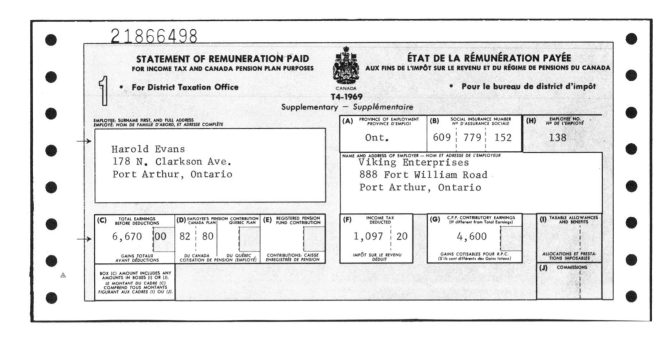

Devices to Assist in the Preparation of the Payroll

The manner in which payroll is prepared depends on the number of employees and the type of office or accounting equipment that is available. An inexpensive technique is the 'one-write' system which makes use of the pegboard or accounting board. It is a flat metal board with a row of pegs on it. Forms are placed into position on the pegs so that by using carbon paper all three basic records are produced with a single writing as shown on the right.

Another method is the Accounting machine (see page 114) which is programmed to enter amounts in appropriate columns and to total these columns. This type of machine has a carriage movement to make the recording process easier. This method also makes use of carbon paper to prepare all three basic records simultaneously.

The most advanced method of preparing the payroll is by means of a computer. However, this method is expensive and usually is used only by large companies that can afford to take advantage of the computer's tremendous speed and capability.

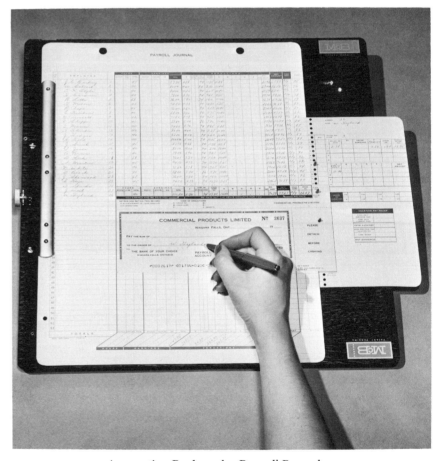

Accounting Pegboard—Payroll Procedure
(Courtesy of The McBee Company)

Bookkeeping and Accounting Terms

Payroll: The total process of calculating and preparing the employees' pays.

Gross Pay: The pay before deductions.

Net Pay: The pay after deductions.

Payroll Deductions: Amounts withheld from the gross pay.

Canada Pension Plan: A Government of Canada sponsored national pension plan.

Unemployment Insurance: A Government of Canada sponsored national insurance plan against unemployment.

Wages: An amount paid periodically to an employee based on the number of hours he has worked or the quantity of goods he has produced. Wages are usually paid on a weekly basis to manual and mechanical workers.

Salary: A fixed amount paid periodically to an employee for his services, regardless of the number of hours he works. Salary is usually set at a certain amount per week, per month, or per year and paid weekly, half-monthly, or monthly.

Commission: An amount paid periodically to a salesman or an agent calculated as a percentage of the amount of goods or services sold.

Personal Exemption: The amount of annual income that a person may earn that is exempt from tax; that is, tax free. The amount varies with the person's marital status and number of dependants.

Employee's Earnings Record: A form used to provide an accumulation of all the payroll data during a calendar year for a particular employee. One is prepared for each employee.

Review Questions

1. Give three main reasons for keeping accurate payroll records.
2. What are the three main methods of calculating the pay for an employee?
3. What information is necessary if employees are paid a wage, and how is it obtained?
4. What is the purpose of the TD-1 form? When is it completed?
5. Why were the Canada Pension Plan and the Quebec Pension Plan introduced?
6. How are contributions to the Canada Pension Plan and the Quebec Pension Plan determined? Who is responsible for contributing?
7. Explain how you would determine the amount of income taxes that an employee must pay.
8. What is the purpose of Unemployment Insurance?
9. Explain who contributes to Unemployment Insurance and how the amount of the deduction is determined.
10. What do the rates for Medical and/or Hospital Insurance depend on?
11. Why does the employer deduct union dues from employees on behalf of the union?
12. What is the formula or equation for calculating the net pay for an employee?
13. Describe the special form used to calculate the net pay for each employee.

14. Describe the steps that are performed to ensure the accuracy of the Payroll Journal.

15. Discuss the advantages and disadvantages of the cash method and the cheque method of paying employees.

16. Describe the three basic records required in payroll accounting.

Exercises

1. The time cards for two employees are given below.

(a) Determine the total number of hours worked each day and the total number of hours worked during the week. (Move the 'In' times ahead to the nearest quarter hour and the 'Out' times back to the nearest quarter hour.)

(b) Calculate the regular and overtime earnings for each. Frank Windsor's regular rate is $2.80 an hour and Ray Peterson's regular rate is $2.60 an hour. (All hours in excess of 40 hours per week are overtime hours paid at the rate of time and a half the regular rate.)

(c) Determine the gross pay for each.

Time Card					
Week Ended		July 23	19		
Soc. Ins. No.		642 393 438			
Name		Frank Windsor			
Day	Morning In Out	Afternoon In Out	Extra In Out	Total Hours
M	7:58 12:01	12:58 5:01		8
T	8:07 12:00	12:51 5:02		7¾
W	7:56 12:03	12:59 5:00		8
T	7:59 12:02	1:01 5:03		7
F	7:57 12:02	12:59 5:01		8
S	'			
S				

	Hours	Rate	Earnings
Regular Time		2.80	
Overtime			
Gross Pay			

Time Card					
Week Ended		July 23	19		
Soc. Ins. No.		643 461 217			
Name		Ray Peterson			
Day	Morning In Out	Afternoon In Out	Extra In Out	Total Hours
M	7:58 12:02	1:00 5:02		8
T	7:59 12:00	12:58 5:01	5:59 8:55	11
W	7:57 12:01	12:59 5:02		8
T	7:56 12:01	12:58 5:03		8
F	7:59 12:01	12:59 5:01		8
S	7:58 12:01			4
S				

	Hours	Rate	Earnings
Regular Time		2.60	
Overtime			
Gross Pay			

2. The Greenfield Real Estate Company pays its salesmen a basic salary of $325 per month plus a 2 per cent commission on the sales they make. For each of the salesmen below, calculate the commission and the gross earnings.

Salesmen	Net Sales
(a) Bob Rennie	$ 90,000.00
(b) Earl Hunt	45,500.00
(c) Gerry Anderson	51,300.00
(d) Allan Milroy	39,800.00
(e) Leonard Downes	61,750.00
(f) Peter Johnson	42,100.00

3. Using the C.P.P. tables on pages 232 and 233, determine the contributions to be made by each of the employees listed below.

Employee	Total Personal Exemption	Gross Earnings
(a) John Anderson	$2,000.00	$225.00
(b) Grant Firth	1,000.00	180.00
(c) Gordon Peterson	2,300.00	176.50
(d) Raymond Charles	2,850.00	217.45
(e) Isaac Reeves	1,550.00	291.18

4. After you have completed exercise 3, determine the following from the tables on page 235 and on page 236.
   (a) The income tax deduction for each employee.
   (b) The unemployment insurance deduction for each.

5. (a) Prepare a Payroll Journal with the following column headings:
   Employee; Employee Number; Total Personal Exemption; Hours Worked (Regular, Overtime); Earnings (Regular, Extra, Total); Deductions (C.P.P., Income Taxes, U.I.C.); Total Deductions; Net Pay; Cheque Number.
   (b) The data below cover the two weeks ending August 12, 19—.

No.	Employee	Hours Worked	Total Personal Exemption	Rate per Hour
731	Alex Willson	88	$2,850.00	$2.75
732	Peter Jones	80	1,000.00	2.20
733	Phil Harris	80	1,300.00	2.68
734	Bob Denver	92	2,600.00	2.60
735	Harold Higgins	80	2,300.00	2.80

Note:

Any hours over 40 hours per week are considered overtime hours and are paid for at the rate of one-and-one half times the regular rate.

Transfer the appropriate data onto the Payroll Journal.

(c) Using the deduction tables in this chapter, calculate the net pay for each employee. Cheques start at number B7648.

(d) Total the columns of the journal and perform the steps to ensure the accuracy of the journal.

---

6. (a) Prepare a Payroll Journal with the following column headings: Employee; Employee Number; Total Personal Exemption; Hours Worked (Regular, Overtime); Earnings (Regular, Extra, Total); Deductions (C.P.P. Income Taxes. U.I.C., Hospital Insurance, Medical Insurance); Total Deductions; Net Pay; Cheque Number.

(b) Each of the employees listed below receives a bi-weekly salary of $175 plus a commission of 1 per cent of the net sales that he makes for the two weeks. Transfer the appropriate data onto the Payroll Journal.

No.	Employee	Total Personal Exemption	Net Sales	Number of Dependants Including Wife	Hospitalization Coverage
35	Eddie Albert	$1,000.00	$12,000.00	0	Public-Ward
36	Bob Cummings	2,000.00	9,800.00	1	Semi-private
37	Al Fraser	2,300.00	16,500.00	2	Semi-private
38	Alex Davidson	2,300.00	12,380.00	2	Semi-private
39	Bob Pettit	1,000.00	9,950.00	1	Public Ward

(c) Each of the employees is enrolled in both the Hospital Insurance plan and the Medical Insurance plan. Use the rates given on pages 237 and 238.

(d) Complete the Payroll Journal and verify.

7. The illustration below shows the column totals from the Payroll Journal of Hudson Fisheries Limited. Prepare the General Journal entries to record the details of the payroll.

PAYROLL JOURNAL   For the _2 weeks_ ended _October_ _16_ 19 _–9_

| Employee | Total Personal Exempt. | Hours | | Earnings | | | Deductions | | | | | | | Net Pay | Cheque Number |
		Reg.	O/T	Regular	Extra	Total	C.P.P.	Income Tax	U.I.C.	Hospital Ins.	Medical Ins	Union Dues	Group Life		
TOTALS				4,982 50	1,612 95	6,595 45	116 35	1021 43	117 60	129 85	143 00	112 50	67 50	4887 22	

8. (a) Prepare the General Journal entries required for exercise 5.
   (b) Prepare the General Journal entries required for exercise 6.

9. Assume that the employees in exercise 6 are paid on a cash basis. Prepare the 'Payroll Currency Requisition'. Cheque A39426 is prepared to obtain the necessary funds. Prepare the General Journal entry to record the cheque.

10. (a) Prepare a payroll with the following headings: Employee; Employee No.; Hours (Regular, O/T); Earnings (Regular, Extra, Total); Deductions (C.P.P., Income Taxes, U.I.C., Hospital Insurance, Medical Insurance, Union Dues); Net Pay.

    (b) Each of the employees listed on page 252 is employed by E-Z Auto Sales Limited. The mechanics are paid an hourly wage as indicated. Any hours over 40 hours per week are paid at the time and a half rate. They belong to the I.A.M. union local and pay $6.25

in union dues each pay period. The salesmen are paid a basic salary of $70 per week plus 1 per cent commission on all sales completed. All E-Z employees are enrolled in both the Hospital Insurance plan and the Medical Insurance plan.

No.	Employee	Total Personal Exemption	Hours Worked	Hourly Rate	Net Sales	Number of Dependants Including Wife	Hospitalization Coverage
481	Dave Durand	$1,000.00	80	$2.75		0	Public Ward
482	Joe Kuchma	2,300.00	80	2.68		2	Semi-private
483	Glen Nyman	2,000.00	86	2.71		1	Public Ward
484	Dave Bower	2,900.00	86	2.59		4	Public Ward
493	Jim Hansen	1,000.00			$16,000.00	0	Semi-private
494	Terry Sutherland	2,600.00			9,600.00	3	Semi-private
495	Ed Milani	2,550.00			12,400.00	2	Semi-private

INSTRUCTION

Complete the Payroll Journal. Use the tables found in the chapter for the various deductions.

(c) Prepare the General Journal entries required for the above payroll. The company uses separate expense accounts for wages and salaries.

(d) E-Z Auto Sales Limited pays their employees in cash. Prepare a Payroll Currency Requisition.

Chapter 14

ADJUSTMENTS FOR FINANCIAL STATEMENTS

One of the chief purposes of Accounting is to accumulate the information necessary for the preparation of the financial statements. You have already studied this aspect of Accounting in Chapter 6. However, before continuing with the work of this chapter you should review Chapter 6.

It has been suggested throughout this text that it is expedient to let certain of the records become temporarily incorrect during the accounting period and to correct them all at one time at the end of the period. This process of correcting the records at the end of the accounting period is known as 'making the adjustments'; the corrections themselves are known as the **Adjustments** or the **Adjusting Entries**.

The first step in preparing the financial statements is to take off a General Ledger trial balance at the end of the accounting period. This is to be done on eight-column work sheet paper. You previously worked with six-column paper; the two additional columns introduced at this time are to be used for the adjustments.

The trial balance figures on the work sheet are taken directly from the General Ledger at the end of the accounting period. As a result, they contain the account balances that are not up to date and which require the making of the 'adjustments'. Although only a few adjustments are discussed at this time, they are important ones and will introduce you to the theoretical concepts involved in making adjustments of all kinds.

Before beginning the study of adjustments a word of explanation is necessary. The topic 'adjustments' is not completely covered in this chapter but carries over into Chapter 15. Therefore, do not expect to be thoroughly informed about adjustments until you have studied both Chapter 14 and Chapter 15.

An accountant may select from two different techniques for the making of individual adjustments. These are: (1) the formal or traditional technique; (2) the short-cut technique. For most adjustments, either technique is equally effective. However, for certain particular adjustments one or the other of the two techniques is definitely superior. You will be informed of these particular adjustments as you proceed through the chapter.

Adjusting Entries— Formal Technique

Let us begin the study of the formal technique of making the adjusting entries by preparing the work sheet for Cassidy Cartage, a service business. The General Ledger trial balance of Cassidy Cartage as of June 30, 19—4, the end of an annual accounting period, is shown in the first two columns of the work sheet shown on page 254.

Adjusting for Accounts Payable

One should not expect to complete the preparation of the financial statements until from two to three weeks after the end of the accounting period. This period of waiting is necessary to allow time for the late arrival of Purchase Invoices from suppliers.

It is not an uncommon occurrence for goods and services to arrive towards the end of an accounting period, but for the Purchase Invoices for these goods and services to arrive after the accounting period is over; that is, in the next accounting period.

The accounting entries for any goods or services purchased should be recorded in the same period as that in which the goods or services are received. Therefore, for the two or three weeks following the end of the accounting period all Purchase Invoices must be examined, and those falling into the category described above must be gathered together and summarized for an adjusting entry.

Assume that the list of Purchase Invoices for Cassidy Cartage in the box below are those for which an adjusting entry is required.

Supplier	Invoice Date	Explanation	Amount
Local Telephone Co.	July 5	Telephone bill for June	$ 15.70
Arrow Garage	July 6	Truck repairs in June	35.50
Frank's Supply	July 6	Supplies received in June	45.21
Star Oil Co.	July 10	Gas and Oil for trucks in June	138.50
Black Lumber Company	July 10	Repairs to building in June	125.00
Public Utilities	July 12	Electricity for June	15.00
Public Utilities	July 14	Water for June	7.81
Jerry's Hardware	July 14	Miscellaneous items in June	20.00

Accounts	Acc. #	Trial Balance Dr.	Trial Balance Cr.	Adjustments Dr.	Adjustments Cr.	P. & L. Statement Dr.	P. & L. Statement Cr.	Balance Sheet Dr.	Balance Sheet Cr.
Petty Cash	1	50 —							
Bank	2	725 41							
Accounts Receivable	3	4 027 56							
Allowance for Doubtful Accounts	4		26 40						
Supplies	5	516 52							
Prepaid Insurance	6	216 —							
Prepaid Licences	7	255 —							
Land	8	8 000 —							
Buildings (Frame)	9	7 280 —							
Accumulated Depreciation Bldgs.	10		2 005 40						
Furniture and Equipment	11	2 950 —							
Accumulated Depreciation F. & E.	12		1 597 40						
Automotive Equipment	13	15 600 —							
Accumulated Depreciation Autos.	14		7 956 —						
Accounts Payable	21		3 047 25						
Sales Tax Payable	22		238 73						
P. Marshall, Capital	31		18 387 21						
P. Marshall, Drawings	32	6 000 —							
Sales	41		28 757 49						
Discounts Earned	42		56 75						
Bank Charges	51	114 92							
Building Maintenance	52	474 37							
Light, Heat and Water	53	472 19							
Miscellaneous Expenses	54	115 70							
Telephone Expense	55	151 30							
Truck Expense	56	5 704 16							
Wages	57	9 419 50							
		62 072 63	62 072 63						

Cassidy Cartage — Work Sheet — Year Ended June 30, 19-4

These Purchase Invoices are summarized into an accounting entry as shown below. Then they are allowed to be absorbed into the normal accounting routine in the new accounting period.

Telephone Expense	$ 15.70	
Truck Expense	174.00	
Supplies	45.21	
Building Maintenance	125.00	
Light, Heat and Water	22.81	
Miscellaneous Expense	20.00	
Accounts Payable		$402.72

This accounting entry is not journalized in the books at this time. It is, however, recorded in the Adjustments column of the work sheet as shown at the top of page 255.

Observe that each of the amounts entered is coded with a circled numeral '1' to indicate that it forms a part of the first adjusting entry.

Cassidy Cartage		Work Sheet				
Accounts	Acc #	Trial Balance Dr.	Cr.	Adjustments Dr.	Cr.	
Petty Cash	1	50 –				
Bank	2	725 41				
Accounts Receivable	3	4 027 56				
Allowance for Doubtful Accounts	4		26 40			
Supplies	5	516 52		① 45 21		
Prepaid Insurance	6	216 –				
Prepaid Licenses	7	255 –				
Land	8	8 000 –				
Buildings (Frame)	9	7 280 –				
Accumulated Depreciation Bldgs.	10		2 005 40			
Furniture and Equipment	11	2 950 –				
Accumulated Depreciation F. & E.	12		1 597 40			
Automotive Equipment	13	15 600 –				
Accumulated Depreciation Autos.	14		7 956 –			
Accounts Payable	21		3 047 25		① 402 72	
Sales Tax Payable	22		238 73			
P. Marshall, Capital	31		18 387 21			
P. Marshall, Drawings	32	6 000 –				
Sales	41		28 757 49			
Discounts Earned	42		56 75			
Bank Charges	51	114 92				
Building Maintenance	52	474 37		① 125 –		
Light, Heat and Water	53	472 19		① 22 81		
Miscellaneous Expense	54	115 70		① 20 –		
Telephone Expense	55	151 30		① 15 70		
Truck Expense	56	5 704 16		① 174 –		
Wages	57	9 419 50				
		62 072 63	62 072 63			

Adjusting for Supplies

The Supplies account is allowed to become incorrect during the accounting period because it is too much trouble to record the usage of supplies as it occurs. As a result, the account balance is incorrect by the cost of all the supplies used up during the period.

To adjust for supplies, it is first necessary to take a physical inventory of the supplies actually on hand on the last day of the accounting period. This involves the preparation of a listing similar to the one shown on the right. Each different item must be counted or estimated and the quantity multiplied by the most recent cost price in order to obtain a reasonable value of the supplies on hand.

The Supplies adjustment debits Supplies Expense and credits Supplies with the amount that will cause the Supplies account to have a balance equal to the Supplies inventory figure. A look at the work sheet for Cassidy Cartage shows that the Supplies account has a balance of $516.52 and that there is an accounts payable debit adjustment of $45.21. This gives the account an effective

```
                    Supplies Inventory
                     June 30, 19-4


  Description                  Quantity    Unit Cost    Value

Envelopes, #10, White           4¾ boxes    $5.50       $23.38
Envelopes, #8, White            4  boxes     4.95        19.80
Envelopes, 8½ x 11, Manilla     1½ boxes     7.50        11.25
Envelopes, 8½ x 14, Manilla     2  boxes     8.75        17.50
Ball Pens, Blue                 ½  gross    72.00        36.00
Pencils, Black, HB              6  dozen     1.50         9.00
Pencils, Black, F2½             8  dozen     1.50        12.00
Pencils, Red                    2  dozen     1.75         3.50
Cellulose Tape, ½"              3/4 box     24.00        18.00
Cellulose Tape, 3/4"            1½ boxes    30.00        45.00
Paper Clips, Regular           15  boxes     1.25        18.75
Paper Clips, Small             10  boxes     1.10        11.00

Gummed Labels, Assorted Colours 1¼ gross    75.00        93.75
Elastic Bands, Mixed            5  boxes     1.05         5.25
                                                       _____
                                                        $395.25
                                                       ========
```

balance of $561.73. To reduce this to the inventory figure of $395.25 requires an adjustment in the amount of $166.48. Accordingly, the adjusting entry for Supplies for Cassidy Cartage is:

Supplies Expense $166.48
   Supplies $166.48

This adjustment is recorded on the work sheet in the Adjustments column as shown on page 256. As with all such adjustments, it is not journalized in the book at this time.

Observe that this adjustment is coded with a numeral '2' because it

happens to be the second adjusting entry on this work sheet.

Too, notice that a line for Supplies Expense has been started beneath the trial balance section. This was necessary because the trial balance did not include a Supplies Expense account. Whenever an adjustment affects an account that is not written in the trial balance section, the account must be written below the trial balance.

EXTENDING THE WORK SHEET

When the accountant is certain that no other adjustment will affect a

Accounts	Acc #	Trial Balance Dr.	Trial Balance Cr.	Adjustments Dr.	Adjustments Cr.	P & L Statement Dr.	P & L Statement Cr.	Balance Sheet Dr.	Balance Sheet Cr.
Petty Cash	1	50 –							
Bank	2	725 41							
Accounts Receivable	3	4 027 56							
Allowance for Doubtful Accounts	4		26 40						
Supplies	5	516 52		① 45 21	② 166 48			395 25	
Prepaid Insurance	6	216 –							
Prepaid Licences	7	255 –							
Land	8	8 000 –							
Buildings (Frame)	9	7 280 –							
Accumulated Depreciation, Bldgs.	10		2 005 40						
Furniture and Equipment	11	2 950 –							
Accumulated Depreciation F. & E.	12		1 597 40						
Automotive Equipment	13	15 600 –							
Accumulated Depreciation Autos	14		7 956 –						
Accounts Payable	21		3 047 25		① 402 72				
Sales Tax Payable	22		238 73						
P. Marshall, Capital	31		18 387 21						
P. Marshall, Drawings	32	6 000 –							
Sales	41		28 757 49						
Discounts Earned	42		56 75						
Bank Charges	51	114 92							
Building Maintenance	52	474 37		① 125 –					
Light, Heat and Water	53	472 19		① 22 81					
Miscellaneous Expense	54	115 70		① 20 –					
Telephone Expense	55	151 30		① 15 70					
Truck Expense	56	5 704 16		① 174 –					
Wages	57	9 419 50							
		62 072 63	62 072 63						
Supplies Expense				② 166 48		166 48			

Cassidy Cartage — Work Sheet — Year Ended June 30, 19–4

particular item on the work sheet, he may extend the item. Both the Supplies line and the Supplies Expense line of the work sheet may be extended at this time. To extend any line of the work sheet you must first find the value of the first four columns; that is, the value of the Trial Balance and the Adjustments columns. Then, transfer this value to the appropriate column of the remaining four.

For Supplies, the value of the first four columns is found to be $395.25 debit, and since Supplies is a Balance Sheet item (asset), the $395.25 is transferred to the Balance Sheet Debit column.

For Supplies Expense, the value of the first four columns is found to be $166.48 debit, and since Supplies Expense is a Profit and Loss item, the $166.48 is tranferred to the Profit and Loss Debit column.

Adjusting for Prepaid Expenses

It is a common business practice to pay in advance for certain expenses that cover a period of time, and to set them up in Prepaid Expense accounts. For example, automobile licences are purchased in advance, usually for a period of one year, and are debited to an account called Prepaid Licences. Similarly, insurance coverage is purchased in advance for periods of one or three years, and is debited to an account called Prepaid Insurance.

With the passing of time, Prepaid Expenses gradually expire and diminish in value. For example, a truck licence costing $60 on January 1, to be in force for a period of one year, is worth $60 on January 1, but gradually diminishes in value with the passing of time. On June 30, the licence is half expired and has a value of $30. On September 30, the licence is three-quarters expired and has a value of $15. Theoretically, the licence (or any Prepaid Expense of this type) has a value relative to the proportion of time remaining in its term.

During the course of an accounting period, however, no attempt is made to keep the Prepaid Expense accounts accurate. Only at the end of the accounting period, for purposes of financial statements, is accuracy of this kind important. And then, accuracy is acquired by means of an adjusting entry on the work sheet.

It is first necessary to calculate the value of the unexpired insurance as of the end of the accounting period. This is done by analysing the insurance policies and preparing an insurance schedule such as the following:

Prepaid Insurance Schedule
June 30, 19–4

Company	Policy Date	Term	Premium	Unexpired Proportion	Prepaid Insurance June 30, 19–4
Admiral	Mar. 31, 19–4	1 year	$44.00	3/4	$33.00
International	Feb. 1, 19–2	3 years	$54.00	7/36	$10.50
Satellite	Jan. 1, 19–3	3 years	$90.00	1/2	$45.00
				Total	$88.50

The adjustment for insurance is one that brings the Prepaid Insurance account into agreement with the Prepaid Insurance calculation. The accounting entry debits Insurance Expense and credits Prepaid Insurance.

The work sheet for Cassidy Cartage shows a balance of $216 for Prepaid Insurance. To bring this into agreement with the insurance schedule figure of $88.50 requires an adjustment of $127.50 as follows:

Insurance Expense $127.50
Prepaid Insurance $127.50

The adjusting entry and the items extended on the work sheet are shown in the illustration below.

Observe that this adjustment is coded with a numeral '3' and that it requires the opening of an Insurance Expense line.

Cassidy Cartage — Work Sheet — Year Ended June 30, 19–4

Accounts	Acc #	Trial Balance Dr.	Trial Balance Cr.	Adjustments Dr.	Adjustments Cr.	P & L Statement Dr.	P & L Statement Cr.	Balance Sheet Dr.	Balance Sheet Cr.
Petty Cash	1	50 —							
Bank	2	725 41							
Accounts Receivable	3	4 027 56							
Allowance for Doubtful Accounts	4		26 40						
Supplies	5	516 52		① 45 21	② 166 48			395 25	
Prepaid Insurance	6	216 —			③ 127 50			88 50	
Prepaid Licences	7	255 —							
Land	8	8 000 —							
Buildings (Frame)	9	7 280 —							
Accumulated Depreciation Bldg.	10		2 005 40						
Furniture and Equipment	11	2 950 —							
Accumulated Depreciation F. & E.	12		1 597 40						
Automotive Equipment	13	15 600 —							
Accumulated Depreciation Autos.	14		7 956 —						
Accounts Payable	21		3 047 25		① 402 72				
Sales Tax Payable	22		238 73						
P. Marshall, Capital	31		18 387 21						
P. Marshall, Drawings	32	6 000 —							
Sales	41		28 757 49						
Discounts Earned	42		56 75						
Bank Charges	51	114 92							
Building Maintenance	52	474 37		① 125 —					
Light, Heat and Water	53	472 19		① 22 81					
Miscellaneous Expense	54	115 70		① 20 —					
Telephone Expense	55	151 30		① 15 70					
Truck Expense	56	5 704 16		① 174 —					
Wages	57	9 419 50							
		62 072 63	62 072 63						
Supplies Expense				② 166 48		166 48			
Insurance Expense				③ 127 50		127 50			

This adjustment is similar to that for Prepaid Insurance. First, it is necessary to calculate the value of the unexpired licences by means of a schedule such as the following:

Prepaid Licences Schedule
June 30, 19–4

Vehicle	Cost of Licence	Term of Licence	Unexpired Proportion	Prepaid Licences June 30, 19–4
3 ton van	$80.00	Jan. 1 to Dec. 31	½	$40.00
½ ton truck	$60.00	Jan. 1 to Dec. 31	½	$30.00
Station wagon	$30.00	Jan. 1 to Dec. 31	½	$15.00
				$85.00

The adjustment for licences is one that brings the Prepaid Licences account into agreement with the Prepaid Licences schedule. The accounting entry debits Licences Expense and credits Prepaid Licences.

The work sheet for Cassidy Cartage shows a balance of $255 for Prepaid Licences. To bring this into agreement with the schedule figure of $85.00 requires an adjustment in the amount of $170 as follows:

Licences Expense $170.00
    Prepaid Licences $170.0

On the work sheet the adjustment (coded '4') and the items extended are as shown below.

Cassidy Cartage — Work Sheet — Year Ended June 30, 19–4

Accounts	ACC #	Trial Balance Dr.	Trial Balance Cr.	Adjustments Dr.	Adjustments Cr.	P. & L. Statement Dr.	P. & L. Statement Cr.	Balance Sheet Dr.	Balance Sheet Cr.
Petty Cash	1	50 -							
Bank	2	725 41							
Accounts Receivable	3	4 027 56							
Allowance for Doubtful Accounts	4		26 40						
Supplies	5	516 52		① 45 21	② 166 48			395 25	
Prepaid Insurance	6	216 -			③ 127 50			88 50	
Prepaid Licences	7	255 -			④ 170 -			85 -	
Land	8	8 000 -							
Buildings (Frame)	9	7 280 -							
Accumulated Depreciation Bldgs	10		2 005 40						
Furniture and Equipment	11	2 950 -							
Accumulated Depreciation F. & E.	12		1 597 40						
Automotive Equipment	13	15 600 -							
Accumulated Depreciation Autos.	14		7 956 -						
Accounts Payable	21		3 047 25		① 402 72				
Sales Tax Payable	22		238 73						
P. Marshall Capital	31		18 387 21						
P. Marshall, Drawings	32	6 000 -							
Sales	41		28 757 49						
Discounts Earned	42		56 75						
Bank Charges	51	114 92							
Building Maintenance	52	474 37		① 125 -					
Light, Heat and Water	53	472 19		① 22 81					
Miscellaneous Expense	54	115 70		① 20 -					
Telephone Expense	55	151 30		① 15 70					
Truck Expense	56	5 704 16		① 174 -					
Wages	57	9 419 50							
		62 072 63	62 072 63						
Supplies Expense				② 166 48		166 48			
Insurance Expense				③ 127 50		127 50			
Licences Expense				④ 170 -		170 -			

An element of risk is involved in selling on credit. Although he may carefully check the credit rating of every credit customer, a businessman cannot be certain of collecting all of his accounts receivable. For a variety of reasons, such as business reversals, death, and bankruptcy, some of his customers may find it impossible to pay off their debts. Consequently, it is necessary to consider the correctness of the value of Accounts Receivable at the time financial statements are prepared.

ALLOWANCE FOR DOUBTFUL ACCOUNTS

At the end of each accounting period, it is necessary to analyse all of the individual customers' accounts for the purpose of determining the total of 'doubtful' accounts; that is, those accounts that may not be collected. This analysis is done by preparing an Accounts Receivable Aging Schedule such as the partial one shown at right. When preparing this schedule it will be necessary to discuss the various accounts with the Credit Manager.

At the end of each accounting period, the ascertained value of doubtful accounts is set up as a credit balance in an account called 'Allowance for Doubtful Accounts'. The estimated true value of Accounts Receivable is shown by the Accounts Receivable account and the Allowance for Doubtful Accounts account which must be considered together. For Cassidy Cartage the estimated true value of Accounts Receivable is shown below in T accounts.

Accounts Receivable	Allowance for Doubtful Accounts
4,027.56	260.45

Estimated true value of Accounts Receivable = $3,767.11

The account, Allowance for Doubtful Accounts, is a 'valuation' account which must be considered in relationship to the Accounts Receivable account. There are other valua-

Cassidy Cartage — Accounts Receivable Aging Schedule — June 30, 19-4

Customer	Account Balance	1-30 Days	31-60 Days	61-90 Days	91 Days and Older	Remarks	Allowance for Doubtful Debts
Advance Associates	156 50	52 00	29 40	75 10		Will be O.K.	
Barley Brothers	251 20	55 00	94 12	102 08		Will be O.K.	
J. Bowman	35 50	35 50				✓	
M. Carey	165 25	102 10			63 15	63.15 is 7 month old disputed item Correspondence with customer is proving fruitless	63 15
Concord Company	346 56	151 00	94 00	73 25	28 31	Slow but sure. Has been a good customer for over 10 years.	
Devon Bros.	95 62				95 62	Item is 10 months old and customer is in bankruptcy	95 62
Durnan + Son	114 56	24 00	90 56			✓	
Empire Traders	26 50	26 50					
Young + Young	16 00	16 00					
	4 027 56	2 461 15	841 90	400 07	324 44		260 45

tion accounts. Each one is related to an asset account and the two accounts must be looked at in conjunction with each other.

ADJUSTMENT FOR DOUBTFUL ACCOUNTS FOR CASSIDY CARTAGE

Having determined the allowance for doubtful accounts figure an adjusting entry is made to bring the account, Allowances for Doubtful Accounts, into agreement with the Aging Schedule. The accounting entry debits Bad Debts Expense and credits Allowance for Doubtful Accounts.

The work sheet shows a credit balance of $26.40 for Allowance for Doubtful Accounts. To bring this into agreement with the schedule figure of $260.45 requires an adjustment in the amount of $234.05 as follows:

Bad Debts Expense	$234.05	
Allowance for Doubtful Accounts		$234.05

On the work sheet, the adjusting entry (coded '5') and the items extended appear as shown at the top of page 260. Observe that since the Allowance for Bad Debts is a minus asset, it is extended to the Balance Sheet Credit column.

Accounts	Acc #	Trial Balance Dr.	Trial Balance Cr.	Adjustments Dr.	Adjustments Cr.	P. & L. Statement Dr.	P. & L. Statement Cr.	Balance Sheet Dr.	Balance Sheet Cr.
Petty Cash	1	50 —							
Bank	2	725 41							
Accounts Receivable	3	4 027 56							
Allowance for Doubtful Accounts	4		26 40		⑤ 234 05				260 45
Supplies	5	516 52		① 45 21	② 166 48			395 25	
Prepaid Insurance	6	216 —			③ 127 50			88 50	
Prepaid Licences	7	255 —			④ 170 —			85 —	
Land	8	8 000 —							
Buildings (Frame)	9	7 280 —							
Accumulated Depreciation Bldgs.	10		2 005 40						
Furniture and Equipment	11	2 950 —							
Accumulated Depreciation F.+E.	12		1 597 40						
Automotive Equipment	13	15 600 —							
Accumulated Depreciation Autos.	14		7 956 —						
Accounts Payable	21		3 047 25		① 402 72				
Sales Tax Payable	22		238 73						
P. Marshall, Capital	31		18 387 21						
P. Marshall, Drawings	32	6 000 —							
Sales	41		28 757 49						
Discounts Earned	42		56 75						
Bank Charges	51	114 92							
Building Maintenance	52	474 37		① 125 —					
Light, Heat and Water	53	472 19		① 22 81					
Miscellaneous Expense	54	115 70		① 20 —					
Telephone Expense	55	151 30		① 15 70					
Truck Expense	56	5 704 16		① 174 —					
Wages	57	9 419 50							
		62 072 63	62 072 63						
Supplies Expense				② 166 48		166 48			
Insurance Expense				③ 127 50		127 50			
Licences Expense				④ 170 —		170 —			
Bad Debts Expense				⑤ 234 05		234 05			

ACCOUNTS RECEIVABLE ON THE BALANCE SHEET

The estimated true value of Accounts Receivable is shown on the Balance Sheet in the manner shown below:

CURRENT ASSETS			
Petty Cash		$ 50.00	
Bank		725.41	
Accounts Receivable	$4,027.56		
Less Allowance for Doubtful Accounts	260.45	3,767.11	$4,542.52

WRITING OFF A BAD DEBT

When it becomes known for certain that a customer's account (or part of his account) will not be collected, the account balance (or part thereof) should be written off; that is, taken out of the books by means of an accounting entry. In the General Journal, an accounting entry such as the following is made:

Allowance for Doubtful Accounts	$63.15
Accounts Receivable (M. Carey)	$63.15

To write off the account of
M. Carey, bankrupt.

Remember that the posting to Accounts Receivable must be made twice–once to the General Ledger and once to the Subsidiary Ledger.

Adjusting for Depreciation

With the exception of land, every Fixed Asset (also known as Capital Equipment) is used up in the course of time and activity and therefore decreases in value. This decrease in value is known as **Depreciation**.

To illustrate the concept of depreciation consider the case of a businessman who purchases a new truck at a cost of $4,000 in order to begin a delivery business. After operating for five years he decides to terminate the business and in the course of its closing, the now used truck is sold for $500. Clearly, over the five-year period it cost the businessman $3,500 to own the truck and just as clearly it was essential that he have the truck in order to conduct his business.

To obtain an accurate picture of the profit and loss of his business, this man cannot ignore the $3,500 cost of the truck. Theoretically, it must be allocated as an expense of the business at the rate of $700 for each of the five years. The question remaining is this: Since it is impossible to make a precise calculation of depreciation until the end of the life of an asset (that is, until the asset is disposed of), by what method is the depreciation calculated during the life of the asset? The answer to the question is: The most common method is to use an estimated rate for calculating depreciation based on rates laid down by government regulation.

NET BOOK VALUE

Valuation accounts are used in conjunction with the fixed asset accounts. They are used to show the total amount of depreciation that accumulates during the life of an asset. At the end of every fiscal period, each fixed asset (with the exception of land) is decreased by the amount of the estimated depreciation. However, the reduction in the value of the fixed asset is not credited directly to the asset account but rather to a valuation account called Accumulated Depreciation.

A fixed asset account together with its Accumulated Depreciation account reflects the estimated true value of the asset. A typical example is the following:

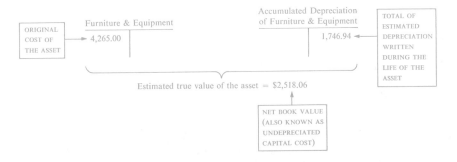

The cost of the asset less the accumulated depreciation gives the estimated true value of the asset.

This is commonly known as the Net Book Value or the Undepreciated Capital Cost. Two accounts in respect to a fixed asset are more informative than one account because they enable the reader to see what proportion of the asset is used up. Without the valuation account this cannot be seen.

GOVERNMENT RATES OF DEPRECIATION

Government regulations include rates of estimated depreciation (also known as 'Capital Cost Allowance') for any possible type of capital equipment. The most commonly used of these rates are:

Brick Buildings	5% per year of Net Book Value
Frame Buildings	10% per year of Net Book Value
Furniture and General Equipment	20% per year of Net Book Value
Automotive Equipment	30% per year of Net Book Value

It is an important point that these government rates are based on the Net Book Value (Undepreciated Capital Cost) of the particular assets.

CALCULATING THE DEPRECIATION FOR CASSIDY CARTAGE

The first step in calculating depreciation is to find out the net book values of the individual fixed assets. These are worked out as follows:

(i) (Frame) Buildings	Less	Accumulated Depreciation Buildings	Equals	Net Book Value Buildings
$7,280.00	—	$2,005.40	=	$5,274.60
(ii) Furniture and Equipment	Less	Accumulated Depreciation Furniture and Equipment	Equals	Net Book Value Furniture and Equipment
$2,950.00	—	$1,597.40	=	$1,352.60
(iii) Automotive Equipment	Less	Accumulated Depreciation Automotive Equipment	Equals	Net Book Value Automotive Equipment
$15,600.00	—	$7,956.00	=	$7,644.00

The second step is to multiply each of the net book value figures by the appropriate rate of depreciation in order to arrive at the respective depreciation expenses for the fiscal period (in this case one year).

ASSET	N.B.V.		ANNUAL RATE		DEPRECIATION FOR YEAR
(i) Buildings (Frame)	$5,274.60	×	10/100	=	$ 527.46
(ii) Furniture and Equipment	$1,352.60	×	20/100	=	$ 270.52
(iii) Automotive Equipment	$7,644.00	×	30/100	=	$2,293.20

Note:
For fiscal periods of less than one year the depreciation must be calculated as follows:
1. Calculate the annual depreciation as shown above.
2. Calculate the number of days in the fiscal period.
3. Compute the depreciation for the fiscal period by applying the following formula:

$$\text{Depreciation for the period} = \text{Annual Depreciation} \times \frac{\text{No. days in Fiscal Period}}{365}$$

DEPRECIATION ADJUSTMENT FOR CASSIDY CARTAGE

When calculated, the depreciation expense figures are set up on the work sheet as expenses and also as additions to their respective accumulated depreciation totals. This is accomplished by means of an adjusting entry (or entries) which debits Depreciation Expense and credits Accumulated Depreciation. For Cassidy Cartage the adjusting entries for depreciation are:

Depreciation of Buildings	$527.46	
Accumulated Depreciation of Buildings		$527.46
Depreciation of Furniture and Equipment	$270.52	
Accumulated Depreciation of Furniture and Equipment		$270.52
Depreciation of Automotive Equipment	$2,293.20	
Accumulated Depreciation of Automotive Equipment		$2,293.20

On the work sheet, these adjusting entries (coded '6', '7', and '8') and the items extended appear as shown on page 264. Because the accumulated depreciation accounts are minus asset accounts, they are extended to the Balance Sheet Credit column.

Cassidy Cartage — Work Sheet — Year Ended June 30, 19-4

Accounts	Acc #	Trial Balance Dr	Trial Balance Cr	Adjustments Dr	Adjustments Cr	P. & L. Statement Dr	P. & L. Statement Cr	Balance Sheet Dr	Balance Sheet Cr
Petty Cash	1	50 —							
Bank	2	725 41							
Accounts Receivable	3	4 027 56							
Allowance for Doubtful Accounts	4		26 40		⑤ 234 05				260 45
Supplies	5	516 52		① 45 21	② 166 48			395 25	
Prepaid Insurance	6	216 —			③ 127 50			88 50	
Prepaid Licences	7	255 —			④ 170 —			85 —	
Land	8	8 000 —							
Buildings (Frame)	9	7 280 —							
Accumulated Depreciation Bldgs	10		2 005 40		⑥ 527 46				2 532 86
Furniture + Equipment	11	2 950 —							
Accumulated Depreciation F+E	12		1 597 40		⑦ 270 52				1 867 92
Automotive Equipment	13	15 600 —							
Accumulated Depreciation Autos	14		7 956 —		⑧ 2 293 20				10 249 20
Accounts Payable	21		3 047 25		① 402 72				
Sales Tax Payable	22		238 73						
P. Marshall, Capital	31		18 387 21						
P. Marshall, Drawings	32	6 000 —							
Sales	41		28 757 49						
Discounts Earned	42		56 75						
Bank Charges	51	114 92							
Building Maintenance	52	474 37		① 125 —					
Light, Heat and Water	53	472 19		① 22 81					
Miscellaneous Expense	54	115 70		① 20 —					
Telephone Expense	55	151 30		① 15 70					
Truck Expense	56	5 704 16		① 174 —					
Wages	57	9 419 50							
		62 072 63	62 072 63						
Supplies Expense				② 166 48		166 48			
Insurance Expense				③ 127 50		127 50			
Licences Expense				④ 170 —		170 —			
Bad Debts Expense				⑤ 234 05		234 05			
Depreciation of Buildings				⑥ 527 46		527 46			
Deprec. Furniture + Equipment				⑦ 270 52		270 52			
Deprec. Automotive Equipment				⑧ 2 293 20		2 293 20			

BALANCE SHEET PRESENTATION

The estimated true value of the fixed
assets is shown on the Balance Sheet
in the following manner:

Fixed Assets			
Land		$8,000.00	
Buildings	$ 7,280.00		
Less Accumulated Depreciation	2,532.86	4,747.14	
Furniture and Equipment	$2,950.00		
Less Accumulated Depreciation	1,867.92	1,082.08	
Automotive Equipment	$15,600.00		
Less Accumulated Depreciation	10,249.20	5,350.80	$19,180.02

Adjusting for Accrued Wages

Certain expenses of a regular nature (such as 'wages' and 'interest') are normally accounted for only on the days that payment is made. From one payment date to the next the liability for such expenses gradually builds up but is not recorded in the books of account. Not until the payment is actually due and paid is the transaction accounted for by means of an accounting entry such as:

Interest Expense	$150.00	
Bank		$150.00

Generally, the date of payment for such expenses as wages and interest does not coincide with the date of the end of the fiscal period. For example, consider the following illustration:

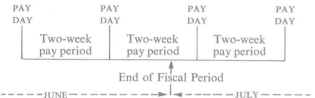

The illustration shows one of the two-week pay periods straddling the date of the end of the fiscal period. Or, expressed in other words, the date of the end of the fiscal period falls between two pay days.

This type of situation poses a problem when preparing financial statements. As at the end of the accounting period, there exists an unrecorded liability–for a portion of two weeks' wages in this case–which must be taken into consideration when accumulating the information for the statements. Items of this nature are known as **Accrued Expenses** or as **Accrued Liabilities**.

The first step is to calculate the accrued liability for unpaid wages as of the end of the fiscal period. This is easiest done by waiting until the completion of the pay period straddling June 30, 19–4, and then computing the portion of the total that pertained to the month of June.

Assuming that the total wages for the two weeks amounted to $262.15 and further assuming that of the ten working days involved six fell in June and four in July, the accrued wages would be computed as follows:

$$\frac{\text{In last pay period, number of working days in June}}{\text{In last pay period total number of working days}} \times \text{Total Wages for the Last Pay Period}$$

$$\text{i.e.} \quad \frac{6}{10} \times \$262.15$$

$$= \$157.29$$

ACCRUED WAGES ADJUSTMENT FOR CASSIDY CARTAGE

Having calculated the accrued wages, it is then necessary to make an adjusting entry on the work sheet. The effect of the adjustment is to increase the wages expense and to set up the accrued liability for wages. The accounting entry debits Wages Expense and credits Accrued Wages Payable.

For Cassidy Cartage the adjusting entry is:

Wages Expense	$157.29	
Accrued Wages Payable		$157.29

On the work sheet, the adjusting entry (coded '9') and the items extended are shown in the illustration below. Observe that, since there was already a Wages Expense account in the trial balance section, it is not necessary to open a new line below for Wages Expense. However, it is necessary to open a new line for Accrued Wages Payable because it is a new item. Accrued Wages Payable is a liability and is therefore extended to the Balance Sheet Credit column.

Accounts	Acc #	Trial Balance Dr.	Trial Balance Cr.	Adjustments Dr.	Adjustments Cr.	P.+L. Statement Dr.	P.+L. Statement Cr.	Balance Sheet Dr.	Balance Sheet Cr.
Cassidy Cartage — Work Sheet — Year Ended June 30, 19-4									
Petty Cash	1	50 —							
Bank	2	725 41							
Accounts Receivable	3	4 027 56							
Allowance for Doubtful Accounts	4		26 40		⑤ 234 05				260 45
Supplies	5	516 52		① 45 21	② 166 48			395 25	
Prepaid Insurance	6	216 —			③ 127 50			88 50	
Prepaid Licences	7	255 —			④ 170 —			85 —	
Land	8	8 000 —							
Buildings (Frame)	9	7 280 —							
Accumulated Depreciation Bldgs.	10		2 005 40		⑥ 527 46				2 532 86
Furniture and Equipment	11	2 950 —							
Accumulated Depreciation F.+E.	12		1 597 40		⑦ 270 52				1 867 92
Automotive Equipment	13	15 600 —							
Accumulated Depreciation Autos.	14		7 956 —		⑧ 2 293 20				10 249 20
Accounts Payable	21		3 047 25		⑩ 402 72				
Sales Tax Payable	22		238 73						
P. Marshall, Capital	31		18 387 21						
P. Marshall, Drawings	32	6 000 —							
Sales	41		28 757 49						
Discounts Earned	42		56 75						
Bank Charges	51	114 92							
Building Maintenance	52	474 37		① 125 —					
Light, Heat and Water	53	472 19		① 22 81					
Miscellaneous Expense	54	115 70		① 20 —					
Telephone Expense	55	151 30		① 15 70					
Truck Expense	56	5 704 16		① 174 —					
Wages	57	9 419 50		⑨ 157 29		9 576 79			
		62 072 63	62 072 63						
Supplies Expense				② 166 48		166 48			
Insurance Expense				③ 127 50		127 50			
Licences Expense				④ 170 —		170 —			
Bad Debts Expense				⑤ 234 05		234 05			
Depreciation of Buildings				⑥ 527 46		527 46			
Deprec. Furniture + Equipment				⑦ 270 52		270 52			
Deprec. Automotive Equipment				⑧ 2 293 20		2 293 20			
Accrued Wages Payable					⑨ 157 29				157 29

Adjusting for Cost of Goods Sold

Because it is a service business, Cassidy Cartage does not require an adjustment for Cost of Goods Sold. However, when preparing a work sheet for a trading business, it is necessary to know how to make this adjustment.

The Cost of Goods Sold adjustment is not easily done by using the 'formal' technique which we have been using. For this particular adjustment, accountants rely on the 'short-cut' technique which handles it very effectively. (It is quite permissible to mix the two methods of making adjustments.)

The short-cut technique for making the adjustment for Cost of Goods Sold is explained fully beginning on page 273, where it is described for the Midway Trading Company.

Completing the Work Sheet

After recording the required adjusting entries, it is necessary to complete the work sheet in the following manner:

1. Extend each line that is not already extended. This means that for each such line the value of the Trial Balance columns and the Adjustments columns must be extended to one of the Profit and Loss columns or to one of the Balance Sheet columns. This must be done carefully and logically. Income and Expense items are to be extended to the Profit and Loss section; other items are to be extended to the Balance Sheet section.

2. Total, rule, and balance the two Adjustments columns.

3. Total, rule, and balance the last four columns of the work sheet. The technique for doing this is described on pages 64 and 65.

The completed work sheet for Cassidy Cartage is shown below.

Cassidy Cartage — Work Sheet — Year Ended June 30, 19-4

Accounts	Acc #	Trial Balance Dr.	Trial Balance Cr.	Adjustments Dr.	Adjustments Cr.	P. & L. Statement Dr.	P. & L. Statement Cr.	Balance Sheet Dr.	Balance Sheet Cr.
Petty Cash	1	50 —						50 —	
Bank	2	725 41						725 41	
Accounts Receivable	3	4 027 56						4 027 56	
Allowance for Doubtful Accounts	4		26 40		⑤ 234 05				260 45
Supplies	5	516 52		① 45 21	② 166 48			395 25	
Prepaid Insurance	6	216 —			③ 127 50			88 50	
Prepaid Licences	7	255 —			④ 170 —			85 —	
Land	8	8 000 —						8 000 —	
Buildings (Frame)	9	7 280 —						7 280 —	
Accumulated Depreciation Bldgs.	10		2 005 40		⑥ 527 46				2 532 86
Furniture and Equipment	11	2 950 —						2 950 —	
Accumulated Depreciation F.+E.	12		1 597 40		⑦ 270 52				1 867 92
Automotive Equipment	13	15 600 —						15 600 —	
Accumulated Depreciation Autos.	14		7 956 —		⑧ 2 293 20				10 249 20
Accounts Payable	21		3 047 25		① 402 72				3 449 97
Sales Tax Payable	22		238 73						238 73
P. Marshall, Capital	31		18 387 21						18 387 21
P. Marshall, Drawings	32	6 000 —						6 000 —	
Sales	41		28 757 49				28 757 49		
Discounts Earned	42		56 75				56 75		
Bank Charges	51	114 92				114 92			
Building Maintenance	52	474 37		① 125 —		599 37			
Light, Heat and Water	53	472 19		① 22 81		495 —			
Miscellaneous Expense	54	115 70		① 20 —		135 70			
Telephone Expense	55	151 30		① 15 70		167 —			
Truck Expense	56	5 704 16		① 174 —		5 878 16			
Wages	57	9 419 50		⑨ 157 29		9 576 79			
		62 072 63	62 072 63						
Supplies Expense				② 166 48		166 48			
Insurance Expense				③ 127 50		127 50			
Licences Expense				④ 170 —		170 —			
Bad Debts Expense				⑤ 234 05		234 05			
Depreciation of Buildings				⑥ 527 46		527 46			
Deprec. Furniture + Equipment				⑦ 270 52		270 52			
Deprec. Automotive Equipment				⑧ 2 293 20		2 293 20			
Accrued Wages Payable					⑨ 157 29				157 29
				4 349 22	4 349 22	20 756 15	28 814 24	45 201 72	37 143 63
Net Profit						8 058 09			8 058 09
						28 814 24	28 814 24	45 201 72	45 201 72

Many experienced accountants utilize two techniques for making the adjusting entries. These two methods are: (a) The formal technique that you have just studied, and (b) A short-cut technique that you are about to study in this section.

Both techniques are employed because not all adjustments can be made using the short-cut technique. In fact, only adjustments that affect one item (e.g., Supplies or Insurance) are suited to the application of this technique.

Let us begin the study of the short cut technique of making adjustments by examining the work sheet for Midway Trading Company after a fiscal period of one year. The trial balance section of this work sheet is shown below:

Midway Trading Company — Work Sheet — Year Ended December 31, 19-4

Accounts	Acc. #	Trial Balance Dr	Trial Balance Cr	Adjustments Dr	Adjustments Cr	P. & L. Statement Dr	P. & L. Statement Cr	Balance Sheet Dr	Balance Sheet Cr
Petty Cash		100 —							
Bank	1	702 12							
Accounts Receivable	6	751 12							
Allowance for Doubtful Accounts			2 50						
Merchandise Inventory	12	074 —							
Supplies		370 —							
Prepaid Insurance		194 —							
Land	15	000 —							
Buildings (Brick)	12	000 —							
Accumulated Deprec. Blgs.			1 711 50						
Furniture + Equipment	3	437 20							
Accum. Deprec. Furn. & Equ.			1 237 40						
Automobiles	7	800 —							
Accum. Deprec. Automobiles			3 978 —						
Accounts Payable			9 461 21						
Bank Loan			9 750 —						
Sales Tax Payable			251 10						
M. Philip, Capital			26 214 87						
M. Philip, Drawings	8	751 —							
Sales			59 168 10						
Sales Returns & Allowances	1	204 30							
Discounts Earned			516 19						
Bank Charges	1	140 26							
Building Maintenance		375 —							
Car Expenses	1	846 50							
Discounts Allowed		749 21							
Duty		315 70							
Freight In.		949 14							
Light, Heat & Water		417 25							
Miscellaneous Expense		116 44							
Purchases	30	616 90							
Purchases Returns & Allow's			1 520 —						
Telephone Expense		484 17							
Wages	7	416 56							
		113 810 87	113 810 87						

Adjusting for Accounts Payable

Any adjustment involving more than one item is best carried out by the formal method described previously. Because the Accounts Payable adjustment usually involves several accounts, it is performed by means of the formal method.

Assume that the Purchase Invoices requiring an adjustment are as summarized at the top of page 269 in the form of an accounting entry.

Car Expenses $147.50
Freight In   42.10
Miscellaneous Expense 12.51
Purchases   1,047.24
  Accounts Payable $1,249.35

This accounting entry is recorded in the Adjustments column of the work sheet in the formal manner as shown below:

Midway Trading Company   Work Sheet   Year Ended December 31, 19-4

Accounts	Acc #	Trial Balance Dr.	Trial Balance Cr.	Adjustments Dr.	Adjustments Cr.	P.&L. Statement Dr.	P.&L. Statement Cr.	Balance Sheet Dr.	Balance Sheet Cr.
Petty Cash		100 —							
Bank		1 702 12							
Accounts Receivable		6 751 12							
Allowance for Doubtful Accounts			2 50						
Merchandise Inventory		12 074 —							
Supplies		370 —							
Prepaid Insurance		194 —							
Land		15 000 —							
Buildings (Brick)		12 000 —							
Accum. Deprec. Bldgs.			1 711 50						
Furniture & Equipment		3 437 20							
Accum. Deprec. Furn. & Equ.			1 237 40						
Automobiles		7 800 —							
Accum. Deprec. Automobiles			3 978 —						
Accounts Payable			9 461 21		① 1 249 35				
Bank Loan			9 750 —						
Sales Tax Payable			251 10						
M. Philip, Capital			26 214 87						
M. Philip, Drawings		8 751 —							
Sales			59 168 10						
Sales Returns + Allowances		1 204 30							
Discounts Earned			516 19						
Bank Charges		1 140 26							
Building Maintenance		375 —							
Car Expenses		1 846 50		① 147 50					
Discounts Allowed		749 21							
Duty		315 70							
Freight In		949 14		① 42 10					
Light, Heat & Water		417 25							
Miscellaneous Expense		116 44		① 12 51					
Purchases		30 616 90		① 1 047 24					
Purchases Returns + Allow's			1 520 —						
Telephone Expense		484 17							
Wages		7 416 56							
		113 810 87	113 810 87						

Adjusting for Supplies

Any single item requiring an adjustment, Supplies for example, can be adjusted by a short-cut technique. However, before the adjustment is made it is still necessary to take an inventory of supplies in the manner described on page 255. Having done this, the Supplies adjustment by the short-cut method is performed as follows:

Step 1. On the Supplies line of the work sheet, write in the up-to-date Supplies figure (assume $192) from the Supplies Inventory Listing. Because Supplies is an asset, this figure is recorded in the Balance Sheet Debit column as shown below.

ACCOUNT	TRIAL BALANCE DR.	TRIAL BALANCE CR.	ADJUSTMENTS DR.	ADJUSTMENTS CR.	P. & L. STATEMENT DR.	P. & L. STATEMENT CR.	BALANCE SHEET DR.	BALANCE SHEET CR.
Supplies	370 —						192 —	

Step 2. On the same line of the work sheet but in the Profit and Loss section, record the Supplies Expense figure. This is found by subtracting the Balance Sheet figure of $192 from the Trial Balance figure of $370. Because it represents an expense, the resultant figure of $178 is recorded in the Profit and Loss Debit column as shown at right.

When preparing financial statements from the work sheet, keep in mind that the $178 in the Profit and Loss section represents Supplies Expense even though it is on a line that reads Supplies.

ACCOUNT	TRIAL BALANCE		ADJUSTMENTS		P. & L. STATEMENT		BALANCE SHEET	
	DR.	CR.	DR.	CR.	DR.	CR.	DR.	CR.
Supplies	370 –				178 –		192 –	

CHECKING MECHANICAL ACCURACY

Many adjustments may be done by means of the short-cut technique. To assist you to perform these adjustments accurately, keep in mind the rule shown at right.

For each line of the work sheet:

The value of the first four columns · · must equal · · The value of the last four columns

Trial Balance		Adjustments		Profit + Loss Statement		Balance Sheet	
Dr.	Cr.	Dr.	Cr.	Dr.	Cr.	Dr.	Cr.

Adjusting for Prepaid Insurance

The Prepaid Insurance adjustment may be performed by using the short-cut technique. However, before making the adjustment, it is necessary to calculate the value of the Prepaid Insurance in the manner described on page 257. Once the Prepaid Insurance figure is obtained, the adjustment by the short-cut method is performed as follows:

Step 1. On the Prepaid Insurance line of the work sheet, write in the unexpired insurance figure from the insurance schedule (assume $112). Because Prepaid Insurance is an asset, this figure is recorded in the Balance Sheet Debit column as shown at right.

ACCOUNT	TRIAL BALANCE		ADJUSTMENTS		P. & L. STATEMENT		BALANCE SHEET	
	DR.	CR.	DR.	CR.	DR.	CR.	DR.	CR.
Prepaid Insce.	194 –						112 –	

Step 2. On the same line of the work sheet but in the Profit and Loss section, record the Insurance Expense figure. This is found by subtracting the Balance Sheet figure of $112 from the Trial Balance figure of $194. Because it represents an expense, the resultant figure of $82 is recorded in the Profit and Loss Debit column as shown at right.

ACCOUNT	TRIAL BALANCE		ADJUSTMENTS		P. & L. STATEMENT		BALANCE SHEET	
	DR.	CR.	DR.	CR.	DR.	CR.	DR.	CR.
Prepaid Insce.	194 –				82 –		112 –	

When preparing financial statements from the work sheet, keep in mind that the $82 in the Profit and Loss section represents Insurance Expense even though it is on a line that reads Prepaid Insurance.

Also, with every one-line adjustment, be sure that it balances in accordance with the rule established on page 270.

Adjusting for Prepaid Licences

For Midway Trading Company no adjustment for Prepaid Licences is required. The reason for this is that the end of the fiscal year, December 31, corresponds to the end of the licence year at which time the value of the licences is zero. If, however, an adjustment had been necessary it could have been done using the short-cut method.

Adjusting for Doubtful Accounts

The adjustment for doubtful accounts may be performed by using the short-cut method. Naturally, before making the adjustment, it is necessary to estimate the total of the doubtful accounts in the manner described on page 259. Once this figure is established, the adjustment by the short-cut method is performed as follows:

Step 1. On the Allowance for Doubtful Accounts line of the work sheet, record the total of the doubtful accounts from the Aging Schedule (assume $143.20). Because the Allowance for Doubtful Accounts is a minus asset, this figure is recorded in the Balance Sheet Credit column as shown below.

ACCOUNT	TRIAL BALANCE		ADJUSTMENTS		P. & L. STATEMENT		BALANCE SHEET	
	DR.	CR.	DR.	CR.	DR.	CR.	DR.	CR.
Allow. Doubt. Acc.		2 50						143 20

Step 2. On the same line of the work sheet but in the Profit and Loss

section, record the Bad Debts Expense figure. This figure is calculated somewhat differently than the previous one-line adjustments. The best approach is to *balance* the 'Allowances' line through the Profit and Loss Debit column. Only one figure will do it–in this case $140.70. You must be specially careful when balancing this line because the trial balance figure can sometimes be a debit figure. The balanced line for Midway Trading Company appears below.

ACCOUNT	TRIAL BALANCE		ADJUSTMENTS		P. & L. STATEMENT		BALANCE SHEET	
	DR.	CR.	DR.	CR.	DR.	CR.	DR.	CR.
Allow. Doubt. Acc.		2 50			140 70			143 20

Keep in mind that when preparing the financial statements the $140.70 figure in the Profit and Loss Debit column represents Bad Debts Expense even though it is on a line that reads Allowance for Doubtful Accounts.

Adjusting for Depreciation

Each of the depreciation adjustments can be performed by the short-cut technique. Before making the adjustments, however, it is necessary to calculate the depreciation figures in the manner described on page 262. For Midway Trading Company these calculations are as follows:

CALCULATING THE NET BOOK VALUES

	ASSET VALUE		ACCUMULATED DEPRECIATION VALUE		NET BOOK VALUE
Building	$12,000.00	minus	$1,711.50	equals	$10,288.50
Furniture & Equipment	$ 3,437.20	minus	$1,237.40	equals	$ 2,199.80
Automobiles	$ 7,800.00	minus	$3,978.00	equals	$ 3,822.00

CALCULATING THE ANNUAL DEPRECIATION FIGURES

	NET BOOK VALUE		RATE OF DEPRECIATION		DEPRECIATION FOR YEAR
Building	$10,288.50	times	5 per cent	equals	$ 514.43
Furniture & Equipment	$ 2,199.80	times	20 per cent	equals	$ 439.96
Automobiles	$ 3,822.00	times	30 per cent	equals	$ 1,146.60

Once the Depreciation Expense figures are calculated, the adjustments by the short-cut method are as follows:

Step 1. On each of the Accumulated Depreciation lines of the work sheet, write in the appropriate Depreciation Expense figure from the calculation schedule. Because they are *expense* figures, they are recorded in the Profit and Loss Debit column as shown at right.

ACCOUNT	TRIAL BALANCE DR.	TRIAL BALANCE CR.	ADJUSTMENTS DR.	ADJUSTMENTS CR.	P. & L. STATEMENT DR.	P. & L. STATEMENT CR.	BALANCE SHEET DR.	BALANCE SHEET CR.
Acc. Dep. Bldgs.		1711 50			514 43			
Acc. Dep. F+d.		1237 40			439 96			
Acc. Dep. Autos		3978 –			1146 60			

Step 2. On the same lines of the work sheet but in the Balance Sheet section, record the new Accumulated Depreciation figures. These figures are obtained by adding the expense figures respectively to each of the trial balance figures. They are recorded in the Balance Sheet Credit column because they represent minus assets. The completed lines are shown at right.

Again, keep in mind that the three figures in the Profit and Loss Debit column represent Depreciation Expense even though they are on lines that read Allowance for Depreciation.

ACCOUNT	TRIAL BALANCE DR.	TRIAL BALANCE CR.	ADJUSTMENTS DR.	ADJUSTMENTS CR.	P. & L. STATEMENT DR.	P. & L. STATEMENT CR.	BALANCE SHEET DR.	BALANCE SHEET CR.
Acc. Dep. Bldgs.		1711 50			514 43			2225 93
Acc. Dep. F+d.		1237 40			439 96			1677 36
Acc. Dep. Autos		3978 –			1146 60			5124 60

Adjusting for Accrued Wages

The Accrued Wages adjustment is one that may be performed by means of the short-cut method. After calculating the accrued wages figure, the adjustment is performed as follows:

Step 1. On the Wages (Expense) line of the work sheet, enter the accrued wages figure (assume $146.54). Because Accrued Wages represents a liability, this figure is entered in the Balance Sheet Credit column as shown at right.

Step 2. On the same line of the work sheet but in the Profit and Loss section, record the adjusted figure for Wages Expense. It is merely necessary to add the trial balance figure to the accrued wages figure and record it in the Profit and Loss Debit column. Or, looking at it in another way, just balance

ACCOUNT	TRIAL BALANCE DR.	TRIAL BALANCE CR.	ADJUSTMENTS DR.	ADJUSTMENTS CR.	P. & L. STATEMENT DR.	P. & L. STATEMENT CR.	BALANCE SHEET DR.	BALANCE SHEET CR.
Wages	7416 56							146 54

the line through the Profit and Loss Debit column; follow the rule on page 270. The completed line showing an expense figure of $7,563.10 is shown below.

In this particular situation, you must keep in mind that the $146.54 in the Balance Sheet Credit column represents a liability even though it is on a line that reads Wages or Wages Expense.

ACCOUNT	TRIAL BALANCE		ADJUSTMENTS		P. & L. STATEMENT		BALANCE SHEET	
	DR.	CR.	DR.	CR.	DR.	CR.	DR.	CR.
Wages	7416 56				7563 10			146 54

Adjusting for Cost of Goods Sold (Periodic Inventory Method)

Trading businesses, which buy and sell merchandise, require an adjustment to determine the cost of the goods that have been sold. This figure is an important one when preparing the Profit and Loss Statement. Service businesses, on the other hand, do not buy and sell merchandise and therefore do not require a Cost of Goods Sold adjustment. Cassidy Cartage, the business used as an example in the early part of this chapter, was a service business and as such did not require a Cost of Goods Sold adjustment. But Midway Trading Company, the business being used currently as an example, is a trading business and does require a Cost of Goods Sold adjustment.

IMPORTANCE OF COST OF GOODS

The biggest expenditure of a trading business is the cost of the merchandise. For every sale that it makes, the merchant must buy and pay for the goods. An item that he sells for $100 may cost in the neighbourhood of $75* making it apparent that the cost of the goods is a very significant expenditure.

Since Chapter 8, you have been making the standard accounting entries to record the sale of merchandise. You have debited Cash or Accounts Receivable and have

* If the cost price of an item is $75 and the selling price is $100, there will be a gross profit or markup of $25. Also, the rate of markup is 25/75 × 100 (Profit/Cost Price × 100) which is 33-1/3 per cent.

credited Sales and Sales Tax Payable on the basis of the selling price of the goods. The merchant and his staff find it no problem in coping with this accounting entry. Since the selling prices of the various goods are prominently displayed on the merchandise itself or in a convenient catalogue, it is an easy matter for the clerk to record the selling price and the sales tax by means of a cash register or a sales slip. For an item costing $75 and being sold for $100 the effect is:

Cash (or Accounts Receivable)	105.00	
Sales		100.00
Sales Tax Payable		5.00

BASIC CALCULATION FOR COST OF GOODS SOLD

But this accounting entry alone is insufficient. It implies that a profit of $100 is made on the sale because it does nothing to record the cost of the goods that were sold. This is not correct; the real profit is obviously only $25.

However, for a number of reasons it is not feasible to account for the Cost of Goods Sold during the accounting period. It is much more convenient to tidy this matter up at the end of the accounting period. It is not a complex matter at the end of an accounting period to calculate the Cost of Goods Sold.

First, the value of the merchandise on hand at the beginning of the accounting period is known to us. This is the balance of the Merchan-

dise Inventory account as listed in the Trial Balance columns of the work sheet.

Second, the value of the merchandise purchased during the accounting period is known to us. This is the value of the Purchases account as indicated by the first four columns of the work sheet. Or, for businesses that have a Returns and Allowances account, it is the Purchase account value less the Purchases Returns and Allowances figure.

The merchandise on hand at the beginning of the period plus the net merchandise purchased during the period gives the total merchandise that was available for sale. Consider the following summary for Midway Trading Company.

Merchandise Inventory at beginning of period		$12,074.00
Purchases of Merchandise during the period	$31,664.14	
Less Purchases Returns and Allowances	1,520.00	30,144.14
Total Merchandise available for sale during the period		$42,218.14

The $42,218.14 figure thus arrived at represents the total of merchandise that was available for sale during the period. But much of this merchandise will have been sold during the period. And, if it was not sold, then it will still be on hand. This statement provides us with the clue to the means of calculating the Cost of Goods Sold. If we take an inventory of goods at the end of the period, and then subtract this closing inventory from the $42,218.14, we will have determined the cost of the goods that were sold during the period.

If the closing inventory of Midway Trading Company happens to be $13,562, the complete basic calculation of the Cost of Goods Sold is as shown at right.

Merchandise Inventory at beginning of period		$12,074.00
Purchases of Merchandise during the period	$31,664.14	
Less Purchases Returns and Allowances	1,520.00	30,144.14
Total Merchandise available for sale during the period		$42,218.14
Deduct: Merchandise Inventory at end of period		13,562.00
Cost of Goods Sold during the period		$28,656.14

Cost of Goods Sold Adjustment

Before the Cost of Goods Sold adjustment can be made, it is necessary to take an inventory of the merchandise in stock on the last day of the fiscal period. This is usually a job that requires considerable time and effort and a great deal of systematic organization. In most cases it is necessary to close down the store or plant until the operation is completed. To take the inventory, it is necessary to count and list every item in stock; to multiply the quantity on hand of each item by its cost price; and finally to total the whole listing.

Once the inventory figure is available, the Cost of Goods Sold adjustment may be made using the short-cut method as follows.

Step 1. On the Merchandise Inventory line, write the opening inventory figure (pick up from the Trial Balance Debit column) in the Profit and Loss Debit column as shown at right.

Step 2. On the same line of the work sheet, record the closing inventory figure (in this case $13,562) in two places:

(a) Profit and Loss **Credit** column;

ACCOUNT	TRIAL BALANCE		ADJUSTMENTS		P. & L. STATEMENT		BALANCE SHEET	
	DR.	CR.	DR.	CR.	DR.	CR.	DR.	CR.
Mdse. Inventory	12074 —				12074 —			

(b) Balance Sheet **Debit** column; as shown at right.

Observe that the Merchandise Inventory line is in balance at this point.

Step 3. Extend the Purchases line and the Purchases Returns and Allowances line to the Profit and Loss section of the work sheet as shown at right.

At this point, the Cost of Goods Sold adjustment is completed. Let us examine it closely to see what it has accomplished.

1. In the Balance Sheet columns, it has provided the correct closing inventory figure for inclusion on the Balance Sheet.
2. In the Profit and Loss columns, it has provided the basic ingredients for the Cost of Goods Sold calculation of a trading business. It should be apparent to you that these figures correspond to those summarized on page 274. You

ACCOUNT	TRIAL BALANCE		ADJUSTMENTS		P. & L. STATEMENT		BALANCE SHEET	
	DR.	CR.	DR.	CR.	DR.	CR.	DR.	CR.
Mdse. Inventory	12074 –				12074 –	13562 –	13562 –	

ACCOUNT	TRIAL BALANCE		ADJUSTMENTS		P. & L. STATEMENT		BALANCE SHEET	
	DR.	CR.	DR.	CR.	DR.	CR.	DR.	CR.
Mdse. Inventory	12074 –				12074 –	13562 –	13562 –	
Purchases	30616 90		ⓓ 1047 24		31664 14			
Purch. Rets + Alls		1520 –				1520 –		

will see how they are included in the Profit and Loss Statement in Chapter 15.

It is an interesting point that almost without exception the Cost of Goods Sold adjustment is done by the short-cut method. Some accountants will use the formal method for making all other adjustments but when it comes time to adjust for the Cost of Goods Sold, they invariably rely on the short-cut technique.

Completing the Work Sheet for Midway Trading Company

The remaining items on the work sheet are extended and the work sheet completed in the manner already described on page 267.

The completed work sheet for Midway Trading Company is as shown below.

Midway Trading Company	Acc #	Trial Balance Dr.	Cr.	Adjustments Dr.	Cr.	P. & L. Statement Dr.	Cr.	Balance Sheet Dr.	Cr.
Accounts									
Petty Cash		100 –						100 –	
Bank		1 702 12						1 702 12	
Accounts Receivable		6 751 12						6 751 12	
Allowance for Doubtful Accounts			2 50			140 70			143 20
Merchandise Inventory		12 074 –				12 074 –	13 562 –	13 562 –	
Supplies		370 –				178 –		192 –	
Prepaid Insurance		194 –				82 –		112 –	
Land		15 000 –						15 000 –	
Buildings (Brick)		12 000 –						12 000 –	
Accum. Deprec. Bldgs.			1 711 50			514 43			2 225 93
Furniture + Equipment		3 437 20						3 437 20	
Accum. Deprec. Furn. + Equ.			1 237 40			439 96			1 677 36
Automobiles		7 800 –						7 800 –	
Accum. Deprec. Automobiles			3 978 –			1 146 60			5 124 60
Accounts Payable			9 461 21		ⓓ 1 249 35				10 710 56
Bank Loan			9 750 –						9 750 –
Sales Tax Payable			251 10						251 10
M. Philip, Capital			26 214 87						26 214 87
M. Philip, Drawings		8 751 –						8 751 –	
Sales			59 168 10				59 168 10		
Sales Returns + Allowances		1 204 30				1 204 30			
Discounts Earned			516 19				516 19		
Bank Charges		1 140 26				1 140 26			
Building Maintenance		375 –				375 –			
Car Expenses		1 846 50		ⓓ 147 50		1 994 –			
Discounts Allowed		749 21				749 21			
Duty		315 70				315 70			
Freight In		949 14		ⓓ 42 10		991 24			
Light, Heat + Water		417 25				417 25			
Miscellaneous Expense		116 44		ⓓ 12 51		128 95			
Purchases		30 616 90		ⓓ 1 047 24		31 664 14			
Purchases Returns + Allow's			1 520 –				1 520 –		
Telephone Expense		484 17				484 17			
Wages		7 416 56				7 563 10			146 54
		113 810 87	113 810 87	1 249 35	1 249 35	61 603 01	74 766 29	69 407 44	56 244 16
Net Profit						13 163 28			13 163 28
						74 766 29	74 766 29	69 407 44	69 407 44

At the time financial statements are prepared it is necessary to make numerous inventories, schedules, calculations, etc. pertaining to the work sheet adjustments and other matters (e.g., bank reconciliation). It is customary to collect all papers and calculations related to the preparation of the financial statements in one file. These papers are known as the Accountant's Working Papers.

Bookkeeping and Accounting Terms

Adjusting Entry: "An entry made before closing the books for the period, to apportion amounts of revenue or expense to accounting periods or to operating divisions, e.g. apportionment of . . . wages between accounting periods when the current period ends between two pay days. . ."*

Taking Inventory: The process of counting, itemizing, and valuing the goods or stock of a business. "The word [inventory] is usually restricted to designate items of tangible personal property which are held for sale in the ordinary course of business, or are in the process of production for such sale, or are to be currently consumed in the production of goods or services to be available for sale."*

Prepaid Expense: "A short term expense prepayment; an expenditure, other than a capital expenditure, which is expected to yield its benefits in the near future and meanwhile is carried forward to be assigned to expense in the near future."*

Doubtful Account:
Doubtful Debt: "An account or note receivable, the ultimate collectibility of which is uncertain."*

Bad Debt: "An account or note receivable that is uncollectible."*

Write-Off: "To transfer to profit and loss . . . all or a portion of the balance in an account previously regarded as an asset or liability."*

Aging: "A process of analysis of receivables by classifying the amounts according to the length of time for which they have been outstanding or for which they have been due. . ."*

---

* Canadian Institute of Chartered Accountants, Committee on Accounting and Auditing Research, *Terminology for Accountants* (Toronto: Canadian Institute of Chartered Accountants, 1962).

Depreciation:	"The gradual exhaustion of the service capacity of fixed assets which is not restored by maintenance practices. It is the consequence of such factors as use, obsolescence, inadequacy, and decay. ."*
Depreciation Accounting:	"An accounting procedure in which the cost or other recorded value of a fixed asset less estimated salvage (if any) is distributed over its estimated useful life in a systematic and rational manner. It is a process of allocation, not valuation."*
Capital Cost Allowance:	"An amount allowed, under *The Income Tax Act (Canada) and Regulations*, with respect to certain assets, in computing a taxpayer's income from a business or property for a taxation year. It may differ from the amount charged for the period in depreciation accounting."*
Book Value:	"The amount at which an item appears in the books of account and financial statements."*
Accrued Expense:	"An expense which has been incurred in an accounting period but for which no enforceable claim will be made in that accounting period by the person who rendered the service. It arises from the purchase of services . . . which have been only partly performed at the time of accounting and hence are not yet billed or paid for."*
Accrued Liability:	"A developing but not yet enforceable claim by another person, which is accumulating with the passage of time or the receipt of the service. It arises from the purchase of services . . . which have been only partly performed at the time of accounting and hence are not yet billed or paid for."*
Cost of Goods Sold:	A classification for financial statement purposes of all costs directly related to the acquisition of the merchandise inventory that was sold during the accounting period.

* Ibid

Review Questions

1. Name the two different techniques for making adjusting entries.
2. Explain why an adjustment is necessary for Accounts Payable.
3. Where is an adjusting entry first recorded?
4. Why are adjusting entries coded?
5. Why is an adjusting entry necessary for Supplies?
6. How does one 'take inventory'?
7. What does it mean to 'extend the work sheet'?
8. What is Prepaid Insurance? Prepaid Licences?
9. What is the first step in making the adjustment for Prepaid Insurance? for Prepaid Licences?
10. Why is an adjustment necessary for doubtful accounts
11. How is the estimated true value of doubtful accounts shown in the books of account?
12. Explain the purpose of the Accounts Receivable Aging Schedule.
13. When is a customer's account written off?
14. In your own words, explain the meaning of depreciation.
15. What is meant by the Net Book Value of a fixed asset?
16. Briefly explain the income tax method of calculating depreciation.
17. Why is an adjustment necessary for accrued wages?
18. Which method (formal or short-cut) is used for making the Accounts Payable adjustment?
19. Which method is used for making the Cost of Goods Sold adjustment?
20. What is the rule for balancing a line of the work sheet?
21. Using the short-cut method, what line of the work sheet is used to make the adjustment for Depreciation of Buildings? for Insurance Expense?
22. Explain the importance of Cost of Goods Sold.
23. How is the closing inventory figure ascertained?

Exercises

1. Calculate the depreciation expense in each of the following cases:

Type of Asset	Asset Account Balance	Accumulated Depreciation Account Balance	Annual Rate of Depreciation	Accounting Period
Building (Brick)	$ 9,572.50	$3,514.21	5%	Jan. 1 to Dec. 31
Building (Frame)	1,263.00	946.50	10%	Jan. 1 to Dec. 31
General Equipment	5,072.13	3,516.20	20%	Jan. 1 to Dec. 31
Automotive Equipment	9,475.43	7,419.21	30%	Jan. 1 to Dec. 31
Building (Frame)	7,500.00	2,946.34	10%	Apr. 1 to Sep. 30
Automobiles	3,500.00	1,050.00	30%	Oct. 1 to Dec. 31
Trucks	15,073.54	8,455.52	30%	Jan. 1 to Mar. 31
Building (Brick)	25,900.00	3,542.10	5%	Jan. 1 to Jun. 30
Furniture	4,406.75	2,120.57	20%	July 1 to Dec. 31

2. A businessman's fiscal year-end is September 30. One of his business expenditures is for truck licences. If he spends $240 on truck licences for the calendar year, calculate the value of Prepaid Licences at the end of his fiscal year.

3. The details of a business' insurance policies are as follows:

Company	Policy Date	Term	Premium
Atlantic	March 15, 19–3	3 years	$ 72.00
Pacific	June 30, 19–4	2 years	120.00
Indian	June 1, 19–4	1 year	84.00
Arctic	September 15, 19–3	3 years	156.00

Calculate the value of Prepaid Insurance as of December 31, 19–4.

---

4. From the following information calculate the accrued wages as of March 31, 19–8, the end of a fiscal period.

(a) Total wages for the two-week period ended Friday April 4, 19–8 are $755.40. The company works a five-day week and the employees are paid every other Friday.

(b) Total wages for the two-week period ended Friday April 10, 19–8 are $804.25. The company works a five-day week and the employees are paid every other Friday.

---

5. A supplies inventory count sheet is shown below.

INVENTORY ITEM	QUANTITY
Rubber Bands	3 boxes
Envelopes #8	10 boxes
Envelopes #10	4½ boxes
Envelopes, Manilla, 8½ x 11	2 boxes
Typewriting Paper, blank	4M sheets
Letterhead Paper	10M sheets
Copy Paper	4M sheets
Carbon Paper, 8½ x 11	2 boxes
Paper Clips	12 boxes
Staples	15 boxes
Pencils, regular	4 doz.
Pencils, red	2 doz.

From the preceding count sheet and the cost price list below, prepare a Supplies Inventory sheet showing the individual items, the quantities, the cost prices, the extensions, and the final total.

Cost Prices

Rubber Bands	.59	per box
Envelopes, #8	$4.90	per box
Envelopes, #10	$5.50	per box
Manilla Envelopes, 8½ × 11	$10.40	per box
Typewriting paper	$6.70	per M
Letterhead	$8.50	per M
Copy paper	$2.50	per M
Carbon Paper	$1.75	per box
Paper clips	.20	per box
Staples	.85	per box
Pencils, regular	$1.10	per doz.
Pencils, red	$1.40	per doz.

Note:

The solutions for the remaining exercises are to be kept for use again in chapter 15.

6. From the following trial balance and additional information, prepare the work sheet for J. P. Gorman, Consultant, for the annual fiscal period ended June 30, 19–0.

J. P. Gorman, Consultant
Trial Balance
June 30, 19–0

Petty Cash	$ 25.00	
Bank	1,047.50	
Accounts Receivable	7,421.00	
Allowance for Doubtful Accounts		$ 7.25
Supplies	300.00	
Prepaid Insurance	280.00	
Furniture and Equipment	2,596.00	
Accumulated Depreciation Furn. & Equip.		1,266.85
Automobile	4,800.00	
Accumulated Depreciation Automobile		1,440.00
Accounts Payable		521.92
Sales Tax Payable		159.10
J. P. Gorman, Capital		4,759.60
J. P. Gorman, Drawings	7,500.00	
Sales		18,072.50
Bank Charges	32.10	
Car Expenses	147.52	
Miscellaneous Expense	61.50	
Rent	600.00	
Telephone	112.00	
Wages	1,304.60	
	$26,227.22	$26,227.22

(a) Purchase Invoices received in July, 19–0 but which pertained to goods received in June, 19–0 were summarized as follows:

Supplies	$35.00
Car Expense	72.50
Misc. Expense	7.40

(b) The Accounts Receivable Aging Analysis showed the doubtful accounts at June 30, 19–0 to be $94.65.

(c) The Supplies inventory taken at June 30, 19–0 amounted to $80.

(d) The Prepaid Insurance schedule as of June 30, 19–0 showed a total of $200 for unexpired insurance.

(e) Depreciation of fixed assets is at government rates.

(f) The accrued wages figure at June 30, 19–0 amounted to $75.

---

7. From the following trial balance and additional information, prepare the work sheet for Dennisson Delivery Service for the half-yearly fiscal period ended June 30, 19–5.

Dennisson Delivery Service
Trial Balance
June 30, 19–5

Petty Cash	$ 100.00	
Bank	570.00	
Accounts Receivable	2,419.51	
Allowance for Doubtful Accounts	10.00	
Supplies	174.00	
Prepaid Insurance	400.00	
Prepaid Licences	1,146.00	
Land	7,000.00	
Buildings (Frame)	21,570.00	
Accumulated Depreciation Buildings		$ 7,046.90
Furniture and Equipment	8,970.00	
Accum. Deprec. Furn. and Equip.		2,946.72
Trucks	18,472.00	
Accumulated Depreciation Trucks		10,407.51
Accounts Payable		3,417.40
Sales Tax Payable		350.00
Joseph Budd, Capital		29,797.06
Joseph Budd, Drawings	8,900.00	
Sales		40,721.19
Bank Charges	115.25	
Miscellaneous Expense	219.51	
Telephone	316.25	
Truck Expenses	6,901.32	
Wages	17,402.94	
	$94,686.78	$94,686.78

ADDITIONAL INFORMATION

(a) Purchase Invoices received in July, 19–5 but which pertained to June, 19–5 were summarized as follows:

Supplies	$ 42.00
Misc. Expense	33.00
Truck Expenses	213.54

(b) The Accounts Receivable Aging Analysis showed the doubtful accounts at June 30, 19–5 to be $77.12.

(c) The Supplies inventory taken at June 30, 19–5 amounted to $125.

(d) The Prepaid Licences schedule showed that the value of unexpired licences at June 30, 19–5 amounted to $412.

(e) The Prepaid Insurance schedule as at June 30, 19–5 showed a total of $215 for unexpired insurance.

(f) Depreciation of fixed assets is at government rates. (Remember that this work sheet is for a fiscal period of one half year.)

(g) The accrued wages figure as at June 30, 19–5 amounted to $316.

---

8. From the following trial balance and additional information, prepare the work sheet of Select Trading Company for the year ended December 31, 19–6.

Select Trading Company
Trial Balance
December 31, 19–6

Petty Cash	$ 25.00	
Bank	5,021.90	
Accounts Receivable	13,295.05	
Allowance for Doubtful Debts		$ 20.10
Merchandise Inventory	10,957.00	
Supplies	100.00	
Prepaid Insurance	180.00	
Furniture and Equipment	5,721.25	
Accumulated Depreciation Furn. & Equip.		1,941.72
Accounts Payable		11,517.20
Sales Tax Payable		245.00
O. Franklin, Capital		14,732.62
O. Franklin, Drawings	12,515.00	
Sales		56,626.27
Building Maintenance	150.00	
Delivery Expense	1,057.15	
Light, Heat and Water	315.19	
Miscellaneous Expense	170.00	
Purchases	30,704.16	
Rent	1,200.00	
Telephone	195.00	
Wages	3,476.21	
	$85,082.91	$85,082.91

282

(a) The Accounts Receivable Aging Analysis showed the doubtful debts at December 31, 19–6 to be $190.42.

(b) Inventories taken at December 31, 19–6 were:
Merchandise $9,567.34
Supplies $22.50

(c) The Prepaid Insurance schedule showed that at December 31, 19–6 the value of the Prepaid Insurance was $136.40.

(d) Depreciation of fixed assets is at government rates.

(e) Purchase Invoices received in 19–7 for goods and ser-

vices pertaining to 19–6 were summarized as follows:
Merchandise $756.30
Building Mntce. $21.00
Miscellaneous Ex. 15.00

(f) The accrued wages at December 31, 19–6 were calculated to be $112.

---

9. From the following trial balance and additional information, prepare the work sheet, of Stirling Sales Company for the year ended June 30, 19–2.

Stirling Sales Company
Trial Balance
June 30, 19–2

Petty Cash	$ 50.00	
Bank	1,292.64	
Accounts Receivable	33,412.94	
Allowance for Doubtful Accounts	5.05	
Merchandise Inventory	35,963.15	
Supplies	506.19	
Prepaid Insurance	396.00	
Land	5,000.00	
Buildings (Frame)	20,000.00	
Accumulated Depreciation Buildings		$ 6,878.00
Furniture and Equipment	4,740.26	
Accumulated Depreciation Furn. & Equip.		2,313.04
Bank Loan		25,000.00
Accounts Payable		17,502.12
Sales Tax Payable		607.50
O. J. Little, Capital		30,333.01
O. J. Little, Drawings	14,904.15	
Sales		151,510.51
Sales Returns and Allowances	1,926.50	
Advertising	1,465.17	
Bank Charges	1,474.10	
Building Maintenance	572.12	
Delivery Expense	3,416.90	
Cash Short and Over	26.70	
Discounts Allowed	2,674.15	
Discounts Earned		742.15
Freight-in	1,946.20	
Light, Heat and Water	375.46	
Miscellaneous Expense	74.12	
Postage	92.04	
Purchases	90,406.56	
Purchases Returns and Allowances		2,472.19
Telephone	675.00	
Wages	15,963.12	
	$237,358.52	$237,358.52

(a) The Accounts Receivable Aging Analysis showed the doubtful debts at June 30, 19–2 to be $402.24.

(b) Inventories at June 30, 19–2 were:
Merchandise $33,592.00
Supplies $155.00

(c) The Prepaid Insurance schedule showed that at June 30, 19–2 the value of Prepaid Insurance was $246.

(d) Depreciation of fixed assets is at government rates.

(e) Purchase Invoices received in July, 19–2, with respect to goods and services received on or before June 30, 19–2 were summarized as follows:

Supplies	$65.20
Merchandise	1,045.57
Building Maintenance	50.00
Delivery Expense	104.32
Miscellaneous Expense	24.05

(f) The accrued wages at June 30, 19–2 were $316.40.

---

10. From the General Ledger Trial Balance of Monarch Marine (after a fiscal period of six months) and the additional information necessary for the adjustments, prepare a work sheet.

Monarch Marine
Trial Balance
September 30, 19–7

Petty Cash	$ 50.00	
Bank	1,046.57	
Accounts Receivable	10,409.50	
Allowance for Doubtful Accounts		$ 26.17
Merchandise Inventory	39,416.50	
Supplies	497.17	
Prepaid Insurance	395.33	
Land	4,000.00	
Buildings (Brick)	7,000.00	
Accumulated Depreciation Buildings		998.37
Equipment	3,469.75	
Accumulated Depreciation Equipment		1,693.24
Delivery Truck	4,200.00	
Accumulated Depreciation Delivery Truck		2,759.40
Accounts Payable		15,609.75
Sales Tax Payable		625.00
Mortgage Payable		3,609.00
B. West, Capital		27,811.73
B. West, Drawings	7,200.00	
Sales Income		75,064.20
Bank Charges	62.50	
Building Repairs	152.87	
Delivery Expense	459.61	
Discounts Earned		315.12
Freight-in	796.14	
Light, Heat and Water	146.19	
Miscellaneous Expense	94.17	
Purchases	42,906.70	
Purchases Returns andAllowances		1,056.92
Telephone	215.90	
Wages	7,050.00	
	$129,568.90	$129,568.90

ADDITIONAL INFORMATION

(a) Purchase Invoices received
subsequent to the year-
end but pertaining to the
fiscal period just ended
were as follows:

Supplier	Explanation	Amount
Jack's Hardware	Paint and materials for repairing buildings	$19.25
King Oil Company	Gasoline and oil for delivery truck	$65.20
Dominion Boats	Boat for resale	$565.00
Best Marine Supply	Merchandise for resale	$175.00
Dandy Cable	Merchandise for resale	$230.45

(b) Depreciation is calculated at government rates (half-yearly fiscal period).

(c) The Accounts Receivable Aging Analysis showed a total for doubtful accounts of $376.45.

(d) Inventories taken at September 30, 19–7 were as follows:

Merchandise $41,759.40
Supplies $255.00

(e) The following insurance policies were in force.

Company	Policy Number	Date	Term	Premium
Circle	34598	March 31, 19–5	3 years	$72.00
Guarantee	234756	June 30, 19–5	3 years	$40.00
Prairie	190645	September 30, 19–6	3 years	$66.00
Select	23114	September 30, 19–6	3 years	$270.00

(f) Wages for the two-week period ended Friday October 5, 19–7 were $214.04. The employees work a five-day week.

Note:

Exercise 11 is for Students who have studied Chapter 13 on payroll.

11. From the following trial balance and additional information for the year ended December 31, 19–5, prepare the work sheet.

General Lighting and Electric
Trial Balance
December 31, 19–5

Petty Cash	$ 100.00	
Bank	1,469.25	
Accounts Receivable	119,007.40	
Allowance for Doubtful Accounts	24.50	
Merchandise Inventory	65,759.10	
Supplies	1,059.26	
Prepaid Insurance	470.50	
Furniture and Equipment	4,942.04	
Accumulated Depreciation Furn. & Equip.		2,574.12
Automotive Equipment	6,574.00	
Accumulated Depreciation Autom. Equip.		2,107.15
Bank Loan		25,000.00
Accounts Payable		41,964.75
Sales Tax Payable		940.60
Employees' Income Tax Payable		219.40
R. Brooks, Capital		93,814.11
R. Brooks, Drawings	9,600.00	
Sales Income		257,906.40
Sales Returns and Allowances	2,065.70	
Advertising and Sales Promotion	1,075.00	
Bank Charges	34.09	
Bank Interest	1,500.00	
Canada Pension Fund Expense	315.90	
Car Expenses	3,951.40	
Cash Short and Over	29.42	
Discounts Earned		1,095.62
Duty	2,964.15	
Freight-in	1,047.24	
Light, Heat and Water	312.95	
Miscellaneous Expense	125.94	
Postage	56.05	
Purchases	162,786.97	
Purchases Returns and Allowances		3,746.15
Rent	12,000.00	
Telephone	941.14	
Unemployment Insurance Expense	400.15	
Wages	30,756.15	
	$429,368.30	$429,368.30

ADDITIONAL INFORMATION

(a) The summary of Purchase Invoices received in 19–6 but which pertain to goods and services received in 19–5 is shown on next page.

Supplies	$	49.50
Furniture and		
Equipment		250.00
Car Expenses		56.55
Freight-in		30.00
Miscellaneous Expense		20.10
Purchase		1,072.16
		$1,478.31

(b) Four accounts were considered to be doubtful. These four accounts are:

Customer	Account Balance
Morgan & Morgan	$342.19
Perfect Company	255.67
J. A. Swift	12.50
W. A. Wallace	150.00

(c) Inventories at December 31, 19–5 were:

Merchandise	$62,056.66
Supplies	$742.00

(d) Details of insurance policies are:

Company	Policy Number	Date	Term	Premium
Northern	90214	Jan. 1, 19–5	3 years	$ 39.00
Alliance	602294	Mar. 31, 19–5	1 year	168.00
Amalgamated	310678	Sept. 30, 19–4	3 years	120.00
Anchor	22230	June 1, 19–4	3 years	90.00
Provincial	123140	Dec. 1, 19–3	3 years	72.00

(e) Depreciation is calculated at government rates.

(f) Wages for the two weeks ended Friday, January 8 amounted to $1,105.12. The employees work a five-day week and are paid for New Year's Day, a holiday.

Chapter 15

COMPLETING THE ACCOUNTING CYCLE

In order to prepare financial statements, one must be familiar with their appearance and organization. There is no single correct form of financial statements, but rather there exist certain acceptable variations each of which is suited to a particular business or situation.

On pages 290 and 291 are shown the Balance Sheet and the Profit and Loss Statement of Fraser and Associates. The statements shown are typical statements for a well-established and profitable trading business. By examining these statements you will see that they are more than just a list of debit and credit items as would appear on a trial balance. On the financial statements, the items are grouped and arranged to provide meaningful information in easily readable form. Financial statements of this type are known as 'classified financial statements'.

The Classified Balance Sheet

The most common classifications on the Balance Sheet are:

CURRENT ASSETS:

Assets that are already in the form of cash or which will be converted into cash in the ordinary course of business within a period of one year. For example, Accounts Receivable are ordinarily collected within a period of one year and are therefore classified as current assets. Current Assets are generally listed in the order of their 'liquidity', that is, in the order of their ability to be converted into cash.

PREPAID EXPENSES:

Expenses paid for in advance. Such expenses are usually used up or expire within a period of one or two years.

FIXED ASSETS:

Assets such as Buildings, Machinery and Equipment which are intended to be used in the operations of the business for a number of years.

CURRENT LIABILITIES:

Liabilities of the business which are due within a period of one year. Current Liabilities are generally listed in the order in which they must be paid.

LONG-TERM LIABILITIES:

Liabilities of the business which are not due for payment within a period of one year. Certain long-term liabilities, mortgages for example, may not be due for several years.

OWNER'S EQUITY:

The owner's share of the business at book value. In other words, the proportion of assets that belong to the owner after providing for payment of all liabilities.

Classified Profit and Loss Statement

REVENUE:

The gross earnings derived from the regular operations of the business.

COST OF MERCHANDISE SOLD:

All of the elements of cost directly connected with the acquisition of the goods which the business deals in. Included is the actual cost of the merchandise as well as any costs involved in the process of transporting the goods from their place of origin to the premises of the business.

SELLING EXPENSES:

All expenses of the business that are directly related to the selling and delivery of the goods.

ADMINISTRATIVE EXPENSES:

All expences of a general nature that are related to the operation of the business. Expenses in this category pertain to such things as the management of the business, the maintenance of the buildings and equipment, and the running of the office.

OTHER INCOME:

Earnings that are not derived from the regular operations of the business.

OTHER EXPENSES:

Expenses that are not related to the regular operations of the business.

Fraser and Associates
Balance Sheet
December 31, 19–9

ASSETS

Current Assets

Petty Cash		$ 100.00	
Bank		1,742.12	
Accounts Receivable	$13,419.05		
Less Allowance for Doubtful Accounts	374.19	13,044.86	
Merchandise Inventory–at cost		15,907.00	
Government Bonds–6½%		10,000.00	$ 40,793.98

Prepaid Expenses

Insurance		$ 416.25	
Supplies		1,530.00	1,946.25

Fixed Assets

Land		$20,000.00	
Buildings–at cost	$75,742.57		
Less Accumulated Depreciation	12,614.30	63,128.27	
Equipment–at cost	$37,407.56		
Less Accumulated Depreciation	18,316.41	19,091.15	
Automobiles–at cost	$10,407.35		
Less Accumulated Depreciation	5,307.75	5,099.60	107,319.02
			$150,059.25

LIABILITIES

Current Liabilities

Accounts Payable and Accrued Charges	$12,409.37	
Bank Loan	5,000.00	
Sales Tax Payable	440.72	
Canada Pension Fund Payable	216.40	
Employees Income Tax Payable	517.42	$ 18,583.91

Long-Term Liability

Mortgage on Property–6%	42,705.16

PROPRIETORSHIP

Owner's Equity

D. Fraser, Capital, January 1		$72,017.21	
Add: Net Profit for year	$31,742.16		
Less Drawings	14,989.19	16,752.97	
D. Fraser, Capital, December 31			88,770.18
			$150,059.25

Fraser and Associates
Profit and Loss Statement
Year Ended December 31, 19–9

Revenue

Sales		$170,984.76	
Less: Sales Returns and Allowances	$ 3,026.04		
Discount off Sales	1,027.19	4,053.23	
Net Sales			$166,931.53

Cost of Merchandise Sold

Merchandise Inventory, January 1		$ 18,414.90	
Purchases	$87,314.42		
Less: Purchases Returns & Allow's $2,016.40			
Discount off Purchases 1,307.51	3,323.91	83,990.51	
Freight-in		2,964.72	
Duty		1,072.12	
Total Cost of Goods Available for Sale		$106,442.25	
Deduct Merchandise Inventory, December 31		15,907.00	
Cost of Merchandise Sold			90,535.25
Gross Trading Profit			$ 76,396.28

Selling Expenses

Advertising and Sales Promotion	$2,504.00	
Delivery Expense	1,594.23	
Salesmen's Commissions	10,234.60	
Salesmen's Car Expenses	5,654.30	
Depreciation of Automobiles	2,185.56	$ 22,172.69

Administrative Expenses

Bad Debts Expense	$ 304.74		
Bank Charges and Interest	502.10		
Depreciation of Building	7,014.25		
Depreciation of Equipment	4,772.79		
Legal Expense	215.00		
Audit Fee	500.00		
General Expense	95.00		
Insurance Expense	128.00		
Supplies Expense	746.12		
Office Expense	216.40		
Postage Expense	155.03		
Rent Expense	84.00		
Telephone Expense	319.54		
Canada Pension Fund Expense	410.34		
Unemployment Insurance Expense	380.42		
Office Salaries	11,442.83	27,286.56	49,459.25
Operating Profit			$ 26,937.03

Other Income

Interest on Investments	4,805.13
Net Profit	$ 31,742.16

Once you are familiar with the form of the financial statements, it is a relatively simple matter to prepare financial statements from the information that appears on the work sheet. It is most important that you are aware of the source of the information for the financial statements. This source of information is the 'work sheet'.

To prepare a Balance Sheet, all of the information is derived from the Balance Sheet columns of the work sheet. It is unnecessary to look elsewhere.

Similarly, to prepare a Profit and Loss Statement, all of the information is derived from the Profit and Loss columns of the work sheet. It is unnecessary to look elsewhere.

So that you may see the relation-ship between the information on the work sheet and the information of the financial statements, the statements of Cassidy Cartage and of Midway Trading Company are shown on the following pages. The work sheets for these two businesses were completed in Chapter 14 on pages 267 and 275 respectively. You should trace the figures from the work sheet to the financial statements to help you become familiar with financial statement preparation.

The statements of Cassidy Cartage and Midway Trading Company follow the form and style described for Fraser and Associates on pages 290 and 291. However, there are some slight differences requiring an explanation. (1) On the Balance Sheets for Cassidy Cartage and Midway Trading Company, no long-term liabilities appear. The reason for this is that neither of these two businesses has any long-term liabilities. (2) The Profit and Loss Statement of Cassidy Cartage is a less classified and much simpler statement. The chief reason for this is that Cassidy Cartage is a service business and consequently has no Cost of Goods Sold section. Also no attempt has been made to separate Selling Expenses. (3) The Profit and Loss Statement of Midway Trading Company is less classified, in that no attempt has been made to separate the Selling Expenses. Also, Discounts Earned and Discounts Allowed are treated as Other Income and Expenses rather than as elements of Revenue and of Operating Expenses.

Cassidy Cartage
Profit and Loss Statement
Year Ended June 30, 19–4

Revenue		
Sales		$28,757.49
Operating Expenses		
Bad Debts Expense	$ 234.05	
Supplies Expense	166.48	
Licences Expense	170.00	
Insurance Expense	127.50	
Depreciation of Buildings	527.46	
Depreciation of Furniture and Equipment	270.52	
Depreciation of Automotive Equipment	2,293.20	
Bank Charges	114.92	
Building Maintenance	599.37	
Light, Heat and Water	495.00	
Miscellaneous Expense	135.70	
Telephone Expense	167.00	
Truck Expenses	5,878.16	
Wages	9,576.79	20,756.15
Operating Profit		$ 8,001.34
Other Income		
Discounts Earned		56.75
Net Profit		$ 8,058.09

Cassidy Cartage
Balance Sheet
June 30, 19–4

ASSETS

Current Assets

Petty Cash		$ 50.00	
Bank		725.41	
Accounts Receivable	$ 4,027.56		
Less Allowance for Doubtful Accounts	260.45	3,767.11	$ 4,542.52

Prepaid Expenses

Supplies		$ 395.25	
Insurance		88.50	
Licences		85.00	568.75

Fixed Assets

Land–at cost		$ 8,000.00	
Buildings–at cost	$ 7,280.00		
Less Accumulated Depreciation	2,532.86	4,747.14	
Furniture and Equipment–at cost	$ 2,950.00		
Less Accumulated Depreciation	1,867.92	1,082.08	
Automotive Equipment–at cost	$15,600.00		
Less Accumulated Depreciation	$10,249.20	5,350.80	19,180.02
			$24,291.29

LIABILITIES AND OWNER'S EQUITY

Current Liabilities

Accounts Payable		$ 3,449.97	
Sales Tax Payable		238.73	
Accrued Wages		157.29	$ 3,845.99

P. Marshall, Equity

Balance July 1, 19–3		$18,387.21	
Add: Net Profit	$ 8,058.09		
Less Drawings	6,000.00	2,058.09	
Balance June 30, 19–4			20,445.30
			$24,291.29

Midway Trading Company
Balance Sheet
December 31, 19–4

ASSETS

Current Assets

Petty Cash		$ 100.00	
Bank		1,702.12	
Accounts Receivable	$ 6,751.12		
Less Allowance for Doubtful Accounts	143.20	6,607.92	
Merchandise Inventory–at cost		13,562.00	$21,972.04

Prepaid Expenses

Supplies		$ 192.00	
Insurance		112.00	304.00

Fixed Assets

Land–at cost		$15,000.00	
Buildings–at cost	$12,000.00		
Less Accumulated Depreciation	2,225.93	9,774.07	
Furniture and Equipment–at cost	$ 3,437.20		
Less Accumulated Depreciation	1,677.36	1,759.84	
Automobiles–at cost	$ 7,800.00		
Less Accumulated Depreciation	5,124.60	2,675.40	29,209.31
			$51,485.35

LIABILITIES AND OWNER'S EQUITY

Current Liabilities

Accounts Payable	$10,710.56	
Bank Loan	9,750.00	
Sales Tax Payable	251.10	
Accrued Wages Payable	146.54	$20,858.20

Owner's Equity

M. Philip, Capital, January 1		$26,214.87	
Add: Net Profit	$13,163.28		
Less Drawings	8,751.00	4,412.28	
M. Philip, Capital, December 31			30,627.15
			$51,485.35

Midway Trading Company
Profit and Loss Statement
Year Ended December 31, 19–4

Revenue

Sales		$59,168.10	
Less Sales Returns and Allowances		1,204.30	$57,963.80

Cost of Goods Sold

Merchandise Inventory, January 1		$12,074.00	
Purchases	$31,664.14		
Less Purchases Returns and Allowances	1,520.00	30,144.14	
Freight In		991.24	
Duty		315.70	
		$43,525.08	
Deduct. Merchandise Inventory, December 31		13,562.00	29,963.08
Gross Trading Profit			$28,000.72

Operating Expenses

Bad Debts Expense	$ 140.70	
Supplies Expense	178.00	
Insurance Expense	82.00	
Depreciation of Buildings	514.43	
Depreciation of Furniture and Equipment	439.96	
Depreciation of Automobiles	1,146.60	
Bank Charges	1,140.26	
Building Maintenance	375.00	
Car Expenses	1,994.00	
Light, Heat and Water	417.25	
Miscellaneous Expense	128.95	
Telephone Expense	484.17	
Wages	7,563.10	14,604.42
Operating Profit		$13,396.30

Other Income and Expenses

Discounts Allowed	$ 749.21	
Less Discounts Earned	516.19	233.02
Net Profit		$13,163.28

Primarily, financial statements are prepared for the use of managers and owners, to inform them accurately of the financial condition of the business and of the results of operation for the fiscal period. Good businessmen usually have a fair understanding of accounting matters and keep reasonably well informed of the financial affairs of the business. For these men, the end of the accounting period is a time of summing up, a time of taking stock, and a time of documenting results.

A few businessmen are ignorant in respect to accounting matters and operate their businesses relatively in the dark. For these men, it is not until after the accounting period is over and the financial statements are prepared by outside accountants that they are made aware of the condition of their businesses. Men in this category, who are not in close touch with the financial affairs of their businesses, run a greater risk of being disappointed by poor results and lack of progress.

All wise businessmen scrutinize and analyse the financial statements thoroughly. In particular, they are on the lookout for unfavourable trends, or areas of weakness that require correction. In businesses that are operating successfully, these are usually few. But in businesses that have a poor profit picture, or even a loss, the areas of weakness are usually painfully apparent. Corrective measures are then imperative.

There are numerous ways in which businessmen use financial statements to obtain meaningful information. A few of these are discussed below.

1. *Current Ratio*
   This is the ratio formed by comparing the total of the current assets to the total of the current liabilities. This ratio shows the ability of a business to pay its debts. It is important because a business that fails to pay its debts when due may be put into bankruptcy by a creditor.

   A current ratio of 2:1 is considered to reflect a safe financial condition; a current ratio of 1:1 is considered to reflect an unsafe financial condition.

   For example, consider the following two cases.

   (a) Current Ratio of Fraser and Associates as derived from the Balance Sheet on page 290.

   Total Current Assets : Total Current Liabilities
   i.e., $40,793.98 : $18,583.91
   Or, by dividing both numbers by $18,583.91 –
   2.2 : 1
   This ratio of 2.2:1 is considered to reflect a safe financial condition.

   (b) Current Ratio of Midway Trading Company as derived from the Balance Sheet on page 294.

   Total Current Assets : Total Current Liabilities
   i.e., $21,972.04 : $20,858.20
   Or, by dividing both numbers by $20,858.20 –
   1.1 : 1
   This ratio of 1.1:1 is considered to reflect an unsafe financial condition.

2. *Gross Profit Percentage*
   This percentage is formed by comparing the Gross Trading Profit figure with the Net Sales figure. For example, the Gross Profit Percentage of Midway Trading Company is calculated from the Profit and Loss Statement on page 295 as shown below.

$$\frac{\text{Gross Trading Profit}}{\text{Net Sales}} \times 100 = \frac{\$28,000.72}{\$57,963.80} \times 100 = 48\%$$

This ratio is an important one because it furnishes the owner with a quick assessment of the performance of the business. He should have some idea of what figure is sufficient to cover the remaining expenses and leave a satisfactory net profit. A comparison of the percentage figure with statements of prior years or in some cases with statements of other companies in the same line of business is useful. If it is found that the Gross Profit Percentage is not satisfactory, it indicates the need either to cut costs, to improve sales, or to increase selling prices.

Comparing Operating Expenses
A percentage comparison of expenses from year to year is a source of valuable information. Such a comparison indicates if any expenses are getting out of line, if there are any unfavorable trends, and where economies can be made in order to improve the profit picture.

In addition to their usefulness to management, financial statements must be made available for other reasons, primarily to satisfy legal requirements. For example, every businessman or incorporated company must submit detailed financial information along with the required annual income tax return. Also, every incorporated company is required to send a copy of its financial statements to each shareholder. Too, chartered banks require annual financial statements from each business to which a bank loan has been made.

Adjusting and Closing the Books

As you are aware, for the sake of convenience during the accounting period, certain General Ledger accounts are allowed to become temporarily out-of-date. As a result, the information contained in the General Ledger cannot be used directly to prepare financial statements. It is from the work sheet that the information for the preparation of the financial statements is obtained.

Once the financial statements have been prepared, the accountant has additional work to do. He must bring the General Ledger up to date and prepare the accounts for the next accounting period. This process, known as 'adjusting and closing the books', is usually done before any transactions of the next accounting period are posted.

Objectives of Adjusting and Closing the Books

The process of 'adjusting and closing the books' has three objectives:

1. To adjust those accounts that are not up to date.

2. To close out all Revenue, Expense, and Drawings accounts. This means to make the accounts have a nil balance. All of the accounts in the Equity section of the General Ledger except the Capital account are affected. They must be closed out in order to make them ready for the next accounting period. Since these accounts are the ones used to accumulate the Revenues, Expenses and Drawings during successive accounting periods, it is necessary that they begin each accounting period with a nil balance.

3. To bring the Equity together again in one account—the Capital account. During the accounting period the owner's total equity is not contained in a single account but rather in several accounts in the Equity section of the ledger. At the end of each accounting period the value of the Equity section of the ledger is pulled together into one account—the owner's Capital account. Therefore, the balance in the Capital account usually represents the owner's correct equity only at the very end of an accounting period, or, which is the same thing, at the very beginning of the subsequent accounting period. Any changes in equity during the period are recorded in the Revenues, Expenses, and Drawings accounts.

Adjusting and Closing Entries

To adjust and close the books of a business it is necessary to journalize and post certain accounting entries known as the 'adjusting and closing entries'. All of the information for these entries is obtainable from the work sheet.

A simplified technique for obtaining the adjusting and closing entries is described below. The technique shown is appropriate for any business or any system. Too, it is appropriate whether the adjustments on the work sheet are performed by the formal method, the short-cut method, or by any combination of the two.

To adjust and close the books, only three steps are necessary:

Step 1. The first step in adjusting and closing the books is to journalize all and only those adjusting entries that appear in the Adjustments columns of the Work Sheet. This step is illustrated on page 298 for both Cassidy Cartage (work sheet page 267) and Midway Trading Company (work sheet page 275).

Step 1 for Cassidy Cartage
(which uses the formal method)

Step 1 for Midway Trading Company
(which uses the short-cut method)

General Journal

Date	Particulars	P.R.	Debit	Credit
June 30	Supplies		45 21	
	Building Maintenance		125 —	
	Light, Heat & Water		22 81	
	Miscellaneous Expense		20 —	
	Telephone Expense		15 70	
	Truck Expense		174 —	
	Accounts Payable			402 72
	Adjusting for Accounts Payable			
30	Supplies Expense		166 48	
	Supplies			166 48
	Adjusting for Supplies Expense			
30	Insurance Expense		127 50	
	Prepaid Insurance			127 50
	Adjusting for Insurance Expense			
30	Licences Expense		170 —	
	Prepaid Licences			170 —
	Adjusting for Licences Expense			
30	Bad Debts Expense		234 05	
	Allowance for Doubtful Accounts			234 05
	Adjusting for Bad Debts Expense			
30	Depreciation of Buildings		527 46	
	Accumulated Depreciation of Bldgs			527 46
	Adjusting for Depreciation of Buildings			
30	Depreciation of Furniture & Equipment		270 52	
	Accum' Deprec' Furn. & Equ			270 52
	Adjusting for Deprec. of Furn. & Equ			
30	Depreciation of Automotive Equipment		2 293 20	
	Accum. Depreciation Auto Equip.			2 293 20
	Adjusting for Deprec. of Auto Equip.			
30	Wages		157 29	
	Accrued Wages Payable			157 29
	Adjusting for Accrued Wages			

General Journal

Date	Particulars	P.R.	Debit	Credit
Dec 31	Car Expenses		147 50	
	Freight In		42 10	
	Miscellaneous Expense		12 51	
	Purchases		1 047 24	
	Accounts Payable			1 249 35
	Adjusting for Accounts Payable			

Step 2. The second of the adjusting and closing entries is obtained from the Profit and Loss section of the work sheet and is one that adjusts some accounts and closes out others. This particular entry is almost the complete reverse of the two Profit and Loss columns.

In detail, this second of the adjusting and closing entries is formulated as follows:

1. Debit each of the individual items appearing in the credit column of the Profit and Loss section of the work sheet to the account named at the left.

2. Credit each of the individual items appearing in the debit column of the Profit and Loss section of the work sheet to the account named at the left.

3. Credit the Net Profit figure (or debit the Net Loss figure) to the owner's Capital account.

When forming this entry, be sure to include all figures appearing in the two Profit and Loss columns of the work sheet, except for the sub-totals and the totals. Also, be sure not to include any additional items. If the figures are picked up correctly from the work sheet, the accounting entry will balance.

Step 2 is illustrated below for both Cassidy Cartage and Midway Trading Company.

Step 2 for Cassidy Cartage
(which uses the formal method)

Date	Account	Debit		Credit	
June 30	Sales	28 757	49		
	Discounts Earned	56	75		
	Bank Charges			114	92
	Building Maintenance			599	37
	Light, Heat and Water			495	—
	Miscellaneous Expense			135	70
	Telephone Expense			167	—
	Truck Expense			5 878	16
	Wages			9 576	79
	Supplies Expense			166	48
	Insurance Expense			127	50
	Licences Expense			170	—
	Bad Debts Expense			234	05
	Depreciation of Buildings			527	46
	Depreciation of Furn & Equip			270	52
	Depreciation Automotive Equip.			2 293	20
	P. Marshall, Capital			8 058	09
	To close out the profit and loss				
	accounts to Capital account				

Step 2 for Midway Trading Company
(which uses the short-cut method)

Date	Account	Debit		Credit	
Dec 31	Merchandise Inventory	13 562	—		
	Sales	59 168	10		
	Discounts Earned	516	19		
	Purchases Returns & Allowances	1 520	—		
	Allowance for Doubtful Accounts			140	70
	Merchandise Inventory			12 074	—
	Supplies			178	—
	Prepaid Insurance			82	—
	Accum. Deprec. Buildings			514	43
	Accum. Deprec. Furn & Equip.			439	96
	Accum. Deprec. Automobiles			1 146	60
	Sales Returns & Allowances			1 204	30
	Bank Charges			1 140	26
	Building Maintenance			375	—
	Car Expenses			1 994	—
	Discounts Allowed			749	21
	Duty			315	70
	Freight In			991	24
	Light, Heat and Water			417	25
	Miscellaneous Expense			128	95
	Purchases			31 664	14
	Telephone Expense			484	17
	Wages			7 563	10
	M. Philip, Capital			13 163	28
	To record adjustments & to close out				
	the profit & loss accounts to Capital				
	account.				

Step 3. The purpose of the third entry is merely to close out the owner's Drawings account to the owner's Capital account. Capital account is debited and Drawings account is credited with the balance of the Drawings accounts which is picked up from the work sheet–Balance Sheet Debit column: Drawings line.

The third and last of the adjusting and closing entries is shown below for both Cassidy Cartage and Midway Trading Company.

Step 3 for Cassidy Cartage
(which uses the formal method)

Date	Account	Debit		Credit	
June 30	P. Marshall, Capital	6 000	—		
	P. Marshall, Drawings			6 000	—
	To close out Drawings to Capital				

Step 3 for Midway Trading Company
(which uses the short-cut method)

Date	Account	Debit		Credit	
Dec 31	M. Philip, Capital	8 751	—		
	M. Philip, Drawings			8 751	—
	To close out Drawings to Capital				

Posting the Adjusting and Closing Entries

After the adjusting and closing entries are journalized in the General Journal, they are posted to the General Ledger.

The General Ledgers of Cassidy Cartage and Midway Trading Company, immediately after posting the adjusting and closing entries, are as shown on these facing pages.

Ledger of Cassidy Cartage
(final position)

Petty Cash #1
			DR. 50.00
June 30			

Bank #2
			DR 725.41
June 30			

Accounts Receivable #3
			DR 4,027.56
June 30			

Allow. Doubtful Accounts #4
			CR 26.40
June 30			
30		234.05	CR 260.45

Supplies #5
			DR 516.52
June 30			
30	45.21		
30		166.48	DR 395.25

Prepaid Insurance #6
			DR 216.00
June 30			
30		127.50	DR 88.50

Prepaid Licences #7
			DR 255.00
June 30			
30		170.00	DR 85.00

Land #8
			DR 8,000.00
June 30			

Buildings #9
			DR 7,280.00
June 30			

Accum. Deprec. Buildings #10
			CR 2,005.40
June 30			
30		527.46	CR 2532.86

Furniture + Equipment #11
			DR 2,950.00
June 30			

Accum. Deprec. Furn + Equip #12
			CR 1,597.40
June 30			
30		270.52	1,867.92

Automotive Equipment #13
			DR 15,600.00
June 30			

Accum. Deprec. Auto. Equip #14
			7,956.00
June 30			
30		2,293.20	10,249.20

Accounts Payable #21
			CR 3,047.25
June 30			
30		402.72	CR 3,449.97

Sales Tax Payable #22
			CR 238.73
June 30			

Accrued Wages Payable #23
June 30		157.29	CR 157.29

P. Marshall, Capital #31
			CR 18,387.21
June 30			
30		8,058.09	
30	6,000.00		CR 20,445.30

P. Marshall, Drawings #32
			DR 6,000.00
June 30			
30		6,000.00	0

Sales #41
			CR 28,757.49
June 30			
30	28,757.49		0

Discounts Earned #42
			CR 56.75
June 30			
30	56.75		0

Bank Charges #51
			DR 114.92
June 30			
30		114.92	0

Building Maintenance #52
			DR 474.37
June 30			
30	125.00		
30		599.37	0

Light Heat + Water #53
			DR 472.19
June 30			
30	22.81		
30		495.00	0

Miscellaneous Expense #54
			DR 115.70
June 30			
30	20.00		
30		135.70	0

Telephone Expense #55
			DR 151.30
June 30			
30	15.70		
30		167.00	0

Truck Expense #56
			DR 5,704.16
June 30			
30	174.00		
30		5,878.16	0

Wages Expense #57
			DR 9,419.50
June 30			
30	157.29		
30		9,576.79	0

Supplies Expense #58
June 30	166.48		
30		166.48	0

Insurance Expense #59
June 30	127.50		
30		127.50	0

Licences Expense #60
June 30	170.00		
30		170.00	0

Bad Debts Expense #61
June 30	234.05		
30		234.05	0

Deprec. of Buildings #62
June 30	527.46		
30		527.46	0

Deprec. of Furn. + Equip. #63
June 30	270.52		
30		270.52	0

Deprec. of Auto. Equip. #64
June 30	2,293.20		
30		2,293.20	0

300

Ledger of Midway Trading Company
(final position)

Petty Cash #1

Date	Debit	Credit	Balance
Dec 31			DR 100.00

Bank #2

Date	Debit	Credit	Balance
Dec 31			DR 1,702.12

Accounts Receivable #3

Date	Debit	Credit	Balance
Dec 31			DR 6,751.12

Allow. Doubtful Accounts #4

Date	Debit	Credit	Balance
Dec 31			CR 2.50
31		140.70	CR 143.20

Merchandise Inventory #5

Date	Debit	Credit	Balance
Dec 31			DR 12,074.00
31	13,562.00		
31		12,074.00	DR 13,562.00

Supplies #6

Date	Debit	Credit	Balance
Dec 31			DR 370.00
31		178.00	DR 192.00

Prepaid Insurance #7

Date	Debit	Credit	Balance
Dec 31			DR 194.00
31		82.00	DR 112.00

Land #8

Date	Debit	Credit	Balance
Dec 31			DR 15,000.00

Buildings #9

Date	Debit	Credit	Balance
Dec 31			DR 12,000.00

Accum. Deprec. Bldgs #10

Date	Debit	Credit	Balance
Dec 31			CR 1,711.50
31		514.43	CR 2,225.93

Furniture + Equipment #11

Date	Debit	Credit	Balance
Dec 31			DR 3,437.20

Accum Deprec. Furn + Equ. #12

Date	Debit	Credit	Balance
Dec 31			CR 1,237.40
31		439.96	CR 1,677.36

Automobiles #13

Date	Debit	Credit	Balance
Dec 31			DR 7,800.00

Accum. Deprec. Autos. #14

Date	Debit	Credit	Balance
Dec 31			CR 3,978.00
31		1,146.60	CR 5,124.60

Accounts Payable #21

Date	Debit	Credit	Balance
Dec 31			CR 9,461.21
31		1,249.35	CR 10,710.56

Bank Loan #22

Date	Debit	Credit	Balance
Dec 31			CR 9,750.00

Sales Tax Payable #23

Date	Debit	Credit	Balance
Dec 31			CR 251.10

M. Philip Capital #31

Date	Debit	Credit	Balance
Dec 31			CR 26,214.87
31		13,163.28	
31	8,751.00		CR 30,627.15

M. Philip Drawings #32

Date	Debit	Credit	Balance
Dec 31			DR 8,751.00
31		8,751.00	-0-

Sales #41

Date	Debit	Credit	Balance
Dec 31			CR 59,168.10
31	59,168.10		-0-

Sales Rets + Allow's #42

Date	Debit	Credit	Balance
Dec 31			DR 1,204.30
31		1,204.30	-0-

Discounts Earned #43

Date	Debit	Credit	Balance
Dec 31			CR 516.19
31	516.19		-0-

Bank Charges #51

Date	Debit	Credit	Balance
Dec 31			DR 1,140.26
31		1,140.26	-0-

Building Maintenance #52

Date	Debit	Credit	Balance
Dec 31			DR 375.00
31		375.00	

Car Expenses #53

Date	Debit	Credit	Balance
Dec 31			DR 1846.50
31	147.50		
31		1,994.00	-0-

Discounts Allowed #54

Date	Debit	Credit	Balance
Dec 31			DR 749.21
31		749.21	-0-

Duty #55

Date	Debit	Credit	Balance
Dec 31			DR 315.70
31		315.70	-0-

Freight In #56

Date	Debit	Credit	Balance
Dec 31			DR 949.14
31	42.10		
31		991.24	-0-

Light, Heat + Water #57

Date	Debit	Credit	Balance
Dec 31			DR 417.25
31		417.25	-0-

Miscellaneous Expense #58

Date	Debit	Credit	Balance
Dec 31			DR 116.44
31	12.51		
31		128.95	-0-

Purchases #59

Date	Debit	Credit	Balance
Dec 31			DR 30,616.90
31	1,047.24		
31		31,664.14	-0-

Purchases Rets + Allow's #60

Date	Debit	Credit	Balance
Dec 31			CR 1,520.00
31	1,520.00		-0-

Telephone Expense #61

Date	Debit	Credit	Balance
Dec 31			DR 484.17
31		484.17	-0-

Wages #62

Date	Debit	Credit	Balance
Dec 31			DR 7,416.56
31		7,563.10	CR 146.54

The objectives of the adjusting and closing entries were set out on page 297. After completion of the adjusting and closing entries these objectives will have been met; that is—

1. All accounts requiring an adjustment will be adjusted.
2. The Capital account will be updated.
3. All other Equity accounts will be closed out.

Note:

The wages account of Midway Trading Company is not closed out. This exception is explained on pages 305 and 306.

Post-Closing Trial Balance

The closing procedure involves the making of numerous postings and calculations of account balances. In all of this, there is plenty of room for the making of mechanical errors. Consequently, in order to be certain that the General Ledger is in a balanced condition to begin the new accounting period, after posting the closing entries it is advisable to take off a General Ledger trial balance, called the 'post-closing trial balance'. This is usually done using an adding machine and paper tape, as illustrated below. The paper tape is headed and stored for possible future reference.

Cassidy Cartage
Post Closing Trial
Balance
June 30, 19-4

```
              0 0 T
          5 0.0 0
        7 2 5.4 1
      4,0 2 7.5 6
        2 6 0.4 5   -
        3 9 5.2 5
          8 8.5 0
          8 5.0 0
      8,0 0 0.0 0
      7,2 8 0.0 0
      2,5 3 2.8 6   -
      2,9 5 0.0 0
      1,8 6 7.9 2   -
    1 5,6 0 0.0 0
    1 0,2 4 9.2 0   -
      3,4 4 9.9 7   -
        2 3 8.7 3   -
        1 5 7.2 9   -
    2 0,4 4 5.3 0   -
              0 0 T
```

Midway Trading Company
Post Closing Trial
Balance
June 30, 19-4

```
              0 0 T  -
        1 0 0.0 0
      1,7 0 2.1 2
      6,7 5 1.1 2
        1 4 3.2 0   -
    1 3,5 6 2.0 0
        1 9 2.0 0
        1 1 2.0 0
    1 5,0 0 0.0 0
    1 2,0 0 0.0 0
      2,2 2 5.9 3   -
      3,4 3 7.2 0
      1,6 7 7.3 6   -
      7,8 0 0.0 0
      5,1 2 4.6 0   -
    1 0,7 1 0.5 6   -
      9,7 5 0.0 0
        2 5 1.1 0   -
    3 0,6 2 7.1 5   -
        1 4 6.5 4   -
              0 0 T
```

Reversing Entries

Reversing Entry for Accounts Payable

When preparing financial statements an adjusting entry is necessary in respect to certain Purchase Invoices that pertain to one accounting period but which do not arrive until the next. This adjusting entry, done by the formal method, gives effect to these Purchase Invoices in the proper accounting period.

Once the adjusting entry for accounts payable is made, the Purchase Invoices are inserted into the accounting system to be processed by the ordinary accounting routine in the new period. It is necessary to do this because they must be matched with the Purchase Orders and Receiving Reports, posted to the Subsidiary Ledgers, and so on. The accounting routine must be adhered to strictly as it is designed for purposes of internal control, accuracy, and efficiency. However, by processing these Purchase Orders by means of the accounting routine, they are entered in the books of the business a second time, this time in the new accounting period. Consequently, these particular Purchase Invoices are recorded in both accounting periods as shown by the following chart.

END OF
ACCOUNTING
PERIOD

Accounting Period Just Ended	Accounting Period Just Begun
+ Effect of certain Purchase Invoices is recorded in the books of the business by means of an adjusting entry.	+ Effect of the same Purchase Invoices is recorded in the books of the business by means of the accounting system.

From the above chart, you can see that the effect of the Purchase Invoices is felt in both accounting periods. But your common sense should tell you that this situation is not right and cannot be allowed to remain.

The situation is rectified by means of another accounting entry, called a 'reversing entry', which is made *early in the new accounting period*. This reversing entry is exactly the opposite to the adjusting entry made previously and completely cancels out the doubling effect.

For both Cassidy Cartage and Midway Trading Company the reversing entries for accounts payable are shown below. These reversing entries are exactly the opposite of the adjusting entries shown on pages 255 and 269 respectively.

July	1	Accounts Payable	402	72		
		Telephone Expense			15	70
		Truck Expense			174	—
		Supplies			45	21
		Building Maintenance			125	—
		Light, Heat and Water			22	81
		Miscellaneous Expense			20	—
		Reversing entry for accounts payable				
		adjusting entry of June 30				

Reversing Entry for Cassidy Cartage

Jan	1	Accounts Payable	1 249	35		
		Car Expenses			147	50
		Freight In			42	10
		Miscellaneous Expense			12	51
		Purchases			1 047	24
		Reversing entry for accounts payable				
		adjusting entry of Dec. 31				

Reversing Entry for Midway Trading Company

The total effect of the reversing
entry for accounts payable is shown
by the following chart.

END OF
ACCOUNTING
PERIOD

Accounting Period Just Ended	Accounting Period Just Begun
+ Effect of certain Purchase Invoices is recorded in the books of the business by means of an adjusting entry (subsidiary ledger excluded).	**—** The opposite effect of the adjusting entry is recorded in the books of the business by means of a reversing entry (subsidiary ledger excluded).
	+ The effect of the same Purchase Invoices is recorded in the books of the business by means of the accounting system (subsidiary ledger included).

The chart shows that the doubling
effect is eliminated in the new accounting period by means of the reversing accounting entry.

Reversing Entry for Accrued Payroll

Reversing entries are necessary for any accounting situation where the following conditions exist:

1. An adjusting entry–*by the formal method*–is made to record an item or items in the accounting period just completed.

2. The same item or items are processed in the new accounting period by means of the regular accounting routines.

Cassidy Cartage used the formal method of adjusting for accrued wages which resulted in six days' wages in the amount of $157.29 being recorded in the accounting period ended June 30. At the same time, the Payroll Department of Cassidy Cartage proceeded in its usual manner to calculate the payroll for the 10-day period ended in July and which resulted in wages of $262.15 being recorded in the new accounting period. Of special importance is the fact that the 10-day wages figure of $262.15 includes the six-day wages figure of $157.29.

The effect of the above is shown by the following chart.

END OF
ACCOUNTING
PERIOD

Accounting Period Just Ended	Accounting Period Just Begun
$157.29 of wages (for 6 days) Recorded by adjusting entry.	$262.15 of wages (for 10 days) Recorded through regular accounting routine.

Because the $262.15 figure includes the $157.29 figure, it is apparent that the $157.29 figure is recorded in both accounting periods. This duplication is corrected by means of a reversing entry which cancels out $157.29 in the new accounting period. The reversing entry is shown below and is exactly the opposite of the adjusting entry made previously, page 266.

July	1	Accrued Payroll		157	29		
		Wages Expense				157	29
		Reversing entry for accrued wages					
		adjusting entry of June 30					

The total accounting effect is shown by the chart below.

END OF
ACCOUNTING
PERIOD

Accounting Period Just Ended	Accounting Period Just Begun
$157.29 of wages (for 6 days) recorded by adjusting entry	$262.15 of wages (for 10 days) recorded through regular accounting routine
	$157.29 of wages (for 6 days) cancelled out by a reversing entry
Net effect: 6 days wages at $157.29	Net effect: 4 days wages at $104.86

Short-cut Technique and Reversing Entries

No reversing entries are necessary for any adjustments performed by the short-cut technique. The accountant is thus relieved of some of his many responsibilities at this busy time.

To illustrate the way in which this works, consider the accrued wages adjustment of Midway Trading Company. This adjustment is performed by the short-cut technique (pages 272 and 273).

After completing the adjusting and closing entries, the Wages account of Midway Trading Company ends up in a credit balance position of $146.54 as shown at right (from page 301).

| Wages | | | | | #62 |
Date	Particulars	P.R.	Debit	Credit	Balance
19–4 Dec 31					7 416 56 DR
31		J.78		7 563 10	146 54 CR

This account has been converted temporarily into a liability account which reflects the accrued liability for wages as of the end of the accounting period, December 31.

When the first payroll is completed in the following period, say on January 9, the wages figure for this payroll will be debited to the Wages account through the normal processes of the accounting system. Assuming the gross wages figure to be $488.47, the Wages account will be debited with that amount. After posting, the account will appear as at right.

| Wages | | | | | #62 |
Date	Particulars	P.R.	Debit	Credit	Balance
19–4 Dec 31					7 416 56 DR
31		J.78		7 563 10	146 54 CR
19–5 Jan 9		J.79	488 47		341 93 DR

This payroll entry, through the normal accounting routine, has produced a debit balance in the account of $341.93. Thus, the account has not only been converted back to its normal status of expense account but has been made to reflect automatically the proper expense figure for the new accounting period.

Full Accounting Cycle

You have now seen the full accounting cycle, that series of progressive accounting steps that must be performed during each accounting period. Specifically these steps are:

Journalizing of transactions
Posting to the General Ledger and
    to the Subsidiary Ledgers   } Performed by junior accounting clerks
Balancing the General Ledger and
    the Subsidiary Ledgers

Preparing the work sheet
Preparing the financial statements   } Performed by the accountant or assistant accountant
Recording the adjusting, closing,
    and reversing entries

Bookkeeping and Accounting Terms

Current Asset: "An asset that, in the normal course of operations, is expected to be converted into cash or consumed in the production of income within one year or within the normal operating cycle where that is longer than a year . . ."*

Prepaid Expense: "A short term expense prepayment; an expenditure, other than a capital expenditure, which is expected to yield its benefits in the near future and meanwhile is carried forward to be assigned to expense in the near future . . ."*

Fixed Asset: "A tangible long-term asset, such as land, building, equipment, etc., held for use rather than for sale."*

Current Liabilities: "A debt owing which will fall due within one year . . ."*

Long-term Liabilities: "A liability which, in the ordinary course of business, will not be liquidated within one year."*

Revenue: "The gross proceeds of the sale of goods and services (generally after deducting returns, allowances and discounts) . . ."*

Selling Expense: "The classification for financial statement purposes of those expenses of an organization relating to the selling or marketing of the organization's goods or services; as opposed to those expenses incurred for other specialized functions such as administration, financial, and manufacturing."*

Administrative Expenses: "The classification for financial statement purposes of those expenses of an organization relating to the overall direction of its affairs; as opposed to those expenses incurred for other specialized functions, such as manufacturing, selling or financing."*

Current Ratio: "The arithmetical relationship between current assets and liabilities, used as a measure of liquidity. It is usually stated as a number representing the amount of current assets expressed as a multiple of the amount of current liabilities . . ."*

Gross Profit: ". . . the excess of net sales over the cost of goods sold . . ."*

Working Capital: "The excess of the total of the current assets over the total of the current liabilities."*

Closing Entry: "An entry made at the end of an accounting period for the purpose of transferring the balances in nominal accounts (revenue, income, expense or loss) to the . . . capital . . ."*

Reversing Entry: "In particular, the plural (reversing entries) refers to a group of entries made at the beginning of an accounting period to bring into account for the period any . . . accrued amounts adjusted at the end of the preceding period."*

---

* Canadian Institute of Chartered Accountants, Committee on Accounting and Auditing Research, *Terminology for Accountants* (Toronto: Canadian Institute of Chartered Accountants, 1962).

Review Questions

1. Explain what is meant by classified financial statements.
2. Name the classifications shown on the Balance Sheet of Fraser and Associates, on page 290.
3. Name the classifications shown on the Profit and Loss Statement of Fraser and Associates, page 291.
4. Do all classified financial statements follow exactly the same format? Explain.
5. What is the source of information for the financial statements? Explain in detail for both the Balance Sheet and the Profit and Loss Statement.
6. Briefly explain the uses to which financial statements may be put.
7. How is the Current Ratio calculated?
8. How is the Gross Profit percentage calculated?
9. What are the three objectives of 'adjusting and closing' the books?
10. What does it mean to close an account?
11. Revenue, Expense, and Drawings accounts must be closed out at the end of the accounting period. Explain.
12. Where does one obtain all of the information for the Adjusting and Closing entries?
13. How many steps are required to adjust and close the books? Explain briefly.
14. What is the purpose of the Post-Closing Trial Balance?
15. Under what conditions is a reversing entry necessary?
16. Can reversing entries be avoided? Explain.
17. List all of the steps in the full accounting cycle.
18. What is Working Capital?
19. Define Current Asset.
20. Define Fixed Asset.

Exercises

1. From the work sheet for J. P. Gorman (Chapter 14, Exercise 6)–
   (a) Prepare the Profit and Loss Statement and the Balance Sheet.
   (b) Journalize the adjusting, closing, and reversing entries in a two-column General Journal.

2. From the work sheet for Dennisson Delivery Service (Chapter 14, Exercise 7)–
   (a) Prepare the Profit and Loss Statement and the Balance Sheet.
   (b) Journalize the adjusting, closing, and reversing entries in a two-column General Journal.

3. From the work sheet for Select Trading Company (Chapter 14, Exercise 8)–
   (a) Prepare the Profit and Loss Statement and the Balance Sheet.
   (b) Journalize the adjusting, closing, and reversing entries in a two-column General Journal.

4. From the work sheet for Stirling Sales Company (Chapter 14, Exercise 9)—
   (a) Prepare the Profit and Loss Statement and the Balance Sheet.
   (b) Journalize the adjusting, closing, and reversing entries in a two-column General Journal.

5. From the work sheet for Monarch Marine (Chapter 14, Exercise 10)—
   (a) Set up the General Ledger accounts in T account form from the trial balance figures.
   (b) Prepare the Profit and Loss Statement and the Balance Sheet.
   (c) Journalize the adjusting and closing entries in a two-column General Journal.
   (d) Post the adjusting and closing entries to the General Ledger T accounts and calculate the account balances.
   (e) Take off a post-closing trial balance of the General Ledger.

6. From the work sheet for General Lighting and Electric (Chapter 14, Exercise 11)—
   (a) Set up the General Ledger accounts in T account form from the trial balance figures.
   (b) Prepare the Profit and Loss Statement and the Balance Sheet.
   (c) Journalize the adjusting and closing entries in a two-column General Journal.
   (d) Post the adjusting and closing entries to the General Ledger T accounts and calculate the account balances.
   (e) Take off a post-closing trial balance of the General Ledger.
   (f) Calculate the Current Ratio and the Gross Profit percentage.

7. The General Ledger Trial Balance of King Chemical Company, after a fiscal period of one year, is as follows:

King Chemical Company
General Ledger Trial Balance
December 31, 19–3

No.				
1	Petty Cash	$ 50.00		
2	Bank	593.74		
3	Accounts Receivable	12,519.50		
4	Allowance for Doubtful Accounts	4.70		
5	Merchandise Inventory	20,416.50		
6	Supplies	575.75		
7	Prepaid Insurance	312.00		
8	Furniture and Equipment	4,010.00		
9	Accum. Deprec. Furn. & Equip.		$ 2,716.50	
10	Automobiles	7,800.00		
11	Accum. Deprec. Automobiles		5,124.60	
21	Bank Loan		15,000.00	
22	Accounts Payable		15,741.62	
23	Sales Tax Payable		672.14	
24	Employees' Income Tax Payable		602.51	
31	F. C. Wallace, Capital		27,441.20	
32	F. C. Wallace, Drawings	15,946.15		
41	Sales		140,567.07	
51	Bank Charges	141.05		
52	Canada Pension Plan Expense	405.00		
53	Car Expenses	3,509.10		
54	Duty	1,075.92		
55	Freight-in	4,074.75		
56	Light, Heat and Water	147.16		
57	Miscellaneous Expense	79.52		
58	Postage	112.40		
59	Purchases	73,416.95		
60	Rent	11,760.00		
61	Telephone	565.70		
62	Unemployment Insurance	286.00		
63	Wages	50,063.75		
		$207,865.64	$207,865.64	

(a) Set up the above information in General Ledger accounts.

(b) Prepare a work sheet for the company for the year ended December 31, 19–3. Use the following additional information:

   (i) The total of the estimated doubtful accounts as shown by December 31, 19–3 aging analysis is $516.90

(ii) Purchase Invoices received in January 19–4 pertaining to goods and services received in 19–3 are summarized as follows:

Supplies	$ 75.00
Purchases	967.25
Car Expenses	135.75
Misc. Expense	74.01
	$1,252.01

(iii) Inventories taken at December 31, 19–3 are:

Merchandise	$18,450.00
Supplies	$ 250.00

(iv) The Prepaid Insurance schedule as of December 31, 19–3 showed the value of Prepaid Insurance to be $116.25.

(v) Capital Cost Allowances are calculated at government rates.

(vi) The gross wages for the first payroll in January amounted to $1,140. Half of this amount pertained to the 19–3 fiscal year and half to the 19–4 fiscal year.

(c) Prepare a Balance Sheet and a Profit and Loss Statement.

(d) Journalize the adjusting and closing entries.

(e) Post the adjusting and closing entries and calculate the account balances.

(f) Take off a post-closing trial balance.

(g) Journalize the reversing entry (or entries).

(h) Post the payroll for the pay period ended January 6, 19–4 from the following payroll summary figures.

Gross Wages	$1,140.00
Canada Pension Plan Deductions	16.70
Income Tax Deductions	78.50
Unemployment Insurance Deductions	13.90
United Appeal Deductions	12.00
Net Wages	1,018.90

(i) Calculate the new balance in the Wages expense account to see if the account reflects correctly the wages expense for the first working week of 19–4.

(j) Calculate the Current Ratio and the Gross Profit percentage.

8. On December 31, 19–4, the end
   of a fiscal year, the General Ledger trial balance of Dominion
   Furniture is as follows:

Dominion Furniture
Trial Balance
December 31, 19–4

No.				
	1	Petty Cash	$ 50.00	
	2	Bank	1,047.21	
	3	Accounts Receivable	10,467.04	
	4	Allowance for Doubtful Accounts		$ 25.94
	5	Merchandise Inventory	12,375.16	
	6	Supplies	362.04	
	7	Prepaid Insurance	243.00	
	8	Land	9,500.00	
	9	Buildings–Frame	7,500.00	
	10	Accum. Deprec. Buildings		2,579.25
	11	Furniture and Equipment	2,150.00	
	12	Accum. Deprec. Furn. & Equip.		1,172.00
	13	Automobiles	4,875.00	
	14	Accumulated Depreciation Automobiles		1,462.50
	21	Accounts Payable		3,076.21
	22	Sales Tax Payable		315.20
	23	Employees' Income Tax Payable		84.50
	24	Canada Pension Plan Payable		31.10
	25	Loan Payable–Due March 31, 19–9		20,000.00
	31	J. K. Smit, Capital		8,706.59
	32	J. K. Smit, Drawings	12,500.00	
	41	Sales		85,904.15
	42	Sales Returns and Allowances	2,074.10	
	51	Advertising	200.00	
	52	Bank Charges	35.00	
	53	Building Repairs and Mtce.	746.09	
	54	Canada Pension Plan Expense	234.00	
	55	Car Expenses	946.80	
	56	Cash Short and Over	13.50	
	57	Discounts Allowed	1,516.15	
	58	Discounts Earned		1,075.21
	59	Duty	357.00	
	60	Freight-in	907.40	
	61	Interest on Loan	900.00	
	62	Light, Heat and Water	112.00	
	63	Miscellaneous Expense	56.50	
	64	Postage	94.60	
	65	Property Taxes	804.90	
	66	Purchases	40,915.78	
	67	Purchases Returns and Allow.		1,010.44
	68	Telephone	212.50	
	69	Unemployment Ins. Expense	151.20	
	70	Wages and Salaries	14,096.12	
			$125,443.09	$125,443.09

(a) Set up the General Ledger of Dominion Furniture as of December 31, 19–4.

(b) Prepare a work sheet for Dominion Furniture for the year ended December 31, 19–4. Use the short-cut technique for adjustments wherever possible. Use the following additional information:

   (i) The total estimated value of doubtful accounts per the aging analysis of $152.

   (ii) Purchase Invoices received in January 19–5 which pertain to goods and services received in 19–4 are summarized below:

Purchases	$1,200.50
Building Repairs and Maintenance	105.00
Car Expenses	41.02
Freight-in	25.00
	$1,371.52

   (iii) Inventories taken at December 31, 19–4 are:

Merchandise	$14,650.00
Supplies	$ 150.00

   (iv) The details of insurance policies as at December 31, 19–4 are:

Company	Policy Date	Term	Premium
Acme	July 1, 19–2	3 years	$ 72.00
Inland	April 1, 19–4	3 years	96.00
Empire	Dec. 31, 19–1	3 years	120.00
Imperial	Sept. 30, 19–4	1 year	36.00

   (v) Capital Cost Allowances calculated at Government rates.

   (vi) The gross wages and salaries for the first pay in January 19–5 totaled $305 for 10 working days. Three working days are in 19–4 and seven are in 19–5.

(vii) The loan payable of $20,000 bears interest at a rate of 6 per cent per annum. Interest payments are made half-yearly on March 31 and September 30. Interest has been paid to September 30 only. (An adjustment is necessary in respect to accrued interest payable.)

(c) Prepare a Balance Sheet and a Profit and Loss Statement.

(d) Journalize the adjusting and the closing entries.

(e) Post the adjusting and the closing entries and calculate the account balances.

(f) Take off a post-closing trial balance.

(g) Journalize the reversing entry (or entries).

(h) Post the debit to Wages and Salaries account for the first pay in 19–5. Calculate the account balance to see if it properly reflects the expense for the new pay period.

(i) Post the debit to Interest on Loan account for the first interest payment on March 31, 19–5. Calculate the account balance to see if it properly reflects the interest expense for the new period.

(j) Calculate the Current Ratio and the Gross Profit percentage.

Summary Exercise

UNIVERSAL LUMBER COMPANY

INSTRUCTION 1.

(a) Read the introductory information and make notes of the business transactions that you will be required to make on your own initiative.

(b) Set up the three ledgers.

(c) Set up the two journals.

Introductory Information

You have taken a position as accountant for the Universal Lumber Company. You are to commence duties on December 15, 19–4, the arrangement being that you are to work with the present accountant until his departure at the end of the month. It is expected that during that time you will become sufficiently acquainted with the company's books, records, and office procedures to enable you to take over full responsibility for their preparation.

During the introductory period you learn the following facts and information:

1. The business is three years old.

2. The owner is James Wiseman.

3. The company's fiscal year coincides with the calendar year.

4. The owner demands interim financial statements at the end of each month, to show in columnar form the results of operation for the month just completed as well as the results of operation for the year to date.

5. In the office there is an adding machine and a calculator which are rented by the company from Office Rentals Co. The monthly rentals of $10 and $15 are due on the fifteenth of each month.

6. The company offers a 2 per cent discount on all sales if payment is received from the customer within 10 days of the date on the Sales Invoice.

7. Sales tax at the rate of 10 per cent applies on all sales.

8. The company has a National Pacific Railway siding. Most of the material purchased is transported to the company premises by rail.

9. On the 15th and on the last day of each month the proprietor draws $625 out of the business.

10. The detailed information in respect to payroll is as follows:

   (a) Pay day is every other Friday. The first pay day in the new year is Friday, January 10.

   (b) All employees are paid on a salary basis.

   (c) The method of payment is by cash. The cash to meet the payroll is obtained by issuing and cashing one cheque for the total amount required.

   (d) The payroll for January 10 is to be made up from the following minimum information:

Employee	Weekly Salary	Exemptions Per TD-1 Forms	Weekly United Appeal Donation	Account to be Charged
C. Barney	$ 75.00	$1850	1.00	Wages
A. Scott	75.00	1300	1.50	Wages
E. Kollar	65.00	2100	1.00	Wages
B. Brody	65.00	2550	.50	Wages
F. Duncan	60.00	2900	1.25	Wages
D. Ellis	90.00	2900	.50	Office Salaries
Accountant (you)	100.00	1000	—	Office Salaries

(Assume for convenience that all employees are over 18 years of age and under 70 years of age.)

(e) Each Monday following pay day the required Unemployment Insurance Stamps are purchased at the local post office and are stamped in the employees' unemployment insurance books.

(f) Employees' income taxes together with employees' and employer's contributions to the Canada Pension Plan deducted at source are remitted to the Receiver General on the fifteenth day of each month following that in which the deductions are made (one cheque).

(g) The United Appeal Fund contributions of the employees are accumulated by the company and remitted to the local organization at the end of each quarter.

11. Sales tax is remitted on the fifteenth of each month for the deductions of the previous month, payable to the Provincial Treasurer.

12. The complete chart of accounts for the business is as follows:

Account Number	Account Name
1	Bank
2	Petty Cash
3	Accounts Receivable
4	Allowance for Bad Debts
5	Merchandise Inventory
6	Office Supplies
7	Prepaid Insurance
8	Land
9	Buildings
10	Accumulated Depreciation (Buildings)
11	Office Equipment
12	Accumulated Depreciation (Office Equipment)
13	Trucks
14	Accumulated Depreciation (Trucks)
21	Bank Loan
22	Accounts Payable
23	Employees Tax Deductions Payable
24	Canada Pension Plan Payable
25	Unemployment Insurance Payable
26	United Appeal Payable
27	Sales Tax Payable
31	James Wiseman Capital
32	James Wiseman Drawings
41	Sales
51	Bad Debts
52	Building Maintenance
53	Depreciation of Buildings
54	Depreciation of Office Equipment
55	Depreciation of Trucks
56	Discounts Allowed
57	Freight-in
58	Insurance Expense
59	Interest and Bank Charges
60	Legal Expense
61	Miscellaneous Expense
62	Office Expense
63	Office Supplies Used
64	Office Salaries
65	Pension Fund Expenses
66	Power Expense
67	Property Taxes
68	Purchases
69	Telephone
70	Truck Expenses
71	Unemployment Insurance Expense
72	Wages

13. The General Ledger trial balance at December 31 was as follows:

	Debit	Credit
Bank	$ 3,846.71	
Petty Cash	100.00	
Accounts Receivable	8,642.81	
Allowance for Bad Debts		93.62
Merchandise Inventory	24,812.55	
Office Supplies	650.00	
Prepaid Insurance	352.20	
Land	12,000.00	
Buildings	17,000.00	
Accumulated Depreciation (Buildings)		2,424.63
Office Equipment	1,339.00	
Accumulated Depreciation (Office Equipment)		653.42
Trucks	11,400.00	
Accumulated Depreciation (Trucks)		7,489.80
Bank Loan		5,000.00
Accounts Payable		11,416.70
Employees Tax Deductions Payable		162.90
Canada Pension Plan Payable		64.56
Sales Tax Payable		1,502.17
James Wiseman, Capital		51,335.47
	$80,143.27	$80,143.27

14. The Subsidiary Ledger trial balances at December 31 were as follows:

Accounts Receivable

Bayvue Village Estates (Nov 30)	$ 2,365.53
Carlton Home Builders (Nov 30)	1,672.16
Evergreen Gardens (Dec 27)	1,848.88
Keele Estates (Aug 23)	120.43
J. Martin (Mar 16)	10.42
B. Starr (Apr 1)	83.20
Superior Construction Co. (Dec 28)	2,542.19
	$8,642.81

Accounts Payable

Lumber Wholesalers	Terms, N60	$5,627.42
Plywood Suppliers	Terms, N60	4,320.60
Wood Moulding Co.	Terms, N60	1,468.68
		$11,416.70

15. The following information is to be used by the accountant to prepare simple financial statements.

(a) *Bad Debts:* The Allowance for Bad Debts is calculated on a specific account basis. The balance in this account at December 31 of $93.62 was to cover J. Martin's account of $10.42 and B. Starr's account of $83.20 both of which were over one year old.

(b) *Prepaid Insurance:* The annual insurance premium is $2,113.20 payable in advance on each February 28th. The Prepaid Insurance account balance of $352.20 at December 31, represents the unused portion (the 2 months of January and February) of the insurance premium calculated as follows:

$2/12 \times \$2,113.20 = \$352.20$

(c) *Fixed Assets:* Fixed assets are depreciated in accordance with the rules and regulations of the federal government. Detailed information in respect to the fixed assets is as follows:

Brick Buildings

Cost Price	$17,000.00

Rate of Depreciation–5 per cent, reducing balance.
Accumulated Depreciation after 3 years is $2,424.63

Office Equipment

Cost Price:	Steel Desk	$ 325.00
	Steel Desk	325.00
	Filing Cabinet	120.00
	Swivel Chair	72.00
	Swivel Chair	72.00
	Typewriter	425.00
		$1,339.00

Rate of Depreciation–20 per cent, reducing balance.
Accumulated Depreciation after 3 years is $653.42

Trucks

Dodge Van	$ 4,600.00
Ford ½ Ton	2,900.00
G.M.C. Stake	3,900.00
	$11,400.00

Rate of Depreciation–30 per cent, reducing balance.
Accumulated Depreciation after 3 years is $7,489.80

16. This business uses a Synoptic Journal and a two-column General Journal in its accounting system. The next page number for the Synoptic Journal is 62 and for the General Journal is 31. (**Note**: This exercise may be done using any system of journals preferred. If some other system is used, the student is to select his own page numbers.)

17. The Bank Reconciliation Statement as at December 31, 19–4 is as follows:

Universal Lumber
Bank Reconciliation Statement
December 31, 19–4

Balance per Bank Statement		$4,228.91
Add outstanding deposit		121.50
		$4,350.41
Deduct outstanding cheques		
635	$ 47.50	
639	156.20	
640	300.00	503.70
Balance per General Ledger		$3,846.71

INSTRUCTION 2.

Record the accounting entries for the transactions in the journals. You are told directly about most of the transactions but some you must remember to originate yourself, from the notes made according to Instruction 1. Post daily to the subsidiary ledgers.

Note:

Students are expected to use current government tables for payroll deductions— Income Tax, Canada Pension Plan, and Unemployment Insurance.

Transactions

January
2 *Sales Invoice*
   –No. 1462, to Ontario Carpentry Co., $625 plus sales tax.
3 *Sales Invoice*
   –No. 1463, to Evergreen Gardens, $575 plus sales tax.

6 *Cash Receipt*
   –From J. Martin, $10.42. on account.
   Purchase Invoice
   –From Industrial Oil Co. Ltd., $54, for gas and oil used in the trucks; N,30.
7 *Purchase Invoice*
   –From Lumber Wholesalers, $1,214.62, for lumber; N,60.

8 *Cheque Copies*
  –No. 641, to Lumber Wholesalers,
   $2,000, on account.
  –No. 642, to Plywood Suppliers, $1,500,
   on account.
9 *Cash Receipt*
  –From Bayvue Village Estates, $2,365.53,
   on account.
10 *Cash Receipt*
  –From Ontario Carpentry Co., $673.75,
   on account.
14 *Purchase Invoice*
  –From National Pacific Railway, $37.14,
   freight on lumber; N,30.
15 *Cash Receipt*
  –From cash sales; $1,412.62; for the
   amount of sales plus the sales tax.
17 *Cheque Copy*
  –No. 649, to Petty Cash; $? ; to replenish
   the Petty Cash Fund for the following
   petty cash vouchers: Office Expense,
   $14.12; Truck Expense, $62.40; Building Maintenance, $19.25.
20 *Sales Invoice*
  –No. 1464, to Bayvue Village Estates,
   $1,250 plus sales tax.
22 *Cash Receipt*
  –From Carlton Home Builders,
   $1,672.16, on account.
23 *Cheque Copy*
  –No. 650, to Wood Moulding Co..
   $1,468.68, on account.
24 *Cheque Copy*
  –No. 651, to Local Telephone Co.,
   $37.50, telephone bill for the month.

27 *Cash Receipt*
  –From Evergreen Gardens, $2,481.38,
   on account.
28 *Sales Invoice*
  –No. 1465, to Carlton Home Builders,
   $982.49 plus sales tax.
  Cash Receipt
  –From Superior Construction Co.,
   $2,542.19, on account.
29 *Cheque Copy*
  –No. 654, to Yorktown Hydro, $47.89,
   hydro bill for month.
30 *Sales Invoices*
  –No. 1466, to Ontario Carpentry Co.,
   $3,687.98 plus sales tax.
  –No. 1467, to Evergreen Gardens,
   $4,846.73 plus sales tax.
31 *Sales Invoice*
  –No. 1468, to Parker Bros., $400.75 plus
   sales tax.
  Purchase Invoice
  –From Lumber Wholesalers, $6,234.65,
   for lumber received; freight prepaid;
   N,60.
  Cash Receipt
  –From cash sales, $1,188.00, for the
   amount of sales plus sales tax.
  Cheque Copies
  –No. 655, to Lumber Wholesalers,
   $4,000, on account.
  –No. 656, to Municipality of Yorktown,
   $23.50, for monthly instalment of prop-
   erty taxes.

INSTRUCTION 3.

Balance the journals and post to the
General Ledger.

INSTRUCTION 4.

Balance the General Ledger and the
subsidiary ledgers as at January 31,
19–5.

INSTRUCTION 5.

Prepare the Bank Reconciliation
Statemtnt as at January 31, 19–5.
The bank statement for the month
of January is shown on page 320.

```
                    CANADIAN CENTURY BANK

In account with:
Universal Lumber Company

|              DEBITS              |              | CREDITS         | DATE   | BALANCE  |
|----------------------------------|--------------|-----------------|--------|----------|
|                                  |              | Balance Forward | Dec 31 | 4,228.91 |
|                                  |              | 121.50          | Jan  2 | 4,350.41 |
| 47.50 (635)                      |              |                 | 3      | 4,302.91 |
|                                  |              | 10.42           | 6      | 4,313.33 |
| 156.20 (639)                     |              |                 | 8      | 4,157.13 |
|                                  |              | 2,365.53        | 9      | 6,522.66 |
| 300.00 (640)                     | 940.61 (643) | 673.75          | 10     | 5,955.80 |
| 27.80 (644)                      | 2,000.00 (641) |               | 13     | 3,928.00 |
|                                  |              | 1,412.62        | 15     | 5,340.62 |
| 1,500.00 (642)                   |              |                 | 16     | 3,840.62 |
| 95.77 (649)                      |              |                 | 17     | 3,744.85 |
| 625.00 (646)                     |              |                 | 20     | 3,119.85 |
| 25.00 (645)                      |              |                 | 21     | 3,094.85 |
| 1,502.17 (648)                   |              | 1,672.16        | 22     | 3,264.84 |
| 227.46 (647)                     |              |                 | 23     | 3,037.38 |
| 940.61 (652)                     |              |                 | 24     | 2,096.77 |
| 27.80 (653)                      | 1,468.68 (650) | 2,481.38      | 27     | 3,081.67 |
|                                  |              | 2,542.19        | 28     | 5,623.86 |
| 37.50 (651)                      |              |                 | 29     | 5,586.36 |
| 25.40 (D. M. For Bank Interest)  |              |                 | 31     | 5,560.96 |
```

INSTRUCTION 6.

Using the following information, prepare the work sheet and financial statements, and record the adjusting, closing, and reversing entries as required at the end of the accounting period.

(a) The Allowance for Bad Debts at January 31 is to allow for B. Starr's account of $83.20 and Keele Estates' account of $120.43.

(b) The lumber inventory at January 31 is valued at $23,773.31.

(c) The office supplies on hand at January 31 are valued at $622.91.

(d) The accrued payroll is to be estimated on the basis of the gross salaries for the period ending February 7 being the same as for the period ending January 24.

(e) There are no unprocessed accounts payable vouchers pertaining to the month of January.

INSTRUCTION 7.
Prepare a post-closing trial balance.

INSTRUCTION 8.
Journalize the following transactions for the month of February. Post daily to the subsidiary ledgers.

February

4 *Non-routine Entry*
   –The G.M.C. truck was in a serious collision and damaged beyond repair. The insurance company, Insurance Underwriters, agreed that Universal Lumber Company could keep the wreck (from which spare parts could be obtained) and that a cheque for $1,205 in full settlement would be forthcoming in the near future.

5 *Cash Receipt*
   –From Keele Estates, $120.43, on account.
   Cheque Copies
   –No. 658, to National Pacific Railway Co., $37.14, on account.
   –No. 659, to Industrial Oil Co. Ltd., $54, on account.

6 *Cheque Copies*
   –No. 660, to Lincoln Motors Limited, $165, repairs to Mr. Wiseman's personal car.
   –No. 661, to Large and Small Ltd., $28.91, C.O.D. order of carbon paper.
   Cash Receipt
   –From Evergreen Gardens, $5,224.77, on account.

7 **Note:**
   Mr. Barney terminated his employment with the company effective at 5 p.m. A Mr. J. Lee was hired to replace him; work to commence on Monday morning February 10. Mr. Lee's salary was set at $60 per week and his TD-1 form showed exemptions of $1,000. Mr. Lee made no other commitments.
   Cash Receipt
   –From Mr. Charles Carlton, owner of Carlton Home Builders; $1,100.29; for balance of account plus $38.18 cash sale of lumber plus sales tax, less cash discounts.

10 *Cheque Copies*
   –No. 663, to John Carmichael, $43.20, painting of buildings.
   –No. 664, to Lumber Wholesalers, $5,000, on account.

11 *Sales Invoices*
   –No. 1469, to Evergreen Gardens, $1,272.68, plus sales tax.
   –No. 1470, to Carlton Home Builders, $3,542.01, plus sales tax.

–No. 1471, to Bayvue Village Estates, $1,672.97, plus sales tax.

12 *Bank Debit Memorandum*
   –$120.43, cheque from Keele Estates, deposited on February 5, was returned– "Not Sufficient Funds".
   Purchase Invoice
   –From Wood Moulding Co., $3,742.62, for lumber; N,30.

13 *Purchase Invoice*
   –From National Pacific Railway Co., $36.24, for freight charges on lumber; N,30.
   Cash Receipt
   –From Bayvue Village Estates, $1,375, on account.

14 *Cash Receipt*
   –From cash sales, $1,431.98, for the amount of sales plus the sales tax.

17 *Cheque Copies*
   –No. 670, to Peter Douglas and Son, $150, cash payment for legal services.
   –No. 671, to Plywood Suppliers, $2,820.60, on account.
   Cash Receipt
   –From James Wiseman, the owner, $3,000, to increase his equity in the business.

18 *Cheque Copy*
   –No. 672, to Tom's Local Garage, $65.42, cash payment of invoice for truck repairs.

19 *Sales Invoice*
   –No. 1472, to Ontario Carpentry Co., $2,288.60 plus sales tax.

21 *Cash Receipt*
   –From Ontario Carpentry Co., $2,000, on account.

24 *Cheque Copy*
   –No. 674, to Petty Cash Fund, $? ; to reimburse the Petty Cash Fund for the following petty cash vouchers: Office Expense, $2.10; Truck Expense, $30.72; Office Supplies, $42.60; Miscellaneous Expense, $21.06.

25 *Purchase Invoice*
   –From Plywood Suppliers, $2,381.11, for lumber; N,60.

26 *Purchase Invoice*
   –From Industrial Oil Co. Ltd., $58.70, for gas and oil used in the trucks; N,30.
   Purchase Invoice
   –From National Pacific Railway Co., $27.01, for freight on lumber; N,30.

27 *Cheque Copies*
   –No. 676. to Yorktown Hydro, $59.10, cash payment of monthly hydro bill.
   –No. 677, to Municipality of Yorktown, $23.50, for monthly instalment on property tax.
   –No. 678, to Local Telephone Co., $37.50, telephone bill for the month.
28 *Cheque Copy*
   –No. 679, to Insurance Underwriters, $2,113.20, annual insurance premium.

28 *Cash Receipt*
   –From cash sales, $1,040.82, for the amount of sales plus the sales tax.
Sales Invoices
   –No. 1473, to Ontario Carpentry, $2,565.53, plus sales tax.
   –No. 1474, to Parker Bros, $1,320, plus sales tax.
   –No. 1475, to Bayvue Village Estates, $680.70, plus sales tax.
Cash Receipt
   –From Parker Bros., $440.83, on account.

INSTRUCTION 9.

Balance the journals and post to the General Ledger.

INSTRUCTION 10.

Balance the General Ledger and the subsidiary ledgers as of February 28, 19–5.

INSTRUCTION 11.

Prepare the Bank Reconciliation Statement as at February 28, 19–5. The bank statement for the month of February is shown below:

CANADIAN CENTURY BANK

In account with:
Universal Lumber Company

DEBITS		CREDITS	DATE	BALANCE
		Balance Forward	Jan 31	5,560.96
47.89 (654)	23.50 (656)	1,188.00	Feb 3	6,677.57
4,000.00 (655)	625.00 (657)		4	2,052.57
		120.43	5	2,173.00
37.14 (658)		5,224.77	6	7,360.63
940.61 (662)		1,100.29	7	7,520.31
27.80 (665)	54.00 (659)		10	7,438.51
120.43 (D.M. for N.S.F. Cheque)			11	7,318.08
43.20 (663)	28.91 (661)		12	7,245.97
		1,375.00	13	8,620.97
165.00 (660)		1,431.98	14	9,887.95
5,000.00 (664)			15	4,887.95
25.00 (666)		3,000.00	17	7,862.95
625.00 (667)			18	7,237.95
1,473.22 (669)			20	5,764.73
913.30 (673)	220.26 (668)	2,000.00	21	6,631.17
96.48 (674)	27.20 (675)		24	6,507.49
2,820.60 (671)	65.42 (672)		25	3,621.47
150.00 (670)			27	3,471.47
23.50 (677)	23.40 (D.M. For Bank Interest)		28	3,424.57

INSTRUCTION 12.

Using the information shown below, prepare the work sheet and financial statements, and record the adjusting, closing, and reversing entries as required at the end of the accounting period.

(a) An analysis of the Accounts Receivable Ledger indicated that B. Starr's account and Keele Estates' account are doubtful.

(b) The lumber inventory at February 28 is valued at $20,667.93.

(c) The office supplies on hand at February 28 were valued at $658.09.

(d) For accrued payroll, estimate on the basis of the gross payroll for the period ending March 7 being the same as for the period ending February 21.

(e) The following purchase invoice received in March pertained to goods received in February:
  Plywood Suppliers' invoice of March 5, $170.50, for lumber.

INSTRUCTION 13.

Prepare a post-closing trial balance.

INDEX

325